TIBET
Abode of the Gods, Pearl of the Motherland

Barbara Erickson

Pacific View Press

Berkeley, California

Library of Congress Catalog Card Number: 97-2611
ISBN: 1-881896-16-1
Printed in the United States of America

Library of Congress Cataloging-in-Publication Data

Erickson, Barbara, 1937–
        Tibet : abode of the Gods, pearl of the motherland / Barbara Erickson.
            p.   cm.
        Includes bibliographical references and index.
        ISBN 1-881896-16-1 (cloth)
        1. Erickson, Barbara, 1937–   --Journeys--China--Tibet. 2. Tibet
(China)--Description and travel.   I. Title.
        DS786.E72   1997
        915.1'50459--dc21   97-2611
                                                        CIP

To my husband John
with love and gratitude

Contents

Acknowledgements

I owe an enormous debt to a trio of friends, Zhang Jichuan, Ngawangthondup Narkyid and Tashi Tshering. Zhang Jichuan made the book happen and supported me in many ways before and during my stay in Beijing. He arranged for my sponsorship, patiently granted me a number of interviews, and introduced me to Ngawangthondup, better known in the United States as Kuno.

Without Kuno's help the present book would be inconceivable. It is impossible to describe the many ways he helped, first with his constant encouragement and support and then with his forbearance and precision in telling his own stories, reading many pages of the manuscript, correcting the spelling of Tibetan words, and introducing me to valuable sources of information. He was enduring and persevering in all of these tasks, and he often went to great lengths to get me what I asked.

It was Kuno who introduced me to Tashi Tshering, my vital support in Lhasa. Tashi kept me alive by feeding me at his home each day and providing me with warm clothes as the Tibetan winter approached. He told me his own history in detail, explained the workings of the old Tibet and the present People's Republic, answered scores of my naive questions and accompanied me to his home village in Namling. I owe much to Tashi's wife Sangye also for her well-cooked meals and many acts of kindness.

There is no way to repay friends such as these. I can only try to produce a book that is worthy of the trust and support they gave.

I have nothing but praise as well for Jin Hongme (Xiao Jin), my interpreter and guide through the Chinese bureaucracy; my sometime nurse, companion and fellow traveler by air, jeep, bicycle, pedicab and foot; my helper in a thousand ways. She was determined, energetic, resourceful and honest, the perfect translator and escort. Her husband, Bugang, was always a kind and intelligent helper as well.

Dorje Tseten, my sponsor, was essential to this project. Without his sponsorship and the arrangements he graciously made on my behalf, I would have been unable to make an acquaintance with Tibet as it is today. Others at the Center for Tibetological Studies were equally helpful, especially Professor Hu Tan, who helped me understand new developments in the Tibetan language.

In the United States Tsultrim Drolma kindly and bravely granted me a number of interviews detailing her own ordeal in Tibet, and her friend Tamdrin patiently acted throughout as interpreter.

And then there are the numerous friends and acquaintances who must remain anonymous, most of them still in Tibet. I am grateful for the hours they gave me, for the risks they took, for their honesty and trust. I hope that their prayers for independence will soon be answered.

A Break in the Bamboo Curtain
(Introduction)

On an icy day in November 1992 I was seated at my desk in a Beijing research institute, warming my hands and preparing to transcribe accounts of Tibet's bloodiest riots from notebook to laptop. My shortwave radio was broadcasting the daily Voice of America news from a corner of the room, but I was paying scant attention—until an item caught my ear. Then I abruptly sat up and took notice. The announcer was speaking of an Australian delegation touring China, a group of lawmakers investigating human rights abuses. They had hoped to check out the situation in Tibet, but the Chinese government had turned them down. Even foreign reporters couldn't get in for a firsthand look, the report went on. China had imposed a news blackout on Tibet.

Voice of America got that story wrong, I thought. I had just spent three months in Tibet, nosing about the offices of bureaucrats, visiting schools and hospitals, and interviewing beggars, monks, nuns, farmers, nomads, and shopkeepers. I had wandered about Lhasa and the countryside, equipped with camera and notepad, asking questions and keeping my eyes open. I was one journalist who had found a breach in the bamboo curtain, and through a series of lucky breaks, I had managed to evade the news ban on that forbidden region.

Voice of America couldn't be faulted for getting it wrong. I wasn't shouting about my expedition into Tibet's bureaucracies and villages; I wanted to keep a low profile so I could take advantage of my security clearance without running into trouble. I wanted enough time to look into the charges that had troubled the Australians and others in the West—accusations of genocide, cultural annihilation, religious repression, environmental plunder, discrimination, and human rights abuses.

I had managed to get the time I needed and also the access, but in the conspiratorial, tense mood of Tibet today I had grown uneasy, and I worried that Chinese officials might suddenly appear and demand my notes. I secured my computer files with a password, disguised the names of sources, and sent a couple of computer disks back to the States via American tourists. But now I was in Beijing, where the atmosphere was less charged, and I was beginning to breathe easy again. I was almost home free.

My journey to Tibet begins on a spring morning in 1991. I am standing on the top of Nob Hill in San Francisco, several hundred back in a line that winds from the portals of Grace Cathedral down to the sidewalk, along California Street, and up Jones. I am waiting to see the Dalai Lama, whose appearance is a feature of the Year of Tibet, a campaign by the Tibetan government-in-exile and its supporters to draw attention to the spiritual leader's homeland. His Holiness, the Nobel laureate, attracts such devotion and curiosity that the crowds have been gathering since sunrise. They are mostly white, in their thirties and forties, in casual, vaguely ethnic, dress.

By my side is white-haired Zhang Jichuan, a Chinese linguist who made his first visit to Tibet in 1955 and returned several times to do fieldwork and research. In one of those developments which send our lives spinning off in new directions, I had happened upon a sign in Berkeley which said that "Mr. Chang," a visiting scholar, was looking for an American home where he could live and practice English in exchange for housework. Since I was about to study Chinese and needed a tutor, I thought it might be a good trade-off. So I called the number listed, and a few meetings later Zhang Jichuan came to live with me and my husband in our Berkeley home.

Now I am with him in San Francisco where he hopes to get a glimpse of the religious leader he last saw nearly forty years ago in Lhasa. It had been a brief encounter. Zhang and dozens of other newly arrived Chinese had attended an audience with the Dalai Lama; His Holiness, then a young man, had granted each of them the traditional blessing for laypeople—the flick of a yak tail to the crown of the head. This time Zhang will see him from a distance, over a sea of heads—a balding red-robed monk speaking from a Gothic pulpit.

As we stand in line, American supporters of the Dalai Lama and his government-in-exile work the crowds, handing out fliers about the Year of Tibet and Chinese oppression during forty years of occupation. One handout informs me that China has been committing genocide in Tibet; over six thousand monasteries have been destroyed; Buddhist studies are outlawed; Tibetan women are sterilized and forced to have abortions; Tibet's environment has been laid waste; medical care, employment, and education are segregated, with the Chinese colonists getting the best of everything; and Chinese now outnumber Tibetans in their own land.

Zhang peruses this flier carefully. Then he shakes his head and says, "They don't know anything about Tibet." What's wrong with it? I ask. Forced abortions? Unlikely, he says. Segregated schooling? Not so. Genocide? No. Political prisoners? Maybe. Religious oppression? Not now. Environmental destruction? Yes and no. Population transfer? Not really.

That night Zhang retires to his room to go over the fliers, and the next morning he emerges to make a proposal: The two of us will write a book on Tibet and set the record straight. He's been doing fieldwork there since the 1950s; he's watched Tibet evolve. And I am a writer, a former newspaper reporter, now a journalism teacher. Together we can give a true account of Tibet under China. I've started to read about that lofty, rugged land, it's beginning to intrigue me, and my journalist's instincts tell me there's a story here. I make some phone calls and find the responses encouraging.

Okay, I say, we'll do it.

At that time, in the spring of 1991, the Tiananmen Square protests and ensuing massacre were not yet two years past, and China was still in lockdown, its leaders fearful that Western influence might once again arouse the masses to rebel. And Tibet was a sore point with China, which had been taking a lot of flak from Western supporters of the Dalai Lama. Foreign journalists had no chance of openly nosing about Lhasa or any other area of the Tibet Autonomous Region, not since a series of riots which began in 1987. They might pass through in tightly controlled groups for a couple of days on staged occasions, or they might make their way into Tibet on tourist visas and talk to Tibetans on the quiet, but beyond that it was no-go. And in 1991, I heard tourists were also limited to escorted groups and charged $100 a day minimum.

I wanted to see Tibet for myself, but it was a forbidden region, barricaded behind an official news blackout. Still, Zhang said, it might be possible. He had asked a Chinese diplomat how a foreign journalist could get into Tibet, and the man had an answer: Find a sponsor, he said, someone who will write a letter of invitation; that will do it. Zhang was willing to try, but he told me not to count on it. He had never joined the Communist Party or curried favor with officials; he had no real clout, but he had a few connections. When he went back to Beijing in October, he would see what he could do.

Meanwhile I was reading and taking in the Year of Tibet in the Bay Area—an exhibit at the Asian Art Museum, film shows, a Tibetan opera performance, and speeches—and at one of these events I witnessed a long-delayed reunion between Zhang and the lecturer. As we entered the hall, the speaker, a lean, sharp-featured Tibetan, strode up the aisle shaking his head. He took Zhang's hands in his. "You, you . . ." he stammered. "I remember . . ." It was Zhang's former Tibetan teacher, Ngawangthondup Narkyid. They had last met thirty-four years before, in 1957, and both had aged. But they knew each other all the same.

In the States, Ngawangthondup went by the name of Kuno, which was easier to pronounce. Before the Chinese took full control of Tibet in 1959 he had been a monk official in the Lhasa government, but he fled with the Dalai Lama after the rebellion of 1959 failed. Now he was serving as the Dalai Lama's official biographer. Several times during his lecture he said that he had once hated the Chinese, but with the help of His Holiness and through meditation, he had shed this burden. Now, he said, gesturing toward Zhang, I can embrace this man. Zhang sat upright in the dark auditorium and beamed his appreciation.

I interviewed Ngawangthondup, who was spending most of his time in Berkeley, lecturing and teaching, and I interviewed Zhang, until he left for Beijing that fall. Both were obliging and patient, and though they had their opinions, they tried to tell me their stories straight, letting me come to my own conclusions. "You will write both the Chinese and the Tibetan points of view," said Ngawangthondup. "That's good. Nobody has done that."

A few months after Zhang returned home, I sat through a conference on Tibet held on the University of California Berkeley campus. It was titled "The Road to Independence" and featured a number of Tibetans in exile, including a brother of the Dalai Lama, Thubten Jigme Norbu, who spoke of decades of violence and destruction and said Tibetans would simply take their independence if China refused to give it to them.

The young Tibetans who followed him at the microphone presented their visions of a new Tibet freed at last from China and also very different from the old Tibet. None called for a return to the past. The pre-1950s Tibet had been isolated and backward. Most of its people were serfs who worked the land and hauled water for wealthy landowners and monasteries; most commoners were illiterate, and almost everyone was ignorant of modern science. But none of the speakers alluded to the conditions of the past. Instead, they spoke of a reconstructed Tibet. They called for democracy and modern techniques in agriculture, industry, commerce, and education.

The speakers held the perspective of exiles experienced in Western and Indian democracy. Since many Tibetans fled their homeland in 1959, after an abortive rebellion against Chinese rule, refugees have settled mainly in India, where the Dalai Lama heads a government-in-exile based in the hill town of Dharamsala. This government has little in common with the political system of the old Tibet. The Dalai Lama serves as chief executive, and an assembly of forty-six members elected to five-year terms serves as a legislature. Members of the assembly represent the three major regions of Tibet and various religious sects; some are Tibetans living outside India. The Dalai Lama may choose to appoint two or three members, and he may also call for sessions of the assembly or dissolve it if he wishes. The exile government also has a judicial commission.

"After independence," said lead panelist Thubten Samdup, "the government-in-exile would be dissolved and Tibetan Autonomous Region officials would remain until the people vote. The Dalai Lama has said that he would have no political role, and Tibet would be a zone of nonviolence and peace." Tibetans would vote on the form of government to follow under independence, but the Dalai Lama has declared that it must count him out as a head of government. He would become a purely religious figure without secular power. The monasteries would likewise become purely religious institutions, unlike those in the old Tibet, which were often involved in running the government.

Other speakers said Tibet needs modern technology, but in the future Tibetans must not tear apart the environment the way, they claimed, the Chinese are doing. An independent Tibet would have solar technology, electrical power, and organic agriculture, they said; it would have carpet and textile industries and sell bottled water from its pristine lakes; it would have Tibetans instead of Chinese running the tourist industry; it would fight illiteracy with education on the Western model where students can speak up and question their teachers, unlike the old Tibet and present-day China.

This image of an independent Tibet was a wish list, the ideal as Tibetans who have grown up in India and the West were seeing it. The only item that had actually materialized was the form of the government-in-exile, and even that, one Tibetan told me, is primarily "practice" for the day when Tibetans can run their own affairs. But everything the panelists said underscored the fact that the old Tibet was dead and Tibetans were not calling for its return. They were counting on achieving independence someday, perhaps, they said, when the People's Republic of China follows the example of the former Soviet Union and splits into separate republics, or perhaps when international pressure on China brings the Tibetans victory at the bargaining table—but most of the speakers at the conference looked beyond that point to their dreams of a new Tibet.

When these speakers referred to Tibet, they meant all the Tibetan ethnic areas of China, the Tibet Autonomous Region (TAR) as well as regions to the east in Chinese provinces where millions more Tibetans live. In the past, these eastern areas—called Kham and Amdo by Tibetans—lay mainly outside the control of the Dalai Lamas in Lhasa, and they were considered parts of their Chinese provinces although generally run by local Tibetan chieftains. Asking the Chinese to return all these regions complicates any negotiations the exile government might have with China. But since the Dalai Lama himself, other powerful leaders in Dharamsala, and large percentage of the refugees come from Kham and Amdo, Tibetans don't stop at the borders of the TAR when they make their demands for greater autonomy or outright independence.

After Zhang returned to Beijing he wrote carefully worded letters which told me that government control was tight. The Communist Party was trying to head off any new stirring of pro-democracy fervor with heavy doses of political education. Zhang and his colleagues spent hours each week in government-mandated classes. The atmosphere was tense, so he was moving carefully. He would wait until after the first of the year to look for a sponsor. It was the only chance of getting me anything better than a tourist visa.

Several weeks passed before he wrote again. He had gone to see Dorje Tseten, a Tibetan who had been headmaster at Lhasa First Primary School when Zhang taught there in the 1950s. After the Cultural Revolution he had served as Chairman of the TAR, and he now headed a research institute, the Chinese Center for Tibetological Studies in Beijing. Dorje Tseten would think about it, Zhang wrote.

Now it was my turn to face the Chinese bureaucracy. I was summoned to meet with Li Weihe, cultural attaché at the Chinese consulate in San Francisco, and I was to bring my résumé and samples of my work. This was an ominous turn, I thought. They will see that damning word "journalist," take note of the news blackout on Tibet, and turn me down. But I would make my bid anyway. I went to the meeting and found Li, a tall Chinese from Anhui Province, to be all business. He gave me a sober once-over. What books have you written? he asked. Only an unpublished novel on Uganda, I said. I used to live there. He lightened up. He had begun his diplomatic career in East Africa. Fascinating place. I agreed. Li looked over my material and asked me some questions. Here you are with gray hair, he said. Will you be able to withstand the rigors of Tibet's high altitude? Its primitive facilities? I spend a lot of time in the mountains, I said, and I managed in Africa. Li nodded. He would see what he could do.

I talked some more with Ngawangthondup and other Tibetans passing through the Bay Area, I read constantly about Tibet, and I watched the news reports on China. The dispatches from Beijing, formerly grim accounts of the post-Tiananmen crackdown, began to sound promising, as China gave signs of opening again to the West. The change was gradual but steady, and the hardline attitude was giving way.

Then in the spring, Zhang wrote that his former boss, Dorje Tseten, had agreed to sponsor the project. There was only one hitch. Zhang himself wouldn't be able to take part; he couldn't get away as he had planned. But I was not to worry. The institute might assign me an interpreter, and they were considering a young Tibetan woman who spoke Chinese, English, and Tibetan. I had only to write to Dorje Tseten, outline my plans, and ask for a letter of invitation from the Chinese Center for Tibetological Studies. The letter would secure me the visa I needed.

The news caught me unawares. I had counted on Zhang as a guide, but I was now left to my own devices, about to take off for the world's highest plateau armed with a meager command of Chinese and no Tibetan. Or maybe it was even worse. Maybe I would not be on my own at all but with one of those Chinese guides who cling like Velcro and steer you to spruced-up model homes and work units. I decided to record all the interviews as a double check, to see if my interpreter—if I had one—was telling it straight. I spent my days listening to cassettes of conversational Chinese and poring over vocabulary lists. It was too late, unfortunately, to work up enough Tibetan, but with some fluency in Chinese I could manage simple interviews on my own.

I took heart from the saga of Alexandra David-Neel, a French opera singer and Buddhist scholar who in 1923 stole into then-forbidden Lhasa on foot, disguised as a pilgrim. She survived on ground barley and butter tea and tramped through Tibet for four months, crossing snow-covered passes as high as 18,000 feet, and sleeping in the open. She was fifty-five years old at the time. David-Neel was my exemplar. If she had managed her trek seventy years ago, then surely I could accomplish my own mission in the age of air travel and antibiotics.

I thought of my brother, who vanished in 1976 during a backpacking trip in southern Thailand. He had become a Buddhist and spent his holidays hiking in the Himalayas. At times he had gazed across the peaks toward Tibet, longing to visit the Land of Snows, but it was then caught in the frenzies of the Cultural Revolution. Before his last excursion, he had written to the Dalai Lama asking for an audience. The reply came saying His Holiness would be glad to grant him an interview, but my brother never returned to learn of this.

Maybe, said my mother, you will find out about Doug when you're in Tibet. Somewhere in a monastery you may meet someone who knew him; perhaps he made his way to a remote hermitage in the Himalayas or is meditating with monks somewhere in Tibet. In my family there was a whisper of hope, almost unspoken, that my journey might be a providential link to Doug, casting light on the riddle of his disappearance.

Zhang Jichuan was at the Beijing airport with his wife and a younger woman when I arrived in July. "I am Jin Hongmei," said the young woman, "the center's interpreter." She placed a white scarf around my neck in the traditional Tibetan gesture of greeting, and she carried a bag with a Tibetan character appliqued on the side. But otherwise she seemed more Chinese than Tibetan, fair-skinned and dressed in Western clothes. And her name was Chinese as well.

Jin Hongmei spent the next four months as my guide, interpreter, and, at times, nurse. She had a Tibetan name, Yudru Tsomu, but her family were Khampa, Tibetans from Sichuan Province, who had been tagged with Chinese names some generations back. She spoke a Khampa dialect at home and had studied Chinese and English in school. During a year in the TAR she had also learned the Lhasa dialect and some written Tibetan. She was twenty-three, bright, earnest and hard-working, and married to a Tibetan. After a couple of days with Xiao Jin ("Little Jin"), I gave up my plan to tape our interviews. For one thing, they were often in Chinese, and I usually knew enough to understand the drift of things. But primarily I had no reason to doubt Xiao Jin. She was a scholar at heart, eager to get the story straight, and meticulous with details. She always tried to get me the facts, unadorned, as I requested.

When we arrived in Lhasa she moved in with her husband's relatives, and I took up residence in the Tibetan-run Snowland Hotel in the heart of the city. It attracted traders and pilgrims and backpacking Westerners. From the balcony I had a view of the Jokhang Cathedral, only a block away; from the street side, the Potala Palace; and to the east and west, mountains rising abruptly on both sides of the valley, so near I could see water coursing down the ravines and prayer flags strung from crag to crag.

Xiao Jin spent the first week rustling up contacts in Lhasa so that we could gain access to officials. None of them would grant us interviews, she explained, unless we used the proper channels. Since the center had its headquarters in Beijing, its staff had to persuade another agency to handle our affairs. That agency would use its own connections to arrange our itinerary.

The Committee of the United Front in Lhasa, a group established in the early days of Communist rule to draw support from a broad coalition, agreed to take us on.

While Xiao Jin hustled, I nursed a sprained ankle and looked around central Lhasa. It was wildly exotic, too dazzling to take in at first. I couldn't sort out the mix of people: Chinese and Tibetan, pilgrims and townspeople, nomads and farmers. I made a circuit of the Barkor, the sacred route around the main cathedral, but I wasn't ready to plunge into the tangle of streets and alleys that surrounded it. It was enough, in those early days, just to find my way to a restaurant and back.

After a week, Xiao Jin had our affairs in order. The center provided us with a pair of bicycles to pedal over the cobbled streets of Lhasa, and we had an itinerary several pages long, devised by the United Front. It was a list of interviews and tours in Lhasa as well as visits to other areas of central Tibet. I looked at it warily. Interviews with local peasants? I asked, referring to the list. Who is going to select them? Tell the staff at the United Front that we want to choose our own people to interview. And I don't want to see so many schools and carpet factories, I told her. Let them know we want free time to nose around on our own.

Xiao Jin reported back. They won't choose anyone in advance, she said. We can arrange our own interviews. No problem. I hoped that was true, and so far all had gone well. I had hours every day to poke about Lhasa on my own; I could talk to Chinese, Tibetans, and Westerners, alone or with the help of friends. Later, when Xiao Jin and I traveled outside the capital we stopped at random—at villages and fields, by lakesides and riversides, at monasteries and markets and shops. We interviewed herders, farmers, beggars, monks, nuns, traders, restaurant owners, street vendors, carpenters, bureaucrats, officials, scholars, teachers, students—Chinese and Tibetans alike. I accompanied a Tibetan friend to his home village and became the first foreigner ever to visit that out-of-the-way settlement in the mountains west of Lhasa. I visited Lhasa's mosque and came to know the city's Muslims, a group rarely mentioned in the literature on Tibet. I went to formal interviews in government offices and conference rooms. And I spoke to people on the street, in teahouses, monasteries, and shops.

My situation was fine for research, but it gave me a bad name with some of the Westerners who came to Lhasa. A couple staying at the Snowland Hotel was cordial and welcoming at first, but suddenly turned chilly when they saw that I had a translator and access to officials, and their suspicions soured my relations with other foreigners for a while. They decided that I must be too cozy with the Chinese who ran things in Tibet. Tibetans, fortunately, remained friendly. They seemed to have a better sense of how the system works and years of practice in learning whom they can trust.

Although the Chinese were willing to let me investigate on my own, they set some limits. They balked at my request to visit Tibetan areas in Sichuan and Qinghai provinces, which lie outside the TAR. Xiao Jin had been hoping to take me to her home village in Sichuan, but the provincial government there squelched that plan. It was a big disappointment. And some topics were off-limits as well, at least with officials, like the controversial power project at a lake near Lhasa.

But I roamed through central Tibet, hung out in Lhasa, and looked for answers to the questions I first asked Zhang Jichuan that spring morning in San Francisco. I also picked up a wary skepticism of official Chinese data: population statistics, legal codes, and programs which appeared only on paper or in the assertions of bureaucrats. These often failed to match reality, and I found that my own eyes and ears gave me the most credible perspective on Tibet.

Note on the Use
of Chinese and Tibetan Words

Chinese words are transcribed in pinyin, the official People's Republic system for transliterating the language. The only exceptions are the words *Kuomintang* and *Yangtze* because they have become so familiar in these forms.

Tibetan words have been transcribed with the help of my friend Ngawangthondup Narkyid according to the Wiley system. We chose to avoid umlauts or the use of *oe* in words such as Shol and wrote them simply with an unadorned *o*. Readers unfamiliar with the Tibetan language should also know that *th* is a strongly aspirated *t*, not like the *th* in "thin" or "that." Likewise *ph* is an aspirated *p*, not an *f* sound. *Kh* is strongly aspirated, but *ch* and *sh* sound as they do in English. *P, t,* and *k* are never aspirated, and to English speakers they often sound like *b, d,* and *g*.

Tibetan names may cause some confusion. Sometimes they are only one word, such as in Ragdi, the TAR official. More often they are two given names, such as Nyima Tsering, without a surname. Tibetans, except for members of the former aristocracy, usually omit surnames and identify themselves with one or two given names. When it is used, the surname traditionally appears first, as in Chinese. An example is the name of the PRC official Ngapo Ngawang Jigme. Ngawangthondup Narkyid is an exception to this. While he is in the West, at least, he places his surname last.

1

Abode of the Gods
(Lhasa and the Communists)

Lhasa's Jokhang Plaza, the heart of Tibet, with its great temple rising from the east end, is filled as usual on this autumn afternoon with traders, pilgrims, idlers, beggars, and amateur dancers. Smoke rises from incense burners in front of the temple, obscuring the rows of prayer flags offered for sale, swirling in juniper-scented clouds around the old woman and her dogs and the old man carving prayer stones—a pair of regulars who take up their stations daily at the foot of a column. Chinese peddlers stand behind their stocks of ceremonial scarves; others pass through the crowds, displaying rows of dark glasses pinned to cardboard placards. The doors of the cathedral are closed, after the morning crush of pilgrims; but before the great portals dozens of Tibetans are rising and falling in devout prostrations.

At the far end of the plaza, pedicabs (called rickshaws here in Lhasa) stand with their canopies of ruffled fabric, waiting for riders, and Tibetan women sit knitting beside carts filled with apples and pears. Nearby stand a pair of gleaming tour buses, disgorging Europeans with video and still cameras. The tourists will make a run through the Jokhang, photographing its dark shrines and towering Buddha image, and they will ascend to the Barkor Cafe for tea and Chinese food, fighting off assaults by the jewelry vendors, women dressed in nomad finery who block their way and hold up turquoise and silver necklaces as they call out, "Lookee, lookee, very old, very good." Some of the tourists will venture around the Barkor, stopping at the stalls offering religious artifacts, wooden bowls, fur hats, fabric, and trinkets. Others will join the circles of onlookers taking in the Jokhang's ever-present impromptu dancers who pass the hat for donations. Today the visitors have a choice of two styles—a quartet of elderly pilgrims in sheepskin who watch their feet as they turn slowly with intricate steps, and a Tibetan youth in an imitation leather jacket and Rambo-style head scarf who is break dancing to the sounds of a ghetto blaster.

The red-robed monks, the nomads in sheepskin, and the golden rooftops of the Jokhang set the plaza apart from any area of China proper and any other religious center of the East. This is unmistakably Lhasa, and Tibetan culture, viewed from the center of the Jokhang Plaza this day, seems very much alive. The tourists will record images of a novel and apparently flourishing way of life, but few will have any inkling that a video camera positioned above an unmarked Public Security Bureau station is scanning the Jokhang crowd. Most will miss the signs that all is not well in the heart of Tibet. And in the midst of the plaza's color and vitality, they will fail to hear my Tibetan friend who speaks with resignation and despair: "Tibet," he says, "is heading for extinction."

After three months in Tibet, I came to agree. I couldn't see it on that afternoon in the Jokhang Plaza, but gradually I reached the same conclusion and understood my friend's dismay. It wasn't that China was committing genocide in Tibet or deliberately strangling Tibetan culture or suppressing the language or discriminating against Tibetans in schooling and health care or looting all of Tibet's natural resources as some have claimed. In the end I rejected those charges and the implication that all Tibetans are innocent victims and all Chinese are greedy, godless plunderers. I came to see that China's hold on that region and the Chinese system of paternalistic despotism are in themselves enough to threaten the survival of Tibetan culture.

The Communists say they liberated Tibet from feudalism. They insist that Tibetans are better off than ever before. They point to the region's roads, schools, hospitals, electric power projects, telephones, and growing prosperity as evidence, and they are right in some of their claims. Tibet is more highly developed today; it has a longer life expectancy and a higher literacy rate. There have been gains. But there have also been losses, and these losses are still accumulating. Some of them are measurable; others are more subjective;

and some are evident only in the light of history and the lessons of other cultures faced with the threat of decay, assimilation, and extinction. To understand this, to assess both the benefits and the drawbacks, I had to go back to the beginning. I needed to comprehend the old Tibet before I could fathom what was going on in the new, and this meant I would have to absorb many reports about the past and also hear Tibetans speak of their lives in the old society.

I also had to find where the truth lay: somewhere, I knew, between the extremes of two opposing camps. The Chinese government claims that pre-1959 Tibet was "a society of feudal serfdom under the despotic religion-political [sic] rule of lamas and nobles, a society which was darker and more cruel than the European serfdom of the Middle Ages," a land where "serf owners literally possessed the living bodies of their serfs" . . . and "ruthlessly exploited serfs through corvée and usury" and barbarous punishments—drowning and beheading serfs, gouging out their eyes, cutting off their hands and feet. Some Tibetans in exile, however, describe the old Tibet as a near-Eden. A brother of the present Dalai Lama, Thubten Jigme Norbu, has written in a nostalgic memoir: "I can imagine nothing more perfect than that Tibet I knew not many years ago." Others have said that the old society fell short of utopia but it was "remarkably successful in meeting the needs and desires of the vast majority of the people" and a "largely tolerant and inclusive society" imbued with the doctrine of compassion.[1]

I had already read accounts by Tibetans, Westerners, and Chinese describing the old Tibet, and I knew it was a land where serfs worked on manorial and monastic estates, a kind of theocracy where the Dalai Lama held primary power. It was also, in part, a secular government in which lay officials shared their authority with monks. Beyond this, it was isolated and primitive in its technology while it was sophisticated in philosophical studies and medical theory.[2]

At the low end of the old Tibetan society were the beggars who roamed the streets of Lhasa. Many of these beggers were convicts, some of whom had lost a hand as a punishment for theft. (The Thirteenth Dalai Lama had outlawed mutilation punishment in 1913, but during the regency after his death in 1933, the practice resumed.) The *ragyapa,* outcasts who collected the dead, also lived on the margins of society along with slaughterers, who performed the impure function of killing animals for food. Then there were the small number of hereditary household servants, who were treated very much like slaves and could be traded to other families, and the poorest agricultural serfs, who lived in stable-like quarters or in small houses of mud or stone and subsisted on little more than ground roasted barley (*tsampa*).

Among the middle range of serfs was the family of my friend Tashi Tshering, who was born in Guchok Village west of Lhasa in 1931. He grew up in a two-story stone house (animals quartered below, the family above) in the midst of barley fields with a view of snowy peaks behind and the sweep of terraced fields before, dropping toward the broad Namling Valley with more snow-topped peaks beyond. Down in the valley, by the Namling River, stood the manor house of the lord who owned the land in the surrounding villages, including Guchok. The serfs worked in the demesne fields of the manor as part of their tax obligation, and their duties were laid out in a written contract. They did not enter into this contract by choice; they were born to it; but it did give them rights and limited the amount of tax they had to pay.

Tashi spent many of his childhood days in the mountains surrounding the village, herding sheep and yaks and passing the hours spinning wool and fashioning shoes and belts for his family's use. He and his fellow shepherds carried tsampa, homemade beer, and, at times, fresh butter to mix with the tsampa. The treeless hills, covered with boulders and brush, were home to wolves which preyed on the sheep, and Tashi still recalls his fear when the pack took a victim and the vultures descended in a great uproar to get their share.

The life of his family was a round of spring sowing and autumn harvest, of tending the sheep, goats, yaks, cows, and donkeys; of laboring in the family fields and also in the fields of the estate below. The village was seminomadic, which meant that the peasants not only cultivated barley but also set off each summer to pasture their herds in the mountains. A small monastery and a small nunnery sat on a hillside beside the village, and on a ridge above lay stone ruins; local people said they had been destroyed centuries back when Mongols sacked the area.

Guchok's villagers were among the 60 percent of Tibet's population that was categorized as agricultural serfs in later counts by the Chinese government.[3] But there were many kinds of peasant serfs, and they acquired many levels of wealth. Most, like Tashi's family, served on the estates of nobles or monasteries. The family sent someone to work for the estate nearly every day of the year, a family member or a hired hand, and they carried their own tsampa and beer when they went; the estate gave them no pay. Other serfs lived in corporate villages under government jurisdiction. The landholding serfs in these villages ran their own affairs as a group, but they were still accountable to officials and had to pay taxes.

There are no statistics breaking the serfs down by income level, so it is difficult to describe a "typical" Tibetan serf. But a common situation was that of a family bound to an estate and required to work the land for a lord. Usually the land was under a steward's care while the owner was in Lhasa. The serf family had the rights to till a set amount of the estate, and they depended on these fields—which yielded barley, potatoes, lentils, and turnips, depending on the altitude—to feed them throughout the year.

The size of the serfs' land determined the amount of taxes they owed, and they paid these with money and in kind—butter, tsampa, wool, labor for dam-building—depending on the region and the estate. In certain villages serfs also paid with herbs, baskets, wood, or special cakes for monasteries. A family might have to give up a son or daughter as well, to serve as a monk, a household servant, or a soldier in the army.

Serfs hated transportation corvée above all other taxes. It obliged them to provide pack animals for anyone with an official permit granting the service, and the serfs had to keep on hand a supply of horses, mules, and yaks, and enough fodder to sustain them. At any time travelers could call on the serfs to carry them along with their goods, a half day's journey at a time.

The transportation tax usually fell on the wealthier serf families, those with hereditary rights to land. They could use their fields as they wished, though they could not sell them, and some of them went into trade on the side, lending grain to other serfs (interest rates were high, 10 to 20 percent). Some improved their lot by becoming favored servants. Through diligence, cleverness, and luck many became wealthy by Tibetan standards, amassing large herds, hiring laborers, and building spacious homes. Still others—45 percent of all agricultural serfs, by Chinese reckoning—paid an annual fee for the right to live and work away from the estate.

The poorest serfs had no hereditary rights to land but were granted sub-sistence fields to cultivate. They carried a lighter tax load, but they still had to grow their own food and at the same time pay their dues in labor. Some of them ran short of grain, borrowed heavily, and fell into debt. If they came to a point of desperation and saw no way out, they would flee their homes and run away beyond the borders of the estate.

When serfs had disputes among themselves, the steward usually acted as arbiter, but a serf could appeal to his lord in Lhasa, and in major cases, he could even take the dispute all the way to the central government. (The outcome, however, usually depended on the size of the gifts he gave the magistrate.)

Nomads, comprising about 20 percent of the population, were likewise vassals of an estate, a high lama, or a monastery. They pastured their herds, which they owned themselves, on the high reaches where nothing but grasses could grow, roaming on land that belonged to a lord, and they paid taxes in hides, butter, and meat each year. They were free to go on pilgrimage, visit relatives, or sell their produce in town bazaars as long as they met their obliga-tions, but they could not ordinarily move their animals to other pasturelands. Some acquired herds ranging into thousands of sheep and goats and hundreds of yaks. They were able to hire other nomad serfs to work as servants.

Although some lords and estate managers abused their power in the old Tibet, serfdom was not synonymous with oppression. An overseer could be arbitrary and cruel, taxing his workers to the limit and beyond, beating the serfs when they did not comply. But often management was lax, and brutality was not the rule. It depended on the individual lord or steward, and overseers had good reason to show restraint: They rarely managed to catch up with runaways, and they knew that if they bore down too hard, they could lose their labor force. Labor was always a scarce commodity in the old Tibet.

Most estate owners left their serfs alone as long as they provided the needed labor—on their own or with hired hands. Even though the law allowed lords to demand their serfs' labor at any time and to deny them the right to marry away from the estate or become a monk, in practice they tended to be lenient. Families and individuals could usually do as they pleased if they paid their dues.

If you were born a serf, however, you expected to remain one for life, although a very few who had served the state exceptionally well—such as skilled artisans or outstanding soldiers—were promoted from serf status to the nobility. And then there was always that slim chance that you could beat the odds, that your son would be recognized as the reincarnation of the Dalai Lama. This could turn your peasant family into wealthy aristocrats overnight.

But in spite of the system's mobility and flexibility and in spite of its legal requisites, the lot of many serfs was hard and full of toil. Often, observers have said, peasant farmers were cowed in the presence of overseers, bowing their heads, sticking out their tongues and gulping in air as a sign of respect.

Life among the old Tibetan nobility—some three hundred families or, according to Chinese data, 5 percent of the population—was leisurely, full of elaborate courtesies and idle pastimes. Their homes enclosed private gardens, and households functioned with a flock of servants who hauled the water, churned the butter tea, swept the floors, watched over the children, and tended the horses. Where the peasants wore homespun, the aristocracy dressed in silk, and the noblewomen wore intricate headdresses strung with semiprecious stones.

The harvests of barley and vegetables, the butter and hides that the serfs paid to their lords went into the granaries and storehouses of the nobles and monasteries. Stewards would sell the surplus grain and send the money in Tibetan *dotsey* notes to the landowners in Lhasa, and there it was stashed away in trunks to be used as needed for silks, jewels, and crafts, for trading ventures and gifts to monasteries. "We had very few expenses," writes one Lhasa noblewoman, "since all of our staples were supplied by our estates. There were no income taxes in Tibet. All we needed to buy at the market was fresh vegetables in season, meat, and a few luxury items from Europe, such as soap, fine tinned goods, and beer and whiskey."[4] This was the ultimate destination for much of a serf's labor.

The aristocrats filled the ranks of Tibetan lay officials, and they were assigned to twelve levels of status. They varied also in their wealth; some owned vast estates; others lived at the level of wealthy peasants or middle-class traders. All of them went in for picnics and lengthy banqueting, and when one was named to an official post, he was expected to put on a five-day feast for hundreds of guests. The entertainment was so lavish, running from early morning to late in the evening with at least a dozen courses at each meal, that many could not afford it. Heinrich Harrer, who spent seven years in Tibet during the 1940s, has described an opulent feast that was held to celebrate the birth of the Dalai Lama's younger brother: "For two consecutive hours the servants served course after course—I counted forty, but that was not the end. To eat through such a dinner required special training. I must be excused from mentioning all the delicacies that were offered to us, but I remember that they included all sorts of Indian spiced dishes and ended up with a soup of noodles."[5]

But it was not only the nobility who threw extravagant parties. Dawa Norbu, born into a serf family in the monastic town of Sakya in the 1940s, writes that his uncle's wedding banquet lasted for a week with feasting from dawn to dusk. The uncle was not a member of the aristocracy but one of Tibet's wealthy commoners.

Within the monasteries, monks—20 to 25 percent of Tibet's male population—also lived in stratified communities. As long as they remained in the monastery, they lost their serf status, but most retained their original social classes, and some spent their lives carrying water and serving higher-status monks. A few who showed promise as scholars could rise to the position of abbot or high lama through years of study, but many acquired only enough knowledge to read the scriptures. Some served as warriors who carried arms, wore red armbands, blackened their faces with soot, and let their hair grow long, training it in coils above their ears. They acted as bodyguards, soldiers, and athletes, and as a kind of SWAT team during festivals, wielding whips and cudgels to keep the crowds under control.

The old Tibet, with its exotic trappings and its medieval structure, had disappeared nearly four decades before I arrived in Lhasa. I was never going to experience that era firsthand, but once I was on the scene I could visit many of the sites and try to imagine them as they once were. I could envision some of the players in the settings they had described to me and thus try for a fuller understanding of times past and the changes of the last half century.

And so, when I looked up at the Potala Palace, majestic and vast, brooding over Lhasa, I thought of Ngawangthondup and Tashi Tshering, my good friends. Ngawangthondup was Zhang Jichuan's former teacher, whom he met again in a Berkeley lecture hall. Tashi Tshering, who grew up in Guchok Village, had come here to Lhasa as a school-age boy. The lives of the two men had converged here in Lhasa, the Abode of the Gods, at the great palace of the Dalai Lamas; and when I arrived in the capital, I tried to envision the city they had known, lost now beneath layers of history and the stir of modern Tibet.

Old Lhasa was a town of some thirty thousand inhabitants, lying in a broad river valley 12,000 feet above sea level and flanked by jagged peaks. In the early 1940s Tibet still slumbered in its medieval isolation, the Potala Palace loomed over a settlement called Shol, and the city of Lhasa was a cluster of houses surrounding the Jokhang Temple a mile away.

Tashi had come to this scene when he was ten years old, plucked from his round of herding sheep and goats when emissaries of the Dalai Lama chose him to join a centuries-old dance troupe. The troupe performed on state occasions, and its traditions had been set in the distant past: He would perform for eight years, and then he would become an instructor and train the next crop of youngsters. Tashi and his father had traveled from Guchok by yak, crossing mountain passes and spending a week on the road, to finally arrive in the capital, where Tashi took up residence in Shol, at the foot of the Potala.

Ngawangthondup was then living and studying in the chambers above, high in the palace. He came from a middle-class family, one which embodied the complexities of Tibetan social structure before the Chinese takeover. His father's family were serfs who served as treasurers for a noble family over several generations. His mother's family were neither serfs nor nobles but hereditary chieftains of an area. They paid taxes directly to the government and owned land and houses staffed by servants.

At the age of seven Ngawangthondup had left his home in the fertile region of Lhokha, south of Lhasa, to join a monastery outside the city. When he showed promise as a scholar, he was selected to enter a Potala school which trained monk officials for the Dalai Lama's government. He lived with senior monks and studied in a large hall overlooking over the Lhasa Valley and Sera Monastery, preparing to become a government clerk.

The Potala today has no court dance troupe and no school for monk officials, and Shol has been enveloped by urban sprawl. To envision Tashi Tshering and Ngawangthondup as they appeared in 1942, I had to turn away from the modern scene and conjure up a young dancer dressed in brocade with a pie-pan hat tied to his head and a student in a wine-colored wrap with heavy felt boots and a pen case of worked steel. Then I could also see the lines of serfs who labored up the steps of the palace carrying buckets of water for the Potala's inhabitants. And I could sometimes imagine the scene below in Shol, its streets empty of trucks, cars, and motorcycles. In those days everyone went about on foot or mounted on horse, yak, or donkey. Old Tibet, with its hidebound resistance to material progress, had eschewed the wheel as a means of transport. In all of Lhasa there was not a single wheeled cart and only a few traders got around on bicycles.

Wandering about the Lhasa of 1992 I tried to get my bearings and situate the events of half a century past. Here, I would think, Tashi came down from the hills and entered Lhasa with his father. And from one of those Potala windows Ngawangthondup watched the Dalai Lama's troops exchange fire with rebel monks during a week of civil conflict. From those rooftops he watched the serfs ascend the wide steps with their burdens and vowed that someday he would design an aqueduct to bring water from the hills. When I passed through the hallways and shrines of the Potala I knew that Ngawangthondup had there, with his fellow students, decided to form a secret society of would-be reformers. (Secret, because they were mindful of Lungshar, a reform-minded noble, who had his eyes torn out when he tried to change the system.) They agreed that when they became middle-level officials, they would dispense justice fairly and work to relieve the heavily taxed vassals of the religious and aristocratic estates. The young students sympathized with the hard life of many serfs and vowed to help them. The fact that they and other educated Tibetans over decades took the risk of supporting reform is evidence that Tibetan serfdom, in spite of its flexibility and legal resources, was often a harsh and unjust lot.

Tashi and Ngawangthondup passed their boyhoods in that somnolent Lhasa of medieval pomp and toiling serfs. It was a city devoted to Tibet's own brand of Buddhism, with its myriad rites and superstitions, austere practices, and lofty principles. Lamaist Buddhism was the basis of its one-thousand-year civilization, and it had flourished and produced a distinctive culture in one of the world's harshest environments. As I trudged through the byways of contemporary Lhasa, breathless and oxygen-starved in the early days of my visit, I came to appreciate the Tibetans' hard-won civilization. It was travail enough to survive at that altitude and in those sterile hills, let alone build a thriving culture.

But because Tibet had held itself apart from the rest of the world, set in a never-changing mold and under the control of reactionaries who fought off any attempts at change, mid-twentieth century Lhasa was about to face the first real threat to its way of life: an influx of outsiders who spoke a different language and disdained the religion and traditions of Tibet. These newcomers were determined to depose the old system and place themselves fully in charge, and they were inflamed with the conviction that they were settling a historic claim and freeing the masses from bondage.

Central Tibet, today known as the TAR, had been something of a remote protectorate of China since the early eighteenth century, while the eastern Tibetan ethnic areas of Amdo and Kham, (now in Qinghai, Gansu, Yunnan, and Sichuan provinces) were ruled for the most part by tribal chieftains. The combined ethnic Tibetan population of the eastern regions, according to Chinese data, was 1.7 million in the 1950s, compared with one million in central Tibet. The Amdowa and Khampa (as the people are called) speak Tibetan dialects which differ from that of central Tibet but with effort they can usually understand one another.[6]

The British had been involved with Tibet since late in the nineteenth century when Great Britain, long the colonial power in India and later the protector of nearby Sikkim and Bhutan, set out to use Tibet as a buffer against Russia. Rather than try to make Tibet into a protectorate, however, the British decided to make trade the basis of their dealings with Lhasa. And in order to sell Indian tea and textiles in Tibet and to import Tibetan wool, carpets, and salt, they signed treaties with the Tibetan government. The history of these agreements, dating from the early years of the twentieth century, underscores the problems Tibet faced in establishing its credentials as a sovereign state.

In 1904, after British troops invaded Tibet and pushed forward to Lhasa, Britain ignored China's claims on the region and signed a bilateral trade agreement with the Tibetan government. But two years later, bowing to Chinese pressure, the British ratified a separate treaty with China which said that China was not a foreign power in Tibet and Britain was the only foreign state with special trade rights there. In effect, it declared that Tibet came under Chinese control without spelling out the extent of that control. The Tibetan government said later that the British had signed the 1906 agreement in secret, and they insisted that the 1904 contract was the true basis for British rights in Tibet.

Then, in 1914, after the fall of the Qing dynasty, Britain sat down with China and Tibet to forge a new agreement. The draft treaty gave China "suzerain" rights over Tibet, meaning that China controlled foreign affairs in the region but otherwise granted Tibet its autonomy. But when the Chinese government refused to go along with provisions setting the eastern borders of Tibet, Britain and Tibet alone signed the agreement, noting that China could not enjoy the rights laid out in the treaty as long as it had not signed. The Tibetans had tried to gain recognition of their independence, but they signed the agreement nevertheless, declaring that it was a draft, not a final document, and that they should have further talks with the Chinese to clarify their status. They also saw it as a guarantee of autonomy, but they still preferred the 1904 bilateral agreement with Britain, which did not give China suzerain (let alone sovereign) rights over Tibet.

At that point Tibet was in fact independent. The Qing dynasty had lost its nominal control in Lhasa after the rebellion of 1911 when a new republican, nationalist government took over, and the Tibetans expelled every Chinese official and soldier. In 1912 the Thirteenth Dalai Lama declared Tibet independent, and it was to function as a sovereign state for nearly forty years. But even as Britain and, later, India, treated Tibet as an independent country, they failed to give it the necessary support in the international community. Tibet was never able to solidify its claims that it was a sovereign state outside of Chinese control.

Once the British set up shop in Tibet, the country began to stir from its medieval moorings. Young Tibetan men attended school in Darjeeling and Britain; an English school was founded in the town of Gyantse; the British built a telegraph line and trained Tibetan telegraphers; an electric plant generated power for a few sites in Lhasa; the Tibetan army was expanded and acquired new arms and modern training (and managed to defeat the Chinese in Kham); and some officials tried to reform the political system and bring about a modern police force, surveys of mineral wealth, and a hydroelectric plant.

But signs of an alien (British) presence in Tibet alarmed the conservative monks and aristocrats who saw it as a threat to their power and the traditional way of life. They managed to persuade the Dalai Lama to rescind most of the efforts at change. The English language school was closed the year after it opened, and the army was cut back once more. Then after the Dalai Lama died in 1933, the reformer Lungshar was arrested, found guilty on trumped-up charges of trying to kill a cabinet member and introduce bolshevism, and punished by blinding. Tibet continued in its ancient rounds, closed to contact with the outside world and lacking the modern army necessary to ward off an invasion.

When Tashi and Ngawangthondup were growing up, World War II was a far-off conflict, a faint rumor from the ends of the earth. But it brought new Westerners to Lhasa, in addition to the British representatives at the trade mission (and the Chinese, who returned to set up an office after the Dalai Lama died): two Austrians who escaped to Tibet from a British prison camp and stayed for seven years, a crew of downed American flyers, and an American survey crew looking into an overland supply route to China.

The Austrians built a second electric plant, and the Americans donated wireless equipment to the Tibetan government. After the war a British wireless operator was stationed in Tibet.

The Chinese saw these contacts with Britain and the United States as attempts to take over Tibet, *their* Tibet. Once the Communists routed Chiang Kai-shek from the mainland in 1949, they began broadcasting their intentions to get rid of the "imperialists" in Tibet and bring the region back to the motherland. This was how China saw it, even though the imperialist faction was nothing more than a handful of men, and no one besides China was claiming Tibet as its own. Russia had withdrawn long before; Britain had ceded its interest to India when that country won independence in 1947; and India, in turn, was not about to get into a major conflict with China over the ownership of Tibet. Now, however, the United States, which had shown little interest in Tibet before Chiang Kai-shek was defeated, began to view Tibet as a possible barrier to the spread of communism. At this point, American officials took a look at sending aid to the Lhasa government.

But the Americans, along with the British and Indians, failed to help Tibet counter the threat from China and gain recognition as a sovereign state.

Even before the fall of the Kuomintang, the Lhasa government realized the danger and tried to win support in Asia and the West. India did send small arms to Tibet, covertly, but no one was willing to go along with Tibet's claim that it was legally an independent nation.

In the autumn of 1950, as Tibet continued its belated and ever-more-frantic effort to gain legal status in the eyes of the world, the People's Liberation Army invaded Tibet from the east and overran the weak Tibetan force. Tibet, in its isolation and its ignorance of foreign affairs, had waited too long to formalize its de facto independence.

Once inside the eastern boundary of Tibet, China halted its troops and called for negotiations. The Lhasa government appealed to the United Nations, the United States, Britain, and India. But once again, as they called for help from the outside world they had resisted for so long, no one came to their aid. They were forced to negotiate with the invaders.

In May 1951, a Tibetan delegation in Beijing signed an agreement which declared that the Tibetan people "shall return to the big family of the Motherland—the People's Republic of China." The contract also held that the People's Liberation Army could enter Tibet, Tibet would remain autonomous under the direction of the central government of China, the existing political system would remain unchanged with the Dalai Lama in charge, and China would take charge of Tibet's foreign affairs. The Chinese would set up a working committee to put these provisions into effect. In all, there were seventeen points.

Then, in what China calls the "peaceful liberation," PLA troops made their way to Lhasa, carrying banners, singing, beating drums. The newcomers brought their culture, with a worldview at an opposite pole from that of Tibetans. They were zealous converts to communism who believed they had wrested Tibet from imperialists and returned it to the motherland, and they were as set on change as Tibet was resistant.

On an autumn day in 1951 both Tashi Tshering and Ngawangthondup joined the crowds who went out to watch the soldiers arrive. They saw a stream of young men and women, tattered and wan from months on the road but smiling as they carried banners and beat drums. Although Ngawangthondup watched in silence, he was troubled by what he saw. He had hoped that the Communists could bring reform, but he didn't like the sight of guns and cannons. He didn't like to see the soldiers put up their tents by the river, where the people of Lhasa used to spend days and weeks picnicking. There were so many of them, and it looked like they had come to stay.

Someone showed me the spot where the troops first pitched their tents. A military station, set behind high concrete walls, stands there now, and the river flows by a stone embankment. But from that site I could look upriver and see the route the soldiers took, down the valley from the east, between the barren mountain slopes. As the troops arrived in Lhasa they crossed the Kyichu River in yakskin coracles. Today, travelers drive across a concrete bridge.

Tashi Tshering used to stand near the river while the soldiers marched in their daily drills, and he listened to the leader shouting, *"Yi, er, san,"*—"One, two, three." The soldiers lent excitement to sleepy Lhasa, but the sight of them—rows and rows of Chinese, regimented and ranked and ready for battle—left Tashi uneasy. The city was changing, and he was both curious and anxious about what was to come. The newcomers set up loudspeakers in their camps, and they broadcast in Tibetan, using words Tashi had never heard before—socialism, imperialists, capitalism. He had never known that there was any way of life beyond that of the Tibet he knew. It was how society was meant to be: perfect, ordered by tradition, proven by centuries of use. But now Tashi turned the new words over in his mind. He was eager to learn about those strange concepts, and in 1957 he left Lhasa and crossed the border to India. He would not return until nearly ten years had passed, when the city was foundering under the assaults of the Red Guards.

Tashi was far from Lhasa when the rebellion of 1959 broke out, but Ngawangthondup was on hand to wield a gun and fight the self-styled liberators. He had been to Beijing to study at the new Institute for National Minorities, and he had hoped at first that China would bring needed reform to Tibet. But he had grown disillusioned with communism and Chinese putdowns of Tibetan culture. By 1957 he had fled back to Lhasa. Now, as a monk official, he became a clerk in the Dalai Lama's government, which operated under an uneasy alliance with the Chinese. Under the Seventeen Point Agreement, the Chinese had tried to gradually gain control while the Tibetan government did what it could to resist their encroachment.

Ngawangthondup worked then in the Jokhang Temple, a short walk from my hotel. Every day I looked out on the golden stupas of the temple roof, and

I always thought of him walking through its maze of shrines and hallways and, in the heat of battle, firing a rifle from beneath the eaves. He was there as Khampa warriors arrived from the east, bringing rebellion to Lhasa, and he was serving in the Dalai Lama's government as tensions grew and finally exploded in warfare.

The Khampa had come from the east, many from beyond the Yangtze River, where China claimed them as part of Sichuan Province. They were mountain people who had often resisted domination by the Lhasa government and gave their allegiance to tribal headmen. But they and the Amdowa to the north of them—also ruled by headmen—were devout Buddhists and Tibetan in culture and language. The Seventeen Point Agreement had no jurisdiction over those who lived in the provinces of China, so the Chinese had early on subjected the Khampa and Andowa to socialist reforms. When the Chinese began to clamp down on Kham's monasteries and tried to take away the Khampa's rifles, local tribesmen took to the hills and attacked Chinese outposts in a series of guerrilla raids. Now the Khampa were fleeing their homeland for central Tibet.

The Lhasa Ngawangthondup found on his return was already changing. Now there were trucks and motorcycles in the roads, maneuvering around the horses and yak trains. The Chinese had built highways to connect Lhasa with Qinghai and Sichuan provinces, and they had spanned the rivers with pylon-supported bridges. Ngawangthondup found that new hospitals and schools had appeared and the markets were filled with Chinese goods: thermos bottles, silks, porcelain bowls, and chopsticks. But he also found the air charged with tension. The Khampa were camped outside of town, and they carried rifles under their sheepskin wraps and recruited local men to join them in fighting the Chinese. Rebel units outside Lhasa were attacking Chinese convoys and garrisons, and in Lhokha to the southwest they were receiving arms from the U.S. Central Intelligence Agency. Both sides were taking losses, and the hospitals were filling with wounded Chinese soldiers.

Ngawangthondup also began to carry a gun, and he put aside his monk's robe to wear the clothes of an ordinary townsman. He wanted to escape attention, and he was preparing to defend himself in case fighting broke out.

Lhasa erupted in open rebellion over an incident that might have drawn little notice in calmer times. Officers of the People's Liberation Army invited the Dalai Lama to attend a theatrical performance, adding an unusual demand: that he leave his armed bodyguards behind. Word got out, and residents of the capital were soon incensed by the rumor that the Dalai Lama was about to be kidnapped. Defiant crowds surrounded his summer palace, and in the center of Lhasa a mob burned a copy of the Seventeen-Point Agreement. On the evening of March 17, 1959, after two shells fell within the grounds of the summer palace, the Dalai Lama was spirited out of Lhasa and began his trek into exile. On the morning of the 20th, mortar fire announced the beginning of war in Lhasa.

When the first shells fell before dawn on March 20, Ngawangthondup was in the Jokhang, and from then on, until he escaped two days later, he found no time to rest. He was twenty-eight years old, a lean, methodical man with a gift for strategy. Together with a Tibetan army officer he took over command of the Jokhang, arming troops, organizing the refugees who poured into the temple, planning attacks. He used a rifle to pick off Chinese soldiers, and as tanks headed for the portals of the great shrine on March 22, he was one of the last to escape.

This story was etched in my mind when I came to Lhasa, and I gradually came to know the sites Ngawangthondup had mentioned: the Happy Light Cinema, which his men seized from a contingent of Chinese soldiers; the streets around the cathedral where Tibetans and Chinese clashed in hand-to-hand combat; Norbulingka, the summer palace, from which the Dalai Lama fled shortly before the battle; and the Lingkor, the pilgrim route around the city, which Ngawangthondup and hundreds of townspeople crossed under enemy fire as they fled the capital. He joined tens of thousands who escaped over the Himalayas to India.

Ngawangthondup and Tashi Tshering weren't around to see the red flag hoisted over the Potala, the lines of prisoners marched toward Norbulingka, the ceremonies granting the serfs deeds to their own land, the gradual emptying of monasteries and nunneries as the state took away their right to tax. Both men lost family members in the harsh reprisals which came after the revolt. Tashi Tshering's brother—who had not joined the rebels—was arrested for hiding a gun from the authorities. He was sent to prison, where he died of starvation. Tashi's family home was confiscated, and his parents and surviving brother were sent to live in a few rooms of an empty monastery. Some of

17

Ngawangthondup's relatives, who had helped the rebels in Lhokha, were captured and sent to prison, where his mother and an elderly aunt died.

The United States and, later, India, continued to supply arms to rebel units in the countryside, and the CIA trained Tibetan guerrilla fighters in Camp Hale, Colorado, but the rebels proved to be little more than a nuisance to the Chinese. The guerrillas retreated to the Himalayan principality of Mustang, on the Tibet-Nepal border, and from there made sporadic raids on Chinese garrisons and convoys, but their attacks failed to loosen Chinese control in Tibet. In the early 1970s, the United States ended its support for the rebels, and in 1975 the fighters laid down their arms.

About the time the guerrillas were regrouping in the mountains, Tashi entered the United States on a student visa, and Ngawangthondup joined the government-in-exile in Dharamsala. Their ways had diverged. Ngawangthondup worked to denounce the Chinese government and return the Dalai Lama to Tibet. Tashi, who was reading Marx and Mao Zedong, decided to join the new rulers of his homeland. In 1964 he re-entered China, eager to help build a new, socialist Tibet, but he was not allowed to go home. He was sent to Shaanxi Province to study with other Tibetans at the Institute for National Minorities. There he was to learn the Chinese language and socialist theory and become a cadre, a member of the professional class which would create a Maoist state in the backward region of Tibet.

While Tashi was in Shaanxi, his homeland was formally inaugurated as the Tibet Autonomous Region, supposedly a semi-independent entity but actually governed from Beijing. Then, only a year later, the Cultural Revolution arrived to destroy whatever government existed in Tibet. Tashi's classes in Shaanxi ended and the students devoted themselves to revolution, the study of Mao Zedong Thought, the exposure of "capitalist roaders," and "struggle sessions" (called *thamzing* in Tibetan), where students and faculty who were branded counterrevolutionary endured hours of abuse.

In late 1966 Tashi and his fellow students returned to Lhasa, joining the contingents of zealous students who had come to smash the "four olds" (traditional culture, habit, ideology, and customs) and replace them with the "four news" (their socialist counterparts). Other packs of lawless youths, Tibetans and Chinese alike, had arrived before them and ravaged the Jokhang Temple as well as monasteries in and around Lhasa. Tashi had come to do the same. "We went to different places," Tashi told me, "looking for things to destroy."

He longed to join the Red Guards, but he was blackballed and viewed with suspicion for having lived in the United States. He could not even visit friends on his own. Whenever he left the group, a monitor wearing a red armband went with him. Nevertheless, Tashi was glad to be of use. He was called on to write slogans in Tibetan, and he humbly carried the broom and bucket of glue when the students went out to paste bulletins about town.

Lhasa now was a drab and cheerless city. No prayer flags flew from the housetops; no incense curled skyward in morning offerings. Chinese chauvinism and prejudice, partially restrained before, now ran unchecked, and the remaining overt signs of faith, Tibetan dress, and even the Tibetan language were derided and punished as backward and counterrevolutionary. Monasteries became political meeting halls, granaries, guest houses, and pig farms. Politicians and bureaucrats were forced out of their offices and consigned to work gangs. Every day they marched out to the fields and labored along with other victims of the Red Guards' zeal.

As Tashi described this Lhasa, the Lhasa of the Cultural Revolution, I found it as difficult to imagine as that of old Tibet. The prayer flags are flying again, and monasteries are crowded with pilgrims. When I stood before the great doors of the Jokhang, watching the devout in their prostrations, it was hard to imagine that not long before, those portals were barred and the people passed them by, eyes downcast, too cowed to make a single obeisance to their faith. When I entered the temple I had to remind myself that the great Buddha statue had once been mutilated and all the side chapels reduced to rubble.

But one day I interviewed an elderly nun, the abbess of a convent on a back street of the Barkor. She had conjured up the scene as it was in 1966, soon after the Red Guards arrived. As she spoke I could imagine her inside the cathedral with a group of fellow monks and nuns who had convened to discuss the Cultural Revolution and what it meant for them, the few remaining inhabitants of their monasteries and convents. In the midst of their anxious deliberations a hubbub of shouts and imperious pounding had broken out at the portals, and when they reluctantly opened the doors, a mob pushed inside and began a frenzy of destruction, shattering the statues of the thousand-armed, eleven-headed Avalokiteshvara, the Seven Mighty Buddhas, the Dharma

Kings, and all their many companions in the dozens of shrines that fill the Jokhang.

As the abbess told her story, she gazed into the dark corners of her convent parlor. "Pah!" she said, making a fist and flinging open her fingers. "Pah!" She was describing the sound of rifles and crowbars as they struck the sacred images. She had returned in memory to that day and was once again running out of the cathedral and through the narrow streets to her nunnery. She had made her way to the chanting hall and found the the statues of saints that she had tended for thirty years lying in dust and rubble on the floor. It seemed that the gods themselves had disappeared from the world, leaving their human devotees bereft and alone in a hostile universe. Now, she asked herself, what happens to faith? And out of her desolation the answer came: Tibet had "come to the end of prayer." This she told me, patiently responding to my questions, her old eyes bright, her hands working her beads.

And even Tashi, one of the rampaging youths, told me that those times plunged him into turmoil as well. He was confused by the high-sounding promises and rhetoric on one side and the cruelty and oppression on the other. He believed in the revolution and Mao Zedong, but he was horrified at the destruction. He saw the city he loved depressed and shattered. He hated thamzing, but he went in obedience, as a witness and participant. Many victims were accused out of resentment or jealousy or simply because they could not defend themselves. "I went to such meetings many times," Tashi told me. "I felt awful, terrible, but I had to say, 'Nice, great, revolutionary.' But it was really cruel and ruthless and not at all convincing. It was always fake; you couldn't believe the charges. Only those who were really infatuated with revolution really believed it. They thought they were responding to Mao's call."

Tashi stayed in Lhasa until the spring of 1967. Then he returned to Shaanxi to still more efforts to weed out the four olds and impose the four news. He didn't see Lhasa again until the spring of 1971, and then it was during a quick passage from the airport to Sangyip Prison on the outskirts of town. Tashi's "imperialist" past had finally landed him in jail, and by the time he returned to Lhasa in handcuffs, he had already spent more than three years in labor camps and prison cells.

Sangyip is one site I cannot describe. For fear of putting all my investigations at risk, I stayed away from Lhasa's detention centers, and so I only know secondhand of that grim establishment, which still holds Tibetans accused of treason and such criminal activities as shouting, "Free Tibet!" in the center of Jokhang Plaza.

Tashi spent more than two years in Sangyip, and then, one cold spring morning, a Chinese prison official called for him and spoke to him kindly, an event so rare that Tashi took it as a good omen. More visits with officials followed, and in May of 1973 he walked free into Lhasa once more. The Cultural Revolution still held the city in its grip, but Tashi spent four glorious days of freedom, visiting friends and an old girlfriend named Sangye (now his wife) before he was escorted back to Shaanxi. He was not allowed to stay in Lhasa; as a former prisoner he had to return to the site of his arrest.

I was coming to see Lhasa in stages: the medieval city moving at a yak's pace, the arrival of the People's Liberation Army, the gradual accretion of roads and buildings, the disappearance of the Dalai Lama and his court, then the razing of temples and the reign of the lawless Red Guards. Tibetans under the Cultural Revolution despaired. They believed, like the old abbess, that they had "come to the end of prayer," that their civilization was dying. I imagine Lhasa then as a city under clouds, the sun, which usually seems so near, blazing in a jewel-like sky just above the mountain peaks, dulled by the grim overcast of captivity.

But then in 1976, Mao Zedong died, and the Cultural Revolution expired with him. Gradually Tibet began to emerge from the enforced commune system and the taboos on religious and cultural expression. But the changes were slow in coming, and in 1979 Tibetans, in a series of mob scenes, gave vent to their anguish and showed the Chinese authorities the depth of their dismay.

To recreate those events I visited Pema, a Lhasa woman in her forties who runs a teahouse in the center of town. She was a schoolgirl during the failed rebellion of 1959, a young wife when the Cultural Revolution seized Tibet, and the manager of a restaurant when delegations from the Dalai Lama arrived in 1979. It was these envoys from India who set off displays of grief and longing and took Chinese officials by surprise.

China, in its eagerness to leave the Cultural Revolution behind, had decided to open Tibet to representatives of the government-in-exile. They wanted to show off the progress of the previous twenty years—the schools, hospitals, roads, and irrigation ditches—and demonstrate the Tibetan people's solidarity with the motherland. In 1979 the Chinese government invited a group of four to travel through the TAR and Tibetan areas of Qinghai Province. Lhasa authorities were so confident of the people's support that they held neighborhood meetings to warn them to behave. We know you hate the old society, the officials said, but please be polite. These visitors are guests of the Chinese government.

It was an autumn morning when the first group arrived in the capital. Pema hurried from her home and made for the Jokhang Plaza, pulling her wrap around her in the chill air. She had heard that the Dalai Lama's elder brother and four other officials from the government-in-exile had arrived and would bow down before the great Buddha in the Jokhang, and she, like thousands of others in Lhasa, was determined to see them. When she rushed into the square, breathless with anticipation, she found the common crowded with people—shouting, weeping, and throwing white scarves into the air.

Pema wanted to touch Lobsang Samten, the Dalai Lama's younger brother; she longed to see his face and receive his blessing. So she pushed into the throng, impelled by her urgency and the pressing current of humanity surrounding her. A group of young men encircled the delegation, trying to hold back the crowd, but some people still managed to reach Lobsang Samten, a slight mustachioed man in his mid-forties, and hoisted him on their shoulders. The frenzied people reached out to touch him, as if he were the Precious One himself. They tore off pieces of his clothing and tucked letters into the folds of his brown wrap—petitions for aid, lists of grievances, and messages for relatives in exile. Lobsang Samten spoke from the center of the mob, shouting to be heard. He said only that the Dalai Lama was in good health; not to worry.

Pema saw him from a distance; she had no chance to touch him or receive his blessing. But she was elated. If the Dalai Lama's brother could stand here in their midst, maybe His Holiness would return and Tibetans could live by their own values as they had before. It was as if the clouds had parted and an image of the Buddha himself had appeared in the sky, showering them with grace.

Tibetans like Pema were heartened, but Chinese officials were dismayed. Throughout the Tibetan regions of China, wherever the delegation went,

Tibetans sobbed and prostrated themselves, exposing their grief over the years of repression and their joy at seeing envoys from their revered leader. And the Chinese were surprised that the delegates had failed to appreciate their achievements. Instead, they had reproached the government. The delegates said they had seen only poverty, anguish, and the ruins of their civilization—tears, ragged clothing, the skeletal walls of razed monasteries, and sacred art used as building material for latrines.

The central government began to take a hard look at conditions in Tibet. In May 1980, Hu Yaobang, General Secretary of the Chinese Communist Party, a moderate and reformer, flew there on a fact-finding tour. After a month in the region, he returned to Beijing, bringing with him the now-disgraced TAR Party secretary, Ren Rong. Hu privately condemned the previous two decades, comparing them to colonial occupation, and he publicly announced a six-point reform program to bolster Tibet's economy, improve education, and restore the damaged culture. These policies still have a profound effect today though no longer officially in place.

Soon after Hu left Tibet, a second delegation arrived, setting off more mob scenes in Lhasa and at the ruined Ganden Monastery. There, at that ancient monastic center, Pema managed to see the delegates. I know the route she took: east from Lhasa, then up a winding dirt road to the ridge where Ganden stands. The monastery is rebuilding now, but the new construction still stands out as occasional breaks of color against the wreckage left from the Cultural Revolution. It is a simple matter to imagine how it looked then, in the summer of 1980: a razed city of jagged, earthen walls.

Pema left at five in the morning and journeyed along a road clogged with traffic and lined with police. She was on hand when the delegates stood in front of the blighted monastery and spoke to the crowd. They said the Dalai Lama himself would come to Tibet, and they urged the people to be patient and work hard in the meantime. Then they sang the Tibetan national anthem, composed by the government-in-exile. "We didn't know the words," said Pema, "so we didn't join in. But we knew the meaning." The mass of Tibetans wept and prostrated themselves, and some shouted, "Long live the Dalai Lama!" "Chinese go home!" "Independent Tibet!"

This time Pema managed to speak to one of the men, a distant relative. She brought her aging mother-in-law forward to meet him, and the man replied kindly. Pema still remembers his words; he said, "Hello, *Sumola* [aunt]. I'm glad to see you, and I will visit you." But the man was never able to come to her home. Officials were growing impatient with the political tone of this delegation, and a few days later the government expelled the five men from Tibet, charging them with advocating Tibetan independence and agitating the public.

The Dalai Lama never returned, in spite of the delegates' promise. Negotiations between the government-in-exile and the People's Republic failed to produce an agreement. But the reforms proposed by Hu Yaobang went forward—an easing of restraints on travel and religious expression, a return of Tibetan language teaching in the schools, tax exemptions, and a flurry of new construction. Now Lhasa came to resemble the city I would come to see in 1992, with a Holiday Inn on the edge of town and devout Tibetans crowding the temples and monasteries.

But Lhasa in the early 1980s was a more sanguine, upbeat city than the one I would come to know. In those days people still believed the Dalai Lama would come home, and China was holding good on reform. In the early 1980s Tibetans could light butter lamps in the temples again; peasants and nomads were freed from the hated communes; individuals could set up shops or peddle goods on the street; hundreds of Chinese cadres were sent back to the provinces; and the Chinese government was planning to replace Chinese with Tibetan as the official language of government. It looked like Tibetans might run their own affairs again, almost as freely as in the old days.

The government put economic reform at the top of its list and brought in Chinese workers to build hotels and office buildings. In 1984 it eased restrictions on tourism and launched an open door policy for all of the People's Republic. Now Westerners began to arrive with cameras and cash, and Chinese came overland by bus from Sichuan, Gansu, and Qinghai. These new Chinese were members of a "floating population" who came for a few months or years to peddle their wares and skills before they returned home. They took rooms in the old city and in the new apartments which sprang up on the outskirts.

This was not what Lhasa residents had hoped for. They might have more money to spend, but they now feared that their way of life was threatened by a flood of newcomers. Worse, there was no more talk of the Dalai Lama's return, and no more delegations came from India. Instead, the city was filling with Chinese who came only to make money, who had no interest in Tibet, its language, culture, or religion.

When I was in Lhasa the Chinese traders, shopkeepers, bicycle repairmen, restaurant owners, cooks, launderers, and vendors were still arriving. The Lhasa of 1987 was very nearly the same city I knew. It took little effort to imagine the city as it was when riots broke out and revealed the growing tension beneath the surface. My hotel was in the center of the city, just where the protesters had gathered and marched and fallen during the time of open resistance. I had read of the riots in newspapers and reports by human rights agencies, but it took some familiarity with Lhasa's old quarter to envision those days of defiance, exhilaration and turmoil.[7]

The first demonstration took place in September 1987, a few days after the Dalai Lama appeared in Washington before the U.S. Congressional Human Rights Caucus. There he had called for the removal of Chinese troops from Tibet and for new talks between the People's Republic and the government-in-exile. He had also accused China of human rights abuses and environmental plunder. Tibetans learned of the speech, and in response, a group of monks marched around the Barkor six days later, on September 27, carrying a homemade Tibetan flag and shouting slogans—"Independent Tibet!" "Chinese Go Home!" "Bring Back the Dalai Lama!" Then they marched down the main street to the TAR headquarters, a sprawling complex behind high walls and security guards, and there police arrested them.

This was followed by another demonstration on October 1 (the anniversary of the founding of the People's Republic), and this one turned bloody. Again a group of monks began circling the Barkor, joined by a growing crowd of civilians, but this time police rushed in from side streets and the demonstration became a riot. A mob set fire to a police station and overturned cars; police shot into the crowd, killing about a dozen unarmed persons and wounding many more. One of the victims was an eight-year-old boy, shot in the abdomen as he tried to fling a rock at the armed men. (He lived, and I have his picture, passed to me by a Tibetan who visited the boy a month after the riot.) Many stood on the side, watching in silence or whistling encouragement.

Several Tibetans told me that a tumult of feeling infected them all, fueling many with unexpected courage. One demonstrator ran from the Jokhang to a hotel three blocks away before he discovered a bullet wound in his abdomen. Some of the rioters acted in a frenzy of defiance and rage. A student monk rushed into the police station, grabbed an officer's gun by the bayonet, and twisted it with his bare hands, wrenching it away and dashing it against the wall before he rushed to a room where a group of prisoners was being held. He hurled himself at the door, and there a policeman's bullet struck him in the head and he fell dead. Friends picked up his body and carried it twice around the Barkor. They were filled, as one of them told me later, with grief, rage, and a kind of wild elation. Then police took the man's body from them and carried it away.

There was another riot during the New Year and Prayer Festival celebrations of March 1988, and another short but bloody demonstration that same year on December 10 (International Human Rights Day). And then in March 1989, rioting broke out again. For three days Lhasa saw protesters setting fire to Chinese shops and skirmishing with police in the streets. The police would wait until a mob was running wild in one section of the old city, and then they would suddenly appear and open fire. The casualties were impossible to count, but informed estimates ranged from forty to 150 dead with scores more wounded. At midnight on the third day the government declared martial law.

Now foreign tourists and journalists were expelled, and police and soldiers made the rounds of monasteries to take monks and nuns into custody. Checkpoints went up on the major streets, and soldiers stopped cars and pedestrians to inspect identification cards. Anyone with a shaven head (thus resembling a monk) and anyone who appeared wounded was suspect and subject to arrest. Propaganda teams visited the convents and monasteries to preach the Party line and warn against "splittist" activities.

Martial law was no longer in effect when I reached Lhasa, at least not an official martial law. It ended a year after the 1989 riots. In 1992 I saw no checkpoints, and the propaganda teams were leaving the monasteries alone, for the time being. But up until a few months before I arrived, the lockdown which followed the June 1989 massacre near Tiananmen Square had affected Tibet as well. Through 1991 Lhasa residents were afraid to speak openly to foreigners, and no one dared sell Dalai Lama photos on the street.

My interpreter, Xiao Jin, warned me that shopkeepers and other commoners would be too wary to talk. That's what it was like when she visited a year before, she told me, so I shouldn't expect anyone to answer my questions. She was clearly nervous. But by 1992, a thaw had set in. Westerners were returning, not only in guided tours, but also as individuals and in small groups, equipped with backpacks and bicycles. I could buy Dalai Lama photos on the Barkor and strike up conversations, discreetly, with almost anyone. Lhasa had changed since the year before, and the fact that I was there, armed with camera and notepad, nosing about government offices and back streets, was one more sign that officials had loosened up.

And yet there were the video cameras which the Public Security Bureau aimed at Jokhang Plaza, the Barkor, and the street where I was lodging. There were those jeeps and a big semi always parked at one end of the plaza, and the men in dark glasses who lingered near them. There were those warnings from knowing friends who told me not to talk too freely; someone might be trying to draw me out. There were the very polite public security men who showed up one night at the hotel and checked our visas. There was all the talk about undercover officers: They dressed like Khampa and walked around the Barkor; they put on monks' robes and entered the monasteries; they were outfitted like shoe repairmen, and they sat all day near the Jokhang.

There was an atmosphere of fear which said to me that martial law, undeclared, was still in effect. It took me a while to make out the signs because the authorities want it to appear that all is well, that only a handful of dissidents, incited by the "Dalai Lama clique," make trouble from time to time. This was Lhasa when I was there, operated under a policy of "outwardly calm, inwardly tight." The central government was stressing control in Tibet, pouring money into its security forces while development in medical care and education languished.

My friend Tashi Tshering, who had originally come to Lhasa to join the Dalai Lama's dance troupe, lives at the center of this new Abode of the Gods. He returned to the city from Shaanxi in 1981, and since then he has taught at Tibet University, retired, and gone into business. The Lhasa where he lives today is still devoted to the old deities but under the control of a new godless creed. The Communist state has tried to replace the Buddhist cosmic view

27

with a materialist and totalitarian society, and the tension between the two creates a city eroded by fear and resentment. Tashi's apartment abuts the Barkor Cafe, where the Public Security Bureau sets up lookouts when protest is in the air. It faces the main command post across the square and the big semi which stands ready to receive prisoners.

During the riots the crowds swirled below Tashi's windows, and he could hear shots and cries and see the smoke of burning cars and buildings. He was, he said frankly, very much afraid. But Tashi has also taken advantage of the new freedoms that came with the reforms. He has traveled to the United States, and he has been making money on his own, selling books and carpets. "I could never have done this even a few years ago," he said in 1991.

This is Lhasa now—tense, wary, and growing steadily more prosperous. It is slowly joining the modern age, but at what cost? That's what I went there to see, and once I gained a sense of the old Tibet and how it grew into the new, I could examine those questions I had first asked Zhang Jichuan that chilly spring morning in San Francisco: Genocide? Environmental plunder? Discrimination? Cultural annihilation? Religious repression? After scanning the past five decades of life in Lhasa, I was ready to look for answers.

2

The Land and Its Survivors (Environment)

China, according to its critics, is razing Tibet—tearing down its forests, carting off its precious minerals, killing its wildlife, and polluting its soil and rivers. Whole species of animals and plants have died out, some say, and the soil has become poisoned and eroded. The critics also charge that Tibet's third largest lake, the pristine and sacred Yamdrok Tso, will soon be sacrificed to provide hydroelectric power for Lhasa. Supporters of Tibetan independence accuse China of exploiting Tibet without a care for its fragile ecology. Before the Chinese came, they say, the people of Tibet lived in harmony with nature and wildlife flourished.

China, however, prefers to talk about development—electrical power, agricultural advances, factories, commerce, telecommunications, and trade. The government claims to have brought modern benefits to a backward region once mired in feudalism. At the same time the Chinese point to tree-planting campaigns, wildlife preserves, and laws designed to protect forests and endangered species as evidence that China is a responsible steward of the land.

The Chinese are correct in saying that they have brought tractors, cars, roads, irrigation canals, and electric lights to Tibet, but the International Campaign for Tibet and its supporters are also correct in noting that since the Chinese took control, the plateau has suffered great losses. The critics may have overstated the case against industrial pollution and the Yamdrok power project, which might possibly ease, rather than aggravate, the burden on the environment. But they are right in sounding the alarm over threats to wildlife and forests. The once-abundant herds of wild yak, antelope, ass, and gazelle have been pushed into the mountains and remotest corners of the plateau. The ancient forests of southern and eastern Tibet are now scarred with barren, clear-cut slopes.

These assaults on the land, some say, result from China's view of Tibet as its "western treasurehouse." They point to the Chinese name for Tibet, *Xizang*, as evidence. *Xi* means "west," and *zang* they interpret as "treasure box," since Chinese script uses the homonym character for depository to reproduce the sound of zang (probably referring to the ancient Tibetan region of Tsang). Xizang, they say, sums up the Chinese attitude toward Tibet as a land ripe for the taking.

In fact, China is not willfully destroying Tibet. It is not so simple as all that. Many Chinese scientists care deeply about the land and its flora and fauna, and China cooperates with international groups trying to preserve Tibet's wildlife. In many cases Tibetans themselves are shooting the rare snow leopards and wild yaks in their mountains. But China as self-appointed warden of Tibet is ultimately responsible for what happens there. It was China's Cultural Revolution that saw the greatest slaughter of wildlife, and it is China which has brought high-powered rifles and chain saws to the region—along with more benign forms of progress. It is also China's lax legal system which allows hunters to ignore laws against the unlicensed pursuit of game.

And Tibetans themselves, despite claims that they are traditionally in harmony with nature, often pay scant attention to the environment. Like many Third World people, they are caught up in strategies for their own survival— getting in the harvest or protecting their herds against foraging wolves. They may complain about scarred, clear-cut hillsides and wonder where the wildlife has gone, but pesticide contamination and air pollution are not among their concerns. Industry and other modern developments are recent arrivals in Tibet, and their liabilities—sources of major controversies in the United States— cause Tibetans little anxiety. Most are unaware of the environmental debate between China and the Tibetan government-in-exile.

Tibetans, however, hold one factor in their favor: their devotion to lamaist Buddhism, which prohibits the taking of life. Many of them pursue musk deer and snow leopards for profit and antelope and gazelle for food, but they often do so with an uneasy conscience. They may give up hunting at the urging of a devout relative or when the gods signal their displeasure with a bout of misfortune. Tibetan religion at least provides a check on unrestrained killing, a more powerful control than the laws of China.

This is what I learned during many bumpy rides through central Tibet and many discussions with officials and commoners. I ranged from the southeastern corner of the Changtang Plateau to the trade-route town of Gyantse, the rich Yarlung-Tsangpo Valley, and out-of-the-way Namling. In Toyota Landcruisers with Tibetan drivers, I crossed passes at elevations of 15,000 and 17,000 feet; skirted glaciers; followed the twisting lakeshore of Yamdrok Tso; explored the soggy margins of Nam Tso, the world's highest salt lake; descended into the raging Tsangpo River canyon at flood time; traversed broad and well-tended valleys; and passed mountain villages, nomad encampments, and isolated monasteries. I also made forays into the offices of Lhasa bureaucrats.

Wherever I went, Tibet's rugged mountains were always in view—features of a barren, forbidding landscape which appears more of a liability than a repository of riches. This desolation is most evident to travelers on the overland journey from Nepal, which begins as an ascent through forested slopes in a landscape of dense greenery. Here fir, pine, and rhododendron press in on both sides of the road; the village houses resemble wooden chalets of the European Alps; the air is bracing and cool with a hint of fog; and the surroundings have a cozy feel. Past the border, through the small town of Khasa, the forest persists, and the road continues to wend upward among the trees, until, abruptly, it opens onto rocks and scrub. Abundance and ease have vanished. Now all is spare and desolate, a harsh, dun-colored region, lofty and impassive. Travelers are stricken by the contrast; they ask themselves what people, what life of any kind, can exist in this pitiless landscape.

This route, then, presents central Tibet in a swift unveiling: Here it is all at once before your eyes—sharp-edged, in dazzling light and dilute air.

In the distance rise jagged peaks, some set in impossible overhangs. They are the shattered crust of Asia, rammed upward by pressure from the Indian subcontinent, which creeps northward at the pace of two inches a year, lifting Tibet, once an ocean bottom, into the world's highest plateau and creasing its surface into a pattern of corrugated, saw-toothed ranges. The average elevation here is 12,000 feet, and the land extends over more than 460,000 square miles. If we took an area twice the size of Texas and raised it above Mt. Rainier or the tallest peak in the Rockies, it would approximate the Tibetan plateau.

Visitors arriving suddenly at this height find their heads begin to throb and their limbs drag like lead. They develop dry coughs, rapid pulses, and swollen hands and faces. They wake in the night, their chests heaving with the effort to breathe, and they discover that climbing a flight of stairs leaves them gasping and limp. They are reacting to the shortage of oxygen at upwards of 12,000 feet. As their bodies produce more hemoglobin and red blood cells, these symptoms subside. But the handful of visitors who black out or cough up pink, foamy sputum or begin to stagger like drunks are suffering from cerebral or pulmonary edema and must descend quickly or die.

The air here is not only thin but dry, although maps show Tibet cross-hatched by rivers and pitted with lakes. Some of the world's great waterways find their sources here—the Salween, Mekong, Yangtze, and Brahmaputra. And yet it is an arid land. From late June to mid-September some monsoon rains manage to advance across the Himalayas, flooding the rivers of southern Tibet. But farther north, beyond other mountain ranges, rainfall becomes scarce; the northern plain is high desert and sparsely inhabited. And even in southern Tibet yearly precipitation is only ten to twenty inches. The air is so dry in Lhasa that you can wash your clothes in the evening, hang them out of doors, and despite the freezing nights, find them ready to wear by sunrise.

If Tibet lay at the latitude of Beijing, it would be uninhabitable, colder than Siberia. But it is at the level of New Orleans and Cairo, and even at an altitude of 12,000 feet Lhasa temperatures can reach more than eighty degrees in summer. Outside of the monsoon season Tibet steeps in sunlight under intensely blue skies, but heat from the sun dissipates rapidly in the thin atmosphere; temperatures rise quickly during the day and plunge at night. At higher altitudes, in the Changtang for instance, where the average altitude is 16,500 feet, summer temperatures can reach one hundred degrees at noon and thirty-two degrees at night. In winter, noon temperatures on the Changtang often rise to forty degrees, dropping to minus thirty degrees at night.

All life in Tibet has adapted to the rigors of its great height and extremes of temperature. Mammals acquire large lungs and rapid respiration rates and grow thick coats against the cold. Cushion plants such as sandwort put out crowded stems and leaves which absorb heat quickly and lose it slowly. The Tibetans themselves have adjusted to the stresses of their lofty land; their blood carries extra hemoglobin, which allows them to draw more oxygen from the air into their lungs. Thus Tibetans can run up mountainsides at 16,000 feet, leaving even the fittest and best-acclimatized lowlander gasping far behind.

Outside the southern and eastern forests with their abundant flora and fauna, Tibet is a land of few choices, and these options grow even more meager as the elevation increases. In the Tsangpo Valley where Lhasa lies, farmers cultivate barley, wheat, rapeseed, turnips, carrots, apples, pears, potatoes, onions, and cabbage. In higher elevations barley is the only possible crop. Higher still, even these fields disappear, leaving nothing but pastureland, up to 17,500 feet. Above that live only the wild creatures—snow leopards, bears, wolves, pika, marmots, and birds of prey.

This harsh land has produced a rugged race which takes the rigors of life on the roof of the world in stride. Nomad children herd their family flocks outdoors, under rain and sleet in summer or bitter cold and fierce winds in winter. Herders tend yaks through the coldest months in mountain camps set at 17,500 feet, and nomads and villagers routinely tend to chores and set out on journeys when blizzards are raging. Pilgrims who make their way to Lhasa often sleep outside on the granite paving stones. Entire families with grandparents and young children camp on the naked ground, with only their sheepskin clothing as bedding and shelter. At dawn you will find them cheerfully brewing tea even after a night of rain.

The landscape is wild still, even though Tibetans have been building houses and monasteries and cultivating fields for centuries. Rivers run free, and much of Tibet is untouched grassland, scrub, and stony waste. Farming and husbandry have only partially tamed this land. The domesticated animals of Tibet—yaks, donkeys, horses, chickens, cows, and pigs—evolved from native wild stock, and some still carry traits much like their free-ranging cousins. Farm chickens fly into trees to roost; small black pigs, kept mainly in the lower valleys, have long fur and sharp tusks; the domestic horse is typical of Central Asian species, scarcely bigger than a pony. In the Changtang Plateau to the north and west, wild yaks mingle and interbreed with the nomads' herds.

Tibetan villages blend into the landscape. Their builders take what lies at hand—mud from the nearest riverbed or rocks from the fields and slopes—and fashion houses which spring out of the earth. Abandoned adobes, stripped of their usable wood, are left to dissolve. Since the larger streams swell during the monsoon rains and carve free-standing walls, mesas, and pillars out of the steep mudbanks, it takes close scrutiny to determine whether they are the work of water and wind or human builders. Deserted houses of stone likewise collapse into rubble, identical to natural ridgetop crags.

As I traveled through this land, I saw no evidence of pollution or of any industry likely to poison the land and soil. The Chinese have opened mines, once considered nearly taboo in Tibet, but these remain humble in scale. There were, for instance, the gold mines I passed near Yamdrok Tso. Two small sluice-flow operations lie off the lakeshore road near the county seat of Nangkartse, but I failed to notice any signs of them although we passed within a few yards of the projects. Only later did I learn that they existed. "You see," said my source, "hardly a large-scale operation." And there is the TAR's first metallurgical industry, an iron-smelting factory, which opened in Lhokha to the southeast of Lhasa in October 1992. It was touted on Chinese television, but it also appeared small-scale, covering no more than a few acres.

In centuries past Tibetans mined iron ore and forged chain links to build suspension bridges, still intact after five hundred years of use. They also dug for gold. But mining was often considered an affront to the gods of mountains and soil. Early in this century, for instance, Tibetans opened a small gold mine near Lake Manasarovar in southwestern Tibet but abandoned it after the god of the mine retaliated with an outbreak of smallpox. In the 1920s a British-trained Tibetan discovered oil southeast of Lhasa, but the government refused to let him develop these reserves. They said it would disturb the environment.

Today, however, Tibet produces gold, coal, limestone, chromite, borax, and gypsum, and geologists have found that the region holds 60 percent of the chromite deposits within the boundaries of the People's Republic. I was told that large-scale mining is a poor business venture in central Tibet, that it is difficult to bring in equipment, given the distances and challenges of travel, and that it is an exacting task to move the ores out to markets. For these reasons, sources told me, mining has as yet made little impact in the TAR.

With better transportation to China proper, however, the mining industry may grow.

But Kham and Amdo have easier access to China proper and have seen something of a gold rush, with local people boring into the mountainsides and leaving open shafts on the slopes. Some miners have died in cave-ins, one Khampa told me, and now the government is trying to exert control. And a native of Amdo said gold mining has turned parts of Golok, a rugged nomad region, into wasteland. The Washington-based International Campaign for Tibet also reports that toxic chemicals used to process gold in Qinghai Province have killed humans and farm animals.

I was not allowed to see those areas of Sichuan and Qinghai, but in central Tibet, where I roamed, there was little industry of any kind. Lhasa has a cement factory and a bottling plant, and the larger cities have carpet factories, but these have produced no obvious signs of pollution. The Kyichu River, which passes through Lhasa, runs clear once the monsoons have passed. Tibetans still flock to the rivers each fall for the annual bathing festival, and fish are visible from the riverbanks.

No one in central Tibet mentioned problems of nuclear waste, but the northern and eastern plateau has suffered from this type of pollution, China's critics say. In April 1993 the International Campaign for Tibet claimed that fifty Tibetans living near research sites and uranium mines in Sichuan Province had died from the effects of radioactive pollution. The group also charges that China has deployed nuclear missiles and dumped nuclear waste on the plateau. A San Francisco nuclear watchdog group, In Vivo Radiation Response, reports that China is opening a new nuclear test site on the border between Xinjiang Province and the TAR. China is highly secretive about its nuclear programs and denies placing missiles or dumping waste in Tibet, but even Chinese newspapers have reported lax controls at nuclear sites.

Although I had no chance to look into nuclear issues on my own, I was able to ask about pesticides, a possible source of pollution. But unlike the United States, where "organic" has become a rallying cry, Tibetans have heard little about these chemicals and the dangers they pose to farmers and wildlife.

August First Farm, a work unit outside Lhasa that is proud of its modern approach to agriculture, began to use pesticides only in 1984. My questions about pesticide dangers seemed to perplex managers there. They could name no more than one chemical they used, something which sounded like DDV. One pesticide is for worms, they said vaguely, and they also have some kind of herbicide. They believe these will cause no harm to humans; no one has fallen ill so far; they use a strong rat poison, and it hasn't hurt anyone; and besides, they teach their workers how to use the chemicals properly. They weren't sure about harm to birds because they grow their vegetables in greenhouses. They had heard of no pesticides outlawed in Tibet or China proper, they said, and since they have to buy these products from a government store, they depend on the suppliers to decide what is best.

At the Agricultural Bureau of the TAR, however, I found more awareness of pesticide dangers. Han Guang, director of the bureau, said the government has been giving free fertilizer and pesticides to farmers because Tibet's living standard is low. (Some Tibetans say the free pesticides are also intended to combat the Buddhist aversion to extinguishing any life.) But, said Han, the farmers wasted the free pesticides, so the bureau now charges them 20 or 30 percent of the cost to the government. He admitted that pesticides have caused "some problems" with birds and other wildlife although he said no people have suffered; they were taught how to use them. But, he said, the government is doing research on pesticide residue in crops, and they "may shut down some factories." It was unclear why, if they have no problems, they might close factories, but his answers at least suggested that the government was mindful of the dangers.

Only once in Tibet did I hear a complaint about industrial development of any kind. One evening, standing on the roof of the Jokhang, a Tibetan waved toward a plume of vapor rising to the west near Drepung Monastery. "You see," he said, "that is the cement factory. The Chinese are bringing us pollution." A frequent visitor to Tibet, one who is fluent in the language and highly knowledgeable, expressed surprise at this. "Must have heard that from a tourist," he said. "No one there talks that way about the environment."

The Tibetans' attitude became clear to me one day when I remarked on the tranquility of the countryside and said modernization brings noise and other problems. My Tibetan companions laughed. Modernization, they said: Its problems are few and its benefits are great. The idea of living in a land where electricity is abundant and reliable, where roads are paved and every family owns a car, and where flush toilets and bathtubs are commonplace held great appeal for them.

But Tibetans shake their heads when they speak of the damage in their forests. The sight of a clear-cut hillside is a shock to the senses, an ugly scar on the land, and since 1959 the southern forests of the TAR and the eastern timberlands of Sichuan have been disfigured by overcutting. This may not be the first assault on the forests, however. Some scientists, viewing the barren mountains of central Tibet and calculating the elevation and latitude, now say the land may have been stripped of its trees centuries ago. The major valleys where Lhasa, Tsetang, and Shigatse lie, they say, are below the tree line, and trees planted recently are thriving. At one time, they surmise, central Tibet may have been rich with forested slopes and valleys.[1]

They can only guess at what used to be, but it is certain that Tibetans have used wood to build for centuries. Where we describe a house as so many square feet, Tibetans traditionally say it has so many pillars—five, perhaps, or nine—to show its size. These pillars are solid wood. The oldest monasteries— those which survived the Cultural Revolution—are also supported by wooden pillars, and I was amazed at the size of them. Many were hewn from single massive trunks and stand some thirty feet high or more. Tibetans began to build monasteries and temples in the eighth century and erected thousands of them, including their seventeenth century wonder, the ue. All of the projects required pillars, wooden altars, roof poles, wooden lintels, and massive wooden doors.

Today Tibetans are still using the timber which remains in their territory for building, cooking, and heating. With the improved economy, they are reconstructing monasteries and putting up new houses, schools, shops, and apartment buildings. Villagers fashion their own mud bricks or gather stones, but they must buy wood for ceilings, pillars, doors, and windows. And in many areas—in Lhasa itself, in monasteries around the city, and in the nomad region of Damzhung—I saw piles of wood brought in for cooking and heating. The residents of Damzhung said local officials ask each family to donate wood to the township school. It comes from an area beyond the hills, they said, where some small trees grow. Damzhung itself is too high to sustain any trees; even carefully tended willows manage to produce only a single stalk and a handful of leaves before they expire. Yet those few trees beyond the hills were torn up for fuel on the command of local officials (who are mainly Tibetan in this area)—even though yak, sheep, and goat dung, which produce brisk and long-lasting fires, are plentiful. You see the dung stacked in mounds outside every home and arranged in rows of dried patties on rooftops.

At the TAR Forestry Bureau in Lhasa, director Yin Binggao said the government is taking notice of the problem. In the 1950s and 1960s, he said, even very good wood was burned as fuel, a great waste. Now the government is trying to set up hydroelectric and geothermal plants and allowing the sale of kerosene for cooking and heating. Lhasa residents say that before the 1980s, when kerosene began to appear on the open market, most householders cooked with firewood. Those who had connections with truck drivers managed to procure illegal gasoline, but now kerosene is everywhere. Still, I saw restaurant owners chopping firewood for their kitchens, and my hotel, Snowland, bought tractorloads of firewood (and dung) for its restaurant.

In a harsh environment like Tibet's it seemed to me derelict to strip so much plant life from the land. This is not the tropics where fenceposts sprout leaves and vegetation grows in riotous abundance. Any forest here is a hard-won victory against the odds, the result of slow, tenacious growth. Even so, the products of Tibet's forests continue to appear as stacks of poles, beams, and firewood hauled to a barren region far from their origins.

Yin of the forestry bureau admitted that Yadong, on the border with Nepal, was overcut after the Chinese took charge in 1959, and this caused erosion and changes in the local climate. Now Yadong is open to the wind and suffers from early frosts, and the rainy season brings landslides and flooding. The best remedy, he said, is to replant trees and ground cover, but reseeding has been difficult because trees are slow to take hold in the high altitude. (American photographer Galen Rowell, who travelled with Yin to the slopes of Mount Everest, west of Yadong, has also reported "trees cut by the thousands" in the Valley of the Flowers on the eastern slope of the mountain. Yin never mentioned this in our interview.)[2]

Tibet's forests include stands of fir, hemlock, larch, and pine, mainly in the southern and eastern counties of the autonomous region, but according to Yin, only a small portion is cut each year. Most of the timber is inaccessible, in high mountains without roads. Almost all the TAR's timber harvest goes for construction within the region, he said. Only since 1990 have they begun to export lumber, and the total has been small, no more than twenty thousand cubic meters in recent years. "I want to stress this," said Yin, "because some people have charged that all of Tibet's timber is being exported to the rest of China."

If you consider the forests of Kham, in Sichuan and Yunnan provinces, as Tibetan timber, then the accusations of overcutting and exporting to China proper are correct, according to all accounts. Yin was referring to the TAR alone, but outside its boundaries lumber moves in a steady stream toward the Sichuan capital of Chengdu and other regions of the interior. Travellers have recorded this on videotape and slides—convoys of trucks loaded with huge tree trunks moving east. They have also recorded denuded slopes and piles of lumber washed up on riverbanks or abandoned by the roadsides.

Khampa who live within access of the main routes also say the forests near their villages have disappeared. "It used to be that you could not walk in many places," said one, "the trees were so thick. Now you can move any-where."

My interpreter Xiao Jin said her village in Kham had also seen overcutting, but the government was trying to remedy the problem. You see signs with slogans about conserving forests, she said, and some areas are off limits. Many Chinese foresters have written about timber issues; there are lengthy bibliographies of articles published in China which address forest conservation, sustainable yields, and timber economics. Some officials and scientists are aware that cutting cannot proceed at a nonstop pace, and the government promotes tree planting.

The Lhasa Environmental Protection Bureau says the agency has planted more than sixteen hundred acres with trees. Every March 12 the bureau oversees a tree-planting day when students and workers go out to set seedlings. They used to plant poplars and willows, but now they are tending toward pines and other evergreens, which seem to fare better. Villagers also plant trees, and most farm settlements have at least a few adobe or stone corrals where the young willows and poplars can grow safe from foraging cattle.

The Tibet Development Fund (TDF), a nongovernmental organization with environmental and social service aims, is hoping to get foreign help for tree planting. The director, Changlo Chen Wangchuk—a broad-featured man with a courteous, deliberate manner—said he envisions small family woodlots as part of the solution. "The people use leaves for the sheep and goats," he said in his careful English, "so they will want to maintain them for their own economic benefit." His plans are in line with the government's recent push toward a market economy based on private initiative, and they are also in line with the findings of an American scholar, Lester Ross, who has researched environmental policy in China. Marxist policy encouraged overlogging, Ross has written, but private operations with effective government regulation and support can help conserve the forests.

Solar power can also save forests, and Tibetans already use the sun's power to heat water for tea. They set kettles to boil in portable devices made of two flexible wings of reflective material curving inward toward a wire frame. These are a common sight on rooftops and courtyards of the more developed areas, where they catch the abundant sunlight of the Tibetan plateau. The TDF is also promoting solar power, according to Wangchuk, and in Lhasa the group is using this source of energy to upgrade bathrooms in the Lhasa Welfare Home compound.

Meanwhile officials depend on other sources of electric power. They have harnessed geothermal energy in a field of geysers north of Lhasa, and this plant provides the bulk of the capital's supply. But the system often goes into overload and breaks down, and if you spend any length of time in the capital, you learn to keep a supply of candles on hand, especially in winter.

With Lhasa's population growing steadily, the government is trying to come up with more abundant sources of electricity, and recently officials have been counting on power from the pristine lake called Yamdrok Tso. The ICT has taken aim at this project, charging that it will destroy the sacred lake and its ecosystem. Before I went to Tibet I heard variously that Yamdrok Tso would be drained, dammed, or diverted. I was eager to take a look for myself.

The lake lies in the mountains more than 2,700 feet above the Yarlung-Tsangpo plain and 14,700 feet above sea level, with a surface area of 245 square miles meandering between peaks and up tributary valleys to form an ornate, serpentine letter Y. It is the largest body of fresh water on the northern side of the Himalayas and stores 530 billion cubic feet. Its waters are turquoise-blue when the weather is fair and so clear you can see pebbles lying in the shallows. In places the shoreline is mossy, spread with purple and yellow wildflowers and riddled with tiny burrows. Small frogs pop into these burrows or leap away when you approach. On the slopes above the lake grow a kind of stinging nettle, wild rosebushes, and shrubs which give off a sweet, pungent odor, like mint.

No one was in the lake or on it when we passed there in September, but we saw one coracle pulled up on the shoreline. Many Tibetans eat no fish or wildfowl, even though both are plentiful. I saw only one fisheater, a large predatory bird skimming over the water. In the shallows of an inlet we passed a flock of ruddy shelduck, sandpipers, and other darting birds like swallows. Yaks with red tassels in their ears grazed on the banks above them.

Along the lakeshore lie villages and occasional barley fields, which were stunted when we passed by even though it was harvest time. We stopped at one of these villages, known as Pede, to ask about the hydroelectric plant now under construction. It is to pipe water from the lake through a massive tunnel to the valley below, generating electricity from the force of the fall. The plan is to let the water cascade downward during periods of peak use and to pump it back to the lake during slack times. The big unknown is what this will do to the shorelines, the lake itself, and the creatures who depend upon it.

Pede clings to the mountainside just above the lake. It is a typical cluster of flat-roofed adobe houses defended by prayer flags, a monument containing sacred objects, and a shrine with an incense burner. We stopped at the top of a slope to talk to a group of women standing in the roadway twisting yarn on the ubiquitous hand spindles. They knew about the electric plant; they'd been told it was all right, that it would do no harm to the lake itself. They didn't know if these assurances were true or not, but they did hope some of the electricity would come to Pede. A wrinkled, toothless woman pointed to her eyes; they were reddened and squinting. "My eyes are so bad," she said, "I can't see in the dark. I even had a bad fall once. We need electricity here." A man fashioning a boot by hand approached and said the plant was all to the good; Tibet needs electricity. But he was less certain that Pede Village would benefit. Maybe they won't send it to us, he said.

Lhasa Tibetans had a similar reaction. They needed electricity, but they worried about the environmental impact. They just didn't know what the effect would be. One woman said she disliked the project, because the lake is sacred, but she also hoped that Lhasa would get more reliable electricity.

In Lhasa I tried to meet with officials who could tell me more about the Yamdrok project. I heard that it had been delayed in 1985 after the Panchen Lama, Tibet's second-highest-ranking spiritual leader then resident in China, said it might harm the environment. Yamdrok, he noted, is not only beautiful, but also sacred, and it is one of Tibet's major lakes. The government postponed work on the plant, ostensibly to study the effect on the ecosystem, and after four years announced that the environment would come to no harm. Crews would therefore begin to tunnel through the mountains to the valley below and move ahead. This much I knew, but I also wanted to hear what was in the environmental report. How much water would they pump out? What would this do to the shoreline? And to the lake's fish, migrating birds, frogs, and herds of yak and sheep? How did they make their assessment? I asked for a meeting with those in charge, but the answer came back: No interviews allowed; the Yamdrok project is secret.

Nevertheless, I picked up some details by "the back door," as they say in China. By the time we visited the lake, crews had already dug one eight-foot-in-diameter tunnel from Yamdrok Tso through the mountain to the valley side, and a chief engineer from Lhasa was in Austria to buy equipment, including the pumps. The project was estimated to cost nearly $128 million and was expected to generate about 200 million kilowatt hours a year. It was to be completed in the year 2000, my source said, but a 1992 white paper on Tibet stated that it would be finished in 1997.

In the summer of 1995, when the government was preparing to celebrate the thirtieth anniversary of the TAR's founding, Lhasa's official newspaper, *Tibet Daily*, reported that the first phase of the project was completed and it was sending power to serve 230,000 people in the Lhasa municipal area (which extends well beyond the city itself into pastoral and farming areas). Some news reports, however, said that the project was "perfectly completed" and mentioned nothing about phases or a later deadline.

But in spite of the upbeat news reports, Lhasa residents said the power plant was still not functioning by the spring of 1996. Blackouts were frequent, and one businessman was seriously thinking of buying a generator. Western technicians working on the project and TIN both reported that a tunnel leading to one of four turbines collapsed in 1995, dropping a thousand cubic meters of rock. One source told TIN there was leakage in the tunnel, that the problem was due to a design error, and that several tunnels were affected. Another said that China plans to re-excavate the tunnel and line it with steel, bringing the cost of the project to $236 million, nearly twice the original estimate.[3]

One Lhasa woman put a religious spin on the project's failure to perform: It is only to be expected when you tamper with a sacred lake, she said, and any attempt to harm the waters of Yamdrok Tso will have to contend with forces beyond the control of engineers. "We tried to tell them," she said.

Meanwhile, planners have begun looking at another hydroelectric source for the Lhasa area. The *Tibet Daily* reported that Drigung, about 100 kilometers north of Lhasa, will become the site of a new station which will become "the key to fulfilling the region's installed-capacity target before the year 2000."[4]

The Yamdrok facility, I was told, was to run water down during the day, the peak period, when the electricity generated brings in more money, and pump it back at night, when demand falls off. Engineers say that pumping more than twenty-seven hundred feet uphill is simple enough and the pumps can handle the job, but the economic balance is less clear. If Lhasa's electric supply is already lacking, it is difficult to predict how much will really be used in peak periods. And it is also costly to pump water upwards that distance, especially when the long drop generates no more power than a much shorter fall would produce. The danger is that return pumping will prove so expensive it will be abandoned.

If no water were pumped back to the lake, it should drop an average of a foot a year. This information apparently comes from the environmental study, which, I was told, was mainly a look at hydrology, the project's water supply, and circulation. There was no information to be had on how this loss might affect the lake's ecology. Chinese reports, at least those available to the public, say only that "a careful feasibility study" determined that "the station will not affect the environment."[5] Any specific details are too "secret" for the public to know.

Certainly the project will affect the land, at least minimally, with new roads and structures. And there are many unanswered questions: How much water will be returned to the lake? Will the state draw water from another source to resupply the lake, or will it hold the lakewater in a reservoir to be pumped back? Will land below the tunnel be flooded? Will the water level fluctuate between night and day? Will fish be sucked into the tubes? If the level drops, what will that do to the shallows and the migrating birds that depend on them? No one could give me answers to these questions, but one source noted that it would make no sense to drain the lake. The Chinese, he said, would never build an expensive plant and then destroy their water supply.

The lake seems a fragile area, best left alone. But, said TDF's Wangchuk, a man who cares deeply for the environment of his native Tibet, Yamdrok is naturally receding. You can now walk across portions that were once underwater. This could be true, because it is the nature of lakes to shrink and eventually disappear, but the future of Yamdrok Tso is especially obscure because of the secrecy surrounding it. If the project provides energy for cooking and heating and if the shoreline remains stable, it could prove more of a boon than a threat to the environment.

But China's refusal to inform its people about a project directly affecting their lives raises suspicions that the government's terse assurances may prove worthless. Among Lhasa residents the dearth of news has spawned rumors that the lake area is being developed for mining—so that the Chinese, it is implied, can more easily extract valuable copper from the lakeside. In any case, even the best-informed Tibetans could only say, "They tell us all will be well, but we don't know."

Tibetans are better informed about the loss of wildlife since 1959, and the damage is also evident to visitors who have read about old Tibet, a land once teeming with herds of ungulates and their predators. During our weeks on the road I never caught sight of a large wild mammal. I saw several woolly hares, a weasel scurrying along the inner wall of a schoolyard, scores of black-lipped pika, a conversational cluster of marmots, and, just beyond Yamdrok Tso, a lustrous golden fox which stopped to watch us before it zigzagged up toward the ridge. These add up to a meager record of sightings for a land once described as a hunter's paradise, swarming with animals. But the large herds are no longer abundant in Tibet. I have seen more wildlife driving the highways of northern California.

Birds there were, but not in huge numbers: vultures (which feed on human corpses during ritual burials), birds of prey, pigeons and doves, ruddy shelducks, sandpipers, other waterbirds, chakor partridges, town-dwelling finches, and an occasional hoopoe, which in flight resembles a flicker with black markings but on the ground displays a topknot like a tiny crested crane.

Before leaving the States I had heard that several species of animals and plants were extinct in Tibet, but no one was able to tell me of one species which had totally expired. The wildlife once visible to travelers, Tibetans say, still exist in the mountains of central Tibet—gazelle, jackals, wolves, lynx, bobcats, antelope, blue sheep, and bears. Musk deer and other ungulates survive in the forests of Kham and southern Tibet, red pandas on the lower slopes of the Himalayas, and wild yaks and donkeys in the Changtang. They have retreated from the populated valleys and byways and several are endangered, but they are not yet extinct.

As we passed herders on the road and stopped to speak to villagers and nomads I asked about local wildlife: What do you see in the mountains? What did you see in the old days? Does anyone hunt in this area? All agreed that the animals had been more abundant before 1959. They used to come near the villages—snow leopards, wolves, gazelle, foxes. Now they have taken refuge in the mountains, the Tibetans said, gesturing toward distant peaks. Many said that hunting, especially during the Cultural Revolution, killed off great numbers because in those days people were hungry and religious observance was suppressed. One nomad said the road near his home has frightened the animals away, and, he noted, there are now more people.

In the farming areas of central Tibet I heard of jackals, which prey on sheep and goats, and gazelle, which occasionally make their way into the valleys. In the higher elevations—the mountains around Yamdrok Tso and the nomad area of Damzhung—herders never failed to mention wolves, which take their sheep, goats, and yaks. (The herders hunt wolves with guns or traps, but they said their best protection is guard dogs.) In the south no one spoke of bears, but in Damzhung the nomads all agreed that bears live in the nearby mountains. One told me there were two kinds and that one species looks almost human.

I always asked about snow leopards, and the answers were as elusive as the big cat itself. In the town of Gyantse one man had heard of snow leopards in the hills, but a woman herding cows on the road said there were none about. Still higher on the road from Gyantse to Lhasa a young man said cryptically that a "mountain tiger" lived in the hills. At 16,000 feet, near a glacier on Mount Kharo, nomad children shook their heads. No snow leopards, they said. In Damzhung, reports conflicted. One nomad would say the leopards still prowled in the hills; the next would say there were none. The replies to my queries indicated that wolves are widespread and bears survive in the Changtang but that the snow leopard is in precarious condition everywhere.

Some of Tibet's animals can be seen in the zoo at Norbulingka, the former summer palace of the Dalai Lama. There, in cages and enclosures, are spotted deer, white-lipped deer the size of elk, monkeys, blue sheep with lyre-shaped horns, a single red panda, several lynx, ducks and geese, pheasants, peacocks, pigeons, foxes, jackals, a wolf with glistening russet fur, and two varieties of bear. The zoo had no snow leopards.

I saw one clear sign of that evasive animal in Tibet: a skin displayed for sale in the Barkor. Vendors there also sold otter skins, dozens of them, which they said came from India. They displayed the hides of tigers and forest leopards, and they sold fox pelts and foxfur hats. Once in the Jokhang Plaza a pair of Khampa offered me a silvery lynx skin for 1,000 yuan, about $150. I also saw a lynx pelt used as a rug at a fair in Sakya.

Tibetans and Chinese prize animals for their fur and medicinal properties. Women from Kham and Amdo trim their clothes with otter fur, and foxfur hats are favorite Tibetan headgear. (A friend of mine said that when a fox appeared on a remote stretch of road, her Tibetan companions began to shout, "*Zhamo! Zhamo!*"— which means "Hat!") Musk, antlers, dried snakes, and bones are used in Tibetan and Chinese medicine, and musk is also used in perfume. All these goods command a price, and the money encourages hunting, even of the most endangered and supposedly protected species.

China outlaws hunting many species in Tibet, and the animals are graded according to first- or second-level protection. A first-level animal can be hunted or captured for research only with the permission of the central (Beijing) government. A second-level animal likewise can be hunted only for research but with the permission of the provincial government. If you are caught hunting a first-level animal without a permit, the central government will set your fine or jail sentence, perhaps $1,000 or less for a wild yak or $200 to $400 for a wild ass.

First-level animals include the wild yak, wild ass, snow leopard, and Tibetan antelope—all found in central Tibet—and the white-lipped deer, takin (an ungainly relative of the musk ox), tiger, Himalayan tahr (a shaggy wild goat), and black-necked crane, all residents of the southern or eastern forests. Second-level animals include the following inhabitants of central Tibet: blue sheep, argali sheep, brown bear, stone marten, Tibetan gazelle, lynx, musk deer, Indian otter, and bar-headed goose; and these forest dwellers: Asian black bear, red deer, serow (a mountain antelope), golden cat, red panda, and small-clawed otter. Wolves and foxes are unprotected.

But the laws were no help to the snow leopard whose pelt hung in the Barkor, nor to the lynx whose lush coat was offered to me in the Jokhang Plaza, nor to the dozens of otters and the tigers and leopards who ended their days as skins for sale in Lhasa's bazaar. The laws were apparently of no help to the deer which contributed musk and the tiger which gave its bones to the "bone-setting plaster" prescribed for my sprained ankle in Beijing, nor to the antelope whose horns were always for sale by the dozens in the markets of Lhasa.

Few Tibetans openly admit to hunting because their religion prohibits the taking of life, but many Tibetans and many Chinese are shooting and trapping the endangered animals of the plateau. Nomads and peasants have few guns and they often resort to traps, but local officials (mainly Tibetan) and Tibetan and Chinese soldiers, equipped with high-powered arms and four-wheel-drive vehicles, are taking snow leopards, wild yaks, blue sheep, antelope, lynx, gazelle, white-lipped deer, and musk deer, not to mention unprotected foxes and wolves. James Halfpenny, an American biologist who worked on the Tibetan Plateau, said the local people hunt with anything from flintlocks to AK-47s and also set out traps. He has seen antelopes "out in the middle of nowhere dragging huge traps on their legs," and he has seen areas where "every single marmot hole had a choke snare." Range ecologist Daniel Miller reports that hunters with high-powered rifles are penetrating the remote Kunlun Mountains of Qinghai Province to kill antelope, gazelle, blue sheep, and wild yak. They sell the meat to markets in outlying towns.[6]

Noting the laws against hunting—with their strict categories of protection—on the one hand and the terrible destruction of wildlife on the other,

TIBET

Westerners have asked what is wrong. How can the hides of snow leopards, tigers, otters, and lynx sell openly in the markets of Lhasa and other cities in China? How can pharmaceutical companies sell medicines advertised as containing tiger bone, antelope horn, and musk? The answer is a fundamental one, which reveals a deep division between China and the West. A Tibetan friend put it this way: "In the West the laws on the books have power, but here they are just words. They have no power. Here it is the person in charge, the individual, who runs things." So even though the central government may pass down regulations and scientists may sound the alarm, county officials can ignore the laws for their own immediate gain. Wangchuk of TDF, for instance, said he appealed to the Commerce Department to crack down on the sale of skins in the Barkor, but officials ignored him. "We gave many suggestions," he said, "but I've seen no attempt to control it." But since my visit, I'm told, the authorities finally responded to pressure and outlawed the open sale of skins in the Barkor, although it still continues out of sight.

Wangchuk finds encouragement, however, in the nature preserves created to protect Tibet's endangered species. The TAR has several major parks including the vast 115,500-square-mile Changtang Reserve, founded in 1993, and the 10,400-square-mile Chomolangma Preserve on the slopes of Mount Everest. Wangchuk said such efforts are paying off, at least in the Himalayan region; wildlife there, devastated during the Cultural Revolution, is making a comeback. But Feng Zuojian, director of the Qinghai-Tibetan Plateau Research Society and a thirty-year veteran in the field of ecology, said the preserves are poorly staffed and poaching continues to take a toll. Some preserves have no rangers at all, he said.

Feng, who works out of a bleak Beijing office building, is a short, balding man dedicated to preserving endangered species. He recites the depressing details with a weary, almost hopeless air—only a thousand snow leopards remaining; county officials, called on to enforce the laws, taking up hunting themselves, forest loss, population pressure, his fears of development in the Changtang.

He concludes that too few people know or care about the danger to wildlife. We need to educate them, he says, and we need to control the growth of human populations and their domestic herds. If not, the animals will grow more and more scarce, and the snow leopard, the most endangered animal in

48

Tibet, will continue to decline. (He can't bring himself to say it will disappear.) Likewise the common otter, the second most endangered, will dwindle to near extinction.

Feng Zuojian and others like him are evidence that all of China is not bent on ravaging Tibet. Threats to the region's environment come from a complex of factors: modernization, population growth, and China's lax system of laws. They come from Chinese and Tibetans alike. It is not a simple case of China tearing Tibet to pieces, as some have suggested. Mining, for instance, has so far made little impact on the landscape of central Tibet; Yamdrok Tso is not likely to lose all its pristine waters.

And yet the critics have good reason to fear, especially for the wild animals which once covered the land in great numbers and for the forests which are becoming, in some areas, barren slopes. Feng and Wangchuk and others like them long for the assurance that those in charge of the land will muster the will and acquire the means to preserve its stark mountains and plains, its forested slopes, its lakes and rivers, and the inhabitants who have managed to adapt and survive in this highest region of the world.

When I was leaving Feng's office, he made a poignant appeal: Please, he said, tell everyone about the rich ecology of Tibet. It has high plateau, subtropical zones, and temperate zones. "The area is so special; it is unique; it has great scientific and economic value," he said earnestly. He was making one more appeal for the wild yaks, argali sheep, otters, and snow leopards, for the sweeping grasslands of the Changtang and the snow-fed waters of Yamdrok Tso; lobbying for biodiversity on the roof of the world.

3

Village, City, and Pastureland (Lifestyle)

When Lhasa protesters demand independence and unfurl the outlawed Tibetan flag and Western sympathizers castigate China for its presence in Tibet, China is outraged and aggrieved. After all we have done for Tibet, they say, how can anyone complain? After all we have sacrificed to bring highways, irrigation ditches, telephones, airports, buses, tractors, sewer lines, and electricity to that formerly barbarous region. . . . Before we liberated Tibet no one cared for the material welfare of the serfs, but now Tibetans are better off than ever before. "Facts have fully proven," declared a pro-Chinese Hong Kong newspaper, "that it is the Chinese government that truly shows concern for the Tibetan people's livelihood and right to survival and development."[1] The government points to a roster of statistics— so many yuan in savings deposits, so many million kilograms of grain, so many kilowatts of electric power, so many construction projects begun and so many completed. The Chinese assert that the central government has bolstered the TAR economy with 35 billion yuan in aid since 1952,[2] and they repeatedly compare the old society—with its primitive technology and stagnant social system—to the new.

Chinese officials fail to recognize the protesters' nationalist sentiments, and respond to their demands and complaints by noting once again that Tibet's economy is growing. Some of China's critics say the government harps on the theme of economic progress because it doesn't understand that Tibetan values are decidedly less materialist than those of the Chinese. They note that many Tibetans are content with subsistence living, with a handful of tsampa and a good wool wrap to keep out the cold, and have little interest in struggling for more. "Why do we need all that?" one Tibetan asked me when we spoke of consumer goods arriving in the shops.

Nevertheless, most Tibetans like the comforts and conveniences of their improving lifestyle, and the Dalai Lama himself has noted the "need to raise the standard of living of the entire population" of Tibet.[3] Moreover, it is true that Tibetans now have a higher life expectancy than they did before 1950, that they travel by airplane, bus, tractor, and horse cart when they once eschewed vehicles on wheels. They can communicate by telephone, even by fax, and no longer must depend on couriers as in the old days. They can reach their towns and cities by road when they formerly journeyed along yak and horse trails. And many of them switch on electric lights when it grows dark instead of relying on firelight and oil lamps.

It is also true that the central government has, since the early 1980s, made an effort to boost the economy of Tibet. When the Dalai Lama sent delegations to the Tibetan ethnic areas of China in 1979 and 1980 and the visitors reacted with outrage to the ravages of the Cultural Revolution—the ruined monasteries and the ragged Tibetans who greeted them with tears— China began to grant special concessions to the TAR. As a result, residents of Tibet have paid fewer taxes than those of China proper, and until 1992 they benefited from subsidies for gasoline, oil, tractors, fertilizer, tea, construction projects, and medical care. China is expanding Tibet's tourist industry and has also provided technical aid—such as yak- and cattle-breeding stations— to improve the lives of nomads and farmers.

In 1994 China's Third National Forum on work in Tibet, held in Beijing, called for still more effort to develop Tibet. The forum initiated new building projects: highway construction, middle schools, tourist facilities, a water supply system, a television receiving station. Half of these, totalling a quarter of the nearly $400 million price tag, are supported by provincial and municipal governments in China proper; the central government is funding the rest.[4]

But China's claims fail to silence the critics, who acknowledge the improving economy and the construction projects, but argue that this is geared toward the ethnic Chinese and Hui (Chinese Muslims) who are steadily arriving in the TAR. The improvements are meant to encourage Chinese to come to Tibet, critics say, and Tibetans benefit only incidentally from the economic growth. In effect, they charge, Tibet is becoming a two-tiered society with the Chinese living at the top of the scale and Tibetans on the bottom. The Lhasa underground group Cholsum Thuntsok asserted in a 1992 flier, "Nowadays China is opening up the whole of Tibet on the pretext of economic development, but in reality it is in order to deny Tibetans rights and work through the endless transfer of Chinese people to live here."[5]

Tibet has its prosperous citizens, its middle class, and its poor, but the classes divide less along ethnic lines than between city and country dwellers, cadres and common folk, merchants and peasants, and those who live in fertile areas compared with those on less hospitable land. And since the breakup of the communes, some families in each sector have prospered while others have fallen on hard times. Once again Tibet has class divisions, but its society is not an apartheid of wealthy Chinese set above the masses of Tibetans. Nor is it as stratified as the old system. Today it has a large middle class, and the material lives of most have improved since market reforms transformed the economy.

As I traveled through central Tibet, stopping unannounced at villages and nomad settlements, I heard farmers and herdsmen declare that they have been faring better in recent years. (All of them were Tibetan; Chinese have moved into cities and county seats, but they remain outside the farming villages and nomad encampments of the TAR.) These herdsmen and peasants said that under the commune system everyone was poor, and hard work brought no rewards, but now that each family is on its own, they have more to eat and some money to spare. Many are able to build new houses, add to their herds, and buy a few items in the market—shoes, caps, thermos bottles, household altars, and battery-powered radios. They also use their money to go on pilgrimages and make donations to monasteries, counting on a good return for these investments in future lives.

None of this was possible, they said, before the reforms, when they were stuck fast in communes, regimented, and working under the control of overseers. In those days, they said, it didn't matter how hard you worked, you could never get ahead. Your harvests disappeared into collective warehouses to be doled out according to the work points you earned, and there was little food to go around.

Communes were established in Tibet in 1966, during the Cultural Revolution. The system robbed former serfs of their land, forced them into work brigades, and subjected them to tedious hours of political indoctrination. Class consciousness was the primary goal, a Tibetan who served as a youth leader in the Cultural Revolution told me, and better harvests were expected to follow once this enlightenment was achieved. But as it happened, farmers and nomads existed on meager—often near-starvation—rations, and the system allowed them no way out; they couldn't even beg for alms.

Tibet emerged from this harrowing experiment after Mao's death in 1976. By 1980 the government was returning commune equipment, land, and animals to the former members and letting each family fend for itself. Since then, although most herders and peasants have found their lives changing for the better, not all have prospered, and the differences sometimes depend on who has the best land. Moreover, price increases and inflation since 1990 have eroded the buying power of ordinary Tibetans. Everything has become more expensive, they say—food, electricity, shoes, rent, kerosene—especially since subsidized rations were cancelled in 1992. Between 1990 and 1994 the prices of butter, tea, and sugar tripled in Tibet, and the cost of electricity went up eightfold.

In a session of the TAR branch of the Chinese People's Political Consultative Conference held in May 1994 in Lhasa, several deputies reportedly asked for relief. One is quoted as saying that "workers' monthly salaries are very low compared with the rising cost of living. Price rises should be more gradual and carefully planned. . . .There is now a strong tendency for the gap between rich and poor to widen . . . and planning must make provision for the income available to the ordinary masses."[6]

Two months later, however, the Third National Forum on Tibet would result in a call for rapid development in the region by integrating the economy of Tibet more fully into that of the rest of China. "Tibet's reform must conform with the framework for ongoing reform of the entire nation in the process of establishing a socialist market economy," Ragdi, Deputy Party Secretary of the TAR, said in a speech reported by *Tibet Daily* in September 1994.[7] It appears that Tibet will get no price controls.

The spiraling cost of living most affects urban dwellers who are on a fixed wage. In farming and nomad areas, Tibetans are highly self-sufficient and more concerned with the weather and the quality of their harvests than with the rising bus fares. This was made plain during my first close-up view of post-reform peasant life. It was at Tashigang Village near Shigatse, which was not on my itinerary but near at hand when we found floodwaters blocking our way across the Tsangpo River. Tashigang was a cluster of adobe houses surrounded by barley fields, and the first farmer we met there was forty-year-old Dorje Tsering, an energetic former soldier dressed in a Mao jacket and cap. He headed a family which included his father, his wife, their three young sons, a brother, and a sister-in-law.

In 1980, when his commune broke up, Dorje Tsering was apportioned a horse and a donkey. Three years later he had saved enough money to build his own mud-brick house of two rooms, one for storage and one for living quarters, with a courtyard surrounded by eight-foot walls. The courtyard served as an enclosure for the family's cows and chickens and as a work area for spinning, weaving, cooking, mending, and preparing rawhide. An overhang off the living area sheltered a loom and a row of benches. By 1992 Dorje Tsering's original allotment of one donkey and one horse had expanded to a horse, eight cows, and forty sheep and goats; he had a cart for the horse, and he was planning to build a new home. He would need only to buy wood for the rafters and poles. The family would make the adobe bricks themselves.

Tashigang Village, set in fertile fields near the Tsangpo, included twenty families, and Dorje Tsering counted himself as an average resident, a member of the middle class of peasants. "There are just a few poor," he said. Most are in the middle. A few are rich and have tractors, but no one has a truck. When we are sowing in the spring, we share one of the tractors." He bought fertilizer and used cow dung to enrich his fields, and the government gave him free pesticides. The family purchased clothes and a few vegetables. They traded with nomads—their barley for yak meat; but otherwise they lived off what they produced: eggs, milk, cheese, barley, and wheat. As Dorje Tsering spoke, seated on the ground in his courtyard, he was spinning wool and cutting strips of rawhide and his wife was at the loom weaving the striped bands of fabric women make into their traditional aprons.

Dorje Tsering said he was content because he paid no taxes and could dispose of the harvest wherever he chose. He took his grain into Shigatse, and he usually sold it to the government, or if he had a surplus, to private buyers as well. "I like the Party," Dorje Tsering said, "because the living is good and I pay no taxes." (By 1995, however, the government was giving signs that tax exemptions were on the way out. A journal article noted that the tax reform had accomplished what it had set out to do and it was time for Tibet to integrate its economy with the rest of China.[8])

Supply lines for Shigatse's electric power passed near Tashigang Village, and a power station stood less than a mile away on the Tsangpo River, but the settlement itself lacked electricity. The village needed a transformer to tap into the supply, Dorje Tsering said. He used an oil lamp when he showed us into his dark storeroom.

But on other visits to rural Tibet, I learned that not all peasants have done so well as Dorje Tsering. At Chantso Village, spread along a gently sloping hillside east of Lhasa, I met seventy-year-old Tsering Drolma, creased and toothless and dressed in a homemade gown of traditional thick wool. She was babysitting her grandson while the other family members brought in the harvest. Tsering Drolma's home, unlike Dorje Tsering's, was dingy with soot, the windows had no glass, and the bright colors of the family altar had dimmed under a film of grime. She described her family as middling well-off for Chantso Village, but they had only two oxen to till the fields, two cows, and no horses, sheep, goats, or yaks. Tsering Drolma's family appeared to be poor on the scale of today's Tibet, in spite of her own assessment, but she gave no hint of why her family had lagged behind others in the village. She only noted that some of her neighbors were "very wealthy," and Chantso boasted four cars and one tractor. Her family grew barley and potatoes, and they collected herbs in the hills (Ganden is famous for its incense), which they sold in Lhasa. There they bought vegetables, butter, and cheese.

Though Tsering Drolma's home was shabby, some houses in Chantso sported freshly painted lintels and doors, and one had a plot of bright flowers outside the courtyard walls. These were most likely the homes of Chantso's wealthy. But no one in Chantso had electricity. Tsering Drolma said this was the biggest problem in the village, and the leaders were petitioning the government to bring power to their homes. Like Tashigang, Chantso stood near a major power plant but lacked the equipment to hook into supply lines.

Post–Cultural Revolution prosperity has also lagged in Guchok, a village in a little-known corner of Namling County, which itself lies off the beaten track. A road from the valley below ascends a riverbed and stops beside terraced fields a quarter of a mile from the village, and you walk the rest of the way. I was able to spend three days there with my friend Tashi Tshering, who once herded sheep and goats in the hills outside Guchok. When he was selected for the Dalai Lama's dance troupe, his family was exempted from taxes (Tashi's service was considered a tax), and they grew wealthy. They came to own two hundred yaks, four hundred sheep and goats, and two houses, but after the abortive rebellion of 1959 they were branded class enemies. They lost their houses and were sent to live in a few rooms of an empty monastery with a few household goods and a tiny remnant of their herds.

During the Cultural Revolution, Tashi said, everyone in Guchok was bitterly poor, worse off than in the old Tibet. But since the reforms his relatives have gradually improved their lot again, although their lifestyle still falls short of former times. Tashi's brother bought back one of the houses and recently added an upstairs room—a small sleeping area with platforms along two walls, a glassless window, and a door covered with a cloth hanging. The house is of stone, two stories high, with rows of yak and cow dung neatly laid out along the margins of the roof. It has a kitchen, storeroom, courtyard, and sheep pen besides the new addition. In 1992 eleven people lived there: Tashi's mother, his brother and sister-in-law with their five sons, a daughter-in-law, and two granddaughters. They had three yaks, thirty sheep and goats, a *dzo* (a yak-cattle cross), three cows, and a donkey.

No one in Guchok owned a tractor, and consumer goods familiar to those who live near urban centers were scarce. Tashi's family members fingered my roll of toilet paper, took a keen interest in my toothbrush, and cautiously took my flashlight apart. They used an earthenware kettle set on charcoal to warm the butter tea, although many in Guchok had thermos flasks imported from China proper. Tashi, who now lives well as a rug merchant in Lhasa, shook his head and sighed. "They're so poor," he said. He had come with bags full of gifts—shirts, blouses, writing tablets, pencils, and erasers—and I had added fruit and candies. All of this bounty disappeared quickly and was cached away.

Guchok, of course, lacked electricity. In all of Namling County, only the county seat and one village had electric power.

When we arrived in Guchok it was harvest time, and the family had risen early to spend the day scything barley. This is the most demanding period of the year, and schoolteachers, students, vendors, and even nuns will leave their posts to help their families in the fields. In the more prosperous areas some farmers use tractors and trucks, but most work by hand and transport the sheaves from field to home on the backs of donkeys and yaks or by horse cart. When the harvest is in, the solid village houses are engulfed by stacks of barley which slowly diminish as the farmers thresh and winnow the grain and store it in bags. Any combination of livestock—cows, yaks, donkeys, and dzo—are hitched together and set to plodding in a circle, trampling the grain. Then women pair off with wooden pitchforks, tossing the stalks into the air and letting the wind separate the barley from the chaff.

In the fall of 1992 the harvest was good in the fertile river valleys near Tsetang, Shigatse, and Gyantse, broad plains which are easily irrigated. When we stopped by fields belonging to Lobsang, a father of seven children in the village of Chungsha Tsome near Shigatse, he was hustling to cut the grain, now tall and golden in early September. Two of Lobsang's children were in school; the rest were out in the field. The eldest daughter sang heartily as she labored, bent over the stalks with her short scythe in hand; the mother hummed; Lobsang worked with quiet concentration. They greeted us politely, but they seemed relieved when I asked if I could take pictures of them at work. They were eager to use every moment of sunlight. With five family members taking part it would still take seven days to finish. The harvest was "good enough," Lobsang said. He seemed content.

But Tashi's family in Guchok was less satisfied, and their meager harvest that year pointed up the contrast between well-situated peasants with good valley land and those who till and reap on the hillsides. Guchok lies on an incline, a sweep of terraced fields dropping toward the Namling Valley below and straddling a clear mountain brook. There is no irrigation system to tap the stream's water supply, and Guchok residents have to rely on rainfall, which had been scarce that year. The barley grains were small and few, a scant yield which could not support Tashi's family through the year. They would have to buy grain, and some of them would travel to nomad areas where they could earn money tanning hides. Their problem was echoed in Tsering Drolma's village of Chantso, also set in a tributary valley rising from broad land below. "None of the fields is near the river," said Tsering Drolma. "We need more water to irrigate."

In the wide valleys, however, the farmers' prosperity was evident. Fields lying in Namling Valley below Guchok yielded potatoes as well as barley, and near the county seat many peasants harvested with tractors. It was the same in Lhokha, near the town of Tsetang, where the soil of the Yarlung-Tsangpo plain and the relatively low altitude support two crops, barley and winter wheat. Here I saw many tractors chugging about the roads and fields; near Tsetang few traveled by horse cart.

But many farmers who carve their fields into hillside terraces lack the security which irrigation allows, and some of them face long treks from home to field as well. In the Tsangpo River canyon between Lhasa and Shigatse, we passed plots sculpted out of every available site; some were strips measuring no more than ten by thirty feet, wherever the sheer walls allowed for leveling, and often there was no village in sight nor any passable road. Farmers who struggle with such conditions often lag behind those in the broad, fertile valleys. Dorje Tsering, who tilled his fields in the Tsangpo River plain, had built a new home in 1983 and was planning to build another soon, while Tashi Tshering's family in Guchok had only managed to buy back one of their former houses and add a single room. Guchok's hillside fields lie at the margins of arable land, but Tashi believed they could be coaxed into yielding richer harvests with the addition of chemical fertilizers. A good irrigation system would also improve matters. At the TAR Bureau of Agriculture an official said that lack of irrigation is a major problem for Tibetan farmers, but the government is too short of funds to help everyone in need.

The fortunes of Tibet's nomads, however, are less dependent on the locus of a few critical acres. Nomad households have rights to a mix of pastureland, and they can maneuver among the various sites and adjust to the needs of their animals. But the nomads, like the peasants, have also divided into rich and poor families since the reforms began. "Now it's up to your own ability," said a nomad in the mountains outside Nam Tso, on the southern frontier of the Changtang. He took a pinch of snuff from a horn container and then he added, "It depends on the labor you have available and your skill." He was

58

one of four seated by a clear stream just below the 17,000-foot Largen Pass. Some families "don't do so well," said one of the men, but he and his companions agreed that almost everyone is better off under the new system.

Among the Pala nomads to the west, American anthropologists found that although every member of the band began with a roughly equal share of livestock in 1981, seven years later the richer 16 percent of the population owned a third of the animals, while the poorer third owned only 17 percent. One family had no animals at all, and those on the lower end were hiring themselves out to the wealthier families to survive. They herded flocks, spun yak hair and wool, and butchered sheep, goats, and yaks. They also received welfare from the government.

The economic differences, the researchers found, were due to "luck, skill, consumption philosophy, and diligence." They also discovered that families who were wealthy (by nomad standards) before 1959 had prospered once again, even though they had suffered most from the "class enemy" label during the democratic reforms and the Cultural Revolution. Two-thirds of the wealthiest Pala families had also been rich in the old days, and all of the formerly wealthy were prospering.[9]

One of those who has done well since the reforms is Wangdu, a nomad of Bagam Village, where we stopped on our way back to Lhasa from the county seat of Damzhung north of the capital. He was an erect and smiling man of sixty-seven married to equally cheerful Thubten Chodron, who was seventy-three. In former times Wangdu was a herdless nomad living in a ragged tent and surviving on what he earned by spinning wool for wealthier neighbors. After the 1959 rebellion, he was given animals of his own for the first time; in the 1970s he moved to a house at Bagam, his "base camp"; and when his commune disbanded he received seven yaks, a goat, and sixteen sheep. In 1992 he had fifteen yaks and seventy sheep and goats and was living with his family of nine—wife, sons, daughters-in-law, and grandchildren—in a solid house built four years earlier.

Wangdu was content, but according to our Nam Tso nomads, his herds were smaller than the average. A typical family in that area had thirty to forty yaks, they said, and the best ones sold on the free market for $200 or more. Goats and sheep brought in a tenth that price. But the government, the nomads said, paid less for livestock, only $85 for a good yak. Wool likewise brought a better price in private sales. But each year local officials required some quota sales to the county. "It depends on how many cadres are in town," the man said; the sales helped support the salaried government workers in the area.

In Pala the research team also found that nomads were forced to make quota sales, although this was illegal under the post–Cultural Revolution reforms. Pala officials did so to fill the coffers of their local agency and make a good impression on their superiors, and they claimed that the sales were voluntary. They paid the nomads just enough to ward off protests to officials in Lhasa.[10] In nomad areas it seemed that local officials were sidestepping requirements of the reforms, but even though the herders could have made more money on a truly open market, they found their standard of living steadily improving.

A thirty-four-year old nomad in Number Three Village of Damzhung said he had an average herd size for the area: thirty-seven sheep and goats and thirty-seven yaks. In 1991 he built a new house for his family of seven at a cost of $350. He had to buy wood, feed friends and relatives who helped with the labor, and pay a painter to decorate the walls and pillars in traditional style. The house had a cement floor, two large rooms, and bright carpets on the sleeping platforms. Like all the homes around Damzhung it also had an attached corral for the animals, a guard dog outside, and conical stacks of yak dung for fuel.

Tibet's nomads can build houses because they move only ten to forty miles from their base camps each year and always return to winter in the same spot. In Damzhung some family members stay in the house year-round while others leave with the herds each spring and return in midsummer or fall. In Pala, where few have houses, the families leave the base camp in late summer and return at the end of December.

The daily round of labor requires herding and milking, and the seasonal chores include the trek to new pastures, shearing (in summer) and slaughtering (in early winter). Nomads also seem to spend a good part of their time searching for stray yaks. During a few hours on the road between Damzhung and Nam Tso we met two groups searching for wandering animals. But the biggest threats to nomad livestock and livelihood are heavy winter snowstorms, wolves, disease, and drought. When snow lies deep on the Changtang the animals can't forage, and sometimes a third or more of a herd will die when heavy snow lingers on the plains. Disease may wipe out all the newborns in one season, and wolves are a continual danger to sheep, goats, and yaks.

The herders trade with peasants for barley, which they roast on sand until it pops and then grind into the staple tsampa. They eat few vegetables compared to farmers, but like them, they too are beginning to acquire consumer goods from itinerant vendors or during journeys to peddle skins, meat, and butter. They buy pots and pans, shoes, hats, shirts, blouses, jewelry, head scarves, metal trunks, radios, cassette players, kerosene lamps, sewing machines, prayer wheels, amulets, and wooden bowls for butter tea.

An abandoned nomad site we visited near the shores of Nam Tso revealed a mixture of homemade and manufactured goods, a traditional lifestyle supplemented with modern amenities. The nomads had cast off fragments of braided yak-hair rope, a broken yak saddle of carved wood, splintered hand spindles, a cardboard carton, beer bottles, and worn sneakers. They had overlooked a wooden tent peg, still in place, and left a pile of dung behind.

Among all the nomads' possessions the most treasured is the yak, which yields horns, hair, fur, tails, meat, hides, and milk and serves as a mount for riding and a beast of burden. Yak parts and yak milk are transformed into tents, rope, religious artifacts, containers, coracles, boots, blankets, dusters, yogurt, butter, cheese, and a cosmetic for women; and yaks, unlike sheep and goats, give milk year-round. Yak milk is twice as rich in butterfat as cow's milk, but yak meat tastes like beef and yak yogurt is hard to distinguish from supermarket yogurt. Yaks also thrive at high altitudes and low temperatures where cattle would perish. In the lower elevations of Tibet cattle are more common than yaks, but in the higher reaches yaks entirely replace cows, bulls and dzo.

Yaks are valuable but not always docile. They will balk at their tasks and shake off their loads, or they will toss their formidable horns. They are also difficult to steer because unlike horses, which are guided by a bit, they are steered by reins passed through their noses. Male yaks have larger bodies and horns and longer fur than females, and they are "scary to look at" (as one resident of Damzhung put it) and truculent. Females are timid and manageable. The males are also stronger and serve as the chief pack animals.

When I visited a yak-breeding project at Damzhung I learned that today's yaks are less profitable than those of the past. They weigh less and yield less milk than their forebears, according to project researcher Li Yuchao. In the 1950s, for instance, the average yak weighed 420 pounds while today it weighs 310, he said. Females (called *dri*) produce a third less milk than they did forty years ago and have a low reproductive rate; when ten dri are bred, only three or four give birth. At the facility in Damzhung, technicians were trying to determine the cause of these problems, and they suspected that overgrazing and inbreeding were factors. They had, however, succeeded in improving yak stock with artificial insemination, one way to break up the cycle of inbreeding.

The facility (known as the Yak Frozen Semen Station) includes a scattering of one-story offices and laboratories and a range where the breeding yaks roam, and it provides one example of China's technical assistance to Tibet. Li said the station succeeded in freezing yak sperm in 1985 and began artificial insemination the following year. Today two-thirds of the inseminated dri conceive (though some abort). Once they achieved this rate, the staff began to visit nomad groups to demonstrate the new approach. At first the herders were suspicious, Li said, and gave them old or sickly dri to work with, but when they discovered that the treated females produced more and healthier offspring, they began to cooperate. Now the station is trying to expand its support to more nomad groups.

Li took us to the facility's pasture where male yaks grazed under the care of four herdsmen. Some were restless juveniles, sparring and feinting in mock fights; others were sedate oldsters; and some of them had wild blood which was apparent in their greater size. Nomads capture young wild yaks and sell them to the facility, but with hunting and population pressure this valuable gene pool is diminishing. Perhaps fifteen thousand are left today, scattered throughout the Changtang. The wild yaks are completely black, but the domestic may be brown or have patches of white. The wild yaks are also twice as large as the domestic. One slaughtered at the station weighed 970 pounds. A crossbred wild-domestic yak might weigh 550 pounds, and a purely domestic animal a little over 300. The crossbreeds can also be dangerous. The largest of them in the Damzhung herd was a threat to anyone but his favored handler.

The animals in this well-tended herd were studs, the semen donors for the station. Their seed is collected in small bags, labeled with the the donor's name, frozen in liquid nitrogen, and stored in canisters. The station takes care to breed each group of dri with the semen of a different yak each year, and before it is sent out, technicians place a drop on a microscope slide to check its vigor. A good specimen will come quickly to life and turn into a field of wriggling sperm darting about in search of a dri ovum. Some of this precious material has been shipped to lower elevations in Tibet for experiments in producing dzo. It proved just as potent with cows as with dri; one trial yielded an 83-percent reproduction rate.

The nomads we visited, however, had never used the breeding program although their own dri produced few baby yaks. One said his herd of fifteen dri produced only one calf a year. Another said that in a good year some seven dri might give birth to two calves. Both said they had heard of the artificial insemination program, but only one had been told that it was effective.

Tibet's nomads and peasants have been doing better since reforms took hold in the 1980s, but they are still poor by many standards and lag behind other rural inhabitants of China. They lack the amenities common in cities—television, paved roads, buses and rickshaws, markets with everything from vegetables to batteries, teahouses, theaters, pool halls, and piped water. But they live in tranquil and often breathtaking settings quite different from Tibet's larger towns with their crowded streets fouled with raw sewage, their packs of dogs and hordes of beggars, and anarchic traffic. In the countryside the work songs of peasants at harvest carry across the fields and blend with the tinkle of donkey bells. The whistles of plowmen trudging behind their yaks weave an ethereal haze of high notes across the valley floors, and the nighttime silence, under a black and star-studded heaven, is broken only by animal sounds—the sudden bray of a donkey, the cough of an ailing sheep, a dog's bark, and, at dawn, a rooster's crow.

It is not only Western visitors and refugees from the cities who welcome the ambience of rural Tibet. Peasants and nomads also believe they have a good deal going, in spite of the hard labor and the simple lifestyle. One Guchok resident who had often visited the capital said to me, "Lhasa has too many people." And nomads, seen as simple and backward by other Tibetans, believe they have the best of all worlds. "The grass grows by itself," a Pala nomad told American anthropologists Melvyn Goldstein and Cynthia Beall. "The animals reproduce by themselves; they give meat and milk without our doing anything, so how can you say our way of life is hard? . . . We have much leisure time . . . farmers come here to work for us, but do we go to work for them? The farmers' lifestyle is difficult, not ours."[11]

Some of China's critics, however, say the government shortchanges the farming and pastoral areas of Tibet and concentrates its development projects and other subsidies on the cities. If China really wanted to help Tibetans, they say, it would provide more support for rural areas, where the bulk of the native population lives and where modern amenities like electricity are lacking. They claim that China is actually benefiting the Chinese cadres and merchants who live almost entirely in and near the towns and cities. "This becomes clear when one studies the deep urban-rural divide in subsidies," the government-in-exile asserted in response to the 1992 white paper.[12] According to government-in-exile supporters, the Chinese hope to attract more Han to Tibet in order to keep political control, and they build and maintain roads purely for military defense.

It is true that China's policies favor city dwellers over farmers and herders, that jobs are harder to find outside the largest cities and that more money goes to urban than rural areas. It is also true that China's registration system—a harsh and demeaning practice by Western standards—favors town dwellers. Registration ties individuals and families to their work sites; it allows them to apply for jobs and attend school only in the areas where they are legally enrolled. A farmer or nomad from an outlying district of Gyantse Prefecture, for instance, has no chance of finding a permanent job at the town's carpet factory because that work is reserved for those registered in the city of Gyantse. To change your registration from rural to urban is "almost out of the question," as one Tibetan put it. But there is one avenue open to country dwellers with enough cash, another Lhasa resident said, and that is buying off officials. It costs at least 1,000 yuan (about $170). If you want to move from city to countryside, Tibetans and Chinese say, the process is easy and requires no bribes.

The registration system may benefit city dwellers, but it was developed for all of China; it is not aimed at Tibet alone. And the bias in favor of urban centers is true throughout the developing world. China, moreover, has not ignored the well-being of Tibet's farmers and pastoralists. They were exempt from taxes from 1980 to the mid-1990s—although they have been forced into illegal quota sales and, it is reported, compulsory labor[13]—while city dwellers have recently begun to pay fees for the right to run market stalls, restaurants, teahouses, and hotels. They also receive other aid—fertilizer, pesticides, cattle-breeding and veterinary programs, technical aid, and welfare payments to indigent families.

The government also builds and maintains roads throughout Tibet, not just where they serve strategic purposes. Travelers along major routes often pass crews of men and women, usually Tibetan but occasionally Chinese, repairing dirt roads with shovels and pickaxes. The crews may camp in white canvas tents near a stream or lodge in a former commune, or they may come from nearby villages. Along the vast Changtang stretch of the Qinghai-Tibet highway they are often the only human beings in sight, and when we ascended the road to Guchok, it was evident that a crew had recently repaired that out-of-the-way track up a dry riverbed. During the 1950s when China was anxious to secure its hold over the region, the new roads were primarily supply lines for the troops, but today, with the army in place, the central government is building and maintaining links with remote nomad and farming areas where Tibetans are the first to benefit.

The network of roads is one of China's major achievements in Tibet, and the government is also justly proud of its oil pipeline from Golmud in Qinghai to Lhasa, one of the few projects completed during the Cultural Revolution. Tibet, in its poverty, could not have funded these developments on its own, but the critics have charged that the Chinese government has taken more out of Tibet than it has put in. "In monetary terms," one tract claims, "the value of Tibetan timbers taken to China far exceeds the amount of financial assistance the government claims to have given."[14]

I gave up on trying to balance these claims with lists of numbers. Chinese data is skimpy and suspect, and the two sides assign different boundaries to that entity known as Tibet: The government-in-exile's Tibet includes Amdo and Kham as well as the TAR; China defines Tibet as the TAR alone. But no matter what the actual tallies may be, the TAR's economy is certainly limited and lagging in comparison to the rest of China. With the development projects, tax breaks, and government support for schools and health care, it appears to be true, as China claims, that the People's Republic is shoring up the TAR with central-government money. As China expert Orville Schell has written,

"Beijing has actually sunk enormous amounts of money into [Tibet], and for all their efforts they've gotten nothing but a terrible diplomatic black eye."[15]

The aid to cities is more immediately visible than that to the countryside. Sizable new buildings like Lhasa's Holiday Inn, post office, and library catch the eye. But in the larger cities an additional effect of the reforms is also evident. Visitors to central Lhasa will see, along with the shrines and incense and the towering presence of the Potala, another traditional feature of Tibet: beggars of all ages stationed near pilgrim sites and restaurants.

In central Lhasa beggars appear beside your table during a meal saying, *"Kukyi, kukyi"* ("Please, please" in Tibetan) and bobbing a thumb under your nose. If you have any leftovers, they will reach inside their wraps for a bowl. Otherwise they will take change, usually in *mao* notes (worth about 2¢ U.S. each). If restaurant owners chase them off, they will gather outside the door. In the streets beggar boys throw themselves at your feet and grab you by the legs, or fling their arms around your waist, or block your way. Some mendicants, along with the monks and nuns who recite prayers for alms, take up stations in the Barkor and flaunt deformed arms or legs.

In the offices of the Tibet Welfare Services Corporation, General Manager Wang Xiejun assured me that the beggars "don't represent the true state of welfare in Tibet." The poor could get help if they asked for it, he said, and the agency supports unemployable citizens—the disabled and retarded—with a variety of projects such as workshops where the clients produce cardboard boxes, printed material, and handicrafts. The beggars, Wang said, bypass their own local welfare services and instead come to Lhasa and other centers because Buddhism encourages the giving of alms.

This is true, to a degree. The nondisabled poor, who meet eligibility requirements, do receive government aid, but only in the locales where they are legally registered, and many beggars are far from home. Wang is also right that many Lhasa beggars are pilgrims, making a circuit from Kham or Amdo or other districts of the TAR and depending on alms as they go. Collecting alms is a traditional feature of the pilgrim journey. Some pilgrims dance and sing in the Jokhang Plaza and pass a hat at the end of each performance. And often monks and nuns will chant and pray near the Jokhang, setting out a small container to collect alms, which they use for the upkeep and repair of their monasteries.

Still others are professional beggars from China proper who travel to Tibet, where the collecting is good. A study outside Tibet found that career beggars return to comfortable homes at night where they exchange their ragged clothes for middle-class attire, enjoy a good meal, and settle in to watch television. My interpreter, Xiao Jin, gave alms twice to a Chinese beggar in the Barkor and later saw him on her airline flight from Lhasa to Chengdu. Her few cents had contributed to his $100 plane ticket.

The Buddhist ethic encourages almsgiving. Each year on Saga Dawa, the fifteenth day of the fourth lunar month in the Tibetan calendar, Tibetans celebrate a festival commemorating the birth, enlightenment, and death of the Lord Buddha. It is a special almsgiving day, and thousands flock to Lhasa where the devout are ready to hand out hundreds of mao notes. One Lhasa woman gave out six thousand of them to as many individuals on that day. Beggars have learned to count on Tibetan generosity, and anyone out of luck or short of funds can go out to collect alms. It is such a certain source of income that an entire village near Lhasa has taken up begging as a vocation.

Beggars of these types—the pilgrims, the Saga Dawa opportunists, and the "beggar village" residents—are, as Wang said, imperfect indicators of Tibet's welfare and economy. But there are other beggars who are driven by poverty or, worse, by their parents, and their presence is more disturbing.

In Shigatse we spoke to an appealing boy of eleven, ragged as most beggars but clean. He was named Chungdak, which means "Little One," and he was from the monastic town of Sakya. He said he had attended school for three years, until his mother told him to give it up and go with her to beg in the city. His mother had returned to Sakya, but he and his older brother stayed on. They had been in Shigatse one year, and, said Chungdak, he was forgetting everything he had learned in school. An older boy, begging at the same restaurant row as Chungdak, was glassy-eyed and listless. He said he was fourteen, but when we asked why he was begging, he turned away without answering. A Tibetan doctor at our table said, "It is probably because his parents are poor and don't send him to school."

In Lhasa a boy of about twelve said he and a friend had run away from their village east of the capital; his friend had returned but he had stayed on. A boy of ten from Kham said he first left home to accompany a holy man to Mount Kailash (a sacred site in western Tibet), but when he returned home he found his family's crops had failed and there was not enough to feed all the children. He then went back to Lhasa to make his way by begging. He was ragged and covered with sores. The twelve-year-old said he slept at the home of relatives, and the younger boy said a family gave him space for the night, but many youngsters said they slept under the overhang of the Jokhang porch.

Lhasa's smallest beggar was a boy around four years of age who often appeared in the Barkor, sitting cross-legged with a bowl before him. He had saucer eyes in a pinched face, like a poster child for famine relief. Once he came into the restaurant where I was eating, trailing a plastic horse behind him on a snarl of cassette tape; it was the only toy ever I saw in his possession. When I gestured for him to come for some dumplings, he took no notice; he was intent on pulling his horse across the floor. He made a brief turn inside the door, holding his bowl before him, and then he left without looking up. He was going through the motions for an adult waiting nearby.

Another beggar boy told this story: He had attended school until the third grade, when his father brought him to Lhasa to beg. The boy had to meet a quota of at least five yuan a day or his father would beat him.

Wang of Welfare Services said his agency has rounded up the beggar children, fed them, and sent them home, but they always return. How about the parents? I asked. Is there no law to punish them for sending their children into the streets? No, he said, we just try to educate the parents. "We may ask an official in the county or township to talk to them," he said. But outside of these feeble efforts, it seemed that no organization in Tibet felt moved to help the beggar children. One Tibetan, acknowledging this, shook his head and said, "This country can kill people by law. Why can't they do something about beggars?"

Among the older beggars was a woman from Lhokha, making the rounds of teahouses in the Barkor. She was sixty-nine, she said, and had come to stay with her son in Lhasa. But her daughter-in-law mistreated her, she said, so she begged to supplement what she received at home. A woman in Shigatse said she begged to support her six children. In Gyantse an official said the town's few beggars are of two sorts: those who have had a run of bad luck and those who don't want to work.

Many of the young men, about eighteen to twenty years old, said they had come to Lhasa as pilgrims and stayed on, surviving on alms. One youth, however, said he couldn't explain why he begged; he just did. There were a few young women of that age, some of them giggling nomad pilgrims making their first attempts at pleading for food and money. But the young men far outnumbered the young women. At that age indigent women often become prostitutes—a growing class in Lhasa, where the floating Chinese population and Tibetan traders include many men who have left their wives behind.

We ran into beggars here and there along the main roads of Tibet. In some villages the children mobbed us for handouts; in others they stood back shyly and watched. But Lhasa and Shigatse, both major pilgrimage sites, were the only towns which attracted crowds of them. At Tsetang, in the fertile Lhokha region, beggars were less in evidence, and we were told that Gyantse, the site of a major temple called Pangon Chorten, had a few low-profile beggars, although we never saw them.

Each of these towns has its own distinctive spirit: Tsetang is growing and prosperous and has a bustling marketplace. Gyantse, on the old trade route, has a rural ambience and few cars; its roadways are filled with bicycles and pony carts festooned with bells. Damzhung, on the road from Qinghai, and the Namling county seat both have a raw frontier feel, with cows roaming the streets and traders arriving from outlying areas to sell hides and meat.

But town dwellers everywhere, even those in backwaters like Namling, have adapted to the reforms in a different manner than the farmers and herdsmen of rural Tibet. Many townspeople are cadres or workers, dependent on monthly wages and lodged in government apartments or houses. They are less likely to build new homes, but they are buying more consumer goods and some are branching into trade. A Lhasa worker—a driver for instance—makes about $50 U.S. a month and receives free housing (although he pays electricity and water charges). His job is to transport staff and visitors in the unit's car, and he will also garner gifts of cigarettes and whiskey from passengers along the way, a kind of "insurance" that they will be treated well. One Tibetan driver had a wife and three children and money to spend on beer, occasional hard liquor, a VCR, and rented videos.

In Gyantse we visited the carpet factory, a collective set up during a lull in the Cultural Revolution. The unit's party secretary, a short, businesslike woman named Paldron, said it had fared badly until the latest reforms allowed the staff to buy wool and sell carpets on the open market. After that, production and salaries took off, and since then the workers, all of them Tibetan, have been paid according to how much they produce. In 1991 their salaries ranged from a low of $14 U.S. a month up to $70 with the average at $46. In 1980, when the reforms began, the average Gyantse Carpet Factory worker earned less than $8 a month.

Professionals such as doctors, teachers, administrators, and researchers earned from $50 to $85 a month or more, including bonuses for working at high altitudes. (Tibet is considered a hardship post for Tibetans and Chinese alike.) They also received free housing. With the extras, their overall earnings were roughly double those in China proper.

Some of the Chinese and Hui floating population are also on salary. At Snowland a family from Sichuan laundered clothes for the Tibetan cooperative which ran the hotel, earning $50 a month per person. The Chinese cook at Snowland, valued for his skill, earned a substantial wage of $117 a month. Both the cook and the laundry workers sent money home to China proper.

Many urban cadres and workers buy and sell on the side or after hours, and with the present rate of inflation, many need this to supplement their wages. One city of Lhasa employee said he puts in eight hours in his office daily, and then, when the inspectors from the tax bureau go home at 6:00, he sets up shop in the Barkor and sells clothes until sundown. He is one of dozens who suddenly appear at that time to avoid paying license fees. These vendors are mainly Tibetan, and they lay out their wares on mats set on the bare cobblestones.

Some cadres have retired and devoted themselves entirely to trade, like my friend Tashi Tshering, who left Tibet University to become a rug-and-book merchant. Workers, peasants, and nomads also have this option, and among Tibetans the Khampa are noted for their mercantile instincts. Lhasa is full of tall Khampa men with red silk tassels in their hair, selling jewelry, skins, *thangkas* (devotional cloth paintings), and other religious artifacts. They buy goods cheaply outside the TAR and sell them in Lhasa at a good profit. Tibetans living in Nepal and India—as well as Westerners, especially British from Hong Kong—have recently been arriving in the TAR to trade. Most of them buy and sell used carpets.

Traders can do well with luck, diligence, and good connections. So can other entrepreneurs such as shoe repairmen, tailors, and even vegetable farmers. Most of these are Chinese and Hui from Sichuan, Gansu, Anhui, Qinghai, and Zhejiang. And some Chinese families raise vegetables on rented land outside Lhasa; they sell to peddlers who take the cabbages, carrots, onions, turnips, and greens to sell in Lhasa. One family of three, vegetable farmers from Anhui, said they make up to $830 a year per person. This is a decent living in Tibet and in China proper.

But in Tibet those who live best are the wealthiest traders and high government officials, including former aristocrats who have been reinstated after returning from exile or from prison. Those who served time were declared "rehabilitated," named to high-ranking but powerless posts, and set up in big houses with cars of their own. They are among the chief "collaborators" with the Chinese government, and Tibetans told me that this, rather than ethnicity, is what guarantees a good living standard. It is not that the Chinese are on the top and the Tibetans on the bottom; it is that the market economy rewards the traders, and the government rewards those who conform. "The cadres are relatively well-off," said one Tibetan. "We cadres are the collaborators, the ones who support the Communist Party, so we're better off." I met a family of visiting Tibetan exiles who found this to be true of their relatives in the TAR. "Those who cooperate with the government have prospered," said one of the visitors. "Those who haven't don't do so well."

In housing as well, Tibetans are not worse off than Chinese. Tibetans live in the center of town, in the old city, where some of the housing stock is rundown, and Chinese tend to congregate in the newly built apartment blocks on the periphery of Lhasa. New housing is more likely to have decent plumbing and electrical wiring, to be sure, but these amenities go not only to the Chinese. The government has built new apartments for Tibetan cadres in Lhasa, and, a Tibetan told me enviously, these have real "water toilets." The new buildings are in traditional Tibetan style, with heavy wooden window frames, ornate lintels, and brightly painted doors. At August First Farm, officials said that several retired workers have built private homes which cost up to $6,700.

Some Tibetan and Chinese cadres live in featureless concrete buildings like those in China proper. Their apartments typically have two bedrooms, a small sitting room and a kitchen with running water. They may have flush toilets as well, but not showers. If not, the family uses a communal flush toilet which serves everyone on the same floor. In the truly Tibetan areas with their older buildings, it is usual to have no plumbing; the family will fetch water from a pump or spigot and use public toilets. These homes, however, have electricity, and many families have television sets, radios, and cassette players. Some of them are well-appointed inside, with stylish furniture, good carpets on the floors and sleeping platforms, telephones, and brightly painted Tibetan-style sideboards and tables. Most homes, though, are crowded by Western standards; a two-bedroom apartment may house six or more family members.

Many Chinese rent rooms in central Lhasa, the old Tibetan quarter, or get free lodging from their employers. The Tibetan-run Snowland Hotel gave rooms to its Chinese workers and to some of its Tibetan workers as well. The cook, Li Shifu (*shifu* is a Chinese term applied to skilled workers), lived in a single barren room furnished with a bed, a desk, a kerosene stove, a small cupboard, and a tottering table. The launderers, a family of seven or so, also called Li, lived in two rooms with several iron beds, kitchen equipment, chairs, and an ironing board; and they shared this space with laundry drying overhead and stacked along the walls.

Other Chinese live in the back rooms of restaurants or shops. In Damzhung, for instance, a family from Sichuan had partitioned off a space inside their restaurant to create a room about six by eight feet where they kept a television and a couple of beds. This room housed two adults and a child, and it seemed a flimsy protection against the cold in that high region. I could see light shining through the roof and between the door and its frame. But the new nomad houses nearby were solid adobe with thick walls.

The finest home I saw in Lhasa housed a highly placed Tibetan cadre. It was a single residence not far from the center of town set behind walls and a garden courtyard. Inside were a sitting room, a well-stocked study with books in a glassed-in case, a room with elaborate carved altars and platforms covered with carpeting and cushions, a bathroom, and a kitchen. The man was about to leave this home, however. The government was giving him a new house worth more than $10,000 as a bonus. But the most expensive homes, I heard, belong to Khampa traders who have made fortunes in the new market economy. Their houses are of stone, in the Tibetan style, and one Khampa reportedly spent about $330,000 on his residence in Lhasa. He could sell it for twice that much, I was told.

At the lowest end were the homeless beggars, and just a step above were Tibetan families living in a kind of shanty-town where they have put together makeshift shelters of plastic, cardboard, bricks, and wood scraps. Many of them are pilgrims who tarry for months in the Holy City; others are resident beggars.

Tibetans are not consigned to the bottom rung in Lhasa. They live at all levels, from the most squalid to the most comfortable. The Chinese likewise vary in their living standards. Some are high officials with many perks, many are middle-level cadres living along with their Tibetan counterparts in assigned housing, others are workers quartered in cramped rooms, and some are traders who rent rooms in old or new neighborhoods.

The local government is also upgrading old houses in the city, and the Lhasa Environmental Protection Bureau has placed housing renovations at the top of its list since the Cultural Revolution, because, officials said, many of the old dwellings are unsound. They are dark and damp, and the supporting pillars are rotting. Around the Barkor and Shol (below the Potala), the government brought in heavy equipment to pull down the old homes (bringing on complaints that China is destroying the charm of the old city), and crews of Tibetans worked at rebuilding. By 1992, the TAR government had spent more than $1 million on upgrading housing stock, bureau officials said. But some residents of the new Barkor buildings have complained that the roofs leak and that the new houses, built with concrete instead of the traditional pounded earth and wooden poles, are poorly insulated. These houses are too hot in the summer and too cold in the winter, they say—but one Barkor resident told me that you can get better quality construction if you bribe the right officials.

The government completed another building project not far from the Barkor, in a spot called Tromsikhang, where an open market has become an enclosed shopping center, the closest thing to a mall in Tibet. Tromsikhang is the bustling heart of laissez-faire trade in Lhasa, a high-ceilinged building covering a city block. It is a vast market sheltered by a roof and sturdy walls, an extension of the bazaars that surround the Barkor and occupy the adjacent alleys. Many members of the floating population from other provinces—Chinese, Hui, and even Uighur from Xinjiang—have stalls here, and I often came to buy snacks, laundry soap, toilet paper, and gifts for the people I interviewed on the road. Tromsikhang has sections set aside for cookies and other sweet baked goods, bottled and tinned condiments from China proper, fruit, meat, butter, vegetables, nuts and dried fruits, and sundries—which include everything from envelopes to peanuts. Tibetans dominate the meat, butter, vegetable, and cookie sections. Chinese and Hui prevail in the fruit, condiment, and sundries sections. This last area is densely packed with merchants; their mounds, bins, and stacks of goods; and customers forcing their way through the crowded aisles. Here you can find items from China proper, India, Nepal, and even Japan: batteries, pencils, candies, juice mixes, packaged cookies, powdered milk, bags of crackers, canned fruits, detergent, bars of laundry soap, writing paper, and plastic bracelets.

Outside—in the streets surrounding the Barkor, near the Jokhang and near the Potala—other merchants set up stands which they stock each morning and clear away in handcarts at nightfall. Across from the cinema on the road leading from the Jokhang you can find household items like thermos flasks and teakettles, shoes, luggage, head scarves, caps, warm-up suits, and rope. At the entrance to the Jokhang Plaza, Tibetan women park carts full of apples, pears, and oranges; and rickshaw pedalers, their cabs draped with flounces of bright material, wait for customers. Traditional Tibetan items and religious artifacts are for sale along the Barkor circuit—woolen cloth, foxfur hats, amulets, thangkas, religious photos and pictures, bells, ceremonial scarves, prayer wheels, jewelry, bales of silk, striped fabric for aprons, wooden bowls for butter tea, sacred scriptures, and strings of prayer flags. Near the Potala, vendors display household items such as bowls, mugs, thermos flasks, and spoons. Also near the Potala stand a new post office (completed during my visit) and a covered outdoor vegetable market.

This abundance and activity are results of the post–Cultural Revolution reforms; they have come about since the mid-1980s and continue today. A Westerner who had visited Tibet in the mid-1980s returned in 1992 to find that Lhasa had acquired scores of new restaurants and produce stalls selling apples, pears, bananas, grapes, and oranges. These were welcome improvements since his former visit, he said, when he dined daily on cabbage—boiled, fried, or stewed. A Chinese who last saw Lhasa in 1987 likewise noted the growth of trade. The city has more vendors and more goods today than in

1987, he said. At that time the area across from the cinema was empty of stalls. Now it is crowded with merchants and customers.

But one Western visitor, an economist by training, noted that Tibet's growing prosperity is built on an artificial base, on funds from outside its own boundaries. If China finds the price too high and someday withdraws its aid, the economy of the TAR could collapse, he said. When I passed these observations on to a Tibetan economist, he told me that they were well-taken. The TAR, he said, needs to develop its own economy with the materials it has at hand, with its exports of wool and carpets, its tourist industry, and the efforts of its own people. This would prevent an economic crash if the supports were ever removed, he said. Although Tibet would never become a force among the world's economies, he believed it could provide a stable and comfortable living standard for its people if it were operating without help from China proper.

China has thus far shown no signs of abandoning its aid to Tibet. With its own economy growing, it can better afford the support; in the face of criticism from the government-in-exile and its backers, the People's Republic is trying to prove that it has brought a better life to a land of former serfs. The government responds to demands for independence by pointing to Tibet's tractors, trucks, electric power, and shops stocked with consumer goods. China hopes to convince Tibetans and outsiders that the TAR will achieve real prosperity if it remains an integral part of the motherland.

But in doing so China forgets the lessons of other lands where control by outsiders brought modern amenities to formerly backward areas. Britain's former colonies, for instance, benefited from roads, hydroelectric power, motor transport, railways, airports, hospitals, universities, libraries, and telecommunications, but this could not hold back the demands for independence. I was living in Uganda when that former protectorate and cast off the British control which had brought modern facilities to its people. Never, during that time, did I hear a Ugandan argue for continued dependence. Likewise, in the TAR, Tibetans are buying tractors and wiring their homes with electricity, but this fails to convince them that the Chinese should stay. They see the new lifestyle as a benefit of the late twentieth century, a global movement which is their due as members of the industrial age.

4

Keeping Well in the Land of Snows (Health Care)

When the exiled Tibetan writer Dawa
Norbu was growing up in the ancient monastic town of Sakya, he watched his
father die. It was a few grains of sand that killed him, grit that blew into his
eyes during a sandstorm and festered there. In their efforts to cure him, the
family first called on a holy lama, Zongchung Rinpoche, who told them to
erect new prayer flags and appease their guardian deities. The lama said one of
those beings, a female named Phuntsok Phodrang, had caused the accident
during a fit of anger, when her malevolence had struck Dawa Norbu's father
at a vulnerable moment in his horoscope. The boy's mother arranged for three
monks to hold a series of rites and appease the goddess, but her husband's
condition worsened, and red growths appeared in the corner of each eye.

Now the family called on a medical doctor who was learned in the centuries-old Tibetan art of healing. The physician, a man of dignified bearing,
who trailed the scent of medicinal herbs in his wake, traveled for two days to
reach Sakya. He scraped out the growths with a penknife and plied his patient
with powders and glistening brown pills. But, the doctor said, the sick man's
greatest threat was his mental state. He must stop worrying and adopt a cheerful
frame of mind, or he would go mad and die. Dawa Norbu's father continued
to decline, he lost the sight in one eye, he was fast losing his sight in the other,
and he often groaned aloud with pain. The physician fed him more herbs and
as a last resort singed the skin on his chest.

This measure also failed, and the family, on the advice of their revered lama, bought a sheep that was about to be slaughtered and dedicated it as a "rescued" life. This meant the sheep would be allowed to die naturally of old age, and the family's act of charity would correct the dangerous spiritual imbalance threatening the sick man. The lama also rechristened Dawa Norbu's father and gave him a new set of clothes—thus making him a new person, one, it was hoped, who was sound in karmic and physical health. Other monks provided the patient with protective relics, and he lay, gaunt and in agony, under a heap of holy ribbons and charms which hung about his neck.

But in spite of these efforts, he continued to weaken, and he expired at last, several months after his eyes had filled with sand. Dawa Norbu, his six brothers and sisters, and their mother had lost their father, husband, and breadwinner, and they had depleted their savings as well. The lamas' rites and the powders administered by the physician had cost them all they had. It was late in 1952, a year after the Chinese had entered Tibet and well before the Communists began their reforms.

After the rebellion of 1959 and the brutal clampdown which followed, Dawa Norbu's family left Sakya and fled to India. They had no contact with relatives in Tibet during the dark years of the Cultural Revolution, and not until 1983 did they meet again with Dawa Norbu's Aunty Dechen—his mother's sister and a former nun—who managed to visit them in India. She recounted the horrors of the previous years and the recent reforms, and she brought them up-to-date on the many changes in Sakya. The Chinese, she said, had built schools, a hospital, and a hydroelectric plant, and the hospital was by far the greatest boon. She herself had undergone an eye operation there, and it had cost her nothing.

Health care was a top item on China's list when the Communists took over Tibet in 1951. Even before they built a network of roads throughout the region, they were sending doctors and medical teams on horseback into farming and herding areas. By 1965, according to Chinese data,[1] Tibet had more than two thousand medical professionals in the field, and some of China's severest critics were beginning to agree with Dawa Norbu's aunt that medical care was the best feature of China's effort to modernize Tibet.

Today the region's health care system is suffering from money problems which threaten to undermine its achievements, but Tibetans continue to benefit, and China repeatedly cites the gains it has made in health services. The central government notes that it has wiped out smallpox, which once ravaged Tibet, killing thousands at a time. By 1992 the government had immunized 85 percent of the TAR's children against polio, tuberculosis, and major childhood diseases. In 1951, according to Chinese sources, the region had no hospital beds; by 1991 it had more than five thousand and averaged 2.3 beds and just over two doctors per thousand residents.[2] Infant mortality, estimated to be at least five hundred per thousand live births (or fully 50 percent) per year before the Chinese takeover, was down to ninety-one per thousand live births in 1991. Life expectancy, China says, rose from thirty-six years—an estimate provided also by Heinrich Harrer, who lived in Tibet in the 1940s—to sixty-five. A Tibetan doctor, however, told me that thirty-six is far too low an estimate, and other Tibetans have disputed Harrer's report that few lived into old age. Perhaps the best information on this question comes from a Western doctor who has worked in Tibet: No one, he said, knows the actual medical statistics for the old society.

Although many of the accomplishments China cites are commonplace today, even among Third World countries, and although some of the data is difficult to assess—smallpox, for instance, was eradicated throughout the world by 1977, and the ratio of hospital beds to population fluctuates so much between health care systems that by itself it is a poor indicator of success—Tibet's progress has been solid for a backward region with vast areas of mountains and wilderness, a scattered population, and a harsh climate. To be sure, the infant mortality rate is well above that of developed countries like the United States, where as of 1992 out of a thousand live births only 8.5 infants died before their first birthday.[3] It is even above that of China as a whole, which had a infant mortality rate of 32 per thousand in 1991. It is also worse than that of neighboring Kazakhstan and Mongolia, and it ranks about the same as Nepal and the African countries of Uganda and Ivory Coast. But it betters the rates in Bangladesh and Laos. Likewise, Tibet's life expectancy rate falls below that of industrialized countries (seventy-five in the United States in 1992) and that of China as a whole (sixty-nine for men and seventy-two for women in 1992), but it is well above that of many African countries, where the average life span is often in the fifties. It also ranks above Bangladesh,

Laos, Nepal, and Haiti. It is near that of its neighbors, Kazakhstan and Mongolia, and the Latin American countries of Nicaragua and Peru. Tibet, ranked among comparable areas of the world, does a better job with life expectancy than infant mortality.[4]

China is not satisfied with citing its accomplishments in Tibet, however; it also insists on painting the former government in the blackest terms to show once again that China truly brought liberation in every sense. "Absolutely no medical treatment was given to the broad masses of serfs and slaves when they fell ill," states the 1992 government white paper, which goes on to say that authorities in the old society were so lacking in compassion that they drove victims of epidemics into the mountains to die.[5]

Dawa Norbu's experience, however, shows that ordinary Tibetans could call on traditional physicians and lamas for help when someone fell ill—although this was often at their own expense. Others confirm that many monks were willing to provide what aid they could when patients and family members sought them out. The problem was that Tibet had no modern medicine to offer, outside of British clinics serving the trade mission. Some Tibetans received modern care at these clinics before the Chinese invasion.

In its efforts to justify its presence in Tibet, China overstates the case against the old society, but it has saved thousands of lives with its network of modern medical practitioners and clinics. The Chinese brought immunization, antibiotics, and modern surgery, all of which, until recently, were provided free of charge to peasants, nomads, and city dwellers. The numbers show that China has improved the health care of ordinary Tibetans.

The Tibetan government-in-exile and its supporters, however, charge the Chinese with discrimination. "Medical care is segregated, with the best facilities reserved for the Chinese," reads an unsigned flier on Tibet. A British magazine made the same statement with a pair of colorful graphs suggesting that Chinese are favored over Tibetans in health care.[6]

I got a different view at Lhasa People's Hospital, a complex of functional concrete buildings off a broad boulevard, where Chinese and Tibetans waited together for outpatient care, sharing the same conditions. The Chinese were members of the floating population and had no registration in Lhasa. They had to pay the normal outpatient fee—equivalent, at that time, to 5¢ U.S.—

and they also had to buy their own medicine, which was supposed to be provided free to those with local registration. (As a foreigner I paid less than $1 to register in the outpatient clinic.)

When I visited hospitals from Gyantse to Lhasa to Damzhung I met Tibetans in charge, at the highest levels of the TAR administration and in county hospitals. This was in contrast to other departments, such as agriculture and forestry, where every official I interviewed was Chinese. According to government data, 80 percent of the TAR's health technicians are Tibetans, and this ratio is even higher in the countryside. Out of eighty-nine doctors and nurses at Gyantse County Hospital only three were Chinese. Out of sixty at Damzhung all but one, a nurse, were Tibetan.

If any group receives superior health care, it is the wealthy or those with good connections—such as high officials or prosperous merchants. Anyone with local registration is supposed to get a medical card to insure free service, but this is often difficult to come by, a Tibetan doctor told me, and it doesn't guarantee that treatment and medicine are available. In any case, only a few kinds of medicine are free. And free service isn't available to workers and cadres in government units—they are supposed to pay first and get reimbursed later by their work units. In 1992 Lhasa residents were already complaining that the wealthy and well-connected fare better than common people, and since then, by all accounts, the differences have become more pronounced. The prices have risen, and a doctor working in Tibet said that if you suffer from "anything complicated or life-threatening, you have to pay."

At the Tibet Development Fund, a nongovernmental organization which runs several health care projects, director Changlo Chen Wangchuk, himself a Tibetan, noted that care is not equally available to city and country people. "We in the cities," he said, apparently referring to well-off urban dwellers, "can get good care by going to other provinces, but local county people can't, those in remote areas." Wangchuk was referring to county hospital patients who need more sophisticated care than the TAR can offer. Tibetans with enough funds and clout (the better-off urban residents) can travel to Chengdu or Shanghai or other centers where the equipment for treatment and diagnosis is available. Those without such advantages make do with local hospitals and clinics and often make their way from rural areas to Lhasa.

Some patients abandon the government hospitals with their lack of medicines and rising fee scale and go to the many private clinics in Lhasa. These are run by government doctors who moonlight in their off-hours or abandon the public sector altogether, and by doctors from China proper. The TAR Bureau of Public Health investigates the clinics, an official there said, and doctors must show the proper licenses and school certificates. But a Tibetan doctor told me that treatment in the private clinics is often substandard. "Aspirin and penicillin shots," he said, "for any kind of illness."

Money and connections make a difference, Tibetans say. One reported that an elderly woman died at the door of a Lhasa hospital because she couldn't pay the $150 inpatient registration fee. At the same time, my informant said, a well-connected woman received free care and then used false receipts to get a reimbursement from her work unit. Many rumors like this circulate in Lhasa, and they underscore the widespread belief that health care is a matter of privilege and wealth.

This is not surprising, considering the complaints Tibetans were making in 1992. Rural folk and city dwellers, the staff of county hospitals, and leading health administrators all were sounding the same theme: Tibet needs medicine, and it needs equipment, and for both of these it needs a big dose of cash.

At Gyantse Hospital we toured the pharmaceutical supply room and passed row after row of bare shelves. The hospital, which serves 560,000 people, had little more than vitamins on hand. In the nomad area of Damzhung, at Lhasa People's Hospital, and at the TAR Public Health Bureau, officials had a ready answer when I asked them to name their most critical problem: Medicine, they replied promptly. We never have enough medicine. When I asked what kind was in especially short supply, they shrugged and said, All kinds.

Village doctor Pempa Tsamcho near Gyantse told me she often sends patients to the county hospital because her shelves are bare. "I have no other way to deal with it," said Pempa Tsamcho, who serves as nurse practitioner for Paljor Lhunpo Village.

When we were on the road, Tibetans we met begged for medicine. At one remote teahouse our driver brought out a packet of headache pills, and the manager immediately put out her hand, even before she knew what sort of drugs they were. Our driver gave her several. At Bagam Village the elderly couple Wangdu and Thubten Chodron pleaded for any medicine I could spare. Thubten Chodron extended her lower lip to show me a scab that refused to heal. I applied a dab of antibiotic lotion, having nothing else on hand, and gave her some more folded into a square of paper. We also left the family with a supply of ibuprofen.

Doctors and nurses have to interpret symptoms and treat patients with outdated equipment. They often lack kidney dialysis machines and blood-test equipment, heart monitors, and electrocardiographs. Gyantse Hospital sorely needed a fiber-optic scope to detect ulcers, according to the director, a heavyset, solemn Tibetan known simply as Phuntsok. With a scope they could make diagnoses that are 90 percent accurate; as it is, they depend on X-rays, which are 70 percent correct. They had fetal monitors and ultrasound machines for obstetrics, gifts from UNICEF; ophthalmological machines for testing vision; and decent microscopes for slide analysis. But they had no dialysis machine to treat patients with kidney failure. At Damzhung County Hospital Director Tsering Dondrup said they had dialysis machines but no technicians to run them. They could take X-rays and perform simple blood tests, but they had no electrocardiograph. "It's hard to diagnose without good equipment," said Tsering Dondrup. "We can observe, but we need the right equipment to do good tests. We can only be 60 or 70 or, at most, 80 percent sure of a diagnosis."

Both Tsering Dondrup and Phuntsok said the government was mandating more sophisticated blood tests, but their hospitals could not perform them; they lacked the necessary tools. Lhasa People's Hospital, better equipped than most, also faced these difficulties. It had incubators for premature babies, a sonogram, and a heart monitor and would soon acquire a CT scan. "But," said an administrator identified simply as Ms. Wang, a cheerful, round-faced woman who was half Tibetan and half Chinese, "we need better X-ray machines, and we only have simple blood-testing equipment. We need better."

The problem was lack of funds, and it was a sign of the changing economic system in China. The medicine was available but in private pharmacies, not in hospitals where it was supposed to be provided free to those with local registration. Lhasa People's Hospital, the largest in the TAR, was chronically short of "the fancier antibiotics," Ms. Wang said. Sometimes the staff asked patients to buy medicine themselves on the open market, and sometimes, when a patient had no funds, the hospital would use its own money to buy what was needed at private pharmacies. Not everyone can afford the prices in these stores, where a course of antibiotics can run from $10 to $20 U.S. This is a steep price for laborers who may earn less than $1 a day and even for relatively well-off drivers who earn about $50 a month.

The hospitals are running short because government support has failed to keep up with costs, health professionals said. Tibet's health care system had received the same amount of funds for several years while population and costs were steadily rising. Gyantse Hospital had been allocated less than $142,000 from the regional government in 1992 to cover the salaries of doctors, nurses, and other workers and the purchase of new equipment and medicine. With a staff of ninety doctors and nurses, this left little to buy antibiotics, not to mention CT scans. Doctors' salaries were low compared to those of other highly trained cadres—at most $50 a month including special allowances for working in a hardship area—so it was not a question of overpaid staff. It was a question of subsidies, and this was where Tibet differed from the rest of China.

China's tracts on Tibet claim that medical care is free in the region, in contrast to every other area of the People's Republic, but this is just what health administrators were objecting to. They were behind other areas, they said, because they could not legally require patients to pay for care. Elsewhere the government had begun to charge patients a percentage of the cost, but Tibet had no such option, and this meant hospitals and clinics had little left to buy medicine and equipment.

Outside of Tibet, China's clinics and hospitals had begun by 1992 to charge patients 10 to 20 percent of the "market" rate (determined by comparing equivalent rates of private sales and computing the cost of office visits relative to doctors' salaries). The system began to change in 1989, when the government decided that free or inexpensive care encouraged patients to waste medicine and take up doctors' time with frivolous complaints. When the Chinese had to pay the market rate, they made fewer appointments, a Beijing doctor told me; the system was no longer overloaded; and there was less burden on doctors and hospitals. And, he said, the patients' fees freed up money to buy drugs and equipment.

For a case of the flu or a bad cold a Beijing patient in 1992 might have paid up to 15¢ U.S. or 10 percent of the cost of an office visit. For a course of penicillin the charge was something like $8 to $10; for a hospital stay, say for pneumonia, it might have reached $350.

Health workers in Tibet hoped for a similar scheme. Costs were high and income was low, they said. Tsering Drolkar, a motherly, plainspoken woman who heads the TAR Bureau of Public Health, noted that cadres were charged less than $1 a day for a normal hospital stay, and $2.50 for a private room. She shook her head. "Just think how much it costs to stay in a hotel," she said. (In Lhasa hotels charged $60 a day at the high end of the scale and less than $3 at the low end.) She was saying that the charges fell far short of covering the costs.

Tsering Drolkar and other health professionals were hoping Tibet's free medical system would soon change. "Possibly the government could give more money for public health," Tsering Drolkar said, "or they could ask the people to pay an amount they can afford." And if the government didn't act, she said, hospitals might ask patients for donations to offset the cost of treatment.

This is happening today, although the "donations" are mandatory rather than voluntary. And cadres, who are supposed to pay first and get reimbursed later by their units, say the units don't always come up with the funds when they're asked. Fees have gone up for outpatients, Tibetans say, and inpatients have to pay $150 just to be admitted. When I asked a Tibetan doctor what would happen if a patient didn't have the money, he shook his head and said, "They would have to borrow it." In effect, Tibetans are beginning to pay for care no matter what is on the books.

In the face of shortages, Tibet's doctors say frankly that they can't treat some diseases. Even in Lhasa, cancer treatment is unsophisticated, according to Ms. Wang. Gyantse County Hospital director Phuntsok, said that although his facility could treat a range of conditions—hepatitis, pneumonia, arteriosclerosis, bone fractures, ulcers, diabetes, meningitis, and other ailments—doctors there could not operate on brain tumors or other forms of cancer. One claimed to treat kidney failure without dialysis, by extracting excess fluid with a needle, but this is at best a temporary measure. Without dialysis or transplants (which no one mentioned in Tibet), patients without functioning kidneys inevitably die.

What happens to cancer patients, I asked, if they can't get good care in Tibet? Some, I was told, go to other provinces. But these were few—mainly well-placed cadres or Chinese who return home. And how about the kidney patients with no access to dialysis? No one answered this. Although 70 percent of the inpatients at Lhasa People's Hospital came from outside the city, county doctors said they sent few patients to the capital, possibly because many of them could do no better there than at home. The implication was that many died for lack of better facilities and medicine.

Nevertheless, there is plenty of healing taking place in Tibet's network of hospitals and clinics. At Tashigang Village Dorje Tsering smiled broadly as he said that his seventy-year-old father had once suffered from tuberculosis but doctors had cured him. When Dorje Tsering's family members fell ill, they could visit a clinic with two village doctors at the headquarters of the former commune two miles away. When we visited Damzhung County Hospital, a nomad girl of thirteen was recovering from appendicitis. She had come from Nam Tso, at least thirty-five miles away and accessible only by a rough track over the 17,000-foot Largen Pass. The director, a surgeon named Tsering Dondrup, had operated on her that day. Standing by her bed in the dark room, he stroked her forehead tenderly.

Tsering Dondrup said Damzhung County was nearly free of measles and whooping cough, which were common before 1985, and health workers had managed to inoculate 90 percent of the county's children. Gyantse doctors said 85 percent of the children in their area had been immunized, and polio, whooping cough, diphtheria, and tuberculosis were no longer serious threats.

Gyantse had just begun to compile maternal death statistics when we visited in 1992. Before 1989 seventy-three women out of ten thousand who gave birth died; in 1990 the rate was seventy-two. According to a UNICEF study based on data for 1990, this placed Gyantse on a par with the Central African Republic and Ghana. The area's rate was well above the regional average for Asia and the Pacific, which was thirty-nine per ten thousand. China as a whole had a fraction of Gyantse's rate, only 9.5, while neighboring Nepal was twice as bad as Gyantse at 150. Neighboring India was better at fifty-seven. Gyantse had a long way to go to reach the European average of 3.6 or the average in the Americas of fourteen.[7]

It was too soon to tell whether or not the statistics showed a trend, said Pasang Tsamcho, deputy director of the hospital. She added, "There are not enough doctors to care for all the women who want to come here to give birth, but they prefer the hospital because they know it is safer." Those who choose to deliver at home have village doctors to assist them, she said. In Damzhung, Tsering Dondrup said some women still preferred home births, especially women living in remote areas. But health education and experience have convinced most of them to use village clinics. As in Gyantse the hospital lacked space to accommodate them all.

In the early days, however, doctors and nurses had to convince the local people that childbirth was safer in the clinics and that immunization would save lives. Some Tibetans (like the Dalai Lama, who was inoculated when he was ten) were immunized against smallpox, thanks to the influence of British medicine. But many were wary in the beginning. "At first," said Phuntsok at Gyantse, "the people resisted immunization because they said they weren't sick. We had to beg and persuade them, but now they know it works."

When the Chinese first arrived with their teams of doctors, Tibetans were slow to take advantage of the clinics. Some monks also opposed the new ways, which threatened to deprive them of patients and income, but in the 1950s, monks were the first patients to show up at the newly built hospital in Lhasa. With this endorsement from the religious establishment, laypersons began to come as well, and gradually the new procedures gained acceptance.

Tibetans began to shed taboos—against germ-killing antiseptics, which were considered sinful for taking life, and against surgery, which had been banned in Tibet ever since a ninth century Tibetan queen died during an operation. In time they learned that modern medicine could cure them; they had only to see the results. By 1962, ten years after the first hospital was built, half the residents of Lhasa were choosing the new system, officials told a pair of British visitors.[8] Today Western medicine predominates in Tibet even though the traditional system with its herbs and powders is still practiced everywhere.

The first doctors trained in modern medicine faced the skepticism and resistance of a conservative society unaccustomed to twentieth century science, and today's physicians continue to struggle with Tibet's altitude, climate, faulty hygiene, vast distances, and endemic diseases. At Damzhung, for instance, the average elevation is more than 14,000 feet, which means that the available oxygen in the air is about 40 percent less than at sea level. This, doctors say, may lead to disorders of the heart and circulatory system. Nomads and farmers also pick up brucellosis from their cattle. It is a disease which causes spontaneous abortions in pregnant animals and often kills them as well; in humans it is rarely fatal, but it brings on weakness and high fever that continue intermittently for several months. Damzhung and fourteen other sites in the TAR have inspection centers to detect brucellosis.

Tsering Dondrup also noted that winter temperatures in Damzhung can sink below minus twenty degrees Fahrenheit. The cold aggravates the misery of arthritis, a common ailment in Tibet and especially painful for nomads who work outdoors with bare hands. A certain form of arthritis causes stunting and deformed joints. It is endemic in Tibet and some areas of northern China, and you often see dwarf-sized adults shuffling about on crutches. Tuberculosis of the bone has afflicted many, doctors said, but this is being eradicated with inoculations. Like most Third World areas, Tibet administers a tuberculosis vaccine called BCG to infants.

Since many Tibetan men smoke nonstop, I asked everywhere about lung cancer, but no one had noticed a high incidence of the disease in the TAR. It may appear in time, however. (In China overall, smoking has increased rapidly with the new affluence, and the lung cancer rate is beginning to rise. Health experts estimate that it will increase fourfold between 1996 and 2025.[9])

Meanwhile in Tibet, stomach and liver cancer are seen as greater threats. "They are prevalent," said Tsering Drolkar, "because there is so much drinking." She had no statistics, however. Such research is still rudimentary in Tibet.

Tsering Drolkar was more concerned with the packs of feral dogs in towns like Lhasa and Shigatse than she was with smoking habits. Her worst nightmare is a rabies epidemic. "It would take only one case," she said, "and it would be a disaster." She had good reason to be anxious. Although strays disappeared from the streets after 1959, they returned after the post-Cultural Revolution reforms. Tibetans believe that feeding these dogs is an act of compassion, and that it is a sin to kill them. So Lhasa today swarms with mongrels that scavenge, breed, whelp, and die—all in public view. In the center of the city, they lie on the cobblestones by day and set up a bedlam of barks, snarls, and yips by night—a cacophony so overwhelming that I could sleep only if I used a pair of earplugs.

Local officials have tried to get rid of the dogs, but according to Zhang Chunyong, party secretary at the TAR City Planning Bureau, each attempt has provoked a backlash of outrage from devout Tibetans. First, Zhang said, the department asked cadres and workers in Lhasa's units to round up dogs, confine them within their compounds, and shoot them. Some units began to comply, but this brought on angry complaints, and Lhasa people gathered strays and took them to Drepung and Sera monasteries for safekeeping. "We respected the religious beliefs," said Zhang, "so we stopped the killing." Then city officials hit on another plan. They built two sets of kennels, collected free-ranging dogs, and divided them according to sex. The males went into one kennel, the females into another. The bureau was prepared to wait for the dogs to die off naturally, but this plan came to grief as well. "The common people," said Zhang, "destroyed the kennels and let the dogs out." He added wearily, "People won't support every decision even when you try to help them."

I asked him for a ballpark figure on Lhasa's dog population. Maybe twenty thousand, he said.

And there are the flies and microbes which breed in Lhasa's open toilets and filthy streets, still more reason for Tsering Drolkar to lose sleep. She has to contend with the Tibetan privy, which is not a pit toilet dug into the earth but a latrine set above the ground. You climb a short flight of steps to a room with a row of oblong holes set in the concrete floor and the piles of excrement visible a few feet below. In the less populated areas—in a small village—for instance, these can be odor-free and endurable (although they are usually protected by no more than a low wall), but near pilgrim sites and major highways and in the cities they can be appalling. The latrine at my hotel was permanently encrusted with grime, excreta, and dirt, and its hole was large enough to disappear through—my constant nightmare. Sometimes the floors of these toilets were covered with squirming larvae.

In Lhasa many pilgrims and other visitors and many residents without toilets in their homes simply use the street. At the Lhasa Environmental Protection Bureau—which proudly points to sixty-two miles of sewer lines built in the capital over the years—officials have tried to tackle the "anywhere will do" issue with educational pamphlets, television and newspaper appeals, and even a tract on cleanliness written by a renowned lama. The message, according to Tsering Wangdu, director of the bureau, is that "when you come to the Holy City you shouldn't act this way." Many of the offenders, Wangdu said, are country folk and nomads who have no experience with modern plumbing, so the city avoids levying fines and tries to persuade them to use public toilets instead.

These, however, are in short supply in Lhasa, and they are heavily used and therefore foul. But Tsering Wangdu said the bureau was planning to build thirteen new toilets in Lhasa by the end of 1992. These, he assured me, would have water.

Although Tibet has come far from the old days when a common morning sight was rows of monks squatting in Lhasa's open spaces, it's obvious that the TAR's sanitary workers could use some help. International aid organizations have donated vans and computers, conducted studies, held conferences, and enlisted experts in communications and solar technology, but no one has provided for Tibet's most pressing need, which is nothing more than a team of good plumbers.

In such conditions dysentery, giardiasis, food poisoning, and other intestinal ailments thrive, and hepatitis has become endemic. In the few months of my visit, I heard of several hepatitis patients—from Tibetan children and adults to a strapping German who had cycled all the way from Berlin across the steppes of Russia only to be felled by the disease in Lhasa. It flourishes not only where nonflush toilets stand a few yards from water pumps but also in restaurants where dogs lie underfoot, flies swarm unmolested, and tables are wiped with stinking rags.

Tsering Drolkar said the public health bureau inspects restaurants and tells the owners to cut food on clean surfaces, provide customers with disposable chopsticks, and keep meat separate from vegetables. They also ask them to use an antiseptic in the dishwater. "But they don't," she added. Her crew of inspectors is stretched too thin, she said, and each individual is dealing with a job that requires three or four.

Sometimes the inspections turn up more than microbes. Her staff caught several Lhasa restaurants lacing food with a narcotic, a sure way, the owners figured, to keep customers coming back. "They put this drug in hot pots," she said. "It was like opium." The Public Health Bureau closed down a number of the restaurants, but she feared that others were going undetected. "Be careful," she told me.

Tsering Drolkar also said, with a touch of defensiveness—she fields many complaints—that her bureau has no jurisdiction over the dog population nor over the flies and rats. She can only urge the departments in charge to take action. Although she is Tibetan, she would like to get rid of the free-ranging dogs. "People here still haven't liberated their thinking," she said. "They think it is wrong to kill any life, even flies."

Like Ms. Wang at People's Hospital, Tsering Drolkar places health education right below medicine as Tibet's major need. "Some minor diseases become serious because people don't know how to take care of themselves," she said. Germs multiply fast in dirty dishes, and they spread quickly when few people bother to wash their hands. In Tibet even the educated may give little attention to hygiene. When a friend of mine stayed at the home of a school principal in a nomad area, she was dismayed to discover that the family members—grandmother, children, mother, and father—simply licked their bowls and put them away. Since guests and family shared the same dishes, she began to scrub them out at the pump after meals. But the principal told her to relax. There's no need, he said. We wash them once a week.

Although educated city dwellers are often fastidious, Tibetans in general are notoriously unwashed. During the yearly bathing festival, families flock to the rivers to launder their bodies and bedding, but in their arid, frigid land baths are less than comfortable and easily ignored. Many countryfolk and poor urban dwellers live happily and unself-consciously under a layer of grime. When we arrived unannounced at Khartse School in Namling County, the children greeted us with their normal complement of runny noses, dirt, and coating of tsampa. Two days later when we returned with advance warning, they sported clean shirts and faces, but their necks remained soot-black.

Tsering Dondrup at Damzhung said dysentery is common, especially in winter and spring when supplies run low, and the people eat food that has been around too long. The staff tries to teach the nomads better hygiene, he said. And at Gyantse, Phuntsok, who directed the public health bureau as well as the hospital, said the county holds a health fair each year to promote awareness of basics like soap and water. The hospital staff had prepared posters of smiling children washing their hands before eating and refusing food that smelled bad.

The major responsibility for health education lies with the village doctors, the descendants of the Cultural Revolution's famous "barefoot doctors." They are the frontline troops in primary health care, and since China joined the United Nations in 1971, they have inspired many developing countries—from Iran and India to Latin America—to train their own community health workers. These doctors are peasants or nomads who undergo a course of training before they return to their communities to give immunizations, deliver babies, treat common ailments, and teach their peers about clean water and sanitation.

During the Cultural Revolution, when the state emphasized rural health care, the barefoot doctors were selected from among the ranks of literate peasants and herders to undergo a three- to six-month training program. Their counterparts today study for a year and must pass an exam at the end of that time. Pempa Tsamcho, forty-six, said she attended a course at Gyantse County Hospital where she learned both Western and Tibetan medicine.

She was in the fields with her thirteen-year-old daughter, the youngest of four children, when we spoke to her. They were spreading rapeseed on mats to dry because Pempa Tsamcho, like all village doctors, works at farm tasks besides serving as a paramedic. When Paljor Lhunpo villagers need help, they look for her at home or in the fields. She keeps no office hours, but she sees an average of fifteen patients a day. She treats their minor injuries and illnesses—colds, diarrhea, headaches, abrasions—and sends those with serious ailments to Gyantse. For this service she earns about $5 U.S. a month.

Village doctors also attend continuing education classes. When we were in Damzhung four of the county's seventy-three village doctors, (serving forty-six thousand square miles and thirty-four thousand people) were attending a seven-day course on maternal and child health. The Swiss Red Cross also helps train, retrain, and supervise village doctors in a joint project with the Tibet Development Fund. Swiss physicians, Phuntsok said, often bicycle long distances to help at village clinics.

Tibetan village doctors face the same problems as physicians in large hospitals—lack of medicine and equipment—and some village clinics contain nothing more than a pair of stools to sit on. A Western doctor who has worked with them also said that the village doctors vary greatly in skill and knowledge. At the Tibet Development Fund, Wangchuk said his group is trying to improve care by training village doctors in traditional Tibetan medicine, which depends on local herbs. "To use just Western medicine in the village is too expensive," said Wangchuk in his careful, accented English. "The cost of Western medicine is too high, but Tibet has good herbs. Therefore, we set up these traditional schools in September 1989, about forty students in each school."

TDF's students will become full Tibetan practitioners. They will study for six years and then return to their home villages. Right now the fund operates two traditional Tibetan medical schools, one in Shigatse and another in Sichuan Province, and Wangchuk hopes to set up another in Nagchu, north of Lhasa. "When we make more progress and have more equipment and medicine," Wangchuk said, "we can train the doctors more in Western medicine, but I think for now we have to use traditional medicine and traditional ways."

Traditional Tibetan medicine is a sophisticated and complex system which developed outside the influence of modern science. Tibetans trace its history back to the fifth century when two Indian doctors brought their learning to Tibet. It began to flourish in the eighth century when the Father of Tibetan Medicine, Yuthok Yonten Gongpo, collected folk remedies, integrated these with four treatises attributed to the Buddha himself, and wrote thirty books on medicine. He drew from both Indian and Chinese sources and promoted a tradition closely allied to Buddhist psychology and spirituality. It includes a pharmacopeia of thousands of herbs, minerals, and animal products and relies on a theory of humors for making diagnoses and prescribing remedies. It has produced elaborate diagrams and charts listing eighty-four thousand illnesses in more than sixteen hundred categories.

To Westerners some elements of Tibetan medicine appear familiar and prudent. Doctors may advise patients to keep warm, exercise regularly, and get enough sleep. They may check tongues, temperatures, and urine samples, ask for case histories, and palpate affected areas of the body; and they may suggest that patients first adopt healthier lifestyles before trying medicine or invasive procedures like acupuncture.

But other aspects reveal a system far removed from Western practice. Tibetan doctors categorize diseases as "hot" or "cold" and describe them as imbalances of wind, bile, or phlegm. When fever is present, they may first "ripen" the body heat and cause it to "burst out" before giving medicine to cool the patient down. They may prescribe medicine to "gather the germs together" before administering a second medicine to attack the disease. They often diagnose conditions by placing three fingers on a patient's pulse and delicately sensing the rate and strength of the beat at various pressures.

For high blood pressure they advise patients to drink thick butter tea and a watery sweet milk tea. They tell patients with cold diseases—such as indigestion and kidney ailments—to avoid goat meat, but they allow patients with both hot and cold diseases to eat garlic. They may suggest eating the fresh meat of animals found in the hills or flour made from old grain.

Westerners, however, can appreciate Tibetan medical ethics which hold that doctors should have compassion for all beings, sympathy for their patients, acceptance of the odors and excretions of the ill, the ability to communicate with patients, pity for the poor, and confident and encouraging bedside manners.

But the canons of medical practice under the old society also had attributes Westerners would reject. According to the Venerable Rechung Rinpoche in his book *Tibetan Medicine,* a doctor "must be of noble birth or he will not be respected by the people" and "he must believe in whatever his Teacher teaches him and have no doubt whatsoever in his teachings." Traditional texts also admonish doctors, who were pharmacists as well as physicians, to collect and prepare medicines with the correct attitude—one of benevolence, compassion, and selflessness. If they fail to do so, the texts warn, the mixtures will lack the spiritual powers to heal.

This last caution underscores the holistic psychic-spiritual-physical unity of Tibetan medical theory. This was evident in the advice Dawa Norbu's father received from the physician: Stop worrying or you'll die of grief. And it was evident in the lama's suggestion to appease the deities and restore the sick man's spiritual balance. Herbs, prayers, and sane attitudes all have a role in healing. Advanced practitioners of meditation may be able to cure themselves; others may benefit from the spiritual state of the healer.

The Communists, of course, reject the religious elements of Tibetan medicine, and students of Tibetan medicine in the TAR usually receive no instruction in the traditional teachings, which call for prayer and exorcisms. The state forbids religious instruction in the classroom, but, one Tibetan doctor told me, "Some teachers take the risk and talk about the Buddhist part of our medicine." In any case, he said, the students know their traditions. "We all know it anyway," he said. "There are the thangkas and the Medicine Buddha, and we can see those."

The Chinese tend to approach traditional medicine as a science, cataloging diseases, quoting the quantities of medicine produced, and deleting any mention of spiritual beliefs, but otherwise they have been inclined to support Tibet's medical heritage. In some ways it resembles traditional Chinese healing. (It has incorporated elements of Chinese, ayurvedic, and Persian medicine into its native system.) Both the Chinese and Tibetan systems treat hot and cold diseases and use pulse analysis for diagnosis and acupuncture and herbs for cures. Tibetan medical doctors, however, have their own variations: Unlike the Chinese they use golden acupuncture needles and apply these to some points of the body, such as the top of the head, which the Chinese omit. Tibetan pulse analysis is also more complex than Chinese.

During the Cultural Revolution, when the Red Guards scorned and attacked nearly every aspect of Tibetan culture, traditional medicine—minus its religious formulas—flourished. Barefoot doctors, for instance, were provided with traditional medical knowledge. Only after Mao died and the Cultural Revolution perished as well did the government once again emphasize modern medical science. Now village doctors learn something of both approaches.

At Menzikhang, the traditional Tibetan medical and astrological center in Lhasa, the staff no longer wear traditional robes but today don white gowns and caps like Chinese doctors and nurses. Chowang Lhundup, deputy director of the outpatient clinic, said the doctors never prescribe meditation for patients now; they stick to physical remedies. But these may include exercises of a religious nature—so many prostrations before the Jokhang, for instance, or so many circumambulations of the Barkor.

The link with Buddhism is more evident upstairs at the Menzikhang where one room contains altars honoring famous Tibetan medical doctors and a library of Buddhist scriptures. The hospital also has a room hung with medicine thangkas depicting diagnoses, cures, and human anatomy, and this last subject includes not only the body's organs and skeletal structure but also energy channels used in tantric practice. An exhibition hall houses glass cases displaying ingredients used in the Tibetan pharmacopeia—precious stones, dried plants, antlers, horns, fungi, a coiled and desiccated snake, minerals, and familiar spices and foods such as saffron, cardamom, caraway, cumin, and sesame. These are ground, combined, and worked into pills, powders and decoctions.

Since 1985 Lhasa has also had an inpatient Tibetan medical hospital with two hundred beds. Patients here must stay for two months at least, Chowang Lhundup said, in contrast to Western-style hospitals. He claimed that it was always full, but we saw many empty beds. The inpatient hospital, like Menzikhang, was cleaner and brighter than others I visited in Tibet; it was an airy, open complex set about with pots of bright flowers. The staff appeared relaxed, unlike the exhausted doctors I met elsewhere. This atmosphere of calm probably has much to do with the role of Tibetan medicine in the new system of health care; it is devoted mainly to chronic, long-term diseases like asthma or diabetes, leaving Western medicine to cope with emergencies and acute cases such as pneumonia, appendicitis, dysentery, meningitis, and heart attacks.

In Lhasa, Tibetan medicine is set apart in its own facilities, but in Gyantse and Damzhung traditional care takes place within the county hospitals. Gyantse, for instance, reserves six of sixty-eight beds for Tibetan medicine. "The Tibetan people like both Western and Tibetan medicine," said Phuntsok at Gyantse, "but they need Western medicine for some problems such as infections and headache. For those ailments Tibetan medicine is too slow." Doctors often prescribe both types of treatment at the same time, he added. Tsering Dondrup at Damzhung said, "We use Tibetan medicine for very slow diseases like arthritis, for which it is very effective, and we use it because the people love it." According to Chowang Lhundup at Menzikhang the people know which diseases are best treated with Western techniques and which do well with traditional cures. They choose their clinics accordingly.

Within Lhasa's traditional Tibetan hospitals, doctors often use the two disciplines in combination; some physicians have been trained in Western medicine as well as Tibetan. "We have some surgery," said Chowang Lhundup, "but it is Western style." When patients arrive with bone fractures, he said, doctors prescribe penicillin if infection is present and then set the bone with splints and bandages. When someone is diagnosed with pneumonia, Menzikhang doctors will bypass traditional medicine and prescribe antibiotics. Sometimes they will let patients choose which approach they prefer, as in the case of the Western tourist who came down with giardiasis. He chose Western and was told to buy the drug Flagyl at a private pharmacy.

Menzikhang is often crowded with outpatients. Some walk in on their own; others are wheeled in on bicycles, supported by family members. During the flu season, Chowang Lhundup said, the hospital treats an average of more than five hundred patients a day and may care for as many as nine hundred at the height of an epidemic. But Western medicine takes a larger share of the overall health care burden. Lhasa People's Hospital averages eight hundred outpatients a day and is only one of four large hospitals in the capital which together contain about fourteen hundred beds, compared to two hundred at the traditional hospital. And considering that Tibetan medical doctors are practicing Western health care, modern science comes out with an even greater edge. One Tibetan doctor told me that young people tend to choose Western medicine; the elderly and those from villages prefer the traditional. "But when there is an emergency," he said, "you go straight to the Western."

Perhaps this is why Western-style doctors are often generous in their assessments of Tibetan traditional care, and some who work in Tibetan medicine tend to promote the traditional type of practice. Chowang Lhundup, for instance, claimed that patients with stomach and liver cancer survive longer under traditional care. Sometimes, he said, doctors at the Western-style hospitals will refer such cases to Menzikhang. He also said Tibetan remedies are more effective in setting broken bones.

The government, however, pays both types of doctors the same. Both earn about $50 a month; both attended medical school tuition-free (although after 1992, I'm told, they had to pay fees) after passing entrance exams. Students at the traditional schools, however, are all Tibetan and need a high level of native language skills to qualify.

As for the exorcisms and prayers of the old approach, these survive outside of the medical establishments. Tibetans may pray to the Medicine Buddha, who is depicted in murals and statues with a dark-blue body sitting on a lotus blossom placed upon a lion throne. In his hand he holds a medicinal plant. Believers may also ward off illness by wearing sacred scriptures or relics or by eating specially prepared and blessed tsampa made into pellets or combined with honey and formed into cones. Nomads often live so far from hospitals and clinics and have so little knowledge of Western medicine that they rely only on "*puja* [prayer], karma, and prostrations," as one Tibetan said. Some Tibetans will also seek out mediums, who fall into trances and become possessed by deities which then announce the cause and prognosis of a disease. The deity is likely to blame an illness on spiritual imbalance or a curse, which can be treated only by ritual means.

These practices have revived since the Cultural Revolution, when religious expression was forbidden. Today local officials are more likely to tolerate them and depend on health education to promote sound practices. The statistics show that China is succeeding in bringing better health to Tibet, but they also show that Tibet remains part of the Third World in its medical profile, and health professionals say that Tibet's gains in health care are now threatened by a funding crisis.

In today's Tibet, the help of a medium may be the best those stricken with cancer or kidney failure can hope for. But for many others the presence of village and county doctors has meant the difference between survival and succumbing to dysentery or pneumonia. If Dawa Norbu's father had come down with trachoma or conjunctivitis—or whatever festering infection began with those fatal grains of sand—only a few years later, he would almost certainly have survived. Antibiotics would have spared his sight, and the assurance of effective help at hand may have soothed the malignant despair which bore him away.

5

Schools for Tibetans
(Education)

In Lhasa I had a ten-year-old friend named Tashi Yumtso, a bright and nimble girl given to pranks. She was a fifth grader at Lhasa First Primary School, and before she began her new school term in the fall of 1992, her family treated her to two days of fun at the Cultural Palace near downtown Lhasa. I accompanied her on one of those excursions, when she dressed in her best—a white straw hat, a green jumper over a frilled blouse, and red pumps—rode the bumper cars, consumed candy and soft drinks, and posed for a photo beside a pond with the Potala looming in the background.

She was celebrating her final moments of freedom before the new school semester began and she would spend her days attending classes or poring over her books at home. Her studies would include Tibetan, Chinese, math, geography, history, natural science, physical education, the arts, and political theory—totaling seven periods a day. She would spend two or three hours on homework most nights, sometimes as many as four or five. Her class was beginning to multiply decimals, and at home she would work out the answers to story problems. For instance: "A half kilo of yarn costs twenty-five yuan. You need one kilo for 230 square centimeters. For a sweater of 1,340 square centimeters, how much yarn will you need, and how much will it cost?" She was beginning her third year of Chinese language with a textbook containing stories and short articles. She would read an assigned story, copy out words and paragraphs up to three times each, and use a new word or phrase in a sentence. Her Tibetan text was more advanced, but it had similar exercises. Sometimes it would ask her to read a story and write down the main points.

. Tashi Yumtso's school, a short distance from home, was free of charge, and when she graduated from the sixth grade she could count on a place in junior high. Her school was also a historic one, the first public institution of learning built in the TAR. Today it has more than two thousand students in grades one through six, housed in a complex of multistoried concrete buildings off a busy street. Its teachers are graduates of normal schools who earn from $56 to $90 U.S. a month.

When I visited the seminomadic village of Guchok, I stayed in a peasant home where my most attentive host was thirteen-year-old Nyima. He filled and refilled my bowl of butter tea and fetched me blankets against the cold night. Nyima was the youngest of five boys and, since Guchok had no school until 1991, he was the first of them to learn to read and write. It was Nyima's uncle, my friend Tashi Tshering, who paid for the construction of the school—a courtyard enclosing a row of classrooms in traditional mudbrick style, set near a mountain stream. Now Nyima was studying two subjects, Tibetan language and mathematics. He could attend the school for three years and then take an exam which might allow him to move up to a township school at the third- or fourth-grade level. (Townships, former commune headquarters, serve four or five villages.)

Guchok's own residents had built Nyima's school with the help of county officials and Tashi Tshering's contributions. About forty students attended in two classes. Their teachers were junior high graduates who had failed the exams to enter senior high. When I visited, both were away taking qualifying tests, and the classes were run by older and more experienced students. Guchok's teachers received $18 to $24 a month in wages, and like all village teachers they were allowed to leave at harvest time to help out in the fields.

The education of Tashi Yumtso and Nyima reveal the best and the worst of schooling policies in Tibet. Lhasa First Primary has an extensive curriculum and high expectations for its students. Guchok School offers only language and math instruction, on the days when teachers are present, and only a fifth of the village children attend. The Guchok student body is also overwhelmingly male; enrollment in Lhasa First Primary is evenly divided between the sexes.

The experiences of these two students have much to say to the critics and supporters of public education in Tibet, to those who charge that Tibetan children are shortchanged in the schools and to the Chinese government which, in its 1992 white paper, states, "Urban [Tibetan] residents, farmers, and herdsmen now enjoy the right to receive education."[1] This implies that education is equally available to all. Here and in other English-language literature on Tibet, the government fails to mention disparities between rural and urban education. It also claims that schooling in Tibet is free although villagers often have to contribute to classroom construction and schools have started to ask parents for fees.

China, of course, points to Tibet's post-1951 progress in education. Only monks and children of the nobility had the chance to learn in the old days, the government claims, while today, according to the white paper, "Education is free. All the study costs of Tibetan students from primary school to university are covered by the government."[2] China also cites its affirmative action efforts for minority students, boarding schools for Tibetans in China proper, and an expanding network of primary, secondary, vocational, and technical schools in the TAR with a total enrollment of 196,000 in 1992.

On the other hand, some critics of China's policies claim that schools are segregated in Tibet, with the best reserved for Chinese. They claim education is used as a propaganda machine to turn out young Communists and to assimilate Tibetans into the dominant Chinese culture. Many charge that Tibetans are not allowed to study their own language. Others, such as TIN and Asia Watch, say nothing about unequal access but note that Tibetans are at a disadvantage because Chinese is the language of higher education. Because of this, they say, Tibetan enrollment falls off as students proceed through high school and on to the college level.

And residents of the TAR have been complaining that the schools, once open to local children free of charge, are now requiring fees which are difficult for many parents to pay.

It is true that China has brought modern schools to a region once ignorant of science and world affairs. It is also true that Tibetan language instruction languishes in some areas, that China views education as a propaganda tool, and that the percentage of Tibetans drops as students proceed through the grades (though the reasons for this are probably mixed). But the debate between the Tibetan government-in-exile and the Chinese government overlooks the major injustice in Tibetan education, which is not a matter of ethnic identity but of locale. A rural child faces difficult odds. At thirteen Nyima was already well behind Tashi Yumtso in education, and he was learning the basics only because of his uncle's generosity. Nyima's education was lagging because the system is stacked against peasant and nomad children. It is not just a matter of allocation of scarce resources; it is also a matter of regulations that work against rural children. Official plans for TAR schools set the minimum years of education higher for city students, and registration laws bar rural children from urban schools. (These conditions are also true in China proper, however, not just in Tibet.) Morever, the gap between city and countryside is an especially grievous handicap to rural youth because their only likely avenue to an urban registration card is success in school.

Villagers, however, are often proud of their simple schools and unaware that they are shortchanged in the present system. At Bagam, south of Damzhung, the nomad Wangdu showed us into the community's newly built village school with its wooden pillars capped by ceremonial white scarves, its outer walls etched with decorative scallops, and its piney white doors and lintels ready for their first application of paint. The windows still lacked glass, and the schoolyard was littered with stones, but the building, with three classrooms, needed only desks to be ready for the first term of the school year.

"This is a good thing," said Wangdu. "In the old days people were stuck in one place and ignorant. Now we have good policies. If students do well, they will go to the township school. If they do well there, they can go to the county school. Some even go to the interior."

Wangdu, a herdless nomad in the old days, never learned to read and write. From his point of view, Bagam School was a marvelous boon for the forty children of the village, and compared with former times, it truly was a step forward.

But Wangdu had no way to size up village education compared to that in Lhasa. Bagam residents had helped build their school with their own labor and donations of money or livestock; city dwellers send their children to facilities constructed by the government. Bagam would have one teacher for three classrooms, and instruction was limited to the Tibetan language and arithmetic. Wangdu most likely knew nothing of Tashi Yumtso's classes at Lhasa First Primary, of the teachers there who earned at least three times the salary of Bagam's lone instructor, nor of the city child's guarantee of securing a place in junior high. At Bagam only the best had a hope of moving up to third or fourth grade. At Lhasa First Primary, sixth-grade graduation and matriculation into secondary school are taken for granted.

At the TAR Education Bureau, a researcher identified only as Zhou tried to put the best face on the differences between rural and urban schools. "Township and village schools," he said, "have more funding sources because the local people donate money and set up foundations for schools." In other words, the cash-poor country people have the right to contribute to their children's education, while city dwellers have only one option—to send their children free of charge.

Zhou, a slender, scholarly man with an air of refinement, also noted that village teachers are less educated than those in the cities "because they are chosen by the villagers and they need to live in the area." They earn less, he said, "because they have fields and livestock, so when they don't teach they can work in the fields." Village schools are private, or "people-run," schools, and city schools are public, or government-supported. A village teacher may have no more than a primary education, he said, but public-school primary teachers are better educated and most of them have graduated from normal school. But, he said, even the village teachers need the approval of the TAR Education Committee.

In its white paper, the government claims that "children of Tibetan farmers and herdsmen enjoy free boarding and education," and that the government, since 1985, has supported needy students with "free food, clothing, and accommodations."[3] I visited one of those boarding schools at Gungthang Township near Damzhung. It was a group of mudbrick buildings surrounded by a wall and set in the treeless plain. It served nomad children from first through sixth grade, who attended in their traditional wraps, unlike city children who wore Chinese sweaters and long pants. At Gungthang I learned that the subsidies had limits and the school suffered for lack of money. The state paid for food, clothing, and lodging only for students in fourth grade and above, said vice principal Tsering Phuntsok, and clothing subsidies for the older children always fell short. So Gungthang had to come up with the funds itself.

Gungthang is a public school, its teachers are well-paid, and it offers an extensive curriculum, but the school has to supplement its funding with produce from a garden maintained by staff and students. It serves its pupils well, however, despite its money problems. It sends many graduates on to high school, and it provides incentives for teachers and parents to encourage learning. Parents of day students sign contracts to insure good attendance, and teachers earn bonuses of $5 to $8 U.S. when their classes earn high scores in countywide tests.

Gungthang is the kind of facility a village-school student may eventually attend by the fourth or fifth grade—with the right exam scores. These scores, according to Zhou at the Education Bureau, depend on the pool of contenders and the number of spaces available, which means that village students are competing for limited space with the better-prepared township students. At "people-run" schools, with their less-qualified, poorly paid, and intermittently present staff, students face a tough battle to reach the same level as those at schools like Gungthang. (One American researcher, investigating education in China proper, called these "certain-failure" schools.)[4]

Zhou said the government was planning some changes in teacher quality and secondary-school matriculation. These would only widen the gap between town and country dwellers, however. It was aiming at a higher percentage of normal-school graduates in public schools, and it was doing away with qualifying exams to enter junior and senior high in Lhasa. Students in public schools there would only have to complete sixth grade to move into secondary school.

The TAR has 900 townships, and, Zhou said, 561 of them had no public primary school in 1992. This meant that Gungthang's school-age children were luckier than most because they had a state-supported school near at hand. They could also attend a county high school in nearby Damzhung. But thirty-six of Tibet's seventy-four counties had no high school. If students in those counties wanted a secondary education, they had to compete for places at the prefectural level or try for a school in China proper. (The TAR has six prefectures and the municipality of Lhasa, which extends well into rural areas, including Damzhung.)

I asked Zhou how many villages had no school at all, but he couldn't say. "Some villages are very small," he said, "with only a few households. It is hard to set up schools or even get statistics." But he did know that many rural children never attend school, whether one is handy or not. This is obvious to anyone who travels through the towns and countryside of Tibet. The children you see in Shigatse, Gyantse, and Lhasa carry book bags and traditional Tibetan wooden slates; they sport the red scarves of Young Pioneers (rewards for the better students), beg for pencils, and sometimes sit in the street doing homework. In rural areas you see children of the same age herding sheep, watching passersby from the roadside, hanging idly over bridges, fetching water, harvesting barley, and gathering dung.

We questioned the young shepherds and peasants of the countryside and found that many of them who lived near major roads or towns had access to village schools, but they often said their schools were closed for the harvest, when teachers were away helping their families bring in the grain. Or they were closed for rebuilding. Or they said they had a school but they didn't attend; their families needed them to watch the herds or work in the field. Those who did attend were usually boys; girls in the same family were likely to stay home. At Khartse Village northeast of Shigatse I asked why the school had only twelve girls out of seventy-five pupils. Because, said the local party secretary, parents find girls useful around the house.

In Namling County, the site of Guchok Village, schools were few. By 1992 Tashi had built two, one at Guchok and another below at Khartse. He was aiming next at two sites across the Namling River from his home. By the fall of 1995, he had built twenty primary schools in the county. They cost $61,000, with 70 percent of the money coming from his own carpet-selling business and 30 percent from donations. Without Tashi's initiative, Guchok and Khartse and many other villages would have no schooling at all. In that area, Tashi said, the population in 1992 was "almost 100 percent illiterate."

His school-building career began when he paid the equivalent of $5,500 to build Guchok's school in his home village, using funds he had acquired from running a private English-language school in Lhasa. It took him five years to negotiate a contract with the county government, and the agreement stipulates that the school belongs to the village and that the county pays for the teachers. The county also helped pay some construction costs.

It takes such private efforts to produce a "people-run" school, and in many areas there is no one like Tashi to pay the costs or even draw up the plans. "It's impossible for the Chinese to build everywhere," said Tashi, "and they don't have the money." Zhou agreed that lack of money is the major obstacle to expanding the school system, and he held out little hope that the government would step up its support. "In the future we can't support all the schools," he said, "so we will ask local people to set up senior high schools and we may ask parents to pay for textbooks." The law requires primary and junior high attendance, he said, so the state can't ask parents to pay for public schools at those levels.

Some things have changed since our talk, however: Schools have been asking for fees even at the primary level, charging for such services as giving exams. Like the health system, education is on the books as "free," but consumers are paying all the same. On the other hand, Tibetans are getting more schools. High-school construction is on the list of Tibet's new building projects, and some of the money for these schools is coming from "donations from twenty-two work units in Shanghai," according to a Xinhua story which appeared in the spring of 1996.[5]

The Xinhua article also said that 70 percent of Tibet's school-age children were enrolled in schools, and if this is true, then it marks a big change in just three years. Fully half the school-age children in the TAR never attended school, Zhou admitted during our interview. Though most of these are nomads and peasants, some city children are also truant. But in spite of the problems with money and logistics, Zhou said the TAR was aiming, by the year 2000, to provide every child with at least four years of schooling. The ideal, he said, would be six years in agricultural areas and nine years in cities.

If half of Tibet's school-age children are playing hooky, as Zhou said, this helps explain the statistics on literacy: Only 44 percent of the population was literate or "semiliterate" in 1991, according to Zhou. (Semiliterates know the alphabet and can spell out simple words.) Some official Chinese publications, however, put it another way: Forty-four percent are illiterate or "semi-illiterate," they say, without explaining the term "semi-illiterate." But the numbers have improved since then, according to a *Tibet Daily* story, which states that by 1995 illiteracy had dropped to 40 percent. In any case, Tibet's literacy rate is low. According to the Central Intelligence Agency World Factbook 1992,

China as a whole had an estimated 73 percent literacy in 1990. This is especially high compared to the TAR because the estimate includes only those who can read and write in their own language, not semiliterates who can read but not write.[6]

China admits that Tibet still has far to go, and it assigns much of the blame to the old society and to Tibet's scattered population, especially in nomad areas. Certainly the vast distances and sparse population of regions like the Changtang create tremendous challenges, but in blaming the former society, China overstates its case. "Before its peaceful liberation," an official report states, "Tibet only had a monastery education for the study of scriptures and a few private schools for the children of nobles and local officials."[7] But even though education in old Tibet was limited, it was not exclusively reserved for nobles and monks, as the government claims.

Fifty years ago, when Tibet still lay dormant in its isolation from the modern world, Nyima's uncle, Tashi Tshering, attended a private school. At the age of thirteen he joined a group of local boys in the home of a Khartse farmer near his village, and seated on the floor of the adobe house, he used a wooden slate to learn the ancient phonetic script of Tibet. Later he studied on his own in Lhasa and eventually made his way to colleges in the United States.

During Tashi's childhood, the premier educational institution in Tibet was the monk-official school in the Potala Palace where Ngawangthondup studied. Ngawangthondup spent much of his time in class, bent over Tibetan woodblock texts, under the strict supervision of monastic teachers. The classroom contained an altar, astrological and medical charts, and a wide window which overlooked the Lhasa Valley and the mountains behind Sera Monastery. Ngawangthondup studied Tibetan history, literature, language, mathematics, Tibetan medicine, astrology, logic, and geography, and after eight years he graduated and became a clerk in the Dalai Lama's government.

When the Chinese arrived, Ngawangthondup was sent to Beijing to study in the new Institute of National Minorities, and there he studied Chinese, Tibetan, history, geography, natural science, and Marxism. The government was training him to become a cadre in the new socialist Tibet, but Ngawangthondup ultimately rejected Marxism and fled to India.

Ngawangthondup and Tashi Tshering today agree that the Chinese brought much-needed science and a broader knowledge of world affairs to isolated

Tibet. But Tashi's story also shows that serfs could acquire learning in the old Tibet, contrary to the assertions of the Chinese. The society was conservative and backward, but some commoners were able to learn and improve their lot. (Tashi's learning, for instance, enabled him to work as a clerk.) Hugh Richardson, who served the British and Indian governments in Lhasa between 1936 and 1950, also noted the private efforts at education and concluded that "a considerable proportion of townspeople acquired a modicum of literacy." Country schools, Richardson said, taught their pupils "sufficient knowledge to enable them to keep rough accounts, write a letter, and read, although not always understand, the sacred books." We also know of literate serfs, such as Ngawangthondup's father, who served as treasurer to a noble family, and other serfs who were highly valued for their skills. Almost all monks also learned to read, although many never learned to write.[8]

When the Communists arrived in 1951 they brought China's traditional veneration for learning. They built schools, and they used them not only to provide Tibetans with modern science and geography, but also to promote socialism. Political theory and China's version of Tibetan history (designed to prove that the region has long been an integral part of the motherland) have been part of the curriculum since the beginning, and the critics are right in saying that China has used education as propaganda.

During the Cultural Revolution students endured heavy-handed indoctrination in class. Teachers rewarded children for informing on their parents, for reporting any criticism of the government they overheard and any signs of religious devotion—references to past lives, mumbled prayers, hidden altars, photos of the Dalai Lama. Tibetan children learned that the Communist Party was the sun, the guardian of the people, the perfect truth; that Mao was both father and mother; that capitalism was a "poison snake." They began the day promising Chairman Mao to behave, thanking him for their liberation, and vowing to always remember the oppression of the old aristocrats and lamas. They were told that Tibet needed the PLA and Red Guards to defend them against the serf-owners and counterrevolutionaries who lurked in ambush to bring back the old system, when landlords tortured serfs and only the privileged lived in comfort. At home, the children heard nothing to the contrary. Their parents could not reveal what they really believed.

Today, however, children receive no incentives to inform on their parents, and political education classes at the elementary level have been reduced to one period a week and contain little more than discussions of school regulations. Still, slogans such as "Warmly Love Socialism" hang in the hallways of public schools and the TAR Education Bureau, children who perform well are rewarded with the red scarves of Young Pioneers (the precursor of the Youth League and eventually, the Party), and state-issued language and history texts contain the expected references to "peaceful liberation" and Mao Zedong. I could hear Guchok children repeating *"Mao Drushi"* (Tibetan for "Chairman Mao") when they read aloud from their school texts.

Tibetan language instruction is also faring better since the post–Cultural Revolution reforms, at least in the TAR. In Lhasa's first public schools, instruction was in Tibetan (except for Chinese language classes), although teachers had to translate their own texts from Chinese. But between 1966 and 1976, when the Red Guards held sway, Chinese was promoted as the language of revolution and almost everything Tibetan was condemned as one of the "four olds." In some areas communes asked members to speak in "friendship language," a combination of Tibetan and Chinese. In others it was outright forbidden to study Tibetan. One Amdowa from Golok told me that he had managed to learn his native script only by hiding Tibetan texts under his sheepskin wrap and reviewing the words when he was out of sight of overseers.

When the Cultural Revolution expired and Tibetans dared once again to light butter lamps and wear their traditional jewelry and hairstyles, the schools returned to teaching Tibetan. But progress was slow, and in 1985 one Lhasa resident decided to take a bold step and appeal to the authorities for change. This was Tashi Tshering, then an instructor at Tibet University. He made a private survey of the schools and composed an open letter to TAR leaders in which he charged that Chinese students, especially those at the college level, were benefiting at the expense of Tibetans, and many Tibetan students had no instruction in their own language.

Tashi cited statistics: In 1985 at Lhasa First Secondary School only 546 students out of a total of 1,451 were studying the Tibetan language even though the majority, 933, were Tibetan. At Lhasa First Primary School nearly half the enrollment was Chinese, and out of one thousand Tibetan students, two hundred had no instruction in their own language.

Tashi wrote this letter at the risk of censure. The repressive atmosphere of the Cultural Revolution still reigned, and typists refused to transcribe his work. But Tashi, who spent more than three years in prison during the Cultural Revolution and managed to clear his name after his release, had learned how and when to speak out. He persisted until he found a typist bold enough to take on his letter; then he mimeographed copies of the seven-page document (written in Chinese) and distributed it to high TAR officials.

It was couched in the requisite Party terminology. He dutifully referred to the unity of the motherland and the "four modernizations" (a post–Cultural Revolution slogan); he declared his trust in the Communist Party, and he politely "begged" TAR leaders to study the issue and take action. But in spite of its rhetoric and decorous tone, the letter was blunt. "We must completely reform the educational system of Tibet," he wrote. "This needs to be done quickly."

Tashi's letter disappeared into the offices of bureaucrats, and he received neither censure nor praise for his effort. No one called him to account, and he continued in his job at Tibet University. But a few years later the TAR took action to correct many of the problems he had pointed out in his letter. In 1989 the region passed down a new policy: Tibetan must be the medium of instruction in all junior high schools by 1993 and in all senior high schools by 1997. This meant the TAR would have to produce more Tibetan-speaking instructors, especially those who taught natural science, where the use of Tibetan had lagged for want of a modern vocabulary.

As a result, many of the statistics Tashi cited have improved. Lhasa First Primary, where half the student body was Chinese in 1985, was three-quarters Tibetan by 1992. It had fourteen classes in which the medium of instruction was Chinese and twenty-four in which the medium was Tibetan. Some Tibetan children attend the Chinese-track classes, at their parents' request, but they also spend some time studying Tibetan. My young friend Tashi Yumtso was in a Tibetan-track class and learned all her subjects, except Chinese, in her native language. Lhasa First Secondary School was two-thirds Tibetan by 1992, and all the Tibetans tracked into the Chinese language classes were required to study their native language. Although Tashi Tshering had found that less than 60 percent of the Tibetan students at Lhasa First Secondary were studying the vernacular in 1985, all of them were receiving some Tibetan instruction in 1992.

The new mandate has also changed the character of Tibet University. It was becoming a genuine university with a range of science and humanities majors, but now it is mainly a teacher training college. Most of the students are Tibetans preparing to teach in their native language. Another group includes Tibetan teachers of natural science who originally learned their subjects in Chinese. They spend from six months to two years preparing to teach physics, chemistry, and biology in Tibetan.

So Tibet University is now providing much-needed educators trained to teach in the Tibetan language. But this also means that Tibetans usually have to leave the TAR to get a good higher education. The TAR government has apparently decided that teacher training is a priority, and it has allocated what funds it has to upgrade elementary and high school education.

Students in the teacher-training programs at Tibet University learn to use vocabulary new to their native language. Although Tibetan once lacked words for modern science, linguists have invented terms to fill the gaps. They have coined words such as *zegyur* for chemistry, a combination of *ze*, which means "material," and *gyur*, which means "to change" (modeled after the Chinese word). They have produced a natural sciences dictionary in Tibetan, full of terms such as zegyur and *tsikor* ("to calculate" plus "machine"), and the teachers at Tibet University are now learning to use this vocabulary in class.

By 1995, according to Lhasa's *Tibet Daily*, the university had seven departments emphasizing the Tibetan language. These included broadcasting in Tibetan, and cultural studies such as Tibetan dance and music. The literature department was emphasizing classical Tibetan literature and offering classes on Tibet's famous *Gesar* epic. The teaching staff, according to the article, was 74 percent Tibetan and 24 percent Chinese, and the 1,334-member student body was 82 percent Tibetan and 17 percent Chinese.

But just three years earlier, many of the policy goals for lower schools still remained on paper and had failed to reach every classroom. At Lhasa Number Eight Middle School (a junior high), thirty out of fifty teachers were Chinese and the Tibetan teachers only taught Tibetan language. The students, mainly Tibetan, learned everything else—math, chemistry, history, physics, geography—in Chinese. One teacher told me he had little hope that the sciences-in-

Tibetan policy would take effect by 1993 as planned. At Lhasa First Secondary School, the region's foremost high school, headmaster Sonam Tobgyel assured me that students in Tibetan-track classes learn their subjects in the vernacular, with the exception of Chinese and English. But when we dropped in on two science classes the teacher in one was both speaking and writing in Chinese in one and the other was speaking in Tibetan and writing in Chinese. Tibet may meet its goal of teaching science in the vernacular, but it still had a distance to go when I was visiting schoolrooms in the region.

And there is a further problem for TAR students who choose the Tibetan-language track instead of the Chinese: Because they are already studying two languages—Chinese and Tibetan—they lose out on English instruction. The Chinese-track students begin to study English in junior high, and Tibetan-track students may, if they are lucky, begin in senior high. Since English is required on the national college entrance exam, Tibetan-track students are at a disadvantage in competing for places in colleges and universities.

Outside of the TAR, in the Tibetan ethnic areas of China proper, Tibetan language instruction often takes a backseat to Chinese. The policy depends on local officials and the ethnic mix of the area and student body. Tibetans from Amdo and Kham in Qinghai and Sichuan provinces told me that Tibetan students often study their own language in primary schools, but high schools usually offer Chinese only. A survey by the International Campaign for Tibet found that Chinese was the main language of instruction in six out of eight selected schools in Sichuan; most of these schools offered Tibetan only as an optional subject four to five hours a week. But at least some children are learning basic subjects in Tibetan in Qinghai and Sichuan: Both provinces publish Tibetan-language textbooks for science and the humanities, and in 1990, Qinghai (at least on paper) began to require young Tibetan children to study their native language from first to fifth grade. The Qinghai students, however, must also study Chinese at the same time, unlike students in the TAR. There, in 1992, the Tibetan-track students were beginning to learn Chinese in third or fourth grade.

The International Campaign's report, *The Long March*, charges that "Tibetans are becoming illiterate in their own language," and this is true for many outside the TAR, where more than half of the Tibetan population lives. But students like Tashi Yumtso and Nyima and those in the purely Tibetan areas of China proper can receive a good beginning in their own language. If they continue to the level of Tibet University, however, they can rely on Tibetan only if they specialize in Tibetan language and literature. All other university majors require fluency in Chinese.

When Tashi wrote his letter to TAR leaders in 1985, he took on more than language; he charged that Chinese students were getting the best the TAR had to offer, while Tibetans were losing out. Again he came armed with numbers: In 1979, out of six hundred TAR students enrolled in colleges and universities only eighty or ninety were Tibetan; the rest were Chinese. In 1984, out of 1,984 students in three institutes of higher education in the TAR, only 666 were Tibetan. At Tibet University two-thirds of the Tibetan students were enrolled in either Tibetan language or Tibetan medicine courses, which meant that Chinese students predominated in all other majors—English, mathematics, science, business, and economics. If the medicine and language departments hadn't required students to be proficient in Tibetan, Tashi said, the Chinese would have outnumbered Tibetans there as well.

Clearly, Tashi concluded, most of the TAR's funding for higher education was supporting Chinese students, and this also meant that more Chinese than Tibetans were being trained to fill high-level positions. He called on officials to guarantee Tibetans equal access to education, spend more money on primary and secondary education, and train more minority personnel.

Tashi never knew if his letter had an effect, but at Tibet University the numbers changed after 1985. In 1992 the school's first Party secretary, Chomphel, insisted that Chinese then made up only 4 percent of the 1,100 students. They were confined to courses in English and tourism, where they were preparing to become tour guides, interpreters, and translators. Since the mandate to prepare Tibetan language teachers came down in 1987, most Chinese could not qualify for any other departments, he said. But according to the *Tibet Daily* article, 82 percent of the students were Tibetan and 17 percent Chinese in 1995. This indicates a 13 percent increase in Chinese enrollment since 1992, if the figures for both years are correct. A June 1994 report by TIN clouds the picture even more; it states that only 45 percent of new entrants to the university were Tibetan in 1994.

By law the university should have a Tibetan enrollment of at least 60 percent. Tibetans are allowed lower admission scores on national exams than

Chinese. Tibetan high school graduates need 220 points out of a possible 640 to enter Tibet University; Chinese need at least 260. The test includes six subjects—Chinese, math, physics, chemistry, biology, and English. Each subject is worth 100 to 120 points.

TAR students looking for degrees in science and the humanities—outside of Tibetan language and literature—have to find places elsewhere, in China proper or abroad. At Tibet University they can only pursue these subjects in the context of teacher training. To gain admission to a university in China they compete with students throughout the People's Republic on national exams, but Chinese policy gives Tibetans and other minorities a break. Admission cutoff scores depend on the performance of the pool of contenders overall and the number of places available, so the requirements vary from year to year. But Tibetans have a 20-point bonus, no matter what the score. If Chinese students need at least 300 to enter a university, Tibetans will need only 280.

The theory is that Tibet and other minority areas such as Inner Mongolia offer substandard education, compared to China proper, and this puts students from these regions at a disadvantage in the exams. Tibet lags, officials say, because it has poorer facilities, fewer trained teachers, and a high teacher turnover rate. Some say Tibetans are handicapped because they have to study Tibetan in addition to Chinese. For these reasons, said one high Tibetan official, standards are lower in Tibet, and many with primary or secondary school degrees should never have been allowed to graduate. Others say there is an additional, cultural factor. A Tibetan who taught in a Lhasa junior high school said her Chinese pupils were diligent and motivated while her Tibetan students had a easygoing attitude. "They didn't work hard," she said. "They just thought about popular songs and clothes. But my Chinese students worked very hard."

In 1984 the central government decided to set up Tibetan schools in China proper for primary-level graduates from the TAR, and now more than five thousand each year attend these junior and senior high schools, located in eighteen sites scattered from Tianjin and Beijing to Shanghai and Yunnan Province. In Beijing I visited a Tibetan school where more than six hundred junior and senior high students (two-thirds of them male) live and study in surroundings that are luxurious compared to those of Tibet University, the

Tibet Academy of Social Science, or any facility I saw in all of the TAR. The complex of buildings, constructed in 1987, is spacious, clean, and well-furnished. Physics, chemistry and biology labs are fitted with gleaming, neatly arranged equipment—beakers, Bunsen burners, shelves of chemicals. In the physics lab each pair of desks has an electric outlet, and in the biology and chemistry labs each pair has a wash basin. The school has an in-house television studio which broadcasts to classes, airs after-school films for recreation, and records programs devised by the students. It also has a sports field, dormitories, and a well-stocked library, which would be the envy of Lhasa First Secondary principal Sonam Tobgyel. He was soliciting funds to build a library for his school of eighteen hundred students when I met him.

On weekends the Beijing students go on in field trips; on holidays the government ships in tsampa and butter tea from Tibet. Each term the school provides professional-quality costumes for drama productions and free instruments for music classes. On the sports field the students learn soccer and baseball from Japanese coaches, and they also play a Chinese game called jewel ball. The funds for all this, according to dean of instruction Xu Xungan, come from the central government, which donates more than $800,000 U.S. annually, supplemented by a small contribution from the TAR.

Each of the eighteen schools in the interior enrolls students from a particular area of the TAR. The municipality of Tianjin, for example, serves Nagchu, and Hubei Province serves Chamdo. The Beijing school was created for nomads from throughout the region. Only Beijing and two other sites have a senior high. Junior high students at each school spend a full year perfecting their Chinese before they begin the regular schedule of classes, adding a year to the usual six (three each in junior and senior high). From then on they have Tibetan lessons six hours a week and learn other subjects in Chinese. In Beijing each class has about forty-five students (two classes in each grade), and students attend school Monday through Friday as well as Saturday morning. They spend their free time engaged in school-related recreational activities—sports, drama, music—or homework. The atmosphere is serious and bustling; after classes, the students fill the library, where they read magazines and books, mostly in Chinese but also in Tibetan.

After four or more years on such a regimen, these students score an average of 100 points higher on national tests than their peers in the TAR, Xu said. Out of ninety-three who graduated in July 1992, eighty-eight went on to universities and technical institutes in China proper. The other five went to Tibet University or minority institutes. Thirty went to Hubei to study hydraulics and were slated to work on the huge YamdrokTso power plant near Lhasa. All are expected to return to the TAR at the end of their studies. The students have racked up a good record, Xu said, partly because they are preselected (out of ten thousand primary school graduates each year only twelve hundred go to China proper) and partly because they've had the benefit of superior facilities and teaching.

But for the Beijing students, 80 percent of them nomads, the transition from Tibet to China can be difficult. They arrive speaking the dialects of their home areas and must learn Chinese or the idiom of Lhasa before they can talk to their peers. They leave the open ranges of Tibet for the smoggy skies and teeming, suffocating streets of Beijing, and they discover shower baths for the first time. At home they have eaten tsampa, meat, cheese, and even noodles with their hands, and now they must learn to manipulate chopsticks and eat rice. Gradually, said Xu, they learn the new ways. "First we teach them to wash their hands before eating, then to use spoons, then chopsticks. Eventually we let them use their hands only when they have tsampa."

Although Tibetan nomads are steadfast Buddhists, the state allows no place for religious practice in its schools. "But when they visit temples and kowtow," Xu said, "no one interferes." The students eventually pick up the attitude of their teachers, however. "After a while," Xu added, "when they go home, they look askance at their own family members prostrating and so on."

The students return home twice in seven years: once after graduating from junior high and again after leaving senior high. By then they prefer rice to tsampa, according to Xu, although they retain a love of butter tea, and by then they are more at home with Chinese ways than Tibetan.

This poses a dilemma for Tibetan parents seeking the best education for their children. Their sons and daughters may earn high scores and admission to top universities, but they will return home more Chinese than Tibetan, accustomed to regular baths, stir-fried dishes, and television, and disdaining the mumbled prayers and prostrations of their elders. So some Tibetans send their children to India, where they can attend schools run by the government-in-exile. In India they will continue to learn Tibetan, get a good grounding in English, and maintain their religion and culture.

These are the issues parents have to weigh, and Tibetans come up with various solutions. A worker in Lhasa told me his wife and two children lived in India while he remained with one child in Tibet. I also heard of a family who sent one child to India and one to China proper to compare the benefits and drawbacks of each. A Lhasa teacher said that after his son spent two years in a TAR school he sent the boy to India because he believed would get a better education there. He would have sent the boy's younger brother as well, but this boy's health was poor. The older son was now fourteen and thinking of returning to Lhasa because living conditions in India were poor and he missed his family. If he returned, his father said, he would have no trouble entering a local school, but he would have to work diligently to catch up in Chinese.

China's critics accuse Beijing of sending young Tibetans to Beijing, Tianjin, Chengdu, and other cities to indoctrinate them and create a corps of educated cadres loyal to China and the Communist Party. This may not be the primary motive for creating the inland schools, but China certainly hopes to make good patriots of its Tibetan students, and the propaganda sways the minds of some young Tibetans. Several have told me that they grew up in Chinese schools believing all that they heard, identifying with the Chinese, and looking down on the Tibetans' religious devotion, casual sexual mores, indifferent hygiene, and disregard for material possessions.

But these same Tibetans say they have had a change of heart as they grew older, that they returned to native values and gained a concern for Tibetan autonomy. This should come as no surprise, when many well-informed Chinese have also turned against the Chinese government. Some educated Tibetans say their schooling has helped them see through government propaganda efforts and take a hard look at the future of Tibet.

By the time he was sixteen, said one Amdowa who was born in 1964, "I thought China was my country and the Communist Party was my spiritual mother." He had also forgotten his native language. When he returned home, he was afraid to talk to visitors; they couldn't understand his accent. Only after Chinese members of his work unit taunted him for being a Tibetan did he begin to think of himself as different and seek out his origins. Then he set off on a personal search that led him to a monastery to study Tibetan and finally, in 1988, to India to join the many exiles who oppose China's presence in their homeland.

When he began his quest, the Amdowa said, he read avidly, trying to make sense of the world and understand his people's history. It was a book by the Italian scholar Giuseppe Tucci which convinced him that the story of Tibet was not the one he had learned in school, and that Tibetans had ruled their own land before 1950.[9] Tucci's work caused him to question China and eventually to flee to India. The book, forbidden reading in China but still passed surreptitiously from hand to hand, was translated into Chinese. It was a text neither of his parents could have read, and the Amdowa had his Chinese teachers to thank that he could make this discovery.

6

Dorje Talks, I Talk
(Language)

From that moment in May 1951 when five Tibetan delegates capitulated to Chinese military strength, affixed their seals to the Seventeen Point Agreement, and ceded their country's independence to the new communist regime, the Tibetan language has been in jeopardy. In an instant the language of some three million people—with its singular and ancient script and rich body of literature—became a minority language, subordinate to standard Chinese. Tibetan then joined thousands of idioms worldwide which exist under the threat of decay and extinction because they have lost status in a political, military, or economic reshuffling.

China has never outlawed Tibetan. On the contrary, it has passed laws and resolutions supporting education in the vernacular for Chinese cadres as well as Tibetans; it has set up newspapers, magazines, television stations, and literary reviews in Tibetan; it has praised Tibetan script as a model for other minority languages; and it has called the language a "treasure" of Tibetan culture. Compared to the British in eighteenth century Scotland or the Spanish in Franco's Catalonia or the Italian Fascists in German-speaking South Tyrol, the People's Republic has taken a lenient, even supportive role regarding minority tongues. And yet, China's claim on Tibet places the language on the threatened species list. All the elements leading to its extinction are in place.

In the 1950s, however, when the new rulers marched into Lhasa, it seemed that Tibetan was in no danger. Chinese cadres set about learning the vernacular, and some spent their spare time studying Tibetan. They were eager to bring their version of socialism to the masses, and since the common people and most aristocrats knew no Chinese, soldiers and government workers needed the language to communicate. Army troops in Tibetan ethnic areas—Qinghai, Gansu, Sichuan, Yunnan, and Tibet proper—found a knowledge of Tibetan essential to dealing with the people now under their control.

The government sought out and trained Tibetan speakers and scholars and promoted research in the language. Even as Tibetans and Chinese negotiated the Seventeen Point Agreement, linguists were busy translating its terms into Tibetan. For this, they soon discovered, they needed a new vocabulary, words which had never appeared in Tibetan before: communism, socialism, the people, feudalism, Marxism, republic. These were new concepts in Tibet, and the scholars had to fill the gaps by adapting Chinese words to Tibetan, resurrecting archaic words, and combining modern words into new forms. Thus they came up with *Markesi Ringluk*, Marxism, which welded the name of Marx to the Tibetan words for society and doctrine; *gungten ringluk,* communism, adapted from the Chinese word; *jingdrol,* liberation, a combination of the Tibetan words for bind and loosen; and *Zhonghua Mimang Jitun Gyalkab,* a hash of Chinese and freshly minted Tibetan words which means "People's Republic of China."

Loudspeakers brayed these new words in daily news and propaganda broadcasts, entirely in Tibetan. Government-supported radio programs and a newspaper, the *Tibet Daily,* repeated them over the airways and in newsprint. Schoolchildren heard them in class. The central government held that all minorities should study in their own languages. Of course, it said in the same breath, they must learn Chinese as well, but native languages would serve as the "major" idioms in minority areas.

When Chinese academics and officials followed this mandate and took up the study of Tibetan, they were becoming familiar with a distant relative of their own tongue, another member of the extensive Sino-Tibetan language family. Like Chinese, Tibetan is monosyllabic, with most syllables carrying a specific meaning, but Tibetan has a greater tendency to combine these syllables and add suffixes. The result is more variety in word length, from *rey* for "yes" to *khyeyrang* for "you" and rambling abstractions like Markesi Ringluk. Tibetan also has four tones, as does standard Chinese, but Tibetan speech is softer, less staccato, than Chinese. Only syllables with long vowel sounds take tones (high, low, falling, or mid-tone). Tibetan contains thirty consonants and to our ears is more plastic and adaptable than Chinese. America and Germany, for instance, are *Amerika* and *Germani* in Tibetan but *Mei Guo* and *De Guo* in Chinese.

The language has had a written form since the seventh century, when an official called Thonmi Sambhota devised an alphabet with the help of Indian scholars. The script, adapted in its present form two centuries later, is phonetic, reads from left to right, and resembles ancient Indian Gupta writing. And, with typical Tibetan conservatism, it has remained constant for eleven centuries while the pronunciation of the spoken language has changed. Thus, what is written *dbus* is actually pronounced *u* and what appears as *rgyal-tse* is in fact the town called Gyantse. The letters can be transcribed into three types of script—capitalized letters for printed texts and signs, a cursive script for formal letter-writing, and a common cursive for informal letters and daily business. The third form is more flowing than the other two, an elegant and minimalist style. Over the centuries Tibetans have carved these scripts into woodblocks in order to print translations of the Mahayana Buddhist canon and original works on subjects ranging from medicine to grammar.

The Cultural Revolution destroyed many artifacts of this thirteen-hundred-year legacy of Tibetan civilization, and the spoken language, although never under direct attack, suffered as well. Chinese replaced Tibetan in schools, government offices, and work units, and some communes asked their members to speak "Chinese-Tibetan friendship language," a mixture of the two. Only in the more remote pastoral and agricultural areas, where the officials were Tibetan, did the language manage to flourish, and there it was often the only sign of true Tibetan identity left.

But even farmers and herders in outlying areas endured occasional linguistic invasions—from officials who addressed them in Chinese, or military propaganda troupes who forced them to recite slogans in the incomprehensible idiom of Beijing. Tibetans were learning, subtly or overtly, that their tongue was inferior to the true revolutionary language of standard Chinese.

Dorje Talks, I Talk

When the Cultural Revolution expired and the Dalai Lama sent delegations to the Tibetan areas of China, the envoys noted that all the public signs were in Chinese, official titles and agencies had been changed to Chinese forms (although they might be written in Tibetan), and Tibetan cadres were giving their children Chinese names to use for official purposes. They found that the major subject in primary schools was Marxism, with Chinese as the language of instruction, and they reported that the Communists had altered the language to conform to their version of reality. The word for "religious faith" had been banished and replaced by derogatory phrases meaning "blind faith" or the the "faith of ignorance." The word for national history, *gyalrab,* was banned as a term for Tibet's traditional account of its past. What Tibetans had once called their history was now demoted to *logyu,* or "individual story" (gyalrab became the term for the history of China). And Tibetan kings had been renamed *lonpo,* ministers, to once again suggest that Tibet had belonged to China over the centuries.[1]

After the Dalai Lama's delegates expressed their outrage at the poverty and cultural erosion they had witnessed and Chinese officials learned of the hysterical crowds which greeted the Dalai Lama's envoys, the government gave the Tibetan language its official support once again. China was not about to rewrite the history textbooks, but it would encourage Tibetan instruction in the schools, and the reformer Hu Yaobang even called for Chinese cadres in Tibet to study the local language. "It should be a required subject," he declared in a six-point plan for rebuilding Tibet. "Otherwise they will be divorced from the masses."

Thus, as Tibetans once again circled the Barkor and prayer flags reappeared on house tops, students and teachers began to speak the vernacular in the schools, and by 1987 the government had formed a working committee to promote the use of Tibetan in classrooms and government units. Since then, Tibet University has been preparing teachers to use the vernacular in class; work units have been told to teach it to Chinese cadres; the government has set up a bureau to translate government documents from Chinese into Tibetan; and hospitals, banks, and post offices have instructions to provide for Tibetan speakers.

And yet, as we visited bureaucrats, teachers, doctors, and academics in the TAR I found Chinese winning out over Tibetan. In offices and conference rooms officials spoke to us in Chinese or a mixture of Chinese and Tibetan. There was only one exception. At August First model farm outside Lhasa, Deputy Party Secretary Dawa used Tibetan with occasional lapses into Chinese. But even as he spoke he referred to a document written in Chinese, and his Tibetan was sprinkled with Chinese words—numbers, dates, the names of fruits and vegetables. And at Tibet University, despite its emphasis on Tibetan-language teaching, Party Secretary Chomphel spoke to us in a medley of the two idioms. As he recounted the history of the school, he referred to a text in Chinese. He escorted us to a composition class offered by the department of Tibetan language and literature, and even there I saw students taking notes in both Chinese and Tibetan. Outside in the hall, lockers were labeled in Chinese, and in the administration building the office directory was entirely in Chinese.

Tibetan playwright Sotse (short for Sonam Tsering) has taken aim at this hybrid of mingled idioms in a play called *Ramaluk*. The title translates to *Neither Goat nor Sheep,* and the meaning is obvious. Sotse visited India and Nepal before he wrote *Ramaluk,* and there he found Tibetan corrupted by English and Hindi, just as it has been adulterated by Chinese in the TAR. "The main purpose of the play was to correct the situation," said Sotse, a restless, wiry man in his forties, "to point out that Tibetans are losing their own language, to call attention to the problem."

At one point in *Ramaluk* a young Tibetan woman calls a meeting of her coworkers and holds forth in a muddle of Chinese and Tibetan, which, Sotse said, he actually heard one day in Lhasa. She makes an attempt at self-criticism and begins her statement in Chinese: "Although I myself . . . " Then she repeats "myself" in Tibetan, reiterates it Chinese, goes on to say "speak" in Chinese, and then "even though" in Tibetan before she quits. In another scene, set in India, a Tibetan from Lhasa speaks to one who has been living in exile. The second says, "I'm going to the bazaar," using the English word "bazaar" in an otherwise Tibetan sentence. The first man is taken aback. In Tibetan his friend has said, "I'm going to the pockmarked face."

Sotse underscores his point when one character, despairing of his efforts to communicate, says, "Dorje talks. I talk. No result." This, he is saying, is where the Tibetan language is heading—into decline and disarray.

Outside my hotel in Lhasa a movie house that showed videos from around the world blasted soundtracks into the streets. These were invariably in Chinese. Directly opposite the video house a Hui noodle shop had also set up loudspeakers to broadcast Chinese-language radio programs at full volume. A block away, below the apartment of my friend Tashi Tshering, another video house played amplified Chinese soundtracks, and nearby on People's Street passersby could hear more Chinese dialogue emanating from Lhasa's main cinema. Every morning in Lhasa and other county seats loudspeakers go into action at 8:00 A.M. Beijing time, piercing the air with shrill martial music and the news in Chinese. (Although Lhasa is two time zones west of the capital, it must, like all of China, follow Beijing time.)

In the heart of Lhasa, the traditional Tibetan quarter, the streets are a din of electronically projected Chinese, and inside Tibetan homes, residents watch Chinese-language television programs—movies, sitcoms, newscasts, and cultural events. At the Arts School of the TAR, where students from throughout the region study performing arts, the principal spoke to us in Chinese, and the instructor in a dance class counted out the beat in Chinese: "Yi, er, san"—"one, two, three." At meetings of the region's governing bodies deliberations are in held Chinese even though some members—in the Religious Affairs Committee, for instance—speak only Tibetan.

Written Chinese is also taking over. A book of Tibetan contemporary art, published in 1991 in Shanghai, contains an introduction in Chinese and Tibetan, but all of the works reproduced in this coffee-table volume are identified in Chinese alone. It is the same with a glossy work on Tibetan ritual masks published in 1989; Tibetan script appears on two introductory pages, and everything else—captions and commentary—is in Chinese. Tibetans we met in commerce or government, like their counterparts elsewhere, rarely failed to produce business cards, and many of these were printed in English on one side and Chinese on the other, with no Tibetan at all. The English side provided a *pinyin* (Chinese romanization) approximation of the Tibetan name—A Wang for Ngawang, Tse Ren for Tsering, Zha Xi for Tashi. When I bought a ticket, changed money, or mailed a package, I came away with a scrap of paper printed in Chinese. My ticket to Samye Monastery, a holy pilgrimage site, held only one line in Tibetan, even though few visitors besides foreign tourists or devout Tibetans make their way there. Pinyin identified the site to Westerners as Sang Ye Temple, and the historical summary on the ticket was entirely in Chinese.

It is obvious to most visitors that Chinese has the upper hand in Tibet, but even so, the government maintains that Chinese is subordinate to Tibetan. At the TAR Working Committee on the Tibetan Language, the agency set up to oversee the reforms of 1987, deputy director Tsering Chogyal said Chinese is designated as a "supplementary language" in the TAR while Tibetan is the "major language." Chogyal, a short man with a lined, weary face, conducted our interview in Chinese, but his business card, at least, was written in Tibetan.

He admitted that his task—to ensure that Tibetan truly serves as the region's "major language"—faces heavy obstacles. For one thing, there is the legacy of the Cultural Revolution, when Tibetan was branded as backward and disappeared from classrooms and public life. And for another, there are those who resist the committee's efforts. "Some people oppose the regulations and fail to implement them," Chogyal said. "People have different views on whether the Tibetan language will help in the construction of Tibet."

I had read that the policy on language reform required that official documents should be written originally in Tibetan by 1990 (not first in Chinese and then translated), but Chogyal denied that the government had ever set a deadline. However, he said, there is a plan to gradually replace Chinese with Tibetan in work units. "It is very difficult," he said, "so it will take a long time." As for promoting Tibetan to the full language of instruction in the schools, that too will be a slow process. "We lack teachers, and we lack textbooks," he said, "so maybe we will have to postpone the 1993 deadline [for junior high schools]."

I had also read that Tibetan was to become the official language of the region by the year 2000, but Chogyal denied this as well. It was never so specific, he said, and besides, China has no official language. That, I learned, is a taboo term. An area may have a major language, but nowhere in China is there an official or national language. The term used by the ousted Kuomintang, *guoyu*, means "national language" and is still used in Taiwan, but the People's Republic replaced that word with the expression *putonghua*, meaning "common speech." I could make no sense of these distinctions until a Chinese academic explained that my problem was political naïveté. Of course China has an official language, he said; you just can't say that. So in the offices of the TAR language committee we spoke of Chinese as supplementary, when it was actually the major language, and we avoided the word "official."

And there was that disparity between my information and Chogyal's insistence that policy goals, outside of education, had never been set to deadlines. No one in China could help me with this, but TIN and an American scholar well-versed in Tibetan affairs both have stated that the government declared by 1988 that Tibetan would thenceforth be the official working language of the TAR. TIN also quotes Xinhua articles from March 1989 which say that Tibetans were required to speak Tibetan at major meetings, that proficiency in Tibetan should be a requirement for government employment, and that by the end of 1990 all official communications should be written primarily in Tibetan.[2] But after the Xinhua articles appeared, the government backed off, and officials began to deny that the goals were ever officially set. The policy now is to emphasize Tibetan instruction in the schools and stop talking about making Tibetan the language of government. (Chogyal was the only one who seemed to think it might happen, and even he said it would "take a long time.")

At the TAR Cultural Bureau, deputy director Hu Jinan repeated the official line. Education is the key, he said. With the new school policies the Tibetan language will survive and flourish. Hu and his Tibetan coworkers, all of them speaking in Chinese, cited the 1987 policy and assured me that all Chinese cadres are required to study Tibetan. Also, they said, each year some thirty movies are translated into Tibetan for audiences in nomad and agricultural areas, and official documents for these areas are originally written in Tibetan, unlike others which are produced in Chinese and then translated.

Officials at the cultural bureau and language committee both noted that the government publishes many volumes of works in Tibetan and dubs television programs and movies in the vernacular. They cited radio programs in Tibetan broadcast to pastoral and farming areas; newspapers, magazines, and journals printed in Tibetan and Chinese; and a Tibetan-language channel on Lhasa television.

There is indeed a Tibetan-language television channel, and undoubtedly many watch it, but Chinese still predominates. The favorite television show among youngsters and adults when I was in Lhasa was a serial adventure story from Hong Kong, broadcast in Chinese. A national news program appears in Tibetan, but it is one day late. Up-to-the-minute information appears in Chinese. There is also a Lhasa video house which presents movies in Tibetan, but this is so much the exception that a Tibetan went out of the way to point it out to me. And there is a bureau where Tibetans toil away at translations of official documents. But these appear first in Chinese, and never, in all my visits to agencies in Lhasa and elsewhere, did I catch sight of a single communiqué in Tibetan.

Likewise there is a directive, on paper, that work units must teach Chinese cadres the Tibetan language, but many simply ignore it. And it seems that those which do comply with the law provide little real learning. A Tibetan from the east, who attended one of these classes to learn the Lhasa dialect, said the Chinese students attended only because they were paid to show up. They made a cursory pass through an elementary text, he said, and then began the same book all over again. At this point he left to study on his own. The situation is similar, a Tibetan teacher said, in Tibetan language classes for native students in the Chinese language track. By law the Tibetan students must attend, but the teaching is often poor, pupils have little incentive to learn, and they consider it an additional burden in their already heavy schedules.

And although there are literary journals in Tibetan, most Tibetan writers use Chinese. Sotse is an exception, and when I asked him to name other Tibetan playwrights, he came up with none who used the Tibetan language. The Cultural Revolution has a lot to do with this. Tibetans educated during those years had no chance to become literate in their native tongue, and many of them are writing today. But there are still other reasons for choosing the majority language, and Amdowan novelist Danzhu Angben (Dondup Wangpon in Tibetan), who writes in Chinese himself, was quick to name them. Books in Chinese, he said, have a better chance of being published. They also have more readers and are more easily translated into foreign languages. Books in Tibetan, he said, have the advantage of "presenting your ideas to Tibetans directly." But this, of course, is true only for Tibetans literate in their own language.

Outside the TAR, where the majority of ethnic Tibetans live, the language has suffered even greater incursions from Chinese. On a visit to four provinces with Tibetan populations (Qinghai, Sichuan, Gansu, and Yunnan) a group from the International Campaign for Tibet found that forms, tickets, brochures, receipts, and instructions were all in Chinese. But away from the cities, in nomad and farming areas, the group met few Tibetans who spoke Chinese; most rural Tibetans were at a loss when they traveled to towns and tried to operate in post offices, banks, and tax bureaus. In bus stations the lone ticket salesman was usually Chinese, and the signs, tickets, and announcements were only in Chinese.[3]

The capitals of these provinces are located outside Tibetan areas, and their populations are mixtures of Chinese, Tibetans, and other minorities. Nomads and peasants who arrive to do business at the provincial level have to manage in Chinese. An Amdowa from Qinghai said the provincial government does not require Chinese cadres to study Tibetan, and primary-school students there study the vernacular only in prefectures designated as Tibetan autonomous areas. Outside these prefectures schooling is in Chinese. Qinghai saw an influx of hundreds of thousands of Chinese after the founding the People's Republic, and Tibetans there have been swamped by Chinese-speaking settlers. Many of them have never learned their ethnic language. "Many young monks who join Kumbum [a major Tibetan monastery in Qinghai]," the Amdowa said, "often can't speak Tibetan because they come from assimilated areas."

And the diversity of dialects in Tibetan also makes it difficult to educate everyone in the vernacular. There are, broadly speaking, three main dialects—that of central Tibet and those of Kham and Amdo—but each group contains subdialects, and sometimes these are mutually unintelligible even between neighboring villages. Some Khampa and Amdowa speak dialects which deviate so far from the standard that schools cannot provide for them. In those areas as well the students learn in Chinese. My interpreter, Xiao Jin, had learned a subdialect at home, and she had studied only Chinese in school.

The variety of dialects also creates problems outside of class. Often Tibetans from different areas resort to Chinese because it is difficult to converse in their respective forms of Tibetan. Even those who have studied Lhasa dialect (now becoming the standard) may understand the words but feel ill at ease speaking it. Lhasa dialect has more tones than that of Kham, for instance; and the Lhasa area, where the old society was heavily stratified, produced a tongue with many honorific terms. Nouns and verbs often come in three levels, each with a different root—one for common folk; another for high officials and monks; and another for those of the loftiest rank, such as the Dalai Lama or his regent. The common word for head, for instance, is *go* while the second-level honorific is *u*, and the common term for mouth is *kha* while the honorific is *shel*. But in Kham and Amdo where the people once belonged to tribes ruled by chieftains, the language contains many fewer words to show veneration or respect. "When Khampa meet Lhasa people," one Tibetan from Sichuan said, "the Khampa often use Chinese because they are afraid they can't use the terms of respect right."

Linguists are looking at ways to standardize Tibetan, and Tibetans themselves are turning to the Lhasa dialect as their common tongue. As a result, the idiom of Lhasa is changing more rapidly than others. Tashi Tsering, director of the Sichuan Province People's Congress, said Tibetans from the three areas who came together to compile a Tibetan dictionary began to use Lhasa dialect among themselves though it was "not quite the standard form." After a few months, he said, they could understand each other. Students at Beijing Tibetan School, which serves nomads from various areas of the TAR, learn the Lhasa dialect to communicate with each other, and Tibetans from all the regions who have lived in exile also speak to each other in a variant of the Lhasa dialect.

Tashi Tsering said a widely used standardized Tibetan based on Lhasa dialect would help preserve the language, and he saw signs that this was coming about. Many in Kham and Amdo, he said, were studying the standard on their own.

But trying to force standardization on a language can create other problems, as some speakers of minority languages have discovered. Those who learn the standard form in school may be at a loss in their native villages, and some nonstandard speakers come to see their own dialects as inferior and abandon them. Or they may find it difficult to understand radio broadcasts and other communications in the standard form. Dialect speakers, faced with these difficulties, may shift to the majority language rather than the standard version of their own idiom.

Tibetan, however, has some advantages in the effort to standardize. Lhasa is the heart of Tibetan identity, and it carries a prestige and integrating force lacking in other minority areas facing the need to unify under a common dialect. Tibetans on their own have naturally assumed the idiom of Lhasa as their common language. Also, the Tibetan script is comprehensible to speakers of all dialects. It was adopted so long ago that it already deviates from standard speech, especially that of Lhasa. (It is closest to the dialect of Amdo, which has retained more of the old phonetic features.)

China has supported efforts to preserve the Tibetan language—promoting a standard dialect, dubbing films, translating documents, publishing magazines and newspapers, teaching the vernacular in school, providing for the use of Tibetan in banks and post offices. But many say this is not enough. Even if students learn the vernacular in school, they will find Chinese more useful once they graduate, and as Chinese takes over, fewer will study it seriously at all. Tibetans point to the steady stream of Chinese arriving to work in the TAR and the dominance of the Chinese language in public life, and they say Tibetan is on the way out. They note that outsiders, and even Tibetans, can get along without it much of the time, and that Chinese is now the language of opportunity.

They have discerned how much the Tibetan tongue has lost since the 1950s when Chinese cadres struggled to learn the language. Today in Tibet only the old-time Chinese know Tibetan, and even many of those who have spent twenty years in the TAR can speak no more than a few words. They simply don't need it anymore. One Chinese academic, fluent in Tibetan, told me that cadres today compare the Tibetan language to a ration card for one place and Chinese to a ration card for the whole country. "People choose to learn the most useful language," he said. Considering the years of study and practice needed to master any language, most decide it is not worth the effort.

Thus Chinese in Lhasa have balked at Tibetan lessons for their children, even when these were mandated by law. In 1990 Lhasa First Primary complied with orders from above and sent Chinese students to Tibetan language classes. "But," said the school's party secretary, a woman named Paldron, "the Chinese parents complained and said that after they return to the provinces the children will never use it." Lhasa First Primary dropped the plan. Chogyal at the Tibetan language committee said such resistance forced the authorities to back off. "It is required for Chinese students to learn Tibetan," he said, "but we let the schools decide." At the education bureau I asked Zhou, who was quick to cite statistics on any issue, whether any Chinese students in the TAR studied Tibetan. "I'm not sure," he said. Then he added gamely, "But each year I see some Chinese names on the list to take the Tibetan language exam. I can infer that some are."

Tibetan parents, on the other hand, often want their children to attend classes in Chinese. At Lhasa First Secondary School one-half to two-thirds of the students in Chinese classes may be native Tibetans. Their parents see no advantage in becoming literate in their native tongue. It is only a burden, many say, to study both Tibetan and Chinese, and university entrance exams require Chinese and English but not Tibetan. Those who choose the Tibetan track may begin to study English in senior high—if at all—while those in the Chinese track begin English at the junior-high level. Since English is required on college entrance exams and Tibetan-track students lose out on English studies, those who seek competency in their own language and the chance for a higher education at the same time face an uphill struggle.

To get into college, secure a job in a government office, or succeed in business, Tibetans need Chinese. The schools underscore this by placing a high value on learning the language of Beijing. The state requires all public-school students to learn Chinese, and the TAR was even considering a move to lower the mandatory beginning level from fourth to third grade. (Outside the TAR, students begin Chinese in the first grade.) Educated Tibetans, therefore, are literate in Chinese, and even the unlettered, especially those in cities, can converse in the undeclared official language of China. I could use my limited Chinese, for instance, with many Tibetan workers—hotel staff, drivers, shopkeepers, street vendors, waiters. Even in remote areas I met unschooled Tibetans who had picked up Chinese in the army or on visits to Lhasa. And then, of course, in every major town and in smaller ones as well, I could speak to the Chinese who predominate in the shops, restaurants, and repair stands.

Tibetan reigns only in the pasturelands and farming villages, and it is seen by some officials as the language of nomads and peasants. At the cultural bureau, Hu and his coworkers, eager to assure me that Tibetan is flourishing, cited the number of movies dubbed in Tibetan each year, the radio programs broadcast in the vernacular, and a calendar published entirely in Tibetan. But in each instance they added that these were specifically for herders and peasants. When they pointed to official documents written directly in Tibetan, they again noted that these were for agricultural and pastoral areas. Chinese has a hold in the towns: Although a fair number of city dwellers—those who have moved to town from the countryside, and older people who never attended school—speak only Tibetan, visitors to urban Tibet get along fine with Chinese alone.

When I remarked that Chinese is the language in evidence at post offices, cultural bureau official Kesang Wangyal explained that this is only reasonable. "It's natural," he said, "because most mail goes to other Chinese provinces, and there no one knows Tibetan, so they have to use it. For example, I'm Tibetan, and when I write to friends, I have to write in Chinese. And also in Tibet many people are illiterate." Kesang Wangyal had summed up the sad state of a minority language: It is a marginal entity in a larger language group. In a truly independent Tibet, letter-writers would have no stronger ties to China than, say, to India or Nepal or countries in the West. And whatever language they might use for international contacts, they could conduct their own affairs in Tibetan.

It is no wonder many Tibetans fear for the survival of their language, now that it has become something expendable, representing only five million people in a nation of more than a billion. Some may also know that similiar efforts to preserve other idioms—in education, publishing, the media, and public agencies—have failed to halt the erosion of many minority tongues. The Celtic languages of Europe, some of them already gone and the rest fading rapidly, have also received help from national governments—television in the vernacular, literary journals, approval for use in the courts, required exams for the military, and language instruction in the schools. These languages have much in common with Tibetan: They were strongest in their native churches, and they also came to be seen as the idioms of rural life. Again, although there was talk about making some of them the official languages of government, this never came about. And, as in the case of Tibetan, it was economic and political integration with larger nations and the influx of non-native speakers that led to their decay.

These defunct and vanishing tongues followed a course that Tibetan is following today. First, they became minority languages, overshadowed by the idioms of their new rulers. Then they became one of two languages in a generation of bilingual speakers, and soon they were dropped altogether in favor of the majority tongue. Each of them, at times, was suppressed by the national government and banned from the schools but later received official support. The arrival of automobiles, airplanes, television, and radios accelerated their decline, and once the process of decay was underway, activists emerged who called for renewal, for laws to mandate the use of the language in offices and legislative bodies. The governments responded by placing the major burden on the schools (though, unlike China, none of them required students to learn the local language), in the hope that classes in Irish or Scots, Gaelic, or Welsh or Breton would create a new generation of native speakers. But the young often saw the old language as an obstacle, and the majority tongue was so firmly entrenched that even the activists carried on their debates in English or French. By the time the calls for renewal were heard, it was too late, and the ancient languages were already moribund.

There is at least one European minority language, however, which has so far managed to evade this scenario. It is Catalan, the Romance language of Catalonia, now an autonomous region of Spain. Catalonia has been part of Spain since the sixteenth century, and it has passed through periods of suppression when the language was outlawed from the schools and public life. Catalonia has also seen a massive influx of immigrants from other parts of Spain—almost 1.4 million outsiders arrived between 1950 and 1975, so many that they made up 40 percent of the population in 1970. And yet Catalan has persisted against the odds. Today, in a truly autonomous region, it is the language of government, and immigrants are eager to learn it. (Native Catalan speakers from Barcelona, where the immigrants equal the natives in population, tend to lace their conversations with Castilian Spanish, however, a sign that even Catalan may be eroding.)

Catalan is a heartening presence in an otherwise dismal roster of minority languages—the Celtic tongues of Europe; hundreds of Native American languages; dozens of African tribal idioms; and, in China, Manchu, and many languages once spoken south of the Yangtze and now known only by the traces they have left in dialects of Chinese. But according to sociolinguist

Kathryn Woolard, Catalan has a crucial advantage over the rest: prestige. It is the loss of prestige that sends many languages into decline. Or, as another linguist put it: "The basic mechanism of language decay starts with social change subordinating the respective speech community to another speech community."[4]

Catalan, however, is a high prestige language, the idiom of an industrialized, economically thriving region. Its capital is the Mediterranean seaport of Barcelona with its centuries of cultural and commercial prominence. The immigrants who streamed into Barcelona after World War II were impoverished city dwellers from Andalusia and other parts of Spain hoping for a piece of Catalonia's wealth. They crowded into urban highrises in new suburbs and went to work for Catalans, who were better educated and wealthier than the immigrant laborers.

Tibet, sad to say, is no Catalonia. In Chinese eyes it is backward, only a few decades out of barbarous feudalism, mired still in superstition, economically depressed, and populated with ignorant peasants and nomads. Where immigrants in Catalonia want their children to learn the local tongue, Chinese parents in Tibet have fought off efforts to teach their children Tibetan. And Tibetan parents often insist that their children attend classes taught in Chinese. These students receive some instruction in Tibetan, but it falls short of comprehensive teaching in their native language.

Another sign of Tibetan's low prestige is the use of Chinese by Tibetan officials and bureaucrats. The Sichuan official Tashi Tsering stood out as an exception. He used Tibetan entirely during our interview, and when I remarked on this, he said, "Some officials in the TAR think they appear more knowledgeable if they speak Chinese." Sometimes, however, it was not the officials who made the choice. At times Xiao Jin preferred Chinese because she found her Tibetan too limited for some subjects. Medicine was one of them, and this touches on another aspect of low-prestige languages: their lack of native technical terms. In Brittany, for instance, French and not the indigenous Breton is seen as the language of the future while Breton is considered a part of the past, an idiom incapable of expressing modern ideas or technical knowledge. Even with the best intentions the push to use Tibetan in science instruction—retraining teachers, inventing new vocabulary, and publishing a special dictionary with the new scientific terms—points up the deficiencies of the language and implies that Tibetan needs shoring up before it can reach the level of Chinese.

So the prestige value of Tibetan is more like that of Breton than Catalan. Both languages now serve "backward" regions of their nations, and their traditional vocabularies have lagged behind social and scientific advances in the modern world. All this widens the gap between them and the majority languages with which they contend. They not only play a humble role on the national scene and no role at all at the international level, but they are also crippled by their backcountry, rough-hewn images. And Tibetan faces not only minority status and low prestige but also an influx of Chinese-speaking workers who find no good reason to study the local tongue.

Some minority languages have revived, to a degree, when their regions won genuine autonomy, but China's centralized hold on Tibet shows no sign of loosening. And some speakers of minority languages who have been cut off from their motherlands when boundaries change, for instance, can cling to the hope that someday they will reunite with the independent nations where their idiom is preserved intact. Or they themselves may migrate. But Tibetans have no such hope. Tibet is the only refuge for those who aspire to keep the language alive. The future of Tibetan depends on what happens in the TAR and the ethnic Tibetan regions of China proper.

Many Tibetans say the only guarantee of survival would be full independence before the language erodes beyond repair. But at the same time most of them despair of this, given China's rock-hard stance on the issue. Instead, some Tibetans speak of cultural autonomy in the TAR with Chinese cadres and traders returned to their homes and Tibetan restored as the language of government. Without such a move, many fear that Tibetan will become a quaint relic of folk history or an endangered species living on in remote preserves. And some acknowledge that even cultural autonomy may only delay the slide to oblivion.

A few Tibetans, however, are making individual efforts against the odds. They study the language in night school, avoid Chinese, and promote Tibetan among foreign visitors. These are Tibet's language activists. I met a handful of them in the TAR, and I especially remember a businessman in Shigatse who was determined and persistent. He had a business card without a single contaminating character in Chinese, and he was ever stopping me to substitute Tibetan words for my Chinese, raising his finger like a school-teacher and asking me to repeat. I gave it a try because I believed he was right, that I should indeed learn Tibetan. But I had already made a start with Chinese, and it hadn't been easy. I had no energy left to begin anew, and I had no chance to become fluent before I left Tibet. I wished him well and hoped he would win his battle against all the forces of history and chauvinism that threatened his native tongue.

7

A Pearl of the Motherland
(Culture)

In the offices of the TAR Cultural Bureau, Xiao Jin and I sit before covered teacups, repeatedly filled by staff members, and pyramids of fruit—the overabundant offerings which I have come to expect at formal interviews. Today we also have before us Vice Bureau Chief Hu Jinan, a moon-faced Chinese cadre, and two Tibetans: Kesang Wangyal, also a vice bureau chief, and Wangchuk, director of the bureau's foreign liaison office. Kesang Wangyal tells me, nodding at the Chinese who shares his title but appears to be his boss, that Hu speaks fluent Tibetan. This is so out of the ordinary in today's Tibet, that I look at Hu for confirmation. He nods modestly, and I offer my congratulations. Kesang Wangyal adds, "Mr. Hu has been in Tibet more than thirty years." This, too, is unusual; most of the old-timers returned to their provinces years ago. So I say, "You must feel you are Tibetan by now." But Hu won't have it. He pauses, and then he says with emphasis, "*Half* Tibetan." This is the most he is willing to concede, but in spite of his less-than-gracious disclaimer Hu is the spokesman today. He is to present us with the official word on Tibetan culture in the 1990s, and he gives it entirely in Chinese.

My first question requires an introduction. I've been mulling over ways to phrase it without raising alarm, without seeming to accuse China of destroying all that is native to Tibet. I say that I have been talking to Tibetan cadres everywhere from Beijing to Lhasa and all of them have told me about their fears for Tibetan culture and the need to preserve it. Could he explain why there is so much anxiety? What are all these people worried about? Hu may not hear the concerns of Tibetans in the street, but he certainly knows that exile groups and the Dalai Lama himself have charged China with "cultural genocide" in Tibet. He is ready with an answer:

"Tibetan culture is abundant and colorful and concerned with all aspects of life," Hu declaims. "Tibetan culture is very valuable, a pearl. It is part of the People's Republic of China, part of China's brilliant culture. Thanks to the peaceful liberation of Tibet, the policy of the Chinese Communist Party is to protect Tibetan traditional culture." He now launches into a forty-minute exposition of official efforts to gather, dissect, and analyze the remaining specimens of pure Tibetan culture. He enumerates pre– and post–Cultural Revolution projects to collect, record, photograph, preserve, collate, organize, publish, and catalogue traditional arts. He points to the restoration of monasteries, the safeguarding of cultural relics, and efforts to record Tibet's great *Gesar* epic, which has been handed down orally for centuries. He notes the publication of books on Tibetan dance and painting, collections of folk literature and proverbs, and the many professional drama and dance troupes in the TAR.

I have read all this before, in official pamphlets on Tibet, but I take down what he has to say. When he is done I tell him that the government's efforts are truly impressive, but they raise another question: Given all these efforts, why do so many people still fear for the viability of Tibetan culture? There is a silence, and then Hu goes on in a louder voice. Of course, he says, people naturally worry because Tibetan culture is a pearl, such a precious entity, and many are concerned because of the open door policy. It has brought outsiders from all over China, and he himself worries about this. Many other nationalities are arriving in Tibet and introducing their own cultures. But, he says, with government support and the innate strength of the Tibetan way of life, this culture will certainly survive.

Hu has hit on an important issue, the flood of outsiders arriving in the TAR, but he has presented this as an influx of mixed ethnic groups, as if Tibet were threatened by contamination from the Uighur and Mongolians of northern China as well as the Han Chinese. But the outside influence most apparent in modern Tibet is Han dress, food, speech, art, literature, music, and customs. This is what Tibetans refer to when they predict the demise of their

137

own society. The danger is that, as it adapts to modern ways, Tibet will lose its own character and become just one more province of China.

This is what exile groups have feared ever since the failed rebellion of 1959 and the exodus of one hundred thousand Tibetans to India and Nepal. China, they have said from the beginning, is deliberately ravaging Tibetan culture. Refugees told of attacks on Tibetan traditions and religion, and their claims gathered strength with a 1960 report by the International Commission of Jurists which said China had "set out to destroy" Tibet's way of life. The government-in-exile then took up the cry of "cultural genocide," and more than thirty years later China's critics still accuse the People's Republic of doing its utmost to exterminate the ancient beliefs and customs of the hardy Tibetans and absorb them into the faceless motherland of the People's Republic.

This debate, unlike that over the environment, is alive among Tibetans throughout China. It is not only the government-in-exile and its supporters who fear for Tibetan society; it is also educated Tibetans who work for the government, cadres educated in Chinese schools, Party members, teachers, and researchers, along with shopkeepers, street vendors, waiters, drivers, rickshaw pedalers, monks, and nuns. They may not use the word genocide or accuse the Communists of deliberate efforts to wipe out everything Tibetan, but they are saying that their culture, forged in a hostile land, will not long survive. They point to many forces eroding the traditional way of life—the pressures of modernization, Tibet's minority status in China's economy and society, the presence of Western tourists, and the recent flood of Chinese traders into the heart of Tibet.

Tibetans have good reason to be troubled. In the eastern regions the culture is indeed floundering under an onslaught of Chinese settlers and decades of rule from Beijing. There, in Qinghai, Gansu, Sichuan, and Yunnan, some Tibetans have come to believe that they themselves have "no culture," that they are a backward people who need to learn from the Chinese.[1] In the TAR many Tibetans fear, with reason, that Lhasa itself will someday become one more Chinese city with a quaint "old quarter" of Tibetan-style buildings and a few well-preserved monuments as signs of its former glory. Then the Jokhang would become a museum, and the plaza, in spite of its present vitality, nothing more than a trading ground, catering to tourists and the eager consumers of a market economy.

China has responded with the litany of projects Hu cited in his Lhasa office. In effect, the government reduces Tibetan culture to folklore, something which can be counted, filed away, and therefore, controlled. It dismisses the Tibetan worldview—diametrically different from that of the dominant Han Chinese—which gives rise to traditional arts and keeps them alive. And officials once again blame any losses on the Cultural Revolution. It was the excesses of those years, Hu said, which damaged Tibetan culture, not present policies or even those that followed the "peaceful liberation." The ten years of chaos were an aberration, the government says, an error which has now been corrected.

In fact, the erosion of Tibet's culture began fifteen years before the Cultural Revolution, as soon as the PLA marched into Tibetan territory and raised the five-star flag. In those early years China completed highways from Sichuan, Qinghai, and Xinjiang to Lhasa; trucks appeared on the streets of the capital; and students began to learn in school that Tibet had always been part of China and Mao Zedong was a benevolent liberator who would rescue them from feudalism. More Tibetans began to use chopsticks and eat rice, musicians learned to play Chinese instruments, and primary-school pupils wore the red scarves of the Young Pioneers over their traditional jackets and dresses.

Then, as the abortive rebellion of 1959 began, the Dalai Lama and his court left Tibet, and with them went the splendor and pomp of the old society. When the rebels had been crushed, officials carried off jewels, gold, and silk-bound manuscripts from manor houses and monasteries and took over the homes of aristocrats who had joined the uprising. The Potala became an empty fortress, and many monks and nuns—denied the taxes that had once supported them—left their monasteries and convents to follow a secular life.

In a sense, the jurists in Geneva were right in saying that China "set out to destroy" Tibetan culture after the rebellion. The Communists aimed to wipe out the serf system and discourage religious practice. But the commission was wrong in the implication that China wanted to crush every sign of Tibetan civilization. During this period, the new rulers still allowed peasants to go about in traditional dress and celebrate their religious festivals. As long as the old customs posed no threat to the state, the Communists usually tolerated them.

The government, however, shattered the old social system when it confiscated the estates of aristocrats and religious orders and gave serfs the deeds to their own land. Zealous cadres (both Tibetan and Chinese) then told farmers and nomads that drinking barley beer and passing their leisure hours in song and storytelling were wasteful and decadent, that they should be working to build the motherland instead. Tibetans, always fond of leisure, found themselves playing less and laboring more under the direction of local officials.

The common folk began to abandon their old form of greeting superiors: bowing low, sticking out their tongues, and sucking in air. They adopted a brisk Chinese nod of the head instead. The few remaining aristocrats no longer passed through the streets clad in silk, riding brightly adorned horses, flanked by servants. Their wives no longer appeared at state functions decked out in elaborate pearl headdresses. High-ranking Tibetan men now went about in Mao jackets and pants, and their women dressed like commoners in plain dresses and aprons.

There were no more processions marking the Dalai Lama's yearly move from the Potala to the Norbulingka summer palace. The court dance troupe, which Tashi Tshering joined at the age of ten, disbanded after centuries of performing on state occasions. Tselobdra, the school for monk officials, with its young students dressed in distinctive red gowns and heavy felt boots, was no more. Its rooms high in the Potala became possessions of the state. The warrior monks, known on sight by their heavy cudgels and the coils of hair over their ears, abruptly vanished, and the ragyapa, outcast collectors of the dead, faded away.

The government formed new, state-run dance troupes, and in this period of "democratic reform" following the rebellion, the musicians began to adopt Chinese instruments, like the two-stringed *erhu*. The dancers still used Tibetan-style choreography and music, but now the songs and skits disparaged the old society and exalted communism. The troupes were also full-time professional companies on salary, unlike the laymen of former times who went from house to house performing for tsampa or ceremonial scarves.

Tibet, after the rebellion, was changing rapidly but still retained much of its native culture. It took the Red Guards, who brought the Cultural Revolution to Tibet in the fall of 1966, to destroy what remained. "Then," said a former dance troupe member, "we dealt only in slogans and policies. There was no traditional Tibetan dancing, only modern Chinese dancing. Tibetans weren't allowed to sing traditional songs. We were told [such songs belonged to] the old Tibet." Drama troupes no longer presented Tibet's traditional operas; they performed Beijing opera instead and Chinese dramas about the Long March and other great moments in Party history.

The youthful Red Guards, many of them Tibetans themselves, incited the local people to destroy entire monasteries, leaving only ruined walls. Some six thousand monasteries in all the Tibetan ethnic regions disappeared; only a half dozen, protected by the army as major monuments, were left standing. The rampaging youth destroyed family altars, thangkas, statues, and prayer flags. They stopped passersby, cut off their braids, and tore off their jewelry. Even polite speech was branded as "old," and routine Tibetan greetings were replaced by quotations from Chairman Mao. Tibetans took to wearing old and patched clothes to avoid assaults by the Red Guards. They tucked their garments into awkward folds and left their traditional hats, aprons, and robes at home.

By 1979, when Tibet began to emerge from the Cultural Revolution, Lhasa resembled other Chinese cities—men in Mao suits and caps, women in pants and straw hats, a sprawl of concrete buildings with tin roofs surrounding the old town. Some women still wore the long wraparound dresses, but now the style was shorter, with pants showing below the skirt.

The first outside visitors—delegations from the government-in-exile and other returnees—were treated to dance shows, but, they said, there was little about them that reflected Tibet. The performances were in Chinese drama and dance forms or an amalgam of other minority styles. "Only rarely does one hear a Tibetan tune," wrote one delegate from India, "and if so the lyrics are new, sung in Chinese style, glorifying Mao and the Communist Party." When another visitor remarked that a Lhasa orchestra had not a single traditional instrument, a Tibetan cadre answered, "We are progressive now." Another Tibetan explained, "This is national minorities music." Travelers in Kham found villagers trying to recall traditional dance routines as they prepared for a festival, the first of its kind in twenty-two years. The dancers laughed at their own clumsy attempts, but the visitors were saddened to see how much had been lost. "Few people were left who remembered all the prescribed movements," one of the visitors wrote.[2]

Heinrich Harrer, the Austrian who spent seven years in Tibet before the Chinese takeover, returned in 1982 and was dismayed at the changes. He searched for the old "greeting spot," where wealthy Tibetans had set up tents to entertain those who were arriving in the Holy City and to send off those who were departing. He could locate the site, but all traces of its former function had vanished. Now, Harrer wrote, it was "one huge grey industrialized zone with ugly buildings." A park with a stone throne for the Dalai Lama was now a "sea of cheap hutments and tin-roofed houses."[3] The Lingkor, the sacred circuit around the city, no longer passed through gardens but followed asphalt roads where buses and trucks lurched over potholed roads. Harrar missed the color of the old days, the brocade finery of the nobles with their furs and oddly shaped hats, the women with their head ornaments, and the singers of tales who once sat in the Barkor reciting magical legends as they spun their hand-held prayer wheels.

Although Harrer wrote that "Lhasa, whose name means 'place of the gods,' no longer bears any relation to that lovely name,"[4] the capital and the rest of Tibet have been making a comeback from the ravages of the Red Guard years. Prayer flags have reappeared on the rooftops, residents burn morning offerings of juniper and pine needles, and pilgrims crowd the Jokhang and Potala. Women's dresses have returned to their traditional length, and Tibetan opera is performed once again. Although the old society is gone, never to return, Tibetans throughout the TAR have brought back much of what was lost—hair styles, village shrines, rivers spanned with prayer flags. In the Changtang, anthropologists Melvyn Goldstein and Cynthia Beall found that by 1988 the Pala nomads had regained their former values and customs. It was a cultural revitalization, they said, thriving under the new policies of reform.[5]

Beall and Goldstein were heartened by the resilience of nomad culture and proclaimed it alive and well "for now and for the foreseeable future." But even those who fear for the end of Tibetan society agree that traditional ways remain in the farming and pastoral reaches of Tibet. They recognize the persistence of their culture in those areas, but they also know that assimilation has followed this same route in other societies—beginning in the cities, spreading to the rural areas, eventually surrounding isolated pockets of the old society, and finally absorbing it altogether. They also know that in the eastern Tibetan regions of Kham and Amdo—in Qinghai, Gansu, and Sichuan—many farming areas are already sinicized, and only the rugged nomad regions remain safely Tibetan—for now. One Amdowa from a peasant family told me that he had adopted a Chinese identity by the time he left high school and had rediscovered his heritage only by living among the nomads. And my interpreter, Xiao Jin, said that although the young people in remote areas of Kham still learn the local songs and dances for traditional weddings, in her own village only the elderly know them.

It is the nomads and farmers from the more remote regions of Tibet, along with the Khampa traders, who lend Lhasa much of its color. They arrive on pilgrimage dressed in sheepskin or peasant jackets of homespun wool. The nomad women pass through the temples and Barkor with their hair braided into a hundred strands, which hang like fine webs down their backs. Their jewelry and their dresses, ornamented with strips of bright fabric and otter fur, indicate their native regions. Men may also wear identifying garb. Those from Lhokha sport striped panels on their jackets. Khampa men attach red tassels to their hair. But the fashion of Kham has caught on with other Tibetans, and men from central Tibet or the west may also appear with their heads swathed in red silk strands.

Many of the old customs persist in the countryside. Some village children and adults still stick out their tongues as signs of respect, and hosts are careful to dab ritual lumps of butter and a dusting of tsampa on kettles of tea and cups of barley beer. Traditional hospitality is also strongest in these villages and encampments. In Guchok, my hosts were so determined to serve me well that they stopped just short of forcing butter tea down my throat, and the family gathered around to bring me bedding against the cold night. They tucked me in and then stood back, smiling and watching me lie in a cocoon of rugs and blankets.

Country villages have also rebuilt their shrines, piles of prayer stones, and incense burners to guard the people and their goods against harm. The peasants once again stack white stones in their fields as offerings to the deities who dwell there. And some areas adopt distinctive building styles. In Sakya, houses surrounding the ancient monastery are painted a steel blue with stripes of white and red. In the broad fertile valley between Gyantse and Shigatse, homeowners tip buckets of paint from the roofs to accent the outside walls with white streaks. In eastern Tibet monasteries are often painted with a row of dots below the eaves.

Clothing styles, like language styles, reveal the currents and spread of Chinese influence, strongest in the cities and less evident in the countryside. Away from Lhasa and other large towns the peasants still dress in homespun clothes and heavy felt boots, and many men have returned to wearing long hair and a single turquoise earring. But even in backwaters like Guchok, some men go about in store-bought jackets, and schoolboys often wear sneakers, Mao caps, and army hats with the Chinese red star. Women and girls put on factory-made head scarves. And even traditional styles have taken on new functions. Today young girls wear striped aprons when they are decked out in their best. In former times aprons were reserved for grown women.

Chinese and Western influence increase as you approach major roads and towns. Close to highway stops and urban centers, peasant and nomad men favor factory-made sweaters and jackets. The women usually stick with traditional dress, but in villages outside Lhasa they resemble their Chinese counterparts, with straw hats, knit vests, blouses, and pants.

Today in Lhasa and Shigatse many educated women have adopted an urban Tibetan style that distinguishes them from the Chinese: blazer and pants, wide-brimmed hat, and long hair. (Chinese women usually cut their hair short and go hatless.) Others wear brown wraparounds over bright blouses; many braid skeins of colored threads into their hair. Older women wear two braids, joined at the back. But urban Tibetan men are indistinguishable from the Chinese, in Mao jackets or Western suits (with a designer label still attached to a sleeve). And schoolchildren in Lhasa and Shigatse dress just like small Chinese, in vests, jumpers, pants, and bright sweaters.

Changes in dress style—now that the Cultural Revolution is long dead—reflect Tibet's gradual shift to a modern society as well as Chinese influence. Residents of most Third World countries are making similar adaptations, and Tibetans in exile likewise conform to the styles of their adopted homes. But China is so eager to convince the world that Tibetan culture is thriving under Chinese rule that it tries to cover up even these predictable shifts in style with staged scenes of local people in "ethnic dress" for visitors and propaganda photos.

The government's 1992 white paper states: "In the cities, towns, and agricultural and pastoral areas in Tibet, most Tibetans still retain their traditional clothing, diet, and housing."[6] This is untrue, but factory workers, students, and even department store patrons are often portrayed in spruced-up finery for photographers and visitors. A Chinese pamphlet shows weavers at the Gyantse Carpet Factory dressed in their holiday best and seated on ornate rugs. In real life they go to work in jackets and sweaters and sit on shabby bolsters.

China has no need to undermine its own image with such transparent distortions. Since the post–Cultural Revolution reforms began in 1980, the government has supported minority cultures, at least in nonthreatening forms such as dress, architecture, and the folk arts. These not only have no overt political stigma, but they also help tourism. In Tibet's cities new residences are going up in traditional style, with ornate and brightly painted lintels, massive window jambs, and flat roofs—identifiably Tibetan. Around the Barkor the city is tearing down old buildings condemned as unsound and replacing them with new ones built, officials claim, on the original plans. "We use new materials," said a staff member at the Lhasa Environmental Protection Bureau, "but they are in Tibetan style."

Some foreigners and Tibetans complain, however, that the new materials destroy the charm of the originals, and it is true that the government makes no effort to save and renovate these historic buildings. The structures have no landmark protection, which often preserves such houses in the United States; they are torn down and replaced. The old houses were made drystone (without mortar), using alternating rows of small stones and large, and this gave them a rustic, textured effect. But the new Barkor buildings are of preshaped granite, like concrete blocks, uniform in size and set in white mortar. And they are new, without the sags, shadings, hollows, and the accumulated memories of long use.

Nevertheless, the local government is trying to balance style with safety and health concerns, and it has come a long way from the Cultural Revolution and even the early years when everything was featureless, grim concrete.

Apartment blocks, schools, shops, and office buildings in this functional style remain, however, in Lhasa and elsewhere, and the new rows of shops (which rapidly fill with Chinese merchants) are nothing but look-alike cells. But new residences carry Tibetan features, and the old drystone technique is still put to use in monasteries and villages.

Government planning, however, could never capture the organic, capricious nature of much Tibetan architecture—like the monasteries and temples with their dark passageways and shrines set within shrines, their unexpected rises, corners, and open spaces. Such complexes have grown, not under an impulse for order, but from a life-force urge to put out shoots, roots, pods, and humps, adapting as they go. Some commercial space also takes on this character, like the hotel where I stayed in Shigatse. To reach the main office we entered a narrow, unmarked alley, passed through a dark storage area, and ascended a ladder to the second floor. The rooms were set about almost at random; two of them, the most luxurious, stood apart with windows on all sides. Ours was tucked in the rear of the building and faced a cattle trough, a hidden watering spot where guests came to wash. In such spaces there is no predictability, like that in government agencies with their identical, functional floor plans: rows of offices facing a windowed corridor. In an organic structural style you must always be ready for surprises.

The playful spirit in Tibetan architecture reflects the native love of spontaneity and fun. Tibetans are given to teasing and horseplay, which sets them apart from the more matter-of-fact Chinese. Young men go in for mock fights, chasing each other around the street and collapsing in laughter. One Tibetan resident of my hotel hung out on the third floor with a water gun, taking shots at victims in the courtyard. At Pede Village on Yamdrok Tso, an elderly woman hammed it up for my camera, as impish as a nine-year-old. The peasants we joined on a ferry passage to Samye Monastery sent around mugs of barley beer and never let up on the jokes: "Hey, there were forty of us; now there're only thirty-nine. Somebody's overboard." Laughter. Then: "No. It's just that you're too stupid. You forgot to count yourself."

In the old days, this sense of ridicule allowed performers to openly burlesque their leaders. Even the lamas did not escape comic portrayals in mime, skits, and song. It was taken lightly, as great fun, even by officials and religious leaders.[7] "During festivals it was allowed," one Tibetan scholar told me. "People could sing satire and make fun of monks and officials, even in Tibetan opera." Today the government allows not a whisper of criticism in public. But in the countryside, the scholar said, some opera performers manage to get away with it. "It's not so obvious now," he said. "It's more roundabout and subtle. You can't do it directly."

Tibetan opera, even under constraint, still conveys the native love of slapstick and horseplay, along with high-flown scenes of goddesses and heroes and skulking villains. The big opera jamboree takes place each year during the Yogurt Festival commemorating the end of former monastic retreats, when commoners once treated the monks to yogurt. Now it is a week-long celebration with performances and picnics at Norbulingka, the former summer palace of the Dalai Lama. (Chinese propaganda claims that only nobles and monks saw these shows in the old days, but Harrer and others who lived in Tibet then insist that the grounds were open to everyone.)

The public opera today takes place under a big top, a traditional white tent with blue designs, while another, more exclusive, performance is held in an inner court. The big-top audience, who pay less than 10¢ U.S. to enter the grounds, form a pushing, heaving mass around the ring. I had to squeeze into this crush of people to see a performance at Norbulingka and there found that the most aggressive shovers were elderly women in braids. But it's possible to move passively, with the tide, and although I began by craning my neck to see around a tall man with a hat, the flow eventually deposited me in front of him. As a newcomer to Lhasa, I was still feeling the deficit of oxygen and wondering if the crush would allow me to breathe, but when the opera began there was no time to worry.

The performance was of *Prince Norsang,* one of a dozen traditional operas which retell Buddhist tales or enact the lives of great lamas. The acting was professional—polished, stylized, and sometimes slapstick, with the heroes, villains, and comic bumblers easy to spot even when you did not understand the dialogue. The dancing was simply Tibetan, neither Indian nor Chinese but with elements of both styles. Sometimes it was acrobatic, with movements designed to show off the performers' tassels and belts, the folds of bright brocade, and the winglike, drooping sleeves which covered the hands and served as banners to waft in the air. Sometimes the choreography was sedate, and once it resembled a cossack routine, with the men's skirts billowing into bell shapes to reveal pantaloons beneath.

Norsang had no yak scenes but other operas have wonderful comic routines where the "yak" (played by two actors, like a horse in vaudeville) dances and rolls over and butts the nomads who are trying to corral it. It is sheer, delightful slapstick and catches both the Tibetans' spirit of play and their close links to pastoral life.

In the old days opera performers were common folk who came to the city once a year to sing and dance during the Yogurt Festival. They inherited this duty and learned the skill from their parents and other relatives. Today they are professional performers who study in the TAR School of the Arts or at institutes in China proper.

But the roving, amateur spirit of Tibetan dance and song continues. In the Jokhang Plaza, pilgrims and locals perform for donations, and in rural areas old-style minstrels show up, dressed in traditional "hunter" costumes of triangular black masks and skirts with tassels hanging from the waist. One of these minstrels performed for us at a guest house in Nangkartse, near Yamdrok Tso. He was an elderly man who chanted in a high singsong, and he recited a folk tale. But my Tibetan companions could not understand what he was saying. Often the lyrics sung in the Jokhang Plaza are just as incomprehensible to Lhasa onlookers. Sometimes the performers speak dialects of Kham or Amdo which the locals can't understand; sometimes the words are in archaic language that the singers themselves only vaguely comprehend.

I watched one family troupe, however, that everyone plainly understood. It included a father playing a wooden flute, a mother beating a drum, three young boys, and a ghetto blaster. In one routine the father danced and mimed with the youngest son, a ragamuffin of four or five. The refrain was accompanied by obscene hip movements, which the boy performed with his father, and this sent the crowd into howls of laughter. The son carried out his routine with childish nonchalance; the father, a lanky man who obviously enjoyed his role, sang his lines deadpan and with a sense of comic timing.

The Jokhang's amateur dance groups always attract crowds. Tibetans are rarely too busy to take time out for a good performance, and it is this love of leisure which supports Lhasa's teahouses, pool halls, movie theaters, beer taverns, and, recently, disco clubs, karaoke bars, and video game parlors. Although barley beer hangouts and teahouses are longtime Tibetan institutions, the rest are incursions from China proper and the West. Many of them are pretty much restricted to male patrons, and a woman who visits a teahouse alone will be taken for a prostitute. Men idle away hours in these spots, downing cups of sweet milk tea, playing checkers or mahjong, talking, and, from sites like the Barkor, watching the crowds pass by.

Tibetans also like to pass their leisure hours in picnics. Usually they seek out a bucolic spot to set up a tent and spread out carpets and sweets, but sometimes they mark off an area on a busy street, using yards of cotton fabric which they wrap around supports to form four walls. Inside they will pass the day playing cards or mahjong or a dice game called *sho-gen*, drinking barley beer, singing, dozing, and eating. During the Yogurt Festival the grounds of Norbulingka fill with these impromptu corrals and tents of white canvas decorated with blue appliques.

I once spent a day picnicking with a Tibetan family at a riverside site outside Lhasa. It was during the four-day holiday to celebrate the founding of the People's Republic, and the family went in a truck and van loaded with rugs, a tent, a table, snacks, a mid-day meal, and drinks. When all was in place we sat on rugs under a traditional white and blue canopy and had our pick of tins filled with cookies, sunflower seeds, candies, peanuts, and fruits. There were barley beer in gallon containers, joint-venture Pabst Blue Ribbon, Chinese hard liquor, and soft drinks. The men spent the day playing mahjong, and at one point we all took the waters. Some of us dipped our heads in the icy river and washed our hair; others managed, with a degree of modesty, to bathe; and some scrubbed their clothes and spread them on the bank to dry.

That day I learned Tibetan drinking rituals, actually an arsenal of tricks to get everyone plastered. There is this one: New friends have to chugalug three times in a row each. (Fortunately the glasses are small.) And there is this: Each time I sing a song you have to drink a glass down. Or: Now you sing a song and we all drink. The only escape is to take off for a walk or pass out.

We also managed to eat: Chinese food reheated on kerosene burners. We ate rice and stir-fried dishes, using chopsticks. This is the rule in many Tibetan families today. They still eat tsampa, usually for breakfast, kneading the barley meal together with butter tea and eating it by hand. They also eat

Tibetan noodles and various soups—like the barley-beer soup with cheese and dried turnip that was our breakfast in Guchok. They go in for meat dumplings, cheese, yogurt, and fried sheep's lungs, all delicious and traditional fare (though the dumplings, I'm told, were long ago imported from China). And everyone loves butter tea, made by adding a pinch of salt to tea and churning it with butter; it's rather like tea with rich cream. But Chinese food and chopsticks are daily fare in urban Tibet, with some local twists, like yak meat in place of beef.

Only a few complain that this culinary invasion undermines the old culture; but some devout Tibetans refuse to eat fish, shellfish, turtle, and fowl. These were traditionally taboo even though fish and waterfowl were always plentiful. Others, however, will eat all of these—a distinct change from the past. But even Tibetans who pay no mind to the old prohibitions won't go near a fishing pole. When a pair of Chinese fishermen approached our picnic spot, the young boys were curious, but everyone else watched them in silence. Only a couple of villages on the Kyichu River were in former times allowed to break this taboo and only because the sites are unfit for pastures or fields and provided no other food source—or so I was told.

A handful of Lhasa restaurants have adapted to Western tastes. One opened in the downtown Banak Shol Hotel when I was there and immediately attracted every youthful backpacker in the area. It served yakburgers, pizza, spaghetti, and apple pie. Another restaurant, with the ambience of a Tibetan teahouse—packed dirt floors and ornately painted coffee tables—offered Tibetan food prepared Western style, that is, with plenty of vegetables. It also began to make cheesecake—an instant success—and put tsampa on the menu so tourists could try it with sugar and milk, like oatmeal. None of them could finish it off. It tastes okay; the flavor is nutty, and the texture is like cookie dough, but a little goes a long way.

Tourists began to show up in Tibet about 1985, and their numbers grew until the riots of 1987, when China forbade individual travel, allowing only tightly controlled groups. (Some savvy travelers managed to evade the ban, however, and came overland by bus.) In 1992, when China eased up again, Lhasa, Shigatse, and other "open" areas saw a new influx of Westerners—group tourists, who stopped only at the major temples and cultural sites, and adventurous cyclists and backpackers. They came from Australia, England, the United States, Holland, Portugal, Israel, Germany, France, New Zealand, Italy, and Scandinavia. Their arrival added a new threat to traditional Tibetan culture.

A French tourist, who first visited Tibet in 1986, told me that much had changed in six years. Tibetans, he said, used to charge visitors the same prices as local residents, but now many of them have come to see Westerners as sources of cash. The Tibetans were becoming more money-conscious. He was right about this attitude toward foreigners. As I passed through the streets of Lhasa I drew calls and even assaults from all sides: "Lookee, lookee, very cheap." "Hallo! Change money?" "Dalai Lama piksha!" and *"Kukyi, kukyi,"* which is the beggar's appeal for funds. When I was traveling I found that the rates for transportation and lodging were triple or even tenfold what citizens of the People's Republic were paying. Some of this is government policy; some of it comes from private entrepreneurs who have taken a cue from the Chinese.

The French visitor estimated that some two hundred backpackers and cyclists were staying in three Tibetan-run downtown hotels during the height of the tourist season in 1992. Many of them had to haggle with Chinese consular officials and border guards before they could make their way to Tibet; it was still on the books that travelers unattached to tour groups were forbidden. What, he asked, will happen if they really open the border with Nepal? So many Westerners are ready to come in from there; if they arrive, he said, Tibet will lose even more of its charm and Lhasa will become another Third World city with a McDonald's franchise and teenagers in blue jeans.

Many Tibetans worry about the worst aspects of modernization and Western culture that have invaded Lhasa. During the sixth assembly of the TAR branch of the Chinese People's Political Consultative Conference, held in May 1994, Lhasa delegates denounced the city's new "cultural markets" visible in the bars, karaoke clubs, discos, video halls, dance clubs, and increasing numbers of prostitutes. These were a bad influence on Tibetan youth and contrary to Buddhist values, they said. As a result, the city government came out with a new regulation requiring entertainment-oriented businesses to take out "cultural business permits." The permits oblige owners to "undertake to serve the people and socialism, pay attention to social benefits, and provide the people with rich, colorful, healthy, and beneficial cultural life."[8]

Many Tibetan artists and writers, however, are using the forms and materials of the West for Tibetan themes and settings. Artists who work in the modern style have learned to use oil paints, formerly unknown in Tibet, and the modern airbrush. They still paint religious images, but they have moved beyond copies of deities and mandalas into portraits of monks in meditation, prayer flags, *mani* stones (carved with sacred script), lines of pilgrims in the dim interior of a monastery, the devout prostrating themselves before the Jokhang. They use religious symbols—lotus flowers, skulls, rosary beads, ceremonial scarves, chalices—in abstract compositions.

They have also taken a new turn for Tibetan art by using secular themes. Nyima Tsering, a Tibetan painter from the Kham area of Sichuan, has compared this change to the Western Renaissance. "In the West, five hundred years ago there was a transition from entirely religious painting to art that included all kinds of subjects. In Tibet, we are just now starting to walk that road."[9] He himself has painted Tibetan deities in everyday settings, and he has been drawn to the "dignity and strength" of yaks, which were once thought too humble to appear in art. Other Tibetan artists paint Tibetan street scenes, portraits of nomads, women at work, still lifes, herds on the vast Changtang, and the weathered walls of village houses. They also recreate scenes from the past—Lhasa without a wheeled vehicle in sight, or noble women with their headdresses.

I only saw this art, however, at Tibet University, in offices, and on the pages of an art book published in Shanghai. I was told that individuals don't buy this art themselves, although many appreciate it and Tibet University teaches modern art along with the traditional.

When Tibetans, and Chinese with an interest in Tibetan culture, spoke to me about modern art and writing, they brought up the subject of politics and censorship. Since there is no public display of political dissent (no oil portraits of the Dalai Lama, for instance) they often commented on how far a particular artist or writer dared test the limits of censorship. They also told me about the occasional subtle signs of dissent which artists managed to work onto their canvases, images that were a kind of code only the artists knew, which they would interpret for trusted friends. A Lhasa artist, for instance, explained that he used images of monks to express his anger and sorrow over Chinese rule, knowing that other viewers would not be able to recognize this until he deciphered it for them.

Likewise they had no taste for the kind of art so prevalent during the Cultural Revolution: scenes of farmers mourning the death of Mao or an idealized version of the "peaceful liberation" of Lhasa with commoners beaming at the Chinese soldiers and the nobility skulking in the background. "I don't like that," said one Lhasa woman decidedly, quickly turning away each time she caught sight of such a portrayal. But some of this art is still published and displayed, along with works based on nonpolitical themes.

A Tibetan who takes up traditional crafts—painting thangkas and murals, carving altars and the elaborate New Year's butter sculptures, or casting statues in bronze—has little to fear from state censorship or official reprisals. The subject matter makes no overt comment on the political scene of today, and the details of these forms were set in centuries past. It is the artist's job to recreate the mandalas, landscapes, and Buddha figures as precisely as possible. They are intended for ritual and worship, not for individual expression, and directions for the composition of each work and its correct proportions, colors, and materials were recorded long ago for artists to follow. Only in Mindoling, a monastery near Tsetang, did I find drawings that seemed to come from the artist's own viewpoint. They were in a mural depicting lamas of the Nyingma order, and their postures and expressions caught the men in living motion, as if they were mingling in a bazaar.

But Mindoling was an exception. Elsewhere murals and statues resemble one another in temple after temple. The major figures are stylized, even rigid, but the backgrounds of many paintings are often full of lively detail. They may include pastoral scenes from mythic lands or the lives of saints, depicted with elephants, monkeys, birds, horses, yaks, and villagers. They are in reds, blues, greens, oranges, and yellows, and in the barren regions of central Tibet they stand out in brilliant contrast to the dun-colored landscape. In style they resemble Indian art with influence from China and Nepal.

Those who work in the traditional style often find commissions in the booming enterprise of monastery restoration. Many of these artists have been working throughout ethnic Tibetan regions, painting columns, roofs, lintels, and walls to recreate as precisely as possible the works destroyed during the

Cultural Revolution. It is this kind of traditional art which is most often seen in Tibetan homes and also sold to tourists.

Today these artists earn salaries and commissions; in the past they resided in a monastery or manor house and worked for room and board. It was forbidden to sell religious artifacts outright in the old Tibet, but these could be commissioned and there was a special term for such transactions. Now the same kinds of religious works are on display in the Barkor, offered to tourists and Tibetans for a price. The styles have remained unchanged, but the commercial art scene is new.

Tibetan writers have also taken up forms heretofore unknown, and they have altered old forms. Traditional literature was handed down orally and consisted of the famous *Gesar* epic, tales of folk heroes, and religious legends. Today Tibetans are writing novels and short stories, dramas, and "cross-talk," a Chinese comic style with two characters trading barbs and witticisms. Poetry has broken out of rigid metrical rules into a kind of free verse. The majority of Tibetan authors now write in Chinese.

Chinese and Tibetan readers gave me no clear consensus on the quality of this literature. One, for instance, said modern Tibetan literature is stagnant because writers have "so many political constraints." But the director of the Tibet Academy of Social Sciences, Majik, insisted that Tibetan literature has been flourishing since the 1980s.

Majik did say, however, that most novelists are setting their stories in the old Tibet, and this, according to other readers, is a sign that authors are avoiding current issues because of their political content. One told me that many novelists and short story writers take refuge in writing fantasy for this same reason. Still another said that Tibetan writing is now constrained by a defensiveness about Tibetan culture. "No one will admit that anything Tibetan is not perfect," she said.

Nevertheless, Tibetans are producing literature and others are reading their work. Lhasa novelist Tashi Dawa is among the most popular. He writes in both Tibetan and Chinese, and he turns out novels, stories, poetry, movie scripts, and cross-talk. He chooses modern settings with Tibetan characters, and his novels and stories are full of love intrigues and adventures.

One who writes exclusively in Tibetan is Sotse, the dramatist, who has written plays, cross-talk, and television dramas. At the end of the Cultural

Revolution he poked fun at the official absurdities of the era in a play titled *Poor People Becoming Richer*. It depicts an elderly peasant who is on his way to sell potatoes in Lhasa when he meets a trio of two officials and a "capitalist roader." The three bombard the old man with demands until he says, "I only grow potatoes in my own field and bring them to sell so I can buy butter for my tea." His helplessness spoke to Tibetans of their own experience. Writing the play was a bold move, one Lhasa resident told me, because Tibet had not yet emerged from the repression of the Cultural Revolution. But the timing was prescient, and, the Lhasa man said, Sotse's play helped "shift the society from the left to the right."

Sotse said his plays usually carry a didactic purpose. Thus, he has written about Lhasa's traffic problems, adultery, overindulgent parents, and idlers who pass their time in tea- or beer houses.

Amdowan novelist and short-story writer Danzhu Angben, a thirtyish associate professor at the Beijing Institute for National Minorities, has also tried to create characters who serve as models of virtue. "We believe novels should educate people," he said during an interview in his Beijing apartment. "For example, you might show that Tibetans are hardworking and show them struggling against natural forces." He thus wrote a historical novel set in Tibet's Tubo Kingdom—which ended more than twelve hundred years ago—to instill pride in Tibetan achievements. And since the kingdom played an important role in Central Asia, he also intended his work to "encourage people to learn foreign languages."

Like Sotse, Danzhu Angben criticized the Cultural Revolution just as it was losing favor. In 1980 he published a short story titled "Yayaya" about an old man who blindly follows authority—lamas and headmen in the old days and Communist officials in the modern period. "The moral of this story," said Danzhu Angben, "is that you should use your own mind to think and act." The play, which presents officials as fallible, would have drawn censure a few years earlier.

Novels, short stories, and cross-talk are forms borrowed from the Chinese, new vehicles for Tibetan themes. And the shapes of the books themselves have also changed. Printing was formerly done by monks using hand-carved woodblocks, and books were oblong, loose-leafed volumes with wooden covers. Today most Tibetan-language books appear in modern form, bound and printed by machine. The old-style printing still takes place in monasteries, but it is a slow process and confined mainly to religious texts.

Since the Cultural Revolution, publishing houses have turned out a high volume of Tibetan literary works, and journals printing poetry, short stories, and essays have appeared. Some of them are designed for specific Tibetan ethnic regions. In Gansu there is one titled *Moonlight,* for instance, and Kham has one named *Kangar Mountain.* Majik, director of the Tibet Academy of Social Science, claims that the proliferation of journals and other publications since 1980 has helped create a boom time for Tibetan literature, with new forms and content and the surge of energy that accompanied many endeavors when the Cultural Revolution ended.

The journals have provided outlets for young writers like Danzhu Angben, who got his start by publishing poetry and short stories in these reviews. But some Tibetans see a danger in the changes occurring today. Writers, scholars, and officials all caution that essential elements of Tibetan culture could disappear in the rush to adopt new forms. "We should use and preserve the best Tibetan folk literature," said Majik, "and also study modern theories of literature from here and abroad, and thus we should develop the best way eventually."

Traditional Tibetan literature drew its imagery from the mountains and villages, from the wilds and village life. Tigers, eagles, vultures, yaks, horses, warriors, and snowy peaks appear in the recitative, repetitive songs of ancient poetry. The early works were often tribal stories of hunting and taming the elements. Later works were edifying Buddhist tales and proverbs, but they used the same wild metaphors:

> *Tise, the icy mountain far renowned,*
> *Its head is covered up with snow; and this*
> *Stands for the whiteness of the Buddha's doctrine.*[10]

Sometimes these religious works contain domestic images, such as beer-brewing, a favorite metaphor of the poet-saint Milarepa quoted above. All this is essentially Tibetan, drawn from homey details, speaking to Tibetan experience.

But today Tibetan experience is changing. In city apartments where adults and children sit in the glow of a television screen, there is little room for the tales of village bards or for riddles and songs. Even peasant children are now more familiar with tractors than with wild yaks and eagles. The old poetry and tales speak of a people and land distant from today's Tibetans, who require new stories and forms to convey their own reality.

This is what Majik was referring to and what other scholars and writers speak of when they say Tibet must modernize and at the same time retain the best of its culture. But Tibetans say that the real question is: Who decides what is Tibetan? Who speaks for our deepest concerns? They note that everywhere in Tibet the Dalai Lama serves as a symbol of unity and hope, but Tibetan literature today (except for that of the exile community) can only mention him as a "traitor" to the motherland and a former "oppressor" of serfs. The influx of Chinese who now outnumber Tibetans in their own capital and the shooting of nonviolent protesters during the 1987–89 riots are anguishing topics for Tibetans. But they cannot publish their sorrow or speak of it onstage, or openly depict it on canvas.

Tibetan artists chafe at these restrictions, but it is not simply the heavy censorship that threatens their society. It is Tibet's minority status within China which creates the greatest risk. When Tibetan authors write in Chinese, they must adapt to Chinese tastes and in so doing adopt a Chinese point of view. As the Chinese language eases out Tibetan, even in the heart of the TAR, it deepens ties to Chinese culture and loosens those to the Tibetan way of life. And when history texts, museum displays, propaganda pamphlets, art, and literature all conspire to present Tibet as a longstanding minority region of a larger nation, reducing its kings to "ministers," and this further erodes Tibetan confidence and pride. The old Tibet, history texts imply, was so ignorant and backward that it could not reform itself, and thus it had to be the Chinese, not Tibetans themselves, who freed the society. In effect, China's version of history says that Tibetans were nothing until the Chinese came along. And Chinese cadres have said openly from the beginning that their own culture is more advanced. This chauvinism also tells Tibetans, subtly or overtly, that they still lag behind the rest of China, but that if they try, they too may become progressive—in other words, they may become Chinese.

It is this ingrained Chinese attitude of superiority which, many fear, will turn the TAR into just another province of China. If Chinese officials, and many Tibetans as well, equate modernization with sinification, Tibet will never find its own way to join contemporary society; it will opt for the Chinese way.

And as Chinese workers continue to arrive in the heart of Tibet, this peril grows constantly greater. The newcomers do not pick up Tibetan dress, speech, food, and attitudes. It is the Tibetans who gradually become more Chinese.

In Tibetan ethnic regions outside the TAR the process is already well advanced. A Qinghai Tibetan, for instance, told a Western reporter, "We Tibetans have no culture, no accomplishments, no history. We've accomplished nothing. Look at our educational level. So few Tibetans can read." Another was more upbeat, but his comments were equally disconcerting. "Now we Tibetans are literate and educated," he said. "Now we are just as good as the Chinese."[11]

A young monk from this same region told me that he too had once adopted Chinese values, but when he began to rediscover his origins, he looked toward Lhasa as the still-solid core of Tibetan culture. There stood the Potala, the Jokhang, and the great monasteries, and there Tibetans were living not in a Chinese province but in an autonomous region. He used to listen to radio programs from Lhasa, traditional Tibetan music with women singing religious and folk songs. Their voices seemed to come from the heart of Tibet, from beyond the mountains where the culture flourished intact. So it had seemed. But when he finally arrived in Lhasa it was 1987 and he found Chinese movies, music, and food; Chinese military trucks; Chinese soldiers on motorcycles. The great Potala had become a showcase, bereft of its purpose.

Lhasa is dying, he thought. Tibetan culture is dying. He had seen this happen to his home village in Qinghai. Now even Lhasa was losing its native character. "I give Tibetan culture fifty years," he said to me, and his was not an isolated voice of pessimism. Many thoughtful Tibetans agree with him. "Tibet is heading for extinction," another said, "within present history."

Young monk in a monastery overlooking the town of Namling

Village doctor Pempa Tsamcho and daughter, in the fields near Gyantse

A man from Lhokha walking the kora (sacred route) at Mindoling Monastery

Wandu, a nomad, at the Bagam Village School, near Damzhung

A student writing in Tibetan at Khartse School, Namling County

View from inside Zhalu Monastery, near Shigatse

The palace of Yumbulagang, destroyed in the Cultural Revolution and rebuilt in 1982

Chinese shop in the town of Namling

Feral dogs in Central Lhasa

*Family dance troupe performing in
...khang Plaza*

*Tibetan Muslim boys at the main
mosque in Lhasa*

Nuns from Penpo, east of Lhasa, chanting and soliciting alms at Norbulingka

Students at Guchok Village School, Namling County

Traditional drystone construction, Drepung Monastery

Drepung Monastery, with intact buildings standing beside the ruins from the Cultural Revolution

Harvesting barley in fields near Shigatse

Ancient iron bridge spanning the Namling River

8

The Children of Chenrezi
(Religion)

Tashi Wangchuk, stooped but still vigorous at seventy-nine years of age, welcomes me to his Beijing home, a Chinese house in the old style—sunlit rooms surrounding a courtyard, gray tile roofs that curl upward at the corners. He is a one-time high official, now retired, and he tells me how he joined the People's Liberation Army when it passed near his Khampa village during the Long March. As one of a handful of Tibetans to throw in his lot with the Chinese in those difficult days, he has remained a loyal Communist ever since, and when he served as chairman of the Qinghai government, he says, he struggled with the Party's most intractable problem among the Tibetan population—the ingrained devotion to lamaist Buddhism. Tashi Wangchuk calls it "the deeply rooted religious-belief problem," and he tells me, over a lunch of Tibetan dumplings and yak meat, that it is the result of poverty and ignorance. "We taught them natural sciences and improved their lives," he says, and thus "lessened the deeply rooted religious-belief problem."

Tashi Wangchuk knows the present line well, and he condemns the Red Guards who razed monasteries and used sacred art as paving stones during the Cultural Revolution. That doesn't work, he says; it just hardens the people's resistance, makes them cling to their faith. The best way is to let Buddhism die "naturally." Meanwhile, it is all right to use religion to gain the people's trust. When he visited Lhasa he kowtowed before the great Buddha in the Jokhang. Not that he really believed it; it was just an act of diplomacy. "Like President Reagan," he tells me, "when he goes to church and bows his head in prayer."

Tashi Wangchuk relates all this with a you-and-I-know-better air, as if I must certainly agree with him. Educated people are above that religious nonsense, his manner implies. In fact, although I am not a Buddhist, I am appalled. He is not the first official to speak this way, but he is the most direct, and his comments express the condescension and contradictions of China's official policy toward religion.

Three years after my visit to Tashi Wangchuk, the Chinese government played out this discordant approach for all the world to see when it spirited away a six-year-old boy named by the Dalai Lama as the reincarnation of Tibet's second-highest religious figure, the Panchen Lama. China then orchestrated the selection of his replacement. The captive boy has become a symbol of religious repression to Tibetans inside and outside the TAR, and a sign that China insists on controlling the practice of Tibetan Buddhism.

The Constitution of the People's Republic of China states in Article 36 that China's citizens "enjoy freedom of religious belief." It also declares, "It is impermissible to discriminate against any citizen who believes or does not believe in religion." But this does not mean the state cannot legally interfere in religious affairs. The constitution only protects "legitimate religious activities," and it forbids using religion for "counterrevolutionary activities." Moreover, these limited guarantees are not for every citizen. Party members are expressly forbidden to believe in religion. The PRC Penal Code is more forthright, declaring in Section 147 that "state officials who deprive people of their religious freedom or interfere with the customs and practices of minority nationalities in serious circumstances will be punished."

China has said repeatedly since the post–Cultural Revolution reforms took hold that the state protects religious freedom in Tibet. It also points to the funds it has spent to rebuild ruined monasteries. But exile groups and human rights monitoring organizations continue to criticize China's management of religious activities in Tibet. Reports by TIN and Human Rights Watch/Asia, Amnesty International, and the International Campaign for Tibet, all released in the spring of 1996, point to broad controls on religious practice, efforts to co-opt and manipulate religious leaders, restrictions on ceremonies and teachings, and arrests of monks and laypersons who oppose the government's handling of the Panchen Lama affair. In response, Shen Guofang of the Chinese Foreign Ministry reportedly said some of the events held up as examples of repression "never happened." He once more called attention to Tibet's economic growth and asserted that "religious beliefs have been protected; we have built many temples."[1]

One of the more revealing pronouncements on religious freedom appeared in a manual published by the TAR Communist Party as a directive from the Third National Forum on Tibet. "We . . . should never let religion spread unchecked," it stated. "There are monasteries which have been opened without permission from the authorities, and there is too much religious activity." It said that religion has interfered with productivity and that some Party members were "quite enthusiastic about participating in religious activities." To correct these problems the directive called on the government to expose the Dalai Lama's intentions to split Tibet from the motherland, "enhance the administration of the monasteries," and "teach Tibetan Buddhism about self-reform and teach them to adapt themselves to the socialist system." By the spring of 1996 attacks on religious belief grew even more shrill when a Xinhua article reported that some cadres "do not realize the deceitfulness, ignorance, and poisoning of religion."[2]

The Buddhism which the Chinese government would like to control for its own purposes came to Tibet from India during the seventh century, twelve hundred years after the Buddha's birth and long after the religion had reached China and other lands of the East. But in spite of its late arrival and some early setbacks, it eventually took firm hold, uniting a tribal society and opening the doors to the influence of India and other countries. As Tibetan Buddhism developed, it became an entire, complex universe, rich in symbolism, practices, literature, and philosophy. It belongs to the Mahayana school of Buddhism, which emphasizes the ideal of compassion and the doctrine of emptiness (a tenet proclaiming the interdependence of all that is). Practitioners gradually, over many lifetimes, work to attain enlightenment, a full understanding of these teachings, which releases them from the cycle of death and rebirth. At the same time Tibetans also embrace tantrism, which maintains that certain rituals can shorten the road to enlightenment. The four major Tibetan Buddhist sects vary in their emphasis on these paths. Some incline to the tantric and some to the long way of study and discipline, but all use elements from each.

Its particular brand of Buddhism is Tibet's chief pride and major preoccupation. Tibetans named their region of high plateau and rugged mountains "the Land of Faith," and in the debate over Tibet's place in the motherland of China, they have always said that they were teachers of doctrine while the Chinese were their patrons. The old Tibetan government was dedicated above all to supporting religion, and for decades sealed its borders against foreigners of other creeds. When the Communists finally breached the barricades, Tibetans called them "the enemies of faith," and when they began to flee into exile, they said their primary reason for leaving their homeland was to escape from Communist constraints on religion.[3]

The Communist government has always said that the religious establishment was a chief oppressor of the masses, and it is true that monasteries taxed their serfs, sometimes cruelly, and often acquired great wealth. But even though Tibetans were aware of this, they revered their lamas. They were reluctant to speak of monastic abuses even after they had fled Tibet into exile. Many refused to believe in Chinese evidence collected to expose monastic greed, or else they excused the monks on the grounds that they were probably unaware of their riches. They found the assaults on their faith demeaning and harsh and said that Communist ideology left them nothing to hope for, neither in this world nor in the next.[4]

The Chinese and their new converts answered that Tibetans were resisting out of ignorance. Education would change their minds, they said. But their critics were not necessarily credulous dupes of the religious establishment. One Tibetan who experienced both the old society and the new is Dawa Norbu, who writes in his autobiography that most monks were "mediocre, though sincere and religious enough," and "few of them lived up to their ideals." But at the same time Dawa Norbu denounces the cruel ridicule directed at the villagers' faith, and he gives evidence that Tibetan peasants could also see past the abuses of the institution to the true basis of their religion. He quotes an "enfeebled old woman," stung by the attacks from the new leaders, who says that the people are well aware of the difference between the true faith and its symbols. Through signs, she says, "the intangible is made tangible. They are the containers of our faith, the pegs upon which we can hang it, like the wooden pegs upon which we hang our ladles." Her response shows that even an unlettered peasant was capable of recognizing the gulf between the tenets of Buddhism and the abuses of the clergy.[5]

Not long after this scene took place, Dawa Norbu's family escaped to India, chiefly, as his mother said, because the Chinese had "deprived us of that most vital freedom" of religion. Likewise, at the end of the Cultural Revolution, it was the loss of religious freedom and the insults to their faith which Tibetans deplored most loudly.

Dawa Norbu was describing the period after the failed rebellion when zealous cadres in Tibet tried to strip religion of its power over the people—dismantling effigies of demons, exposing the wealth of the monks, and preaching materialism. At this time the International Commission of Jurists reported that China was committing religious genocide in Tibet by killing Buddhist leaders and outlawing the practice of Buddhism. But these assaults eased in 1962, and religious expression revived, to a degree. Then, during the Cultural Revolution, Buddhism (and every other faith) came under direct attack, and even the most trivial expression of devotion was banned. From 1966 to 1976 not a single prayer flag flew in Tibet. Mao's portrait hung in monastery chanting halls, and Marxist materialism was the only creed allowed.

And yet, as soon as the restraints eased, government officials learned that Tibetans had failed to conform to Marxist predictions that religion would disappear in the light of science and socialism. They poured out their fervor on envoys from the Dalai Lama, in pilgrimages, and in determined reconstruction of the razed monasteries. Although the Communists and some of their Western sympathizers had foreseen a swift end to lamaism (the few remaining monks would be the last, they said, and the old rites would die away), only a few decades later they had to abandon this prognosis.

This failure of theory, along with the central government's wish to prevail in the hearts and minds of its people, has evoked a testy, conflicted approach to religion from Party leaders. They make much of Tibet's new freedoms, but they still advance the atheist creed of Marxism. They also suspect that religious expression is more than individual piety, that it is a statement of defiance and separateness, and this deepens their distaste for the faith. Their suspicions are correct: Tibetan identity is linked to the practice of Lamaist Buddhism more than to language or geography or any other element of the culture. To be Tibetan is almost synonymous with being a believer (although a small percentage of Tibetans in Lhasa and Shigatse are Muslims, and some practice Bon, a religion that predates Buddhism in Tibet). To walk around the Lingkor turning a prayer wheel, to prostrate yourself before the Jokhang, to replenish butter lamps before an altar is to say, "I am not Chinese. I am Tibetan."

So today the government mistrusts and decries popular faith and tries to discredit Tibetan Buddhism while claiming to respect individual belief. It allows Tibetans to make pilgrimages and light butter lamps because suppression of religion hasn't worked and because China hopes to convince the rest of the world of its tolerance. At the same time the state fears the power of religion and wants to control it. And while it scorns "blind faith," it promotes unquestioning faith in its own creed.

China faces a further dilemma with Lamaism, which draws such fervent devotion from the country's Tibetans and Mongolians. Because the monasteries are the heart of resistance to Chinese rule, the government would like to forbid religious practice altogether. But this would alienate the people and invite all-out defiance, and it would also destroy the profitable tourist industry, which brought in $11.3 million in foreign exchange in 1995.[6] On the other hand, complete freedom would allow the monasteries to grow and become centers of nationalism. So China has decided to impose controls on monks but let laypersons perform their devotions while it subtly attacks their faith and waits for them to shed their "superstitions" in the light of scientific knowledge and material advancement.

When China takes aim at Tibetan piety, its targets include Bon, Tibet's native religion. The government places Bon followers—the Bonpo—in the same category as Buddhists, even though the two faiths arose from different foundations. A number of Bon devotees remain in Tibet, but their creed has absorbed so much from Buddhism that it is often hard for outsiders to tell the monasteries, rituals, and tenets of the two apart. The Bonpo, however, walk around sacred sites and spin their prayer wheels counterclockwise instead of clockwise as the Buddhists do, and they revere not the Lord Buddha but a founder named Shenrab. Bon was originally an animist cult teeming with spirits, and when Buddhism arrived its followers converted those beings for their own use and interpreted them in the light of their own philosophy. Tibetan Buddhism thus became populated with an array of deities taken from the native Bon as well as from Indian tantrism.

The crowd of benevolent and threatening gods peering from murals, altars, and thangkas may give the impression that Tibetan Buddhism is a superstitious cult. But the deities are not central to the faith. Behind them stands Lamaism's basic teachings, which hold that all beings can achieve enlightenment. And many of the cherished saints are *bodhisattvas*, great practitioners who have reached spiritual awakening but who renounce nirvana and choose instead to return to the round of worldly existence in order to work for the salvation of all. The reincarnations of bodhisattvas are called *tulkus,* and they are usually discovered as young children and brought to live in the monasteries of their predecessors. The great majority have been male. Tulkus and other highly learned practitioners including great teachers and doctors of Buddhist philosophy are called lamas, and for this reason Tibetan Buddhism is often called Lamaism.

The present Dalai Lama, the fourteenth, is the most revered tulku and is seen as the reincarnation of Chenrezi or the Bodhisattva of Compassion. His lineage goes back seventy-four lives to a Brahmin who lived at the same time as the original Buddha himself (also known as Shakyamuni), and he passed through several reincarnate lives in India before appearing in Tibet in 1391 as the first Dalai Lama. At that point his story became linked to Tibet's own origin legend. It goes like this: A hundred years after the birth of Shakyamuni, Chenrezi, in the form of a monkey, and the goddess Tara, in the form of a rock demoness, produced a tribe of monkey offspring. These gradually became human beings, set up a village, and began to sow barley. In time they peopled the entire land. Thus Chenrezi—and, in a sense, the Dalai Lama—became the father of all Tibetans and at the same time the patron saint of the Land of Snows.

The monkey legend is one of many Tibetan Buddhist tales, yet another myth in a tradition which encourages an abundance of stories, symbols, and forms, and it points up the procreative impulse of the faith, its fertility and inclusiveness. To walk into a Tibetan temple is to enter a realm where seemingly any sight, sound, smell, and shape might appear—as an icon, as an offering of praise and supplication, or as a symbol of demonic forces. A monastery shrine, for instance, may contain clothed and gilded statues of Shakyamuni, of previous Dalai Lamas, founders of sects, protective deities, and great lamas. These may be tiny figures encased in cubbyholes, like a collection of storybook dolls; or life-sized figures aligned on an altar; or immense sculptures many yards high. They are often draped with ceremonial scarves and jewelry, and they sit before an array of offerings—grain, tsampa, vessels containing water and barley beer, butter lamps of all sizes, money, flower bouquets, peacock feathers, photos of the Dalai Lama and Tibet's other great lamas, sprigs of dried grass, strings of white petals, and corncobs. The interiors of the shrines are dim, but the glow of butter lamps reveals brightly painted columns; thangkas; banners of pleated cloth in red, green, yellow, and white; stacks of scriptures; and—in the monasteries once famous for their warrior monks—decaying leather armor, rifles, knives, swords, and shields.

Murals in vivid colors cover the walls of monasteries and temples, and these may depict the thousand Buddhas (who are to appear on earth during this eon), guardian kings, pastoral scenes of the Pure Land (a Buddhist paradise), the lives of saints, mandalas, or protective deities (guardians of the faith). The latter usually flank the entryways to monasteries and look down on visitors with fierce and lowering expressions, crowned with skulls, holding a sword in one of their many hands, and surrounded by flames. (At first I found them grotesque, but later, when I thought of them as guardian attendants, I began to appreciate their power and savagery.) The walls may also contain niches for relics, scripture, and clay figurines. Some shrines are open to men only, and women who visit there sanctuaries must send in their hatas or butter for lamps with a male friend or a helpful monk.

Within the halls and shrines of the monasteries monks chant scripture and prayers, sometimes singly, sometimes in formal rows accompanied by bells and sonorous eight-foot-long brass horns. They may also blow on conch shells or chant in low vibrating tones. To enter a dim hall with its gilded figures seated in state on the main altar, its pillars wrapped in scarves and banners, its shadowy side altars ranged along the outer walls, and its flickering butter lamps—and there catch the sound of monks chanting in the recesses of the monastery—evokes a sense of occult power. Then it is easy to understand the awe of pilgrims who pass through the major shrines in long, snaking lines, touching their heads to the altars, rubbing their hands over the carvings, and leaving what offerings they can afford.

The faithful express their devotion and, many believe, gain protection from harm by going on pilgrimages and by performing dozens of acts of piety. They prostrate themselves before altars, temples, and high lamas; they circumambulate holy mountains and other sacred places, always clockwise; they burn offerings of incense in the morning, set up home altars, and donate money or labor to monasteries. They recite *om mani padme hum* or reproduce it in dozens of forms. This is the mantra of Chenrezi, which is a succession of syllables whose sounds have a vibrational quality. When repeated they help break down the illusions barring the way to enlightenment. Some interpret it as a prayer for the good of all sentient beings. Tibetans carve these sacred syllables on stones and yak skulls, which they use to build walls and cairns; they spell them out with white stones on hillsides; and they repeat the prayer endlessly by turning prayer wheels that contain other mantras and scriptures inside and "om mani padme hum" embossed on the outside. They suspend prayer wheels over streams so the words spin continuously in the current; they turn smaller prayer wheels in their hands, clockwise; and they send the mantra skywards in "wind horses" or prayer flags—squares of red, yellow, and green cloth on which the precious syllables and other prayers are printed. They string rows of prayer flags on cords and suspend them across streams and rivers and between mountain crags; they wrap them around columns, attach them to branches, and raise them over rooftops and shrines.

Tibetans honor previous Dalai Lamas, great teachers and practitioners, the founders of sects and monasteries, and the early kings who brought the faith to Tibet. They often pray to the goddess Tara, who in her green form represents the motherly aspect of compassion and serves as the patron goddess of Tibet and in her white form represents the fertile aspect of compassion, or generosity. They also honor local deities of fields and mountains, setting up small shrines of white stones in their barley fields and erecting larger structures at the boundaries of villages. They call to the spirits when they reach the tops of mountain passes, shouting *"Lha-gyallo! Lha-sollo!"* ("May the gods be victorious!"). And they pay homage to a throng of other entities, such as Manjushri, the bodhisattva of wisdom, and various tantric deities who are depicted in sculpture and in paintings copulating with their female consorts (thus symbolizing the union of wisdom with "skillful means" or compassionate action).

Tibetan Buddhism seems to embrace all that exists in the material and spiritual realms. In a stark land it provides a sense of endless possibilities, a teeming world of color and form against a backdrop of barren hills and valleys. It is a creed with few requirements for the mass of believers, and in its popular, lay form, one which prefers mystery to explication, a sense of awe over the rational, and the elusive over the tangible. Thus it allows legends, images, and rites to accrue in unruly abundance. It has given rise to oracles like the deity Nechung, who was consulted on every major decision confronting the old government. Nechung and other such beings spoke through mediums who went into trance during elaborate ceremonies. They are still consulted by the government-in-exile. And it has embraced fortune-telling, sorcery, and spirit possession. Although the Chinese government has forbidden these as "abnormal" religious practices, such beliefs persist in Tibet today, mainly in the rural and pastoral reaches.

And yet, despite the overlay of superstition and the pantheon of spiritual beings, Buddhist practice in Tibet is also disciplined, austere, and ascetic, especially in monastic life. Hermits retire to caves, and there contemplate the meaning of emptiness and detachment. Monks and nuns swear off alcohol, and many take vows of celibacy; they rise early in the morning to meditate alone in their rooms, follow prescribed rites and courses of studies, and read volume upon volume of commentary on the teachings of the Buddha. To become a doctor of Buddhist philosophy a monk must study for fifteen to twenty years and pass a series of increasingly rigorous examinations.

To the learned monks and nuns, the deities and gods are not malevolent and kindly spirits to call upon or placate with offerings; instead, they are symbolic figures, aspects of emotional energy which may be evoked during meditation. By learning to concentrate on mandalas that represent these beings, serious practitioners visualize the three-dimensional diagrams with the deities at their centers. The aim is to discipline the conscious mind in order to increase wisdom and compassion and, eventually, attain enlightenment. The mandalas themselves are also considered true images of ultimate reality.

In Tibet such training is reserved for those who enter monasteries and convents. I met not a single layperson who meditated, and the faith of peasants and nomads is especially superstitious and credulous. Near Samye Monastery, Tibet's oldest, we passed a miniature city of stone houses built on the side of a sand hill. Pilgrims had made these simple structures, none more than a foot high, out of a few flat rocks so that their souls would have dwelling places when they died. I tried to see it as a whimsical rite, a gesture not of belief but of tradition. Xiao Jin, however, said the builders took the business seriously. Above, in the main temple of the monastery, a sign listed seventeen blessed relics, including a statue of the goddess Tara "which has been known to speak" and the skull of the great master Shantarakshita. "When pilgrims pay their respects," a notice in English read, "they will receive the benefit of removing obstacles to life and health and ultimately be aided in realizing the four sacred embodiments of primordial wakefulness."

During our trip to Samye we gave lifts to various pilgrims and took with us an elderly aunt of Xiao Jin's husband who wanted to pay homage to Samye. As we drove over the back roads and made the rounds of monasteries, they mumbled their prayers, praising the saints and the goddess Tara. "This is a pilgrimage to Songtsen Gampo [the first Buddhist king]," intoned an old man from Kham. "This is a pilgrimage to Tara." He also recited a common prayer to the goddess. The elderly aunt prayed for protection. "I have had misfortunes in my life," she said to whatever deity she was invoking. "May these be cut away; may you protect me from more misfortune in the future."

They saw religion as insurance against harm, an appeal to higher authorities for the best deal in present and future lives. When I took this topic up with a monk, he smiled and said, "That is right, and unfortunately that is also the problem even with some monks. They are ignorant. They don't know that Buddhism is to change the mind slowly, slowly, over many lifetimes, to make a bad mind into a good one, to help us with right thinking, speaking, and acting." Another monk from Qinghai, now living in India, said to me, "I wish the people of Tibet could make their spiritual level higher. Between my teachers' lives and the people's lives I saw a long distance, a spiritual distance."

But even though much lay practice is superstitious and benighted, it buoys the people's spirits and gives them peace. The devout elderly, who often spend their final years making the rounds of temples and going on extended pilgrimages, appear content and kindly. And for Tibetans of all ages, religious rites provide drama, diversion, and festivity. There is, for instance, the autumn thangka festival at Drepung. Crowds pour out of Lhasa to watch the unveiling of an enormous, appliqued banner of silk, laid out on a hillside behind the monastery. As incense rises from the stony mountain slopes and rows of red-robed monks haul at the veil which covers the thangka, the figure of Shakyamuni slowly appears in brilliant color, surrounded by guardian deities and saints of the dominant Gelukpa sect, to which the Dalai Lamas and Panchen Lamas belong. A clang of cymbals announces the start of the unveiling, and sonorous horn blasts mark the full appearance of the Buddha, when at last a final yellow veil is drawn away from the face. The deep overtones of horns sound reverence and devotion, and then, in due and stately time, higher-pitched horns add a note of joy.

Lhasa is an empty city on this day. It seems no one is left in the heart of town. All the buses head for Drepung, and the steep road to the monastery is clogged with foot traffic. Many circumambulate the monastery and set up picnics on the grounds.

We found a similar spirit in Sakya, an ancient monastic town outside Shigatse when we arrived during a ceremony of masked dances performed by the monks of the monastery. Thousands of peasants from the surrounding countryside had come to watch the solemn dances and spend the day picnicking. They were dressed in their best and in a holiday mood, and some set up elaborate tents near the dance field.

In spite of the split between lay and monastic practice, Tibetan Buddhists come together during such events to celebrate their faith. And in their daily lives, the most devout make an effort to follow the precepts shared by all major religions—the admonitions to give to the poor, to tell the truth, and to harm no one. These maxims have left a mark on Tibetan behavior. Tibetans are liberal givers of alms and rarely show impatience with the pesky beggars of Lhasa. They are also generous with friends and visitors, pouring out gifts of fruit or sweets with overflowing abundance, giving away personal adornments and household items. I learned to hold back on praise when I visited Tibetans; I was too likely to find the owner taking off a pin or picking up a bowl and insisting I take it with me. Giving is considered an act of compassion, and this is the precept I most often heard from devout Tibetans: "Be compassionate." Although many lacked a full understanding of their creed, they often took the major precepts to heart.

Another maxim, which prohibits the taking of any life, places Tibetan Buddhists in a dilemma. In Tibet's harsh climate and terrain there is little to eat besides barley and meat—sheep, yak, beef, wild game, and, in some places, pork. Tibetans must slaughter their animals to supply themselves with enough food for the year, but their creed labels this a sin. In the past, they solved this problem by creating an outcast group of butchers or calling on Muslims to do the job. During the Cultural Revolution, however, nomads and farmers were forced to kill their own animals. Since then some have continued to do this chore themselves, but others now pay poorer nomads and peasants to do it for them. Even those who choose this solution, however, often recognize the inherent conflict between eating meat and practicing their faith, and they take it as a contradiction they have to live with.

The government and Party view this vast world of Tibetan Buddhism, with its array of spirits, its color and vitality, and its path of contemplation and good deeds, as a threat. They give the faith little credit for its teachings of compassion and pacifism. These tenets are scarcely mentioned in the government's literature on religion, which tries to maintain an impartial tone and at the same time subtly belittle Buddhists and their creed. Buddhism, according to a government pamphlet, took hold in Tibet because the nobles and monks forced it upon the people. "People had no choice," the pamphlet reads, but to accept the only religion—Tibetan Buddhism. (The pamphlet is incorrect in saying the people had no choice. In Kham some Tibetans became Christians, and in Lhasa and Shigatse, Tibetan women married Muslim traders and converted to Islam. Moreover, Bon has persisted through the centuries in spite of its early rivalry with Buddhism. [7]) In its choice of illustrations the pamphlet emphasizes the more bizarre features of Tibetan Buddhism: the fierce protective deities; a savage tantric figure with two heads and sixteen arms, depicted coupling with his consort; a dancer with a deerhead mask performing a ceremony to drive away ghosts. A caption beneath the photo of a nun spinning a prayer wheel in a sooty cave notes, with barely concealed sarcasm, that she is "cultivating her moral character."[8]

In a booklet titled *Social History of Tibet, China*, provided by the Cultural Palace of Nationalities in Beijing, religion gets scant attention, except for two macabre paragraphs listing human and animal parts used in ceremonies. One ritual required "four human heads, ten sets of human intestines, pure blood, impure blood, earth from ruins, widow's menstrual blood, leper's blood, various kinds of meat and flesh, human and animal hearts," and more. Another required "a set of human intestines, two human heads, blood, and a whole human skin." The Chinese government is content to give the impression that Tibetans conducted ritual human sacrifice, and it also fails to date these passages, which could have been written many centuries in the past.[9]

It is true that tantric ceremonies—esoteric rites to attain spiritual power—sometimes call for human skulls as drinking vessels and thighbones as ritual objects, but these are easily come by without resorting to murder. Tibetans have traditionally disposed of their dead in "sky burial," cutting the corpse into pieces and feeding it to vultures at sacred funeral sites. This is considered the ultimate sacrifice, the giving of oneself to nature, and it is performed by monks who pray as they carry out the final rites in prescribed order. It may be grisly, but this is the worst that can be said about it, and even today it provides tantric practitioners (and tourists) with a source of human skulls and bones. The flesh and blood for the ceremonies listed in the *Social History* were most likely acquired in the same way, and the rituals themselves, though bizarre, were probably of the kind that certain tantrists performed. By handling what is normally taboo, they aimed to break down the barriers of illusion, exorcise demons, and confront their own fears and rage. The Cultural Palace booklet makes no effort to explain any of this and lets the two passages stand as its sole comment on religion in Tibet.

The subtle and blatant put-downs of Tibet's faith may be offensive, but Tibetans consider them less of a threat than government control of monasteries, religious associations, and Buddhist leaders. This last tactic is an effort to win over the masses by promoting and publicizing major religious figures who have joined ranks with the government. (The Party has used the same strategy with the aristocracy in minority areas, preaching the primacy of the working class while joining up with its alleged oppressors.) Even as they attack religion, they proudly bring forth Buddhist leaders who collaborate with them—or seem to do so. In *Tibet Transformed,* published in Beijing, author Israel Epstein dismisses Tibetan Buddhism as the benighted fantasies of the ignorant and brands it as an "exploiting system" and "an ingenious political tool" which once imposed "theological terror" on the masses. And yet, along with liberated serfs and smiling Party leaders, the book features photos of

Dorje Phagmo, a woman tulku (identified as "Tibet's only female Living Buddha") who returned from India and took a position in the government, and of the Tenth Panchen Lama, then a member of the National People's Congress. The Panchen Lama is shown reading Buddhist scriptures.[10]

The Tenth Panchen Lama is the best known of those Buddhist leaders who fraternized with the Chinese government. His link to China goes back in history to his predecessors who played the Chinese off against the Lhasa rulers to secure their own power. He grew up in a Chinese-controlled area and was courted by the Communists when they took command. His monastery, Tashilhunpo in Shigatse, had always—until 1995—received lenient treatment from the government, but the Panchen Lama also spoke out against the excesses of religious persecution and intervened on behalf of monks who ran into trouble with the authorities. He died at Tashilhunpo in 1989 at the age of fifty-one. (Some Tibetans say the circumstances of his death are highly suspicious, coming just after he spoke out for the Dalai Lama's return.)

From the beginning, the Communists tried to promote the Tenth Panchen Lama and insisted that he was "co-leader" of Tibet along with the Dalai Lama. In fact, the Panchen Lamas traditionally governed a fiefdom much smaller than that of the Dalai Lamas and held less secular power. Today, the Tenth Panchen Lama's portrait appears in government publications as if he is the chief object of reverence among the people, while the Dalai Lama is either ignored or mentioned in texts as a traitor to the motherland. Tibetans themselves, especially those who live near his base, Shigatse, admire and pay homage to the Panchen Lama, but the Dalai Lama is first in the hearts of all Tibetans.

The Tenth Panchen Lama now sits in state at Tashilhunpo, his mummified body gilded and clothed in brocade. He, like his predecessors, has his own stupa within the monastery grounds and also a memorial hall, paid for in part by government funds. These structures and their occupant now overlook the grounds where a mass revolt took place in 1995, only to be swiftly and harshly put down by truckloads of troops.[11]

Immediately after the Tenth Panchen died, China and the Tibetan government-in-exile both began the search for his reincarnation. The head of the Chinese government–appointed search committee was Chadral Rinpoche, a tulku respected by Tibetans. He was the abbot of Tashilhunpo and the head of the Democratic Management Committee of the monastery, an organization set up by the government to run the affairs in each religious house. Like the Tenth Panchen Lama, he walked a fine line between observing government-required formalities and serving his faith. He kept the nationalist sentiments of his monks in check; the monastery was never chastised as others had been for contributing to antigovernment demonstrations; it appeared to thrive, with a large population of monks and a series of building projects. The government rewarded Chadral Rinpoche with a house and an expensive car.

From India the Dalai Lama tried to send delegations to Tibet to aid in the search for the Eleventh Panchen, but the government refused his requests. The Chinese did, however, allow Chadral Rinpoche to send him an official letter in 1993, requesting his guidance and giving some details of the search. In Dharamsala, the Tibetan religious hierarchy consulted the oracle Nechung on how to proceed.

In the tradition of the Gelukpa order, to which both the Panchen Lama and the Dalai Lama belong, reincarnations are found through divination: dreams, ritual, visions, visits to a sacred lake. These and reports about possible candidates help narrow the search to certain regions and households where likely boys of the right age are found. The searchers then visit the homes of the most promising candidates and subject them to various tests: offering them possessions of the former lamas to see how they will react, conversing with them, and having them draw lots.

The results of this process pointed to six-year-old Gendun Chokyi Nyima, from Lhari District in Nagchu, a nomad area. He appeared to be the Eleventh Panchen Lama, the tenth reincarnation of the original Panchen Lama who had first been born in the fifteenth century. Some in Tibet say that the boy bore on his arms the marks of ropes that bound the Tenth Panchen during a struggle session, that he greeted an aged monk from Tashilhunpo as an old friend, and that his first words in infancy were, "I am the Panchen; I sit on a high throne."

In Dharamsala the Dalai Lama received word of the boy and consulted the Nechung oracle, who twice verified that Gendun Chokyi Nyima was the true reincarnation of the Panchen Lama. Some say that Chadral Rinpoche and his search committee were favoring the same child; others say it is uncertain whether the boy was ever on the official list of candidates. But whatever the circumstances, on May 14, 1995, before either the search committee or the Chinese government could announce the final decision, the Dalai Lama declared that the boy from Nagchu was the authentic reborn Panchen Lama. Soon after this Chadral Rinpoche was arrested; he has been detained ever since.

One report has it that the search committee had already chosen the new Panchen and leaked this news to the Dalai Lama, that the Chinese learned of this and withdrew the boy's name, and that the Dalai Lama then decided to announce the discovery of Gendun Chokyi Nyima. Another report says that the central government and Chadral Rinpoche were at odds over government demands that the committee select the boy from lots drawn from a golden urn—a procedure, the Chinese said, established long ago by the emperor (but actually used only twice to select a Panchen Lama and never before in the Jokhang). Hearing that Chadral Rinpoche was in difficulty over this, the Dalai Lama made his announcement.

In any case, the young child disappeared soon after his name was released to the world. Witnesses say that security police appeared at his home and escorted his family to Nagchu airport. No one has seen them since, and for over a year Chinese officials denied any knowledge of where he was. They also tried to vilify the boy and his family, charging that he once drowned a dog and that his parents are "notorious among their neighbors for speculation, deceit, and scrambling for fame and profit." The Dalai Lama was denounced for "his vicious intention of disrupting Tibet's stability and undermining China's national unity through religious means." Then, under pressure from the UN Committee for the Rights of the Child, the government announced in June 1996 that Gendun Chokyi Nyima had been "put under the protection of the government at the request of his parents" because he was "at risk of being kidnapped by Tibetan separatists."[12]

After the arrest of Chadral Rinpoche, fifty Party officials moved into Tashilhunpo Monastery to scrutinize the monks, trying to discover any signs of opposition to the government. Those who rejected Gendun Chokyi Nyima as the reincarnate Panchen Lama were granted extra food rations. Those who refused were warned to change their attitude. In July the monks were assembled to hear Party chiefs read a denunciation of their former abbot, Chadral Rinpoche. The loyal monks jeered, and many refused to sign a proclamation denouncing the abbot. The next morning police moved in to make arrests. Pilgrims waited outside the gates, which remained closed while truckloads of police passed through the crowd. In the late afternoon six military trucks and two jeeps drove into the monastery, and that night police went to hotels in Shigatse telling tourists to leave town the next day.

As a result of the crackdown more than thirty monks were taken to Shigatse's main prison. They arrived badly bruised and bleeding, some with broken teeth. The Chinese announced that Chadral Rinpoche was undergoing medical treatment and had been removed from his post. More monks were arrested in following weeks.

Finally, six months after the Dalai Lama announced that six-year-old Gendun Chokyi Nyima was the Eleventh Panchen Lama, the central government convened a group of selected Tibetan Buddhist leaders in Beijing, held them under guard in a military hotel, and demanded that they agree to choose a new Panchen Lama by drawing names from three contained in the golden urn. Prime Minister Li Peng was to have final approval. It is said that some monks continued to resist and upheld the right of the Dalai Lama to recognize the Panchen Lama's reincarnation, but the new leadership of Tashilhunpo was compliant. Official photographs published in Chinese newspapers show the monks lined up behind President Jiang Zemin with Liu Huaqing, deputy head of the Central Military Commission, in full uniform.

Two weeks later, in late November, the government staged a chilly predawn ceremony in Lhasa's Jokhang cathedral with armed guards stationed on the roof. It began with a senior Chinese official dressed in suit and tie reading a firm warning to the assembled monks that religious decisions are only valid if approved by the government. Then an elderly monk reached inside the urn to extract the name of six-year-old Gyaltsen Norbu written on an ivory tile. The procedure was broadcast on state television, showing a wide-eyed child in a yellow silk hat handing a ceremonial scarf to Deputy of State Council Li Tieying. To one side stood a row of smiling Chinese in business suits, a world apart from the red-robed monks who avoided the camera with bowed heads and downcast eyes.

In December Gyaltsen Norbu was enthroned in Tashilhunpo monastery, then taken to Beijing where he was photographed with the Chinese leadership. Since then the Chinese have released news stories aimed at bolstering the status of their chosen Panchen. Xinhua quoted a Tashilhunpo lama, Kenchen Tsering, as saying that pilgrims are flocking to the monastery and that some have been moved to tears by the boy. "All Tibetan Buddhists trust this choice," the lama is reported to have said.[13]

In fact, Tibetans have no regard for the government's choice. They call him "the Party Panchen," because it is said that his parents are staunch Party members and not practicing Buddhists. Gendun Chokyi Nyima's photo is secretly reproduced and held with reverence inside Tibet. Tibetans say that the people of Lhasa and Shigatse (the seat of the Panchen Lama), once longtime rivals, are now united by a sense of common opposition to the Chinese. And the government, in spite of its claims that the people are accepting the official choice, is taking no chances: Gendun Chokyi Nyima, who turned seven in April 1996, was still missing, along with his family in the fall of that year.

When I was in Lhasa another young Tibetan boy, a Khampa nomad, was enthroned as the reincarnation of a high lama. The ceremony took place at Tshurpu Monastery outside the capital, and although it was not without controversy, it was held in public view during daylight hours, unlike the ceremony set up for Gyaltsen Norbu. Both the Dalai Lama and the government had approved this child as the reborn Karmapa, head of the Kagyupa sect, and his arrival in Lhasa and investiture at Tshurpu brought out crowds of the devout. Although his was no predawn, tightly controlled ritual, some followers of the Kagyupa sect dispute his selection, and they have enthroned a second Karmapa in Sikkim.

The Tibetan Karmapa is named Ugyen Trinley. He was eight years old at the time of his installation in 1992, and he now carries the title of the Seventeenth Gyalwa Karmapa. Tradition holds that the second Karmapa, recognized in the thirteenth century, was the first tulku in Tibet's history. The lineage is revered as an incarnation of the active aspect of Chenrezi, and the Kagyupa sect is the smallest of the four major orders in Tibetan Buddhism. (The others are Geluk, Nyingma, and Sakya.)

Whether the boy is a genuine rebirth of the Gyalwa Karmapa or not, it is true that the Chinese have made much of his discovery and enthronement. Government dignitaries were present at the hours-long rite, and the government is quick to mention the enthronement as evidence that Tibet enjoys freedom of religion. The installation ceremony also appeared several times on state-run television. A few weeks before it was held, pictures of the boy—appearing well-fed and imperious—showed up in restaurants and homes in Lhasa and on vendors' tables in the Barkor.

But even those who accepted Ugyen Trinley as the true Karmapa were grumbling that the government was courting the Kagyupa, especially the young incarnate's regents—who will run the sect until the boy reaches maturity—by providing cash to renovate and paint the monastery and by handing out other perks. A Western visitor who made a journey to Tshurpu shortly before the ceremony claimed that the monks there had sold out and were solidly pro-Chinese. And a young Lhasan told me, "The Karmapa has been approved by the Nationalities and Religious Affairs Commission, and he will be a Chinese puppet like the Panchen Lama. In twenty years this Dalai Lama will be gone, and then the Karmapa will be old enough to be a tool for them." He sighed. "The Chinese are very clever." A monk agreed. "Yes, that is what we are afraid of," he said, "that they will take him to Beijing and make him side with them."

But Tsurphu's monks may not be so compliant as the Western visitor suspected. In October 1994 after the young Karmapa made an "apparently forced" visit to China proper and reportedly said he supported the Party and prayed for Mao Zedong, at least some of the monks protested and five were arrested.[14]

In spite of the controversies, Tsurphu, which lost its highest tulku in 1959, now has him back again. Other monasteries are less fortunate. In many throughout Tibet the reincarnations of founders and great teachers are no longer honored in the flesh but in faded photographs placed reverently on altars. "We have no tulku now," said a monk at Sakya. "One is in America, and one is in India." At Zhalu Monastery outside Shigatse a monk said the community lost its only reincarnate lama when he fled after the rebellion. He died in exile, and his successor was found in India.

Since 1959 the TAR has lost most of its lamas. Nobody could tell me how many reincarnates there used to be or even how many there are now, but all agree there were once thousands. Drepung Monastery, for instance, had 600, but now the entire Lhasa area has no more than thirty. During the Qing dynasty (1644–1912) a census found 160 highest rank tulkus in all of Tibet, but today there are only a handful.

The tulkus began to disappear after the rebellion of 1959, when Chinese officials sent monks to prisons and work camps, abolished the serf system, and forbad the recognition of new reincarnations. Hundreds of tulkus fled over the Himalayas, following the Dalai Lama. Some remained in Tibet but left their monasteries, married, and took up secular lives. I ran into several in Lhasa and Chengdu; they had all gone into teaching, research, or publishing.

When the Cultural Revolution arrived, and the Red Guards forced many monks and nuns to disrobe and marry, hundreds, perhaps thousands, went into hiding, going about in laymen's clothes and working in the fields and factories. Some of them joined an underground circuit, staying in the homes of devout Tibetans who took turns sheltering them. A young Amdowa from Qinghai told me that when he was a schoolboy he discovered refugee lamas hiding out in a shed on his family farm. They sat in the dark storage shack, reciting mantras, and they spoke to him of their religion. But they refused to teach him to write Tibetan. If they did, they said, it could lead to their discovery and arrest.

When one of these tulkus in hiding passed away, there was often no way to search for his successor. And as others became secular teachers or researchers, they lost the aura of sanctity, and this undermined their lines of succession as well. In the late 1980s, however, China, relaxed its policy and allowed the naming of several obscure tulkus without interfering in the process. Minor tulkus are returning to all areas of ethnic Tibet. Likewise, in the West and among the exiles in India and Sikkim, reincarnations are still appearing. Several have been found in Switzerland, where there is a large Tibetan exile community; others have been recognized in Bhutan, Spain, Seattle, Maryland (a female reincarnate), and California. Some have also been identified in Tibet and smuggled out to India, and a few tulkus from India have quietly made their way back to Tibet. China, which views tulku succession as a political game rather than a spiritual tradition, protests whenever a reincarnation is discovered outside its borders.

The tulkus are among the thousands of monks who have disappeared since the failed rebellion, and the drop in numbers has transformed Tibet's monasteries. Before 1959 at least 15 percent of the male population was assigned to monasteries, and altogether there were from 110,000 to 133,000 monks and nuns in two thousand monasteries in central Tibet (not counting those in Amdo and Kham). A year after the rebellion half of them were gone; the population had dropped to fifty-six thousand in seventeen hundred monasteries. And by the end of the Cultural Revolution the numbers had sunk to a fraction of what they had been before. Only eight monasteries and nine hundred monks and nuns had survived those years. (A dozen monasteries remained in all Tibetan areas.)[15]

But since the mid-1980s, young Tibetans have been choosing religious life again. In 1992 the government counted forty thousand monks and nuns in fourteen hundred monasteries, a fortyfold increase in little more than a decade. But in spite of the revival, the population is still below the 1960 count and represents only a fraction of the pre-1960 census.

Some say the change has led to at least one advantage over the old days, when families sent boys to join monasteries at the age of seven or eight: Many of them would never have chosen to spend their lives in prayer, but now most new monks enter religious life on their own. As a group, the monks of today are more dedicated, better practitioners of Buddhist precepts. (Nuns were always a smaller proportion of the population, and even in the old days most of them freely chose the religious life.) "I think almost all monks are more obedient to the *dharma* [Buddhist way] now," a young monk told me, "and they treasure the religion more."

Tibetan exiles say that independence would not bring back the old system in monasteries. The numbers would be higher than they are now under government constraint, but they would never return to the pre-1959 levels. Church and state would be separate, they say, and freedom of religious choice and practice would be guaranteed. In this independent Tibet, the monasteries would support themselves with donations and the labor of the monks, as the exile monasteries in India do now.

No one expects the monasteries to grow to their former size, and the loss of numbers appears to be a permanent change in the once powerful monastic system. Some of the great monasteries of Tibet now have less than a tenth of their former populations. Drepung, which had an official census of 7,700 and an unofficial count of ten thousand,[16] said they had five hundred when we visited in 1992. Sera, which once had 5,500 officially and something like seven thousand unofficially, said they had four hundred; Samye, the region's first monastery, which once had three thousand, told us they had 120.

Tashilhunpo had nearly eight hundred monks in 1992, making it the largest monastery in the TAR: at its peak it housed four thousand. And then there are hundreds of small monasteries which have never revived. Guchok Village once had two small establishments, a monastery and a nunnery, but these are in ruins now, and there are no plans to rebuild.

Still, the numbers are up since the early 1980s and continuing to rise, and visitors to the eastern regions say the religious revival is even stronger there. In Chengdu I heard of one Kham monastery now up to a third of its former strength, and one which is even larger today than it was in 1951, up to seventy monks from a former count of fifty. In Amdo, Kirti Monastery is also over its earlier population, with two thousand monks in 1990 compared to 1,800 in 1959.

The counts would be higher if the government did not interfere in monastic affairs. It is unwilling to let the monasteries and convents grow to their full potential, which, if the authorities left them alone, would be determined by the number of applicants and the amount of money donated by the laity for their support. China uses quotas, expulsions, and limits on registration cards to keep the numbers down.

The Nationalities and Religious Affairs Commission sets up ceilings for all monasteries and nunneries—six hundred at Drepung, five hundred at Sera, four hundred at Ganden, and one hundred at the Jokhang Cathedral, I was told by an official of the committee. Anyone wanting to legally enter a monastery or nunnery needs approval from the Religious Affairs commission, his or her work unit, local officials, and provincial officials as well as the monastery. With these endorsements in hand a novice who has moved from the countryside to a Lhasa monastery should be able to get a new registration card. That would be a simple procedure in other government units, but it is not so in religious houses. There the government seems to purposely delay and obstruct, and few new monks and nuns have the papers they need to live legally in the city. At Ani Tsamkung Nunnery, with ninety-nine residents, only three elderly nuns had registration cards. At Ganden, of the four hundred residents only the abbot and a few of the older monks had registration. Drepung monks said they had one hundred registered out of a population of five hundred; and at the Jokhang, they said they were above 50 percent, with forty-three registered out of eighty-four. Monks and nuns without official residency are vulnerable to security sweeps. After major riots police have entered monasteries and sent home members who lacked local registration.

At Ani Tsamkung abbess Tenzin Sangmo said that each year the number of applicants grows, and the convent could take in more but it lacks the space to house them. "We don't have room in the hall for everyone to sit when we have prayer in common," she said. The nunnery once owned some rooms across the cobbled alleyway from the main building, but these were confiscated during the Cultural Revolution, and now, even though the convent has applied to the government for their return, the rooms have not been given back.

The government has also expelled monks and nuns arrested in demonstrations or suspected of pro-independence activities are expelled; and many monasteries have lost their most promising scholars and leaders this way. "Many of the nuns who went to prison," said the old abbess, "were really good nuns, very, very smart. It's a pity for them because they had a real future." At Drepung a monk said, "Many, many monks have gone to prison because of the riots. Two hundred were sent away." They were among the best students, another monk said, and although Drepung leaders pleaded for their return, the government refused. Some were sent back to their villages under a kind of house arrest, and there many still wait, hoping that the government will relent. But others have given up and married, and still others have fled to India.

Monasteries also lose out on restoration funds when their members join demonstrations. Although monasteries run mainly on voluntary donations from the laity, the government has financed the rebuilding of major sites damaged during the Cultural Revolution. But at Ganden and Drepung, which qualify for restoration money, monks said frankly that the government has held back on funds due them because some of their members took part in protests. Officials told them to clean up their act first. Some of Ani Tsamkung's nuns have also marched against Chinese rule, so it is no surprise the convent is having trouble getting its confiscated apartments back.

Ani Tsamkung, which was trashed and used for thamzing (the "struggle sessions" staged to punish counter-revolutionaries) and Red Guard meetings during the Cultural Revolution, receives no money for restoration work. Individual donations have paid for all of the cleanup, rebuilding, and painting. This is the case at most monasteries, even though the government reports spending millions of yuan on reconstruction. It is true that the prominent sites such as the Potala, the Jokhang, and Tashihunpo in Shigatse have received government money, but these are on the tourist circuit, and—with the exception of the Jokhang—most have played no role in the independence demonstrations. At Tashihunpo—considered to be a compliant monastery before the Panchen Lama affair—a lavish stupa and a memorial hall for the deceased Tenth Panchen Lama went up with the blessing and funding of the government.

Although the government finances restoration work at some sites, it holds that monasteries should all become self-supporting. The only monks and nuns who receive salaries are the few who serve on Democratic Management Committees, the administrative councils of the larger monasteries. The others are supported by their families, donations from the laity, and whatever else the monks can do to bring in cash: guiding tourists, making amulets and other religious objects, charging fees to enter the temple and to take photographs.

The government discourages contributions to monasteries but allows them if they are "freely given and small in quantity." When the gifts are, in China's view, too many or too large, officials have campaigned against religious donations. One document called the practice of generous gift-giving "shocking," and said it was the cause of "broken families, stealing, high interest loans, factionalism, increased instability . . . and a damaged image of Party and government." Officials have also acknowledged, however, that 90 percent of Tibetan Buddhist monasteries are built with private donations and 90 percent are run on donations from the general population.[17]

When monks and nuns take part in protests, they not only jeopardize restoration funds but also bring on tight government control. In 1992 Drepung was under especially heavy surveillance. Many of its monks took part in the early protests, and it had not only lost members, it was also under guard. Both times I visited Drepung, I saw armed police standing, guns at the ready, at the entry driveway, and security forces hanging about with two-way radios. Drepung, Sera, Ganden, and other monasteries, like Zhalu near Shigatse, have been in trouble because a few of their monks raised their fists and shouted, "Chinese go home!"

Government control has also cut into the numbers of school-age monks. In the old Tibet boys typically joined a monastery between the ages of seven and ten, but today you see few boy monks, especially in the urban centers. Tashilhunpo seemed to be an exception. I saw many there who were perhaps ten to twelve years old—even though the government forbids monasteries to admit anyone under eighteen. (Major tulkus like the Karmapa and Panchen Lama are apparently exempt.) Away from the cities some monasteries were taking boys at the traditional age of seven or eight. But near Lhasa, where control is tight, I saw very few under the legal limit, and those were in their teens. (The older monks always said the young ones were "temporary" or "not real monks.")

Before 1959 monasteries included monks of all ages, the larger establishments were organized into colleges, and the best students trained under accomplished masters and doctors of Buddhist studies. Most monks learned to read but not to write,[18] and many worked as servants for those of higher status. Today, however, monasteries have a few older monks, almost none who are in their forties and fifties, and plenty of men in their twenties. With many of the well-trained lamas living in exile and only a few elderly ones left to pass on traditions, the monasteries have no way to teach doctrine and perform rites as they did before. And with new government policies that put almost all monks to work at least part of each day, they have less time for study.

When we visited Zhalu Monastery outside Shigatse the community had two monks in their seventies and more than sixty in their twenties (not counting five who were dismissed for taking part in demonstrations). In the old days Zhalu had a repertoire of fifty-two ceremonies, such as ritual dances and offerings on festival days, but now they can only perform five. "There is no one to supervise and teach the rest of them," a young monk said. Ganden in 1990 had only two philosophy teachers: it once housed hundreds.

Without the older generation of teachers, monasteries can't impose the discipline they once required. "It is much more lax than it was in the past," said Shenyen Tsultrim, a lean, scholarly former monk now at the Tibet Academy of Social Sciences. "The teachers don't follow strict regulations now." At Ani Tsamkung, abbess Tenzin Sangmo said, "It's very bad now. Before it was very strict; they prayed and studied. Now they have to work for a living and go out and get exposed to many influences. I don't know what to do with so many young people. Discipline is the big thing."

As she spoke, a dozen young nuns were seated in a dark room below the chanting hall printing scripture on woodblocks, cutting the papers, and rolling them in silk to sell to the Jokhang. The temple buys them to insert in statues, and thus the nunnery gains some income. The nuns worked patiently, sometimes in silence, sometimes singing to pass the time. They would keep at it, one said, "as long as the old nun tells us to do it." One had been making scrolls for over a year. After serving their time in the printing room the young nuns gradually move on to other duties such as tending shrines, like the one down a narrow path from their workspace. There another young nun prayed and watched over a tiny sanctuary with a statue of Songtsen Gampo, the king who introduced Buddhism to Tibet, and a pit where the great king is said to have meditated.

The nuns, like members of religious houses throughout Tibet, spent much of their day performing such tasks—tending butter lamps, conducting tours, collecting donations from visitors, and producing holy objects to sell. On the upper floor of a temple in Ganden monastery, monks sold packets of holy scripture tied with colored string. These were to be worn around the neck as amulets to ward off evil spirits and cure disease. One young monk sat before a miniature stupa, using the peak of the figure as a mold for stamping out pellets of kneaded tsampa. He flipped them onto a cloth to dry before they were sold as remedies for spiritual and physical ailments.

In the Jokhang, monks who spoke English or Chinese worked as tour guides, taking groups around to the major shrines and explaining the rites and symbols. This left them little time for studies, and one of the monks, Nyima Tsering, has spoken publicly of his frustration. When he first arrived in the Jokhang, he said, he was eager to learn about his faith, but he found himself sweeping floors, tending butter lamps, and keeping an eye on visitors. "Nobody taught us the scriptures," he was quoted as saying in a *China Daily* article. "If we didn't do the chores required, we would be asked to leave."[19] When I spoke to him some weeks later, he took up the same complaint. He wanted to become a doctor of Buddhist studies, but how was it possible when he could only study early in the morning and after ten o'clock at night? The Jokhang needed more monks, he said, so they could take turns working and studying, and the temple was appealing to the government to allow more of them to stay. One hundred would be a bare minimum, he said; two or three hundred would be ideal.

The problem Nyima Tsering cited is not an accident, one monk said. "The Chinese are destroying religion in Tibet gradually," he told me. "Monks have to work too hard and don't have enough time to study, so they don't know enough about their own religion. Some of the most knowledgeable, educated monks were arrested for demonstrating and not allowed to return even though the abbots pleaded and said they were needed." With many of the best scholars dismissed from religious life and others in exile, no one is producing original works. "Buddhism is study," he said, "but we have no time the way things are. This way, the government is slowly strangling religion. If there is no change, there will be only the temples and altars and no more tradition of learning." When I suggested that Buddhism might emerge from the radical changes of recent years even stronger than before, he shook his head. Like others I spoke to in Tibet, he saw the content of Buddhism as already fixed and perfect, in need of no real reform. "We must teach the doctrine as it is," he said.

The government, however, has created Buddhist colleges in Beijing, Amdo, Kham, and the TAR. At these schools students can devote more time to learning. I met several who had attended two of them—Nechung near Lhasa and Kumbum in Qinghai Province. Critics have charged that the colleges teach Chinese propaganda and history in an effort to produce government collaborators. But if this is true, the government has failed: All the students I met were Tibetan nationalists. I was told that some from Nechung were shot to death during demonstrations.

The Tibetan Buddhist Association, set up in the 1950s as an advisory body to the government, is reputed to be a puppet group controlled by the Chinese. Witnesses to the 1988 riot at the Jokhang told me of their satisfaction in seeing association bigwigs and Party leaders hurriedly sliding down ropes to escape from the temple. But one dissident monk told me that the association "has some good people but no real power," that the Nationalities and Religious Affairs Commission is more likely to intervene in the operation of monasteries. The commission decides on quotas and which applicants get registration. But the line of command actually extends beyond the local agency itself. An official at the commission made it clear that the staff there is only following orders from Beijing.

China, of course, hopes to use both the Buddhist Association and Religious Affairs to control the slippery issue of religion and the restive monks and nuns who raise their fists in the Barkor and spread "splittist" propaganda. The government also tries to take command at the monastery level through the Democratic Management Committees, which were set up after the 1959 rebellion to run affairs in religious houses, in effect taking power away from the abbots and other traditional leaders. Some say the committees are staffed with collaborators and informers, and this is true in some monasteries. A monk from Kumbum told me that some monastery leaders were pro-Chinese and did whatever officials asked. But another monk from a monastery near Lhasa said he trusted everyone in his community and was only wary of those who visited from outside.

When riots broke out in the late 1980s the government went over the heads of the management committees and sent in "work teams," groups of Party educators who give political education classes and try to identify troublemakers. Tsultrim Drolma, a former nun who escaped to India and now lives in the United States, said that in the spring of 1988 a team of three arrived at her convent, Chupsang Gompa, set in the hills outside Lhasa. They stayed around the clock, and every day they called the nuns together in the chanting hall, took roll, and lectured them on China's version of Tibetan history. They admonished the nuns to avoid conflicts with the government—or else—and listed all that China had done on behalf of Tibet. After a few days of this, Tsultrim Drolma was so incensed that she decided to go to Lhasa and hold a demonstration with friends. There she was arrested and imprisoned.

The work teams spent five full months at Drepung and Ganden after the first riots, and one monk at another Lhasa monastery said the team members at first encouraged monks to speak their minds openly and share their worries about Tibet. "People said what they were worried about," he said, "what they really thought of the government policies and the problems here. But then they gave us the lessons in political science and told us the West was bad and Tibet was a part of China, and then everyone was afraid to say any more."

In 1992 the work teams were less in evidence, but they returned at the end of 1993, according to TIN, and have been more active since then.[20] In

June 1995 the government announced a new category of monastic administrator, the temple registration official, who was to report directly to these work teams. Tibetans have begun to call these officials "temple police."

When a work team tried to crack down on the display of Dalai Lama photos at Ganden Monastery on May 7, 1996, the monks rebelled, and the conflict escalated into a fight with police and work team members. TIN reported that three monks were shot and wounded, and two monks were possibly killed. Some fifty were arrested, and reports say that the monastery was left nearly deserted and was closed to the public for at least three months. The rebellion apparently spread to other convents and monasteries, TIN reported, citing a Japanese tourist who saw two truckloads of wounded Tibetans, mostly monks and nuns, near a Lhasa hospital.[21]

Some monasteries have come under orders to put on trumped-up performances for foreign visitors. A monk from Kumbum said the residents were told what to say and do when visitors came. They were to inform on each other, especially if one of them accepted a photo of the Dalai Lama. When a United Nations delegation was scheduled to arrive in 1985, the Kumbum monks were called back from vacation and others were brought in to fill the monastery and chanting hall. Then they were told to hold a prayer ceremony as if this were the normal routine. "I was very suffering," said the monk, "because it was just playing, a performance, not really sacred. I was angry because they wanted to hide the truth." He left the hall and fled to his room. There, he said, "I stood before the Dalai Lama's picture and cried and cried and said, 'I have to leave here, this terrible place. I can't use my own mouth or mind. I am no better than a machine.'" More than a year later, in the middle of winter, he fled to India, riding a bicycle all the way from Qinghai to Lhasa over the frozen Changtang before crossing the border in 1987.

This kind of pressure and interference with monastic affairs only stiffens the resistance of many monks and nuns and makes commoners nervous. They remember the Cultural Revolution, and they know that the state is officially atheist. Thus, many devout Tibetan cadres who long for the Dalai Lama's return dare not risk their government jobs by making a show of their devotion. In their offices and in the sitting rooms of their homes they hang photos of Mao Zedong meeting with the Panchen Lama and Dalai Lama. These images are safe and ideologically correct. But inside their bedrooms they set up altars displaying the Dalai Lama's photo alone. In Lhasa at least, these still remained in the spring of 1996, even though in 1994 the government had announced that Party members and cadres would not be allowed to possess or display such photos.

The Panchen Lama affair has convinced many observers that China is not keeping its promise to allow religious freedom. The absurd situation of an atheist government selecting the reincarnation of a lama born five centuries ago has angered and frustrated Tibetans and their sympathizers, outraged human rights groups, and made the young captive into a martyr. To force his substitute on Tibetan Buddhists only deepens the growing bitterness and resentment in Tibet. Although peasants and nomads have been somewhat remote from the tensions of Lhasa and thus less likely than urban dwellers to openly rebel, they are among the most devout followers of the Dalai Lama and take the attacks on him as insults to their faith.

Tibetans know they have no guarantee that China will fully protect their religious rights. The government may have pledged this protection on paper, but Chinese officials believe they have the right to decide what is "too much" religion, who the religious leaders should be, how many monks each monastery should have, which monasteries should be built, and what constitutes "legitimate" religious practice.

Chinese officials fail to acknowledge the reality of faith in something beyond the here and now. They seem to take religion as an assortment of quaint customs, a kind of meaningless formality which they must allow and sometimes endure. And they link religion with minority affairs, as if it is a cultural issue for minorities only. But they do understand that a faith can hold supreme power over its followers, and this they find insupportable. The only legitimate power, in their eyes, is the state. Thus they constantly tell Buddhist believers that true devotees put patriotism above all, even above the constitution or any abstract principle such as justice or equality.

So China's approach to religion is riddled with irony. When the Chinese came as "liberators" to Tibet, they expected the masses to thank them for destroying the power of the religious establishment. Instead, tens of thousands fled, primarily to continue worshipping as they always had and to follow their religious leader into exile. The monks and nuns branded as "parasites" have now become Tibetan heroes and martyrs, symbols of resistance to the new oppressors, who have taken over the role the religious establishment once had, that of imposing control from above. And officially atheist China presents itself as the guardian of tradition in discerning the selection of reincarnate lamas.

In the old Tibet many religious leaders used their power as a way to exploit the masses, but they were betraying a creed that called for detachment, humility, and the renunciation of worldly power. Chinese leaders may find it difficult to comprehend the attraction of the sacred, but China likewise is betraying its promise of "protecting religious belief" and prosecuting those who interfere with the free practice of faith. No matter how many pilgrims wend their way through the Potala, leaving their offerings before the shadowy shrines, the images of a young boy held captive, a closed midnight ceremony in the Jokhang, and a contingent of monks held under guard in a military hotel in Beijing belie the claim that Tibetans are free to worship as they please.

9

"The Final Solution"
(Population)

"They had these mobile clinics which went from village to village," said Rinchen Khando Chogyal of the Tibetan Women's Association in Dharamsala. "They would just get the women together and get them sterilized. Even women who were pregnant in their ninth month were made to abort their children." She was a slight, soft-spoken woman and she gazed shyly into the camera as she added her voice to a series of accounts exposing Chinese oppression in Tibet. She was appearing briefly during the television program "Compassion in Exile," aired by the Public Broadcasting Service in the summer of 1993 and listed in the *New York Times* "Television Highlights" for the day. The program presented Chinese rule in Tibet as a series of horrors directed against a gentle and peace-loving people.

It was not the first time American audiences had heard stories like this. A film called *Lung Ta: The Forgotten Tibet,* shown throughout the U.S. in 1992, asserted that the Chinese invasion of Tibet "led to genocide" and the death of 1.2 million Tibetans from harsh prison conditions, torture, and famine. Hundreds of thousands of Tibetan women and young girls were forcibly sterilized, the narrator of *Lung Ta* went on. "Mothers," he said, "were strapped to special machines and had their babies cut to shreds within their wombs." And now, he said, the Chinese have added another element to this all-out attack on the Tibetan race: population transfer, a deliberate policy to fill the region with

Chinese settlers, who already outnumber Tibetans—7.5 million to 6 million—in their own land.

In a *New York Times* column that appeared September 15, 1995, A.M. Rosenthal writes about "the ouster of millions of Tibetans from their own land and their replacement by handpicked Chinese . . . About two million out of six million Tibetans killed or forced out of their country." He is "heartsore," he says, "that nobody mentions the genocide, ethnic cleansing, and unwritten embargo that are destroying this lovely land in the Himalayas."

The accusations become even more grisly and explicit in a flier titled *Facts About Tibet,* issued by supporters of the government-in-exile. "Forced abortions and sterilization of Tibetan women are common," it reads. "In Chamdo, Tibet's third-largest city, fetuses have been found in storm drains and hospital garbage bins." The flier also denounces population transfer and tags it with a label from Nazi Germany. The policy, it claims, is China's "final solution" to the Tibet problem.

These are alarming charges: claims that China is using its birth-control laws to exterminate an entire ethnic group. Viewers and readers would naturally react with horror and outrage, and some might wonder what the Chinese themselves have to say about these issues. But China's response is never mentioned in these articles and films; it's as if the Chinese government has remained silent in the face of such accusations, admitting guilt by default. And hearing nothing but the atrocity stories repeated on printed page and screen, many Americans have come away convinced that China is out to destroy Tibetans as a race. When National Public Radio held a *Talk of the Nation* program on Tibet in the fall of 1993, a caller said matter-of-factly, "It's common knowledge, the genocide."

The Chinese embassy refused to take part in the talk show, but the People's Republic has elsewhere answered the critics who charge it with willful extermination of an entire people and a deliberate attempt to swamp the remnants of the race with imports from China's teeming cities and countryside. In newspaper articles and pamphlets, China cites numbers to support its claims.

To begin with, China insists that the ethnic Tibetan population is greater today than at any time in the past. Before the Chinese takeover, government tracts say, Tibet was underpopulated, with only 1 million inhabitants in all of the central region and no more than 1.7 million in Amdo and Kham. Other estimates—with the exception of one claiming 15.4 million—place the pre-1950 combined population of central and eastern Tibet in a range from 1 to 4 million. In 1990, according to a government-sponsored booklet titled *Figures and Facts on the Population of Tibet*, there were over 2 million in the TAR, another 2 million and then some in Amdo and Kham, and some 400,000 elsewhere in China, a total of 4.6 million, double the 1953 population. By 1995, according to a *Tibet Daily* article in February 1996, the TAR had a population of 2.39 million, 2.32 million of them permanent residents. Tibetans can thank socialism, the liberation of serfs, better nutrition, and improved medical care for this. Considering the numbers, the booklet asks, how can anyone accuse China of killing more than a million Tibetans? The charge of genocide is a "fantastic lie."[1]

And, according to government publications, there is no plan to carry out a "final solution" of population transfer in Tibet. The Han Chinese in the TAR numbered only 79,000 in 1995, 3.3 percent of the population, according to the *Tibet Daily* story, while Tibetans "and other minorities" totalled 2.31 million. Some Chinese have gone to Tibet as cadres or construction workers, to help build the economy of the region, the government says in its 1992 white paper, and those who have arrived to do business and work as craftsmen are just passing through, trying to make a living as members of China's floating population. No one could call them settlers, and there are only a few of them anyway.

Which side has the story right? You can't have both genocide and a twofold population increase at the same time. And if only 3.3 percent of the TAR is Han, there's no immediate threat of outnumbering the natives with immigrant Chinese. If China's statistics are even close to being accurate, how can the critics argue that there is a campaign to wipe out the entire race?

The genocide charge is an old one in the battle between the government-in-exile and Beijing. It surfaced in 1959 when tens of thousands of refugees fled over the Himalayas to escape communist rule and began to relate stories of Chinese atrocities: bombed villages, the shooting of innocent civilians, the deportation of twenty thousand children for indoctrination in China, the killing of some two thousand monks, and the forced settlement of millions of Chinese in Tibet. When these accounts showed up in Western newspapers, the Geneva-based International Commission of Jurists decided to take a look and found a prima facie case of genocide directed against Tibetans, enough evidence to warrant an investigation. The commission set up a Legal Inquiry Committee on Tibet, and the following year the group came back with its report: It had uncovered clear signs that the Chinese were killing monks and trying to wipe out religious practice. Thus, said the panel, China was committing "genocide against Buddhists." It was also violating the human rights of Tibetans with arbitrary imprisonment, torture, and confiscation of property. The report concluded that "large numbers" of children had been sent to China, but it came up with no hard evidence that the Chinese were trying to destroy Tibetans as a race or nation.[2]

The committee, which based its conclusions on refugee accounts and Chinese documents, found the government guilty of a narrowly defined genocide in 1959, but the word has stuck as a blanket term for China's activities in Tibet. "The Chinese have been committing genocide in Tibet for a long time," an otherwise knowledgeable American said to me just before I left for the TAR. The Chinese may cite all the numbers they want, but no one is listening. In this case, however, the truth is on China's side. Tibetans are more numerous today than at any time in recent history. Population growth has been rapid and continuous, and there is no sign that China wants to wipe out the Tibetan race.

But the ghoulish tales of genocide are only part of the population debate, albeit the most sensational. There is still the question of coercive birth-control practices, which in fact have been adopted in Tibet. And there is also the issue of Chinese settlers, the "final solution" condemned by the International Campaign for Tibet. In this last case the critics have good reason to cry foul: The thousands of Chinese flowing into Tibet each year are the biggest threat to Tibetan identity and peace in the region. And in Kham and Amdo the new arrivals are moving into areas once held by Tibetan farmers alone.

Lhasa residents mutter about the newcomers—the peddlers and repairmen who have flooded into the city since 1984—but no one could give me any firsthand accounts of forced abortions, although most said they had heard of them. Coerced abortions were another matter. Women were pressured into abortions, I was told, with the threat of losing bonuses and other benefits at work and knowing that babies born after the family has reached the two-child limit will not get registration cards. But Tibetans acknowledged that family planning regulations give special dispensations to minorities: Tibetan cadres and workers were allowed two children, and peasants and nomads, in 1992, had no real restrictions at all. But Han Chinese could have only one child per couple. In the cities and countryside I met many Tibetan families with four or more children: one Lhasa high-school student had eight brothers and sisters; a Lhasa elementary-school student came from a family of four; a peasant family near Shigatse had seven children; one nomad family north of Lhasa had five children; another had eight. The average family in Damzhung, according to hospital administrator Tsering Dondrup, had three or four children. Phuntsok, head of public health in Gyantse, said the average family in his rural county had four.

But the large Lhasa families had managed to produce their offspring before 1985 when birth-control regulations went into effect for urban Tibetans in the TAR. This was five years after the one-child-per-family rule was imposed upon Han Chinese throughout the People's Republic in response to China's urgent need to check the population growth. Tibetan city dwellers with government jobs were then restricted to two children (though up to 1990 some laborers were allowed to have three), and the state, in its usual intrusive and autocratic style, told cadres and workers not only how many children they could have but also how they should be spaced. Couples may have their first child whenever they want, but they are expected to get permission for the second. The ideal spacing between births, says the government, is three years, and it encourages families to adhere to this by granting a four-month vacation to women who wait the accepted length of time. The government also gives a year's paid vacation to mothers who choose to be sterilized after the first child.[3]

Couples who defy the two-child limit must pay a fine and hospital costs for additional births, and often face harassment and threats from employers and officials. And the additional children themselves suffer. Those who are born third or later receive no registration card, and this means they are denied schooling, jobs, free medical care, and other normal rights of city dwellers.

But in rural and pastoral regions of the TAR, the peasants and nomads I met seemed unaware of any restraints on family size, and doctors in Gyantse and Damzhung said they teach the farmers and herders about birth control and let them decide on their own. Tsering Dondrup of Damzhung County

Hospital—which serves thirty-four thousand nomads north of Lhasa—said, "We don't have any limits on the number, but we try to educate people so they will ask for sterilization. They are beginning more and more to ask for it because they know their living standard is low if they have more children."

The Tibetans I met never spoke of birth control as a Chinese plot to exterminate their race. Many of them, in fact, supported family planning just as Tsering Dondrup did in Damzhung. In Guchok Village my friend Tashi Tshering told his niece, pregnant with her fifth, that she shouldn't have so many children. "It keeps the family poor," he said. And in the western Changtang area of Pala, a nomad woman with a large family asked American researchers to help her get birth-control "medicine."[4] In Lhasa several families I knew chose to have only two or three children, sometimes spaced widely apart, well before the birth-control policies went into effect. And some career-minded Tibetan women decide to have one child when they could legally give birth to two.

Outside the TAR, regulations also allow Tibetan cadres and workers to have two children, but enforcement depends on local officials. In some counties they are strict, holding to the two-child limit, hounding families until the wife has an abortion, and even setting quotas on the number of births allowed in a prescribed area each year. In other locales, mainly small towns and peasant villages, officials are more lenient, allowing up to three children per family and charging a one-time fine for a fourth.[5]

It was in these eastern regions that the wholesale forced abortions and sterilizations allegedly took place. Two monks from Amdo, who escaped to India in 1988, reported that a mobile birth-control team had pulled into a Tibetan village in Qinghai the year before, set up a tent, and sterilized all the women of childbearing age. The women screamed and protested, the monks said, but the medical crew went about its work methodically. Then they aborted the fetuses of all the pregnant women as well, tossing them onto a pile outside the tent. The story conjures up nearly as much horror as the Nazi Holocaust, but so far no one has been able to pin it down. TIN reported that they could find no evidence to support the monks' tale. Stories of individual forced abortions and even the murder of newborns have come from other refugees in India, but, TIN noted, "Most of the accounts of physical force, deception, or infanticide are secondhand. Few are corroborated by other reports." The stories persist, however, and TIN found them disturbing enough to warrant more research.[6]

Then there is the claim that 1.2 million Tibetans have died as a result of the Chinese occupation. This number comes up frequently—in fliers, television specials, and films—and government-in-exile spokesmen work it into interviews. I have yet to see a breakdown or anything near a precise accounting, but the exile community points to many mass fatalities: the resistance fighters of the 1950s; guerrillas who continued the fight for more than a decade after the Lhasa revolt; refugees who expired crossing the Himalayas, in Indian road crews, and in disease-ridden camps; victims of thamzing, which began in 1959 and reached a peak during the Cultural Revolution; peasants and workers who starved to death during the Great Leap Forward and the Cultural Revolution; and thousands who died in prison camps.

Both sides could debate the numbers endlessly and never shed light on the question. China's own statistics are often suspect, and the exiles have no way to arrive at an accurate tally themselves. Tibetans in India, for instance, say ten thousand died in three days of fighting during the Lhasa rebellion. But this was fully a quarter of the city's population, and when I interviewed those who were there during the battle, they mainly spoke of damage to buildings, although it seems that many Tibetans died defending the Dalai Lama's summer palace. I never heard of a death during a thamzing session, but I was told that an elderly Muslim leader died after he had been paraded through the streets of Lhasa in disgrace. Tibetans told me they dreaded thamzing, but it was the humiliation they feared rather than death at the hands of a hostile mob. Although China's critics have said that thamzing victims were buried alive, crucified, scalded, stoned, shot by their own children, hanged, beheaded, and disemboweled, I never heard a whisper of such stories in Tibet.

And yet the exiles and their supporters are right in noting that many died because of China's errors and outright oppression. During the late 1950s Tibet proper was exempt from the Great Leap Forward mandates, but Tibetans living in Sichuan, Qinghai, Yunnan, and Gansu were not. They suffered the famines of 1958 through 1961, which were the result of government policies. In those days, an Amdowa from Qinghai told me, everyone was desperately hungry, and his mother once watched a woman eat a clove of garlic picked out of a human stool. Reliable estimates place the total famine-related death toll in all of China during that era at at least 10 million and quite possibly 30 million.[7] Most of the victims were peasants, and undoubtedly many were Tibetans living in Kham and Amdo where the Great Leap went into full effect, unlike in the TAR.

After the 1959 Lhasa uprising, China came down hard on everyone suspected of links with the rebels, and here again the critics are right in charging that harsh measures killed off a large number. The count may not be in the tens of thousands, as the exile sources claim, but there is no way to compute the actual score. It is enough to know that a great many families lost relatives in prison, and most of these prisoners starved to death. During the famine years, inmates forced into hard labor were issued scanty rations of grain, and even the young and healthy expired. One of them was Tashi Tshering's younger brother, who was a robust peasant in his twenties when he was arrested for failing to turn his pistol over to the authorities. He served only a few years of a fifteen-year sentence before he succumbed. And not a few prisoners were driven to suicide. In Sakya soon after the failed revolt, according to Dawa Norbu, three inmates killed themselves within a few weeks. A monk jumped into a toilet pit and stabbed himself in the heart. Then, after officials confiscated the prisoners' weapons, a former official managed to hang himself with a belt. When the authorities took possession of the prisoners' belts, another monk tore his robes into shreds, fashioned a noose, and hanged himself.[8]

China may have brought modern medical care to Tibet, but it also managed to kill off many Tibetans with famine and incarceration. And it drove massive numbers to flee over the Himalayas to India, Nepal, Sikkim, and Bhutan. Some 100,000—a tenth of the population—soon followed the Dalai Lama into exile. The exodus has slowed in recent years, although Tibetans continue to make their way across the high passes.

The critics describe these journeys as desperate flights to freedom. "The flood of refugees continues to this day," said the narrator of "Compassion in Exile." "They risk their lives escaping from Tibet so that they can freely practice their Buddhist religion, help maintain their culture, and be near their cherished leader." Even children make the trek over the mountain passes, he went on, because "conditions are so bad in occupied Tibet" that their parents send them as a last resort. "Many," he added, "have died on the way."

But in the TAR I often met Tibetans who had gone to Dharamsala and then returned—some legally, some with paid guides, and some with generous bribes to border guards. They went to see the Dalai Lama, attend school, visit relatives, and to experience something of the wider world. There was, for instance, a cheerful, rotund young woman I knew in Lhasa, a village girl who had come to the city to work. Like many young people, she was searching for the right job or the right boyfriend, something to give her life stability, but she had yet to find what she needed, and she decided to try India. She traveled to the border, but there the sentries stopped her and sent her home. She returned unharmed but mildly chagrined. If she had taken a thousand yuan—about $150—to pay a guide, she would have made it over the border. That was all. Her journey was no reckless bid to escape oppression, and it held no more danger than crossing the frontier at El Paso.

TIN, however, reported in its 1996 document *Cutting Off the Serpent's Head* that Tibetans have been "routinely beaten" when they try to cross the frontier to or from India. The report claims that China is trying to stop the flow of information between Tibet and the outside. But no one I asked could confirm this. It's a matter of luck, Tibetans said, and how you react. Some guards are brutal, but others will just send you home.

When I was in Lhasa I also met the father of a teenager studying at the government-in-exile school in Dharamsala. The man had sent his son to India to get a good education and learn English. The entire family had traveled to India, enrolled the boy in school, and then returned to Lhasa. The mother was visiting her son when I was in Tibet, and she persuaded him to come home. He then entered a school in Lhasa with no difficulties. When I asked the father why families sent their children to India he listed a number of reasons: Poor families strapped for funds send their children away to receive free schooling, food, and lodging provided by the government-in-exile; others want their children to learn English in India; and some have a difficult child on their hands and send him off to learn discipline. Of course, he added, the troublesome child is often a problem in India also. Then, he said, there is a fourth group of older ones who go on their own. They are runaways of sorts who go for adventure or to protest "the present situation" (meaning the Chinese occupation). And then there are a few families with more than the allotted two children. They may send their "illegal" sons and daughters to India because they have no registration cards and are barred from city schools.

Since my visit to Lhasa, the government has demanded that cadres with children in India bring them back. Many complied after they were told they would otherwise lose their jobs.

The real refugees today are those who have taken part in protests or "splittist" activities and flee to India in a risky bid for freedom; some of them have already been imprisoned. But overall the refugee movement today is no heavy drain on the population.

China's critics, however, still insist that Tibetan areas have been engulfed by an invasion of Chinese settlers, so many of them that they now outnumber natives 7.5 million to 6 million. This calls up visions of Chinese farmers tending fields and herding pigs on the Tibetan plateau and hordes of Chinese pressing into former Tibetan strongholds, and it is true that the Chinese are coming in a steady stream, riding over the mountain passes and across the Changtang in buses and trucks, traveling all the way from Anhui and the coastal province of Zhejiang. But most of those who come to the TAR remain in or near urban centers or along the major highways and tend to avoid farming villages and nomad settlements. Those alarming numbers, even taking the eastern regions of Amdo and Kham into account, cannot be substantiated. When Asia Watch looked into the figures, the human rights organization decided that the exiles' charges had no basis in fact. The claim that 7.5 million Chinese now live in Tibetan areas "cannot be accepted," Asia Watch said in a 1990 report. And even though the rights group had no precise statistics of its own, it was certain the number was much lower.[9]

On the other hand, Chinese government tallies are often dubious, especially when it comes to sensitive issues like the ethnic makeup of Lhasa. A Tibetan friend warned me in advance that I would never get my hands on the actual number of Chinese in Lhasa. "You'll never get that," he said, "never." Still, I had to hear what officials were saying, and I tried at several agencies. Just as my friend had said, none of the numbers reflected the Lhasa I saw all about me.

I stayed in the old city, the most Tibetan area of the capital, where most of the residents were natives, and even there Chinese and Hui rented rooms and worked in local hotels, restaurants, and shops. And many others arrived during the day to peddle ceremonial scarves and sunglasses and set up repair stalls. As I pedaled my bicycle along the major thoroughfares I heard Chinese spoken on all sides, and when I left the old city I entered neighborhoods with Chinese shops and apartment buildings, Chinese characters on the storefronts, and rows of Chinese restaurants. One day when I was riding through the suburbs west of Lhasa, I found myself in a wholly Chinese community, which had grown up around a military station. Off-duty soldiers hung out near Sichuan restaurants and teahouses, and faceless concrete apartment buildings lined the road. Then, suddenly, the bland concrete structures gave way to a Tibetan village of mud-brick houses topped with prayer flags, hemmed in by the sprawling developments—a reminder that this was Tibet after all. But just as abruptly the shops and apartment buildings closed in again, and the Tibetan enclave was left behind.

Such is the reality of present-day Lhasa, and anyone who has looked around the city can see that Chinese now make up the majority—even if the official word is otherwise. There are unofficial counts, however. Before I began making the rounds of government agencies I made friends with a Chinese who was well-acquainted with Lhasa and also knew many of its leading citizens and officials. These well-connected Chinese and Tibetans, my friend said, reported that six or seven out of every ten Lhasa residents were non-Tibetan, mainly Chinese and Hui. By this accounting, Tibetans made up only 30 or 40 percent of their own capital in 1992. Considering the numbers of Chinese soldiers, peddlers, repairmen, construction workers, and government cadres I saw in the city, this tally seemed close to the mark, and later a Tibetan researcher and a Western diplomat with access to off-limits material both told me they agreed with the count. Since then, by all accounts, Chinese have continued to pour into Lhasa and other parts of the TAR.

More evidence comes from Lhasa's main mosque, where the native Tibetan Muslims have been engulfed by an exploding population of newcomers. Hai San, the seventy-year-old administrator of the mosque, told me that the Lhasa Hui—mostly traders from Qinghai and Gansu—numbered seven thousand in 1992, while the hometown population of Tibetan Muslims came to only two thousand. On festival days this makes for a crowded mosque.

"Then," he said, "we need a loudspeaker, and many people have to stand outside because about five thousand come. And in the old days, Friday prayers would attract about two hundred. Now we get twice as many."

If the Muslim percentages applied to Lhasa as a whole, this would mean that three-quarters of the city was non-Tibetan in 1992. An article in the Katmandu magazine *Himal* comes up with a similar estimate: Lhasa in 1994, it says, was 20 to 30 percent Tibetan, counting only the civilian population. *Himal* gives the city a population of 300,000 to 400,000, twice most estimates, possibly because it refers to the entire Lhasa municipal district, which functions like a prefecture and extends into nomad and farming areas.[10]

But the public, official numbers tell a different story. Staff at the TAR Planning Department said that Lhasa had a population of 125,000 registered residents and that the floating population amounted to only 25,000, or one sixth of the total. Given that some members of the floating population are Tibetan, this put the itinerant Chinese and Hui at a small fraction of Lhasa's whole. Then to further confuse the issue, one academic told me the floating population of the city was 60,000, and another insisted that the itinerant population of the entire TAR was a little more than 38,000. But the most reliable information adds up to this: Lhasa had a population of about 150,000 civilians in 1990, and more than half of them were Chinese and Hui; taking the military into account, some 70 percent of the city was non-Tibetan.

Then there's the question of how many Chinese have moved into the TAR. Tibetan exiles and some of their Western supporters have charged that the region has at least 2 million Chinese, who now outnumber Tibetans. The Chinese government, however, says in its 1992 white paper that only 5 percent of the TAR population is non-Tibetan—meaning Hui, other minorities such as Uighur and Mongolian, Han Chinese, and tribal groups from the southern frontier areas. This would put the total of non-Tibetans at 100,000. But the claims of exiles and the Chinese government both appear to be far off the mark. Because the rural areas, where more than 80 percent of the population lives, are solidly Tibetan, Chinese are still a distinct minority in the TAR, contrary to the exiles' charges. But they also number far more than the government claims. In the late 1970s, for instance, the Central Intelligence Agency estimated the Chinese population of the TAR at 234,000, and this was well before the floating population began to arrive. The Chinese have reported

120,000 Han civilians in the TAR from 1976 through 1980 and 250,000 to 300,000 Han including military in the year 1975. The 1995 census citing 79,000 Han in the TAR cannot be valid.[11]

Such are the frustrations of dealing with statistics in China. They usually obscure rather than clarify. Lists of precise numbers, broken into categories and printed in government documents, don't compute; the groupings are incomplete, imprecise, and overlapping; one document contradicts another; and significant data—like the number of Chinese soldiers in Tibet—are rarely mentioned. And there is no way of knowing whether any of the numbers are accurate or even if the government is able to make an exact count of certain groups like the job-seekers now on the move throughout the People's Republic. The Chinese citizens are used to this. When I told a Chinese academic about my efforts with this muddle of numbers and groupings, he nodded knowingly and said, "Just use your eyes."

Monitoring groups like Tibet Information Network and Asia Watch, however, have wrestled with the numbers, sizing them up in light of visitors' accounts and any other evidence at hand. They accept China's claim that the Tibetan population has roughly doubled since the 1950s, inside the TAR and in the eastern regions of China proper. And what I learned of rural and pastoral areas in the TAR supported this. The nomad settlement of Bagam, south of Damzhung, grew from twelve households in the 1950s to thirty-eight in 1992. Takna Village in Namling County contained about nine hundred inhabitants in the early 1950s and has two thousand today. And Lhasa's native Muslims, which numbered six hundred in 1959, now total three and a half times that many.

But the groups also support government-in-exile charges that Chinese and Hui are flooding into land that until recently was occupied solidly by Tibetans. TIN, using China's own statistics, has reported an overwhelming influx into Kham and Amdo. In the 1950s Tibetans made up the majority of Qinghai Province, TIN says in its 1991 document, *Defying the Dragon,* but by 1982 they formed only 20 percent. In the province's six Tibetan autonomous prefectures, the Chinese population grew more than a tenfold in the thirty years between 1953 and 1982, from 40,000 to more than 500,000. In the same period, in the four autonomous prefectures and two autonomous counties spread from Gansu to Yunnan, the Chinese population doubled.

"These figures indicate an overall 350 percent increase in the Chinese popula-tion of specifically Tibetan-designated areas outside the TAR," TIN noted. "Over the same period, official statistics show that the Tibetan population outside the TAR increased by only 38 percent, from about 1.5 million in 1953 to 2.08 million in 1982."[12] The autonomous counties and prefectures are supposedly compact Tibetan communities, but some of them already had Chinese majorities in 1982, before the open-door policy took effect. By 1990 the numbers and percentages of non-Tibetans were certainly much higher.

Many of these Chinese in the provinces are members of the floating popu-lation, as in the TAR, according to an informal survey by the International Campaign for Tibet. But others were sent to those areas, and still others went to take advantage of the extra benefits offered in hardship posts. ICT found that more than 70 percent of the Chinese interviewed in Kham and Amdo had arrived since 1980. Most of them were restaurant and shop owners. The survey team reported that many areas of Sichuan Province which had Tibetan majorities in the 1982 census are now overwhelmingly Chinese.[13]

"My village was very small," a Qinghai resident told me. "Before the 1950s there were one hundred Tibetans and one or two Chinese families. It was very Tibetanized; we spoke Tibetan; we practiced Tibetan Buddhism. Suddenly very many new Chinese were coming, because of the government policy. By 1968 it was half Tibetan. Now there are about thirty-five Chinese families and only eight Tibetan ones. Many people just left and went to no-mad areas." The newcomers, he said, came from Hunan, Shandong, and Gansu. Many settled down as farmers.

Another Qinghai Tibetan told a Western visitor that he had never seen a Chinese face until 1946, when the Communists were heading toward victory. Now, he said, the land where he grew up is filled with Chinese hamlets. Ti-betan herdsmen, he said, have been forced to pasture their animals higher in the mountains.[14]

Some Tibetans are saying that they themselves have helped accelerate the process in the east. In Amdo many young men have left their villages to join monasteries or the exile community in India, an elderly Tibetan said, and the young Tibetan women who remain are marrying Hui and leaving their own culture behind. In Kham, he said, men are abandoning their farms to become traders. As they leave, land-hungry Chinese move in to rent the fields and grow produce. Only the high plateau where the nomads roam has remained safe, for now, from Chinese settlement.

Native residents of the TAR include not only Tibetans but also tribal groups of the southern frontier zone like the seventy-five hundred Monpa, who practice Tibetan Buddhism, and the sixteen hundred Lopa, hunters and animists of the rugged mountain jungles. Many natives are Tibetan Muslims, which the government counts as Hui even though they themselves say this is incorrect, that they are really ethnic Tibetans. They speak Tibetan, eat Tibetan food, wear Tibetan dress, and adorn their mosque with Tibetan symbols and script. And their language is even more conservative than that of other Lhasa residents. They say "Bapung," for instance, for Drepung Monastery, using an old form which has died out among other groups. But in spite of this, the government lumps them together with the Chinese-speaking Hui who live in Gansu and Qinghai and in small communities throughout the People's Republic. I brought this up with a staff member at the Nationality and Religious Affairs Commission and said that Tibetan Muslims object to this label, but he shrugged as if that was irrelevant. It made no difference what they claimed; the government alone would decide who these people were.

Lhasa has about two thousand Tibetan Muslims and Shigatse another thousand. Both groups are said to be descendants of traders and missionaries who began to arrive some seven hundred years ago from Kashmir, Nepal, Saudi Arabia, and Persia and married into the Tibetan population. They are Sunni Muslims and take a relaxed attitude toward some of the more demanding aspects of Islam—such as Ramadan, the month of strict fasting. Many eat during the daylight hours of Ramadan, one said, although this is usually taboo. But otherwise they follow the orderly rites of Islam, making their ritual ablutions and praying in their tidy, well-swept mosque (where simplicity and structure reign not far from the tumult of the Jokhang). Since the early 1980s they have been joined by thousands of Hui from Gansu and Qinghai, traders who continue to flock into Tibet. The Hui all speak Chinese, and, in contrast to the well-educated Tibetan Muslims, many are illiterate; they devote themselves to business and commerce. They tend to marry early, in their teens, and, some told me, many Hui who move in and out of Tibet defy China's laws against bigamy and take one wife in the TAR and another in their home provinces. In Lhasa, Tibetan Muslim women dress in the local long dresses and striped aprons, but they wear a kind of mantilla which hangs down the back, unlike the caps and bandannas which the Buddhist women set on the crowns of their heads.

The Tibetan Muslims of Lhasa and Shigatse are natives, full members of Tibetan society over centuries, but the Hui who join them at the mosque are members of the floating population, Chinese-speaking outsiders who come to work in the towns and cities. Many reports on Tibet describe them and the Han traders as settlers and immigrants who are sent by the government or induced to come as part of a government policy of population transfer, considered by Tibetans inside and outside the TAR as the gravest threat to their identity. They know what happened in Xinjiang Province where the native Uighurs (people of Turkish stock) once predominated. Since 1949, according to TIN, the Chinese population of Xinjiang has grown from 200,000 to somewhere between 5 and 7 million. The Chinese may before long outnumber the 6 million Uighur in their own land. TIN also notes that the Inner Mongolia Autonomous Region has lost its cultural identity since it was colonized by Han and Hui. It now has 8.5 million Chinese inhabitants and only 2 million Mongols.[15]

Many Chinese in Tibet are not part of the floating population but government employees, cadres who work in offices and members of road crews and construction teams, and they have been brought in by their units or enticed by higher pay. But whenever I spoke to the newly arriving Chinese and Hui they told me they had come on their own initiative, to make money in China's newest frontier. They were taking advantage of economic reforms which allowed them to strike out on their own as individual entrepreneurs. When they left home they gained the chance to take part in the new market economy. Most of them were peasants or small traders who had few opportunities at home. They had come from Sichuan, Qinghai, and Gansu, which border the TAR, and also from faraway Anhui and Zhejiang. Some had been in Tibet for four or five or even nine years, and many had arrived in the past year or the past few months. Some, like a Hui acquaintance of mine from Qinghai, fifty-four-year-old Ma Zhongyuan, had come and gone more than once. He first arrived in 1984, when he set up a hotel in Lhasa. He remained for five years, went home to Qinghai in 1989, and returned to Tibet in 1992 for a stay of several months, this time dealing in wholesale fabrics. Then he left for Qinghai again, planning to come back to Lhasa soon.

In Snowland Hotel, three members of the Li family from Sichuan Province worked as employees of the Tibetan cooperative which owned and managed the facility. They ran the laundry, which took in washing from a booth in the street outside—suits, shirts, hats, dresses, skirts, jackets. They had been at it for two years although some members of the family had arrived in Lhasa much earlier. One had come in 1983, and the others had followed. They were still coming, and the fifth member, a younger brother, showed up when I was there. Some of the Lis worked outside the hotel.

In Sichuan they had lived in a small town where they sold "daily life objects," such as combs, stationery, pencils, twine, and brushes. There, they said, one person could make $17 to $35 U.S. in a good month. At Snowland they earned a steady $50 each. Without ration cards they had to pay higher prices for basic goods before the system ended in 1992, but they still came out ahead and had enough to send money home each month.

It was the same everywhere: The Chinese said they had come to Tibet because they could make more money here, two or three times as much. On the outskirts of Lhasa, Chinese families were raising vegetables on rented land. A family from Anhui grew turnips, cabbage, green onions, and potatoes on less than an acre leased from the military. "We came here," said a teenage boy who was flooding the rows with water pumped from the nearby river, "because there was no land in Anhui and people in our village said you could make money in Tibet." The villagers had been right; at home, where they faced heavy competition from other farmers, a pound of cabbage sold for only five *fen*, or about 1¢ U.S., but in Lhasa it sold for eight times as much. The boy had come to Tibet in 1989, and he had yet to make a visit home.

Down the road a family of three from Sichuan was renting one and a half acres from a transportation company. They had been in Tibet six years, and in 1989 they shifted from peddling household wares to farming. In Sichuan, they said, land was at a premium, and they had only one *mu* per person (a mu is about one-sixth of an acre); here they had three mu each. Back in their home village of Mian Yang, a single person made perhaps $170 U.S. a year raising pigs, rabbits, and vegetables. In Tibet they made three times that.

Every two or three years they returned to Sichuan, spending $50 for the bus trip north across the Changtang then south to their home.

In an alley behind the Barkor I spoke to a seamstress from Zhejiang who had set up her treadle sewing machine on the cobblestones. In her hometown she was one of many women who could sew, she said, and so she had few customers. She had come to Tibet where there was less competition, and now she was doing better, charging up to 20¢ U.S. for a quick repair job. In Lhasa she had found that fewer women had machines or the skill to use them.

Other Chinese said they had come because a brother or sister or uncle had already set up in Tibet, or because they had failed the high school entrance exam at home, or because their parents were too poor to send them to school. All had heard that they could make a good living in Tibet.

In Damzhung, Sichuan and Hui restaurants lined the road. They served travelers and the scores (perhaps hundreds) of Chinese soldiers stationed nearby. Even in Namling, a backwater well off the main roads, Chinese had set up small shops and were selling matches, thermos bottles, liquor, tea, candy, dried noodles, cigarettes, padlocks, and other small items. And on a corner in the sleepy town a Sichuan restaurant served noodles, rice, and stir-fried dishes. The owner had been in Namling for eight years.

In Lhasa the Han and Hui filled the sidewalks and storefront shops along every thoroughfare. They set up treadle sewing machines by the filthy curbsides, hung a handful of zippers from the spool pin, and waited for customers. They acquired a few dozen pairs of dark glasses and laid them out on a sheet of cardboard. They set out cleats, soles, heels, and swatches of leather and inner tube and went into the shoe-repair business. They got hold of a hand pump, a few bicycle seats, spokes, reflectors, rubber patches, and tools and waited for cyclists with flat tires or wobbly wheels. They set up shop under awnings on People's Street and the Barkor, offering socks, sweaters, thermos bottles, blankets, luggage, water carriers, shoes, baby clothes, candy, fruit drinks, cigarettes, and toilet paper. They arrived with instant-picture cameras and brightly painted carts and began to operate mobile photography studios, snapping color shots of tourists, soldiers, and pilgrims. They wheeled narrow stalls onto street corners and sat in the cramped spaces repairing watches. They rented storefronts and opened restaurants, or they stocked the shelves with fabric, ghetto blasters, television sets, baked goods, dresses, suits, or cosmetics. They bought silk ceremonial scarves in China and brought them to the Jokhang Plaza and the Barkor where they hung them over sawhorses and sold them to pilgrims. Much of the time they waited, knitting, reading novels, dozing, or scanning worn English-language textbooks. They were ready for any opportunity. When the rains arrived, one family latched onto a supply of boots, loaded them onto a truck, parked at a busy intersection, and conducted a brisk business from the rear of the truck bed. A young man from Sichuan made an oven out of an empty oil drum and did well selling baked potatoes near the Jokhang Plaza.

If any of them were part of a government plan to overwhelm the Tibetan population, none was aware of it. They were hard-working peasants and village shopkeepers who took time out to answer my questions with simple grace, and all of them had decided on their own to move to Tibet. Many had come because they had relatives in the military, and this gave them the necessary connections to rent land or storefront space from the army. Others had relatives who had been sent to work in construction crews.

Good connections often give the Chinese an edge in the job market, and the exile community has made much of that fact, saying it allows the newcomers to take jobs from Tibetans and leaves many unemployed. Not a few Tibetans, however, blame themselves. "Tibetan workers, barbers, rugmakers, and shoemakers lose out," said one longtime Lhasa resident, "because the Chinese are more aggressive; they are hard-working, efficient, and money-conscious. But Tibetans are less aggressive; they are lazy, less money-conscious, and engaged in their religious activities." Amdo native Dorje Tseten, former chairman of the TAR, told me, "The Tibetan people are more interested in the future life than the present. The Chinese save the money they earn. Tibetans will spend it all. A Tibetan will rent out his rickshaw to a Chinese and sit in front of the Potala all day drinking barley beer. Maybe the Khampa will buy jewelry cheaply and sell it at a high price in Lhasa, but Lhasa people say it is too hard to do this. They refuse to do many kinds of work."

It is true that the Tibetans love to play and the Chinese in the TAR work nonstop. At Snowland the Li family was up at dawn, and the younger son began immediately to haul on the courtyard pump, filling washtubs with icy water so he could scrub the heavy clothes by hand and set them out to dry in the first rays of the sun. During the day he also ran errands for a Tibetan neighbor of mine, rushing up the stairs with hot water and earning a few pennies for his efforts. (This same neighbor later complained to me that the Chinese were always in charge and the Tibetans always on the bottom.) But the Tibetan women who cleaned the rooms and corridors and, very occasionally, handed out fresh bed linen arrived about nine thirty to make a pass along the balconies with their brooms, entering a few rooms if the doors happened to be open. Sometimes they splashed a bucket of water over the floor of the foul latrine. Then, about ten thirty, they sat down for butter tea and gossip. In the course of the day they managed to show a few rooms to arriving guests and perhaps move some furniture. Maybe once a month they washed the bed linen. They moved languidly, smiled often, and sometimes one of them would break into song. They could be charming, and I grew fond of them. But as a guest who had to endure the horrific toilets and sleep on grimy sheets I often wished they could show something of the local Chinese work ethic.

This is what Tibetans mean when they criticize their own people, especially Lhasa residents, for laziness. The jobs are there, they say, but the Chinese win out because they are more ambitious and willing to work hard. When I asked a manager at Tibetan-run Snowland why the hotel hired Chinese to do the laundry, he said they had originally taken on Tibetans, but after a good start the workers slacked off. So they began to hire Chinese. The Li family was the second group from Sichuan, and the Chinese had proved to be better employees, with more staying power. Snowland was owned and run by a cooperative of Tibetans, and their experience was not an isolated one.

Many Lhasa Tibetans, even strong nationalists, find themselves hiring Chinese. They often employ Chinese carpenters, who, they say, work faster and don't demand the traditional Tibetan payment of barley beer. And one young Lhasa woman told me she hired a Chinese tailor to make her New Year's outfit after a Tibetan quoted her a high price for giving short notice. She was sorry to encourage Chinese workers, she said, but also frustrated with her own people. "It's our own fault," she said, referring to the dominance of Chinese in many trades.

Some Tibetans also note that the old society had no place for shoe and bicycle repairmen. In those days all but the rich made their own footwear, and no one traveled on wheels of any kind. So Tibetans today lack the skills to compete with the Chinese in these areas. The newcomers, they say, have an unfair advantage.

But others reject any suggestions that Tibetans themselves are partly to blame. They place the responsibility on the Chinese newcomers and the government which allows them to come. There was, for instance, the Tibetan carpenter who had once supported himself by making the elaborately carved and painted tea tables, altars, and cupboards found in every home. I spoke to him near the east end of Lhasa's Beijing Road, where cabinetmakers prepared and sold their furniture from storefront workshops. "I was a carpenter for ten years and now I just sell," he said, seated cross-legged on the sidewalk next to a container of beer. "Now I get 10 yuan [less than $2 U.S.] for selling a 350-yuan cabinet. The Chinese are taking over because they sell cabinets cheaper. They build a standard cabinet in four days. Tibetans take seven to eight days. But the Chinese work isn't as good; they don't take as much care."

I made a count and found that out of thirteen cabinet shops, eight were run by Chinese. But even this number was deceiving. The Tibetans often bought the cabinets readymade from Chinese carpenters and only applied the paint themselves. A few years earlier nearly all the shops had been Tibetan-owned and -run. And another factor has accelerated this process, some Tibetans said: Many artisans who would normally carve, paint, and build the ornate cabinets were presently at work restoring monasteries. The cabinet shops may be typical of Lhasa business as a whole, if figures reported in *Himal* magazine are correct. An unofficial count in 1993, it reports, showed that Tibetans owned 10 to 15 percent of Lhasa's business, the government owned 8 or 9 percent, and Han and Hui owned the rest.[16]

In Lhasa, Shigatse, and Tsetang, the largest cities in central Tibet, Chinese and Hui continued to arrive during my visit, and in each of those cities new storefronts were going up. I would stop and ask who owned the new buildings and who would occupy them. Sometimes the builder was the local government, and other times it was a private developer. In Lhasa, for instance, I spoke to a crew of Chinese workmen putting up storefronts for a Tibetan owner. In Tsetang a mason at work on a new row of shops said he was working for the prefectural government. The new occupants, everyone agreed, would be largely Chinese. They would open restaurants, beauty parlors, video parlors, photography studios, bakeries, and shops selling everything from vinyl flooring to television sets.

The Chinese and Hui were able to make a living in Tibet because few there had the skills or desire to compete with them and because the local economy was bolstered by subsidies from the central government and tax breaks. The subsidies have also become an issue among Tibetan exiles. Tibet gets special treatment, China's critics say, not to help out the local economy but to encourage Chinese to move to the TAR. This is what they call the "final solution"—a scheme to attract thousands from China proper each year. The exile community and some nationalists in Lhasa were also charging that China had decided to send one million "settlers" to the TAR in 1992. But other Tibetans dismissed this as a rumor.

In any case, China's motives are rarely clear, given the secrecy surrounding government decisions and the obscure layers of command. It could be that China grants Tibet special treatment not to encourage immigration but to stifle dissent at home and criticism from abroad. And some regulations, at least until 1992, worked against the influx of outsiders. The government, for instance, levied higher taxes on the floating population of vendors and repairmen to give an advantage to those with local registration. Lhasa residents selling goods in the Barkor were paying 2 percent less in taxes in 1993 than those with temporary residence permits, and the cost of a business license was 3 percent cheaper for locals. Outsiders also paid higher rent for Barkor stalls, and when Tibetans complained that Chinese artisans were getting the restoration jobs in monasteries, officials made sure the work went to local people. TIN, in its 1996 report, *Cutting Off the Serpent's Head,* however, has said that China raised taxes on Lhasa's street vendors and shopkeepers in 1994, setting off a protest demonstration.

But at the same time the floating population has also benefited from Tibet's overall tax breaks, even though Tibet's economy lags behind that of the rest of China. The vegetable farmers from Anhui and Sichuan would have faced levies on their produce in China proper, but they paid nothing in Tibet. Although bicycle and shoe repairmen did pay taxes in Tibet, they were charged a rate lower than that in their home provinces. And those on government salary also got some perks: extra pay for working at high altitudes and in cold climates. These apply to local Tibetans as well as to Chinese.

Up to 1992 China made no consistent effort to smooth the way for outsiders who came to Tibet. Members of the floating population not only paid higher taxes and fees, but they also had to buy staple goods at nonsubsidized prices on the open market and often paid more than local residents for medicine. But still the Chinese and Hui found it worthwhile to come. The government was not openly inviting the new arrivals, but at the same time it was not discouraging them. The policy then, many Tibetans said, was a kind of laissez-faire stance. China had set the process in motion by sending Han to work on building projects in Tibet and by adopting an open-door policy along with the market economy. And then—even if this meant that Chinese were changing the face of Lhasa and beating out Tibetans in the job market—the government saw no reason to staunch the flow. It simply let it happen.

The government could make an effort to reverse the effects of its policies in Tibet, if it had half a mind to do so. In 1991 it sent home thousands of job-seekers from the north who had crowded into booming Guangdong Province and camped out in the capital city's railway station. "Why, then," a Tibetan asked, "don't they decide the Chinese are a burden here? Why don't they send them home, too?" The government could also take less extreme measures to ease the situation. Officials could simply tighten controls already in place. The transients can now legally enter the TAR by bringing letters from the authorities in their hometowns, documents that spell out just where they are going in Tibet. With this the vendor from Qinghai or the cabinet maker from Zhejiang can take out a business license and get a temporary residence card. The government could put a limit on new business licenses or residence permits, or it could stop the issuing of letters of transfer into the TAR. But so far, in spite of the obvious discontent in Lhasa, the government has made no move to do so.

In fact, in December 1992 the government took down the roadblocks between the TAR and Chinese provinces and in November 1993 made it easier for new arrivals to get business permits. Moreover, TIN notes in *Cutting Off the Serpent's Head,* China's Third National Forum on Work in Tibet, held in Beijing in 1994, opted for a policy to "open the door wider in Tibet" and "encourage traders, investment economic units, and individuals to enter our region to conduct different sorts of enterprises." A document reporting on the forum stated baldly, "We should continue to import Chinese and other nationalities." The forum also called for sixty-two new construction projects, which would require the importation of Chinese labor. And the Tibetan official Ragdi openly welcomed Han in an interview reported in *China's Tibet,* an official publication, late in 1994. "Tibet is part of China," he said, "and thus it is perfectly proper for the Han to move into Tibet. . . . In order to further develop our economy, culture, science and education, and public health, we need more people like these to come to Tibet."[17]

So far, however, the government has not openly encouraged non-Tibetan settlers in the TAR, but Tibetans nevertheless fear that China could do so. "The central government has no restriction on their coming here," said a young Lhasa resident, "no policy at all. But so far the Chinese plan hasn't been to send a whole lot of settlers to Tibet. It is just possible that this is the case, but I have no proof. I have never seen it with my own eyes." Nevertheless, he went on, if China did adopt such a plan, Tibetans would have no way to resist. "Then," he said, "Tibet would be swamped. It would be a tremendous change. All would be over." And even without a clearcut call for colonization, he said, the government could decide to give the temporary workers permanent residency, and that, too, would be a disaster. He was one of the Tibetans who said that Lhasa residents were unable and often unwilling to compete with the newcomers, but he also believed that Tibetans should have a chance to develop the region on their own.

He had good reason to worry. Even though China insists that the Chinese and Hui are only passing through Tibet, their numbers are increasing steadily. They may be itinerant, but they are ever more numerous. And even though the government white paper claims that lowlanders find the land and climate so harsh that they "can hardly adapt to them," many Chinese told me that they were beginning to see Tibet as their home, at least for many years to come. It's okay here, the vegetable farmers said, once you are accustomed to the weather. "I'm used to it now," said one of the Li sisters. "I just miss the fresh vegetables in Sichuan." The Snowland cook, Li Shifu, has even come to prefer Tibet over Sichuan. "The weather's not so humid," he said.

And although the launderers, farmers, and vendors have no registration in Lhasa, the system requiring legal residency is breaking down in the new market economy, and the government itself has helped accelerate that process. When I visited Lhasa First Primary School, Party secretary Paldron said the school was now enrolling the children of traders even if they had no registration. The parents had to pay a $17 U.S. fee, but for the first time the government was allowing these children to receive an education in Lhasa. With such advantages, the itinerant shopkeepers, vendors, farmers, and repairmen will have less reason to hurry home.

And with each wave of newcomers, Tibet becomes more comfortable for the displaced Chinese and Hui. "The new ones from the interior at first found it difficult here," said Hai San, the leader of the Lhasa mosque. "They weren't used to eating tsampa and drinking butter tea. But now there are Muslim restaurants here, and they can cook in their homes." (They do, however, have to put up with Lhasa's feral dogs, which are unclean and contaminating according to Islamic law.) Now there is no need for Han or Hui to eat Tibetan food in Lhasa, Shigatse, or even in many small towns in Tibet, and there is no need to learn the Tibetan language. The newcomers can move into Chinese neighborhoods where they find the familiar ambience of home.

In the 1950s the inhabitants of central Tibet warily watched events in Tibetan regions to the east, where socialist reforms came early. The Dalai Lama's brother fled his monastery in Qinghai and came to the Potala so he could alert the Lhasa government to the Communist agenda. Then as the Khampa in 1956 and the Amdowa in 1958 rose up against the Chinese, the fighting sent hundreds of refugees to central Tibet, where they spread tales of atrocities and attacks on monasteries. It was the presence of these mutinous newcomers which ignited the Lhasa rebellion of 1959.

Now Tibetans in the TAR are watching the east again as the Chinese arrive, pouring over the borders from the teeming provinces of the eastern lowlands. They know what has happened in some areas of Qinghai, Gansu, and Sichuan, and they fear that their region will be subsumed in a tide of Han and Hui. The government-in-exile likewise views population transfer as the gravest threat to Tibetan identity.

But China shows no sign of changing course. The government may have no policy for outright colonization of Tibet, but those in charge know that the influx of Chinese into the region helps tighten their hold. Since the riots of 1987 to 1989, the leaders have even more reason to welcome the demographic changes, no matter what inspired them in the first place. Given the crowding of the lowlands, the growing economy of Tibet, and the Chinese and Hui communities ready to accommodate newcomers, China has no need to adopt a new policy—for now. The situation, in the government's view, is taking care of itself.

10

Han Go Home!
(Tibetan-Chinese Relations)

One autumn day, when I was walking by Lhasa's Kyichu River with a young Amdowa woman, my companion stopped beside a broad granite stairway built into the bank and told me it was there, on those steps, that she learned firsthand about the petty harassments Chinese face daily in the Tibetan capital. My friend, whom we shall call Drolma, used to sit on the steps of the embankment during her early days in Lhasa, sunning herself and reading. She had been educated in Chinese urban schools, and the riverside vista made her nostalgic for the mountains and bracing air she had known in her home village. Drolma said she relished the time she spent by the river, but often she was startled to find her quiet moments broken by a hail of pebbles tossed from above. Sometimes she could ignore the intrusion, but at other times she would turn around to find a Tibetan—an elderly woman or a child or a youth her own age—eying her suspiciously. "Hey!" she would call in the dialect of Lhasa . "What are you doing?" The reply was always the same. "Sorry," they would say. "I thought you were Chinese."

Drolma was light-skinned, and she wore pants, blouses, and bright sweaters like a Han woman, and because of this Tibetans often mistook her for one of the outsiders. She soon learned to wear the blazers and straw hats of local Tibetan women and to speak out to passersby in the local idiom, announcing as best she could that she was Tibetan, too. Drolma found these precautions necessary because the residents of Lhasa, where the intruders now outnumber the natives by a good margin, find many ways to say, "Han go home!"

Those were, in effect, the first words that I heard spoken between Chinese and Tibetan when I arrived in the city. After settling into my hotel, I stepped out to look around the Jokhang Plaza, and there I struck up a conversation with a young Chinese peddler carrying a placard hung with sunglasses. He had arrived the year before, he told me. "Well," I asked, "are you going to stay here or go home?" Before he could answer, an elderly Tibetan stopped and said, "Are you going back or not?" Then he turned his back on us and walked away. The vendor laughed uneasily and told me, yes, he would return sometime, maybe in a few months.

The peddler got the message, and he also got off easy. Those few words of pointed sarcasm were less humiliating than a shower of spit or a sprinkling of pebbles and less damaging than a beating. He was well aware of that. Chinese in Tibet know they are unwelcome, even if they happen to have Tibetan friends, lovers, or spouses. Many stay away from the central, Tibetan area of Lhasa at night, and those who venture out after dark do so warily. "When I'm in the streets then," said Li Shifu, the Snowland Hotel's Sichuan cook, "I keep my head down and avoid trouble."

Tibetans also treat Chinese tourists with chilly correctness, another way of saying, "We have to put up with you, but you can see how we feel." When I took a Shanghai teacher to a Tibetan restaurant, the waitresses—who had always been chummy with me, full of talk and kind attention—turned sullen and abrupt. Male customers were sitting nearby with their shot glasses of sweet tea, and they turned their heads to stare. My friend, a kindly man who was eager to sample Tibetan food, seemed to miss the signals, but I was uncomfortably aware. Other vacationing Chinese told me they could find no bicycles to rent or no one to give them clear directions around the city. Westerners, however, found all this easy to come by. I have also seen monks tending the entrances to monasteries and demanding fees from Chinese while they let foreign tourists in for free.

Some Chinese visitors may pass through Lhasa without getting the message, but those who make their living in the streets or on construction crews know how deep the resentment lies. They have experienced the truth which the government prefers to deny or ignore: After more than forty years of Chinese rule, Tibetans want the Han and their government to go away. Even those who frown on petty harassments and criticize their own fellows for laziness take offense at the growing Chinese presence in their midst. The pebble-tossers express what virtually all of their compatriots feel.

It's not that Tibetans haven't spoken out before now. There were, of course, the rebellion of 1959, the turbulent and tearful welcomes granted the Dalai Lama's envoys at the close of the Cultural Revolution, and the riots of 1987 to 1989. On each of those occasions Tibetans were saying that they resented the Chinese presence in their land. They have been trying to express this for more than four long decades, but the Chinese government has refused to listen. Instead, the leaders in Beijing have preferred their own interpretation of those events, which drew support from thousands of Tibetans—educated cadres and simple nomads alike.

The government claims that discontent in Tibet has always been the work of outside agitators. Even Tibet's de facto independence before 1950 was, according to the 1992 white paper, "cooked up by old and new imperialists out of their crave [sic] to wrest Tibet from China," as if the Tibetans would never have thought of such a thing on their own. The riots of the 1980s, which took place well after the reforms had begun, were clearly, the white paper says, "incited by the Dalai [Lama] clique and plotted by rebels who were sent back to Tibet." Once the rebellions were put down, the common people gave a collective sigh of relief. An official news report stated, "The masses universally declared: We feel a sense of security with the PLA patrolling the streets. We will cooperate in implementing the State Council's martial law decree and completely smash the separatist conspiracy." And even after grievously wounding Tibetan religious sentiment in the Panchen Lama affair, the government failed to recognize that Tibetans had any reason to resent its actions and continued to say that nationalist fervor was the fault of the Dalai Lama and hostile Western forces.[1]

But anyone who spends time with ordinary Tibetans quickly learns that they hardly need foreign provocation to send them into the streets in protest. A young Tibetan academic who watched the first protests in the fall of 1987 said many people joined the monks and nuns who were shouting their defiance in the Barkor, and many on the sidelines whistled encouragement or yelled slogans: "Chinese go home!" "Dalai Lama, ten thousand years!" "Independent Tibet!" "The Dalai Lama is our Precious Jewel!" My friend was also elated to see such open resistance, but he was afraid—he didn't know who in the crowd might belong to Public Security—so he kept silent. "I wanted to stand back and watch," he told me, "but people were behind me pushing me forward so they could see, too." He saw that even elderly people had fallen into the spirit of the occasion. They tugged at the armed police and public security forces, who were clubbing the protesters, and begged them to stop. "They are unarmed," the older Tibetans said. "Leave them alone."

China has claimed that the riots resulted in "severe losses" to the property of Tibetans,[2] as if the protesters had not singled out Chinese passersby, shops, and restaurants for their fury. In fact, the mobs promptly torched a Chinese restaurant, and a Chinese pharmacy with a reputation for price-gouging. "The Chinese shops began to close," my friend said. "Tibetan shops stayed open." Later, during three days of rioting in 1989, Chinese and Hui shops burned again. "Many restaurants, especially," said a Tibetan woman who had a close view of the rampaging crowds. "But," she added, "no Tibetan stores were burned."

The numbers of political prisoners and arrests in the TAR say a lot about Tibetan opposition to Chinese rule. Tibetans know what will happen if they shout "Independence!" in the Jokhang Plaza, and yet they still choose to speak out, risking imprisonment, torture, and the loss of their jobs. TIN has documented over a thousand political arrests in Tibet from 1990 to 1995. About 44 percent of those arrested were monks and 23 percent nuns. More than 80 percent were under thirty years of age, and the detainees came from city and countryside. Since 1987 they have included bank employees, high school students, teachers, businessmen, quarry workers, nomads, carpenters, farmers, masons, merchants, construction workers, accountants, drivers.[3]

Lhasa is the center of resistance, but protests take place in the ethnic Tibetan areas outside the TAR and, increasingly since 1992, in rural reaches and remote monasteries. Amnesty International and TIN say farmers and nomads have been putting up posters, demonstrating, and organizing resistance groups. In the Gyama Valley, nationalist protests by farmers over three years led to thirteen detentions, and in Kyimshi in southern Tibet a rebellion resulted in thirty-five arrests.[4]

HAN GO HOME!

From 1990 to the end of 1995, according to TIN, the number of documented political prisoners throughout the TAR—including those in detention centers who have not been sentenced—has shot up from one hundred to more than six hundred. Drapchi Prison, for judicially sentenced prisoners, showed an increase of 270 percent with 274 political prisoners in 1996.[5]

By 1994, the time of the third forum, Chinese leaders were no longer claiming that resistance was limited to a few monks and nuns or the more militant Tibetans who belonged to the underground. "Some cadres were hoodwinked by the publicity of the Dalai clique about nationalism," a high official charged. And a 1994 TAR report said, "Splittist forces showed a tendency of spreading into cities and towns as well as farming and pastoral zones."[6]

The riots, the nearly universal veneration for the Dalai Lama in defiance of Chinese attacks on him, the constant complaints about the Han population in Tibet, the harassment of Chinese workers, the numbers of arrests for "splittist" activities—all belie government claims that Tibetans are content with Chinese rule. Peasants and nomads and city folk as well may prize their economic gains since the 1980s reforms, and they may appreciate the benefits of modernization and education, but at the same time they will tell you that they resent the alien power in their land. The truth is that the great majority of Tibetans are fearful of Chinese control, and they have often tried to say so by whatever means they can. Virtually all of them, even those who live in remote areas away from the influx of Han, fear the power of the central government to intrude on their lives.

Some Tibetans are driven to outright resistance, risking torture, the loss of their jobs, jail sentences, and death; others resort to petty assaults; members of a small underground, active even during the Cultural Revolution, have organized protests and occasional acts of sabotage; and still others choose to watch events from the sidelines, afraid of putting their livelihoods in danger. But whether they take action or hide their dismay, Tibetans say they have plenty to complain about and numerous reasons to resent China's control of their land.

In the fall of 1951 Lhasa residents greeted the newly arriving PLA troops with suspicion, sullen silence, and jeering hostility, but the invaders, all agree, reacted with discipline and restraint. The troops were on their best behavior in the early days, following Mao's directives to show respect for local customs and to take "not one needle" from the commoners. "Even if a pickpocket took a soldier's gun," former monk official Ngawangthondup recalled, the soldier "just reported it to the local police. And the common Chinese were ordinary human beings who liked our little enjoyments. People began to think the soldiers were nice." But, he added, "I can't say they trusted them."

For the fact remained, no matter how well they conducted themselves, that the soldiers were outsiders. Tibet had not asked them to come; it had fought them on its eastern borders and lost, and soon the presence of thousands of troops put a strain on food supplies and sent prices soaring. "Han go home!" signs first appeared in Lhasa only a few months after the soldiers filed down the broad valley and crossed the Kyichu on rafts.

During the early years of an uneasy alliance between the Tibetans and Chinese, the Communists tried to win the people's trust and admiration by building roads, hospitals, and schools, but they also managed to insult them with subtle attacks on the Lhasa government (still nominally in charge) and Tibetan Buddhism. Then in the 1950s Khampa and Amdowa began to appear in ragged bands, fleeing the bombings, pillage, and mass arrests which followed the uprisings in their homelands. They found many willing to listen to their stories, and central Tibetans began to join them in guerrilla campaigns against the PLA.

When the Lhasa insurrection broke out in 1959, the great majority of Tibetans sympathized with the rebels.[7] A few had given their loyalty to the new rulers, but most placed their faith in the Dalai Lama. As the young leader fled over the Himalayas to India, tens of thousands followed him into exile, and more would have fled if the Chinese had not sealed the borders and tracked down fugitives.

The Communists, in spite of their claims that only a handful of aristocrats were behind the rebellion, scoured the land for sympathizers and carted thousands off to jail. They confiscated estates and monasteries and hauled away truckloads of artworks, brocades, housewares, and religious artifacts. In Beijing I visited a library of Tibetan works in the Cultural Palace of Nationalities, and there I saw row upon row of silk-wrapped Tibetan texts. These began arriving in 1959, the archivist told me. I couldn't understand why they showed me this firsthand evidence of looting. The texts had no place in Beijing.

But other articles, taken between 1959 and the early years of the Cultural Revolution, traveled even further and turned up in the shops of Hong Kong. Some gold and silver works, it is said, were melted down and used to secure foreign exchange. The state may have benefited from some of this pillage; individual officials certainly cashed in on the rest. Tibetans remember the plunder, and they blame the Chinese once again.

But the Communists also made some needed changes. They freed the serfs from their estates and granted them their own plots of land. This, it would seem, should have won the hearts of the toiling masses, and I asked a few aged men and women, former serfs, what it had been like: How did they feel when they finally possessed deeds to the fields they had once tilled for others? I had seen Chinese films which showed emancipated serfs dancing with joy as they burned the old certificates of ownership and received title to valley and hillside plots, and I wondered if these men and women would express a sense of relief and gratitude.

The former serfs said their lives had suddenly taken new directions. "My life changed a lot," said Tsering Drolma, who now lives in a hillside village near Ganden Monastery. She had once hauled water and gathered herbs for the monks, but in 1959 she was granted five mu (five-sixths of an acre) of her own to cultivate. Former serf Sonam Wangdu, of Tashigang Village near Shigatse, said he was glad to be relieved of the manorial taxes he had found so burdensome—levies exacting transportation corvée, herbs, barley, and butter. In Bagam, a pastoral area north of Lhasa, a grandfather named Wangdu said he had received his own livestock at last. He was thirty-four at the time, and until then he had supported himself by spinning and shearing for wealthier nomads.

But none of them spoke with enthusiasm of those times. Life became a bit better, they said, or it was "okay," but that was all. Their responses were decidedly tepid, and I wondered if the bitter years of the Cultural Revolution had clouded their memories. But I also knew from studies and firsthand accounts of that time that the former serfs had still other reasons to downplay the supposed benefits of those days. They had been freed from the old system of castes and ranks, but they were now consigned to a new society with its own class labels. Although the land was theirs on paper, they could not always cultivate it as they wished. "All this was of little use," writes Dawa Norbu of the years immediately after the 1959 rebellion, "when our crops were appropriated, and we were made to work extremely hard on near-starvation rations." And although the serfs may have gained in status, they also saw others —monks, for instance, and commoners with the wrong class labels—made to suffer unjustly.[8]

One of the victims of the new policies was Norbu Tsering, then a teenager and the illegitimate son of a nobleman who fled his ancestral estate in Gyantse during the rebellion. Along with his mother and two siblings, he was banished from the manor house where he had lived—surrounded by such luxuries as table tennis, a gramophone, and imported foods from India and the West— and sent to live in the stable-like quarters of former serfs. Norbu Tsering was ostracized and denied the schooling and other perks granted the newly emancipated poor. His face and hands swelled from malnutrition, and his mother was publicly humiliated in thamzing.

There were many families like Norbu Tsering's who felt the cruel weight of oppression even in the first days of "liberation." And the one-time serfs who escaped the label of class enemy also found themselves enduring new burdens. The Communists imposed their own taxes, which they called patriotic contributions to the motherland, and forced the peasants to attend political education sessions and witness thamzing. The land may have been theirs, on paper—but in many areas at least, the crops were not. Officials took a good portion in duties and most likely sent much of the grain to China proper, which was in the grip of famine.[9] Former Sakya resident Dawa Norbu has told how the Party rationed the local peasants' harvests, leaving them just enough to survive; the newly emancipated serfs of Sakya found themselves laboring more and eating less; and they had to till the fields and build irrigation canals in mandatory mutual aid teams controlled by local Party members. Many flinched to see their revered monks and abbots hauled off to work camps or forced to labor in the fields, and they themselves endured insults to their faith as zealous cadres tried to wean them from Buddhist beliefs.

Some Tibetans have said that the harsh measures eased after 1962 when moderates took control from Mao Zedong, and Tibetans found they could practice their faith more openly once again and control a greater portion of their harvests. But the thaw ended in 1966 when the Cultural Revolution engulfed the entire republic. The Red Guards, both Tibetan and Chinese, battled each other, the Party, and even the PLA, and they set out to suppress everything that hinted of the old society. In China proper they tore down temples and destroyed works of art, but in Tibet their revolutionary fury went further, revealing Chinese chauvinism and contempt for Tibetan culture. Tibetan hairstyles and clothes were suspect, and many local people adopted Chinese dress to avoid censure. The rampaging Red Guards tore down prayer flags and piles of prayer stones, and they forced musicians and dancers to perform Chinese works in the Chinese language.

And now nomads and farmers lost even the titles to the land they had won in the "democratic reforms" of 1959; they were organized into communes, where they endured Maoist sloganeering, indoctrination, thamzing sessions, and the bullying of petty officials. The commune system also brought them near starvation; there was no incentive to work, and harvests were poor.

When Mao died and the Cultural Revolution lost its grip, peasants and nomads were released from the communes (the memories of this moment evoked wide grins from the farmers I interviewed), and China began to talk to the government-in-exile once again. When the delegations arrived from Dharamsala, Tibetans hoped and expected that the Dalai Lama would return. But gradually their hopes faded as talks broke down, and when the Dalai Lama stepped up his denunciations of the Communist Chinese, Tibetans supported him with the first protests of 1987. They were also demonstrating against the influx of Han and Hui, which was changing the face of Lhasa and transforming their heartland into one more outpost of China. When they took to the streets, police and soldiers shot unarmed demonstrators and battered monks and nuns with cudgels. The government responded to these atrocities by blaming the protesters and absolving the security forces, and Tibetans took this whitewash as one more sign that they could expect no justice from the latest round of leaders in Beijing.

Since the riots, Tibetans said, the military presence has grown in Lhasa, and this has added to their resentment. "Look," a young man said to me one day as we were passing through Lhasa. He nodded toward a military base where soldiers were strolling about. "There are many, many soldiers here, mostly Chinese," he said. He had traveled through much of China, so I asked if he noticed more soldiers in Tibet than elsewhere. "Yes," he said, "many more." Later, when I approached Drepung Monastery in a bus, I had the same experience. A young Tibetan nudged my arm and quietly pointed out two guards, guns at the ready, standing at the foot of the entrance drive.

The masses of Chinese have also endured (or expired under) famine, purges, repression, and attacks on traditional culture (while they, like the Tibetans, have also benefitted from the material gains of the past forty years) and they point to the former regime—the Gang of Four and the errors of Mao Zedong—as the cause of their sufferings. Tibetans, however, blame the Chinese. The Chinese drove their Precious One into exile. The Chinese brought the Cultural Revolution, which left only a dozen monasteries standing out of thousands. The Chinese have attacked their most sacred beliefs and ridiculed their way of life. They know that if the Chinese had not come, they would never have suffered such losses and insults. They have little hope that the central government will ever serve their real interests. As one young Tibetan said to me, "During the Cultural Revolution China destroyed a thousand years of Tibetan culture. If we don't run our own affairs again, maybe there will be a second and a third Cultural Revolution. The problem is, the Chinese are over us. They are our real leaders."

But in spite of the failed experiments in socialism, the Chinese insist that Tibetans should be grateful. They point to hospitals, schools, power lines, roads, tax exemptions, and billions of yuan in subsidies as evidence of their good intentions. They were shocked by the riots of the late 1980s; they really believed that Tibetans wanted nothing more than a new airport or power plant to keep them happy, and their blindness to spiritual and nationalistic concerns pointed up a vast gulf separating the Tibetan and Chinese points of view. Chinese academics and administrators told me insistently to compare the old Tibet to the new. If I did that, they said, I would realize how much China has done for the once-backward region. They were thinking of the new roads and hospitals; they showed no regret at the losses (and they probably knew little about the true state of affairs in the old society). When I visited the Chinese Consulate in San Francisco upon my return, an official questioned me anxiously about Westerners' impressions of Tibet. "Did they find it poor?" he asked.

Han Go Home!

It never occurs to those in charge that Tibetans are asking for more than material gain. Although the Chinese complain of the humiliations they suffered under Japan and the West, they fail to understand the Tibetans' nationalism and ethnic pride. They are likewise baffled by the Tibetans' preference for the spiritual over the material. Even the most sympathetic Chinese shook their heads when they told me that poor Tibetans often give their entire savings to monasteries. "You go see," one said. "Watch how they leave hundred-yuan notes on the altars." This was not only foolish in their eyes, it was wrong. They seemed to be saying, "What can you do with such people?" In the same spirit another told me, with obvious indignation, that Tibetans burn so much butter in votive lamps that the region has to import more from outside. I could never understand why the Chinese were objecting, why they should care what Tibetans did with their own money. But Chinese society harbors a decidedly worldly outlook on life, and this inability to understand the spiritual values of Tibetans is a major source of tension.

Chinese insensitivity to Tibetan ethnic pride adds to the growing resentment. There is, for instance, the Cultural Palace of Nationalities in Beijing, where visitors are shown two exhibits on Tibet, one to prove that the region is an inseparable part of China, and another to paint the old society as an unrelieved system of injustice and oppression. The second exhibit displays instruments of torture and photographs of mutilated convicts, beggars, the hovels of the poor, and the plush drawing rooms of aristocrats. There is no mention of the Thirteenth Dalai Lama's ban on torture and other pre-1950 reforms nor any admission that some serfs, like the family of my friend Tashi Tshering, grew rich, amassing large herds and constructing comfortable homes. But at the end of this diatribe the government manages a condescending pat on the back. It sums up the display: "Over a long period of historical development, the Tibetan nationality has created a brilliant culture and made outstanding contributions to the formation and development of China as a multinational unified country." Then it adds that the feudal system blocked progress until the Communist Party took over in 1959.

The exhibit, of course, is designed to persuade viewers that Tibet is better off under Chinese control. It is almost to be expected that the official "history" of Tibet would skew the facts, but even more disturbing is the effect this

227

has on Tibetans themselves. What are they to make of their own culture, the inheritance of over a thousand years, if it is presented as nothing but a primitive and barbaric past? The Chinese are telling them: This is how you messed up on your own. Without us you can't do anything right.

Chinese dissident Wei Jingsheng noted the poisonous effects of this kind of indoctrination in a 1992 open letter to Deng Xiaoping. "Due to the propaganda of the last forty years," he writes, "cadres in Tibet (and in other areas, too) have had a deep-rooted discrimination against the Tibetans which, in turn, has deepened the hatred among the Tibetans against the Han." He goes on to give an example from his own life: "My parents do not know any Tibetans and have not done any research about Tibet. Whatever they knew about Tibet was what the Communist Party had told them. In their minds, Tibetans were half humans and half beasts. So it was only natural that when I planned to marry a Tibetan girl, what I got from them was the strongest opposition and they even threatened to sever all relationships with me." His parents relented, once they came to know their son's fiancée, but her parents were so outraged by the reaction of Wei's family that they managed to prevent the marriage.

Some Tibetans admitted to me that they, too, bought this spin on the old Tibet; they believed that they could not govern on their own, and they learned to look down on the superstitions of rural folk. By the time he was in his late teens, one Tibetan told me, he felt contempt for his native culture, and he thought the nomads were insane to give their money away to the monks. "They didn't care for buying a television or furniture," he said. "I thought this was wrong. I wanted to tell them prayer was useless." In time he came to value the accomplishments of his ancestors, and he now resents the regime that turned him against his own people.

Some told me they experienced Chinese disdain for Tibetan accomplishments and culture in more direct ways. One said a Chinese visitor to Lhasa told him Tibet had no bridges until the PLA arrived. "That's not true," the Tibetan said. "We've had steel chain-link bridges since the fifteenth century. They are still standing." But, he said, the man refused to believe him. Another, a monk who worked as a tour guide in Kumbum Monastery said Chinese tourists, especially soldiers and Party officials, laughed at his explanations of thangka paintings. "That's superstition," they would say. "It's a lie. You should leave here and go to Beijing to study communism." He found the common Chinese to be ignorant of Buddhist precepts. "Some," the monk said, "would ask me how many children I had. They also didn't respect the monastery. They would turn the prayer wheels the wrong way and even with their feet. They would take pictures where it was not allowed."

The history of past abuses, the put-downs of Tibetan culture, the disregard for human rights, the stream of Chinese entrepreneurs seeking their fortunes in the Tibetan homeland, and the absence of real autonomy in the TAR have poisoned relations between Tibetans and Chinese, between Tibetans and Hui, and even among Tibetans themselves. A young Chinese woman told me with obvious pain that she had come to Lhasa with sympathy for the Tibetan cause, but the Tibetans who ran the hotel where she lodged began to bait her with a series of petty harassments. They tried to raise her rent by five yuan (less than a dollar) a day, but she refused to pay. Then they said she would have to pay for showers, which are normally free for guests, and finally, when she returned from an excursion outside Lhasa, they told her they had no room, even though she had previously had an entire floor to herself. "It got to the point," she said, "where they verbally abused me for being Chinese, so I said, 'Okay, I'll just leave.' But when I took my suitcase away, I discovered that someone had slashed it." After this she found herself taking a sour view of all Tibetans. "I would let the Tibetan rickshaw drivers go by," she said. "I would wait for a Chinese one." When she saw where her feelings had led her, she tried to shake off her resentment. "It has to end somewhere," she said.

Some Chinese, however, make no effort to rise above the ethnic feuding. A Qinghai Tibetan, fluent in Chinese, said he used to seek shelter with Chinese when he traveled on his own to Lhasa. Some would refuse to let him in until he said, "Maybe you think I'm Tibetan. I'm really Chinese." Then they would welcome him. "Many Chinese don't like Tibetans because they know Tibetans hate them," he said. Again in Lhasa he posed as a Chinese and mingled with soldiers and workmen. One day he was shocked to hear an army officer say soldiers have to kill dissident Tibetans. "Otherwise," the officer said, "they will never accept our rule in their hearts. It's because they hate us. If we don't kill some of them, they won't respect us. Talking with them is useless."

Although Tibetan Muslims have lived peacefully in Lhasa and Shigatse for centuries, the Hui who arrive today from Qinghai and Gansu are little different from Han Chinese in the eyes of local Tibetans. They speak Chinese—they have no dialect of their own—and they are just as competitive as the Han. Hui at the Lhasa mosque said Tibetans ask them, "Why did you come here? When are you going home?" They may be minorities, but they, too, are invading Tibetan territory. A young Hui from Gansu said Tibetans treat him a shade better than they treat the Han Chinese, but, he added, "They do harass us. Sometimes they take things from my stall, and they don't pay. Sometimes they try to steal Tibetan customers away. They come to them and speak to them in Tibetan."

A Tibetan Muslim, the owner of a teahouse beside the mosque, sided with the Lhasa Buddhists against his coreligionists. "It's a big problem," said the man, a heavy-set Tibetan in a cloth hat, "all the Hui coming from Qinghai and Gansu. They're all so ambitious. They take business away. They're bad people. They drink and run around with women and cheat you." But his brother, younger and taller and dressed like a Pakistani in a long shirt with slit sides, took a different stance. "We're all Muslims," he said, "all brothers." The mosque administrator, Hai San, also spoke well of the Hui. "Because of them I have had to learn Chinese well," he said. "And sometimes they help the mosque when we need money."

But Hui shops burned during the three-day riots of 1989, Lhasa residents staged three protests against Hui in the winter of 1995, and relations between the government and Lhasa's Muslims—both Tibetan and Hui—appear to be cozy. As soon as the Cultural Revolution ended, the authorities gave back a good-sized school to the Muslim community. In the fall of 1992, on the fifth anniversary of the first demonstrations, I saw men dressed like Hui, in blue Mao suits and coolie hats, in a row at one end of Jokhang Plaza, all of them standing tensely at attention and facing in the same direction. One of them was talking to a beefy man with a two-way radio who stood on the balcony of the Barkor Cafe. I saw many of these real or phony Hui hanging about the plaza on normal business days. During my early weeks in Lhasa, I tried to strike up a conversation with one, but he was curt and standoffish. In time I learned about these agents in Hui dress. That morning in the plaza I knew

Tibetans would notice this inept deployment of covert agents and find even more reason to resent the Hui in their midst.

And then there are the Tibetans allied with the Chinese, who also earn the scorn and mistrust of their own ethnic group. A few of these collaborators are exiles who have returned from abroad, responding to government promises that their confiscated property will be returned. "Nobody will talk to them," a Tibetan told me. "Everyone looks down on them." Some Tibetans in security agencies have gone so far as to inform on dissidents and bash the skulls of protesters, and Tibetans naturally see them as traitors, as part of the system they are fighting. Sometimes Tibetans turn their rage on any symbol of collaboration with the Chinese government. During the riot of March 1988, protesters overturned and torched two cars owned by the Tibetan Buddhist Association, a government-controlled group of religious leaders. That same day TAR Deputy Party Secretary Ragdi, a Tibetan, escaped from the besieged Jokhang by sliding down a rope. Tibetans were elated to see his undignified scramble to safety. They laughed again the next day when Ragdi appeared on television, waving a rope-burned and bandaged hand in the air as he ranted against "splittists," protesters, and "the Dalai clique."

But Tibetans don't always agree on who is a collaborator. After I visited a government agency dealing with sensitive political issues, a Lhasa resident told me scornfully that the Tibetans there held high positions because they had bought into the government line. But another said, "They seem to go along with policies, but they really try to do what they can for Tibet. Some of them have warned me to be careful because police came around asking for me." This man also gave me a visible sign that Tibetan cadres often oppose the Party in secret: a half-dozen letters written by Americans on behalf of Tibetan political prisoners. A worker in a government agency had found the letters in the trash, unopened, and took the risk of smuggling them out to dissidents. And then there were the Tibetan soldiers who helped monks escape from Chinese troops storming the Jokhang. The soldiers hurried the monks into their rooms and locked the doors from the outside. "The Chinese soldiers didn't know the Jokhang so well," one of the monks said, "so they didn't find us."

Although some Western accounts have labeled the late Panchen Lama a collaborator who sold out to the Chinese—he refused, for instance, to go along with the 1959 rebellion—the Tibetans I met mourned his death. Because he had connections with the Party, they said, he was able to force some concessions from the government and occasionally lighten the weight of oppression in Tibet. He spent fourteen years in prison—from 1964 to 1978—for supporting the Dalai Lama's return and condemning state suppression of religion; he later risked censure by speaking out again; and in 1988, when a monk challenged him in an open meeting, he stepped in to prevent the man's arrest. The following year, when the Panchen Lama died at age fifty-one of an apparent heart attack, the government wasted little time in hauling the outspoken monk off to prison.

Tibetans also told me that former aristocrats play along with the authorities but at the same time express their true feelings in ornate, elliptical language which eludes the higher ups. They have been known to speak on state occasions with all the appearance of praising the Party when they are actually putting it down. The less educated have also learned this game. There was the elderly woman, for instance, who said that life today is wonderful "because of how the water flows. It used to flow around the Barkor, but now it just goes through it." She was making an ironic reference to the Chinese in her homeland. Other Tibetans write their protests on the walls of buildings and inside latrines, even on high-school blackboards, risking arrest if they are caught. And some have been taking a stand in a more dramatic but still anonymous fashion, exploding bombs in front of official buildings and residences. Several have gone off in Lhasa since 1994 and also in Nagchu, the home of Gendun Chokyi Nyima, the boy who disappeared after being named Panchen Lama.

Still other Tibetans, like those who work for the Public Security Bureau and other "sensitive" agencies, are forced to make tough decisions between ethnic loyalty and their jobs. They may be asked to inform on dissidents, and then, a woman told me, "Some look for new work, some stay." But those who remain, another Tibetan said, "are all conflicted in their minds. They do it for political and economic gain, but they are still Tibetans."

A Lhasa woman told me that during the 1989 riots, she found herself caught up in a demonstration in the Barkor, and there she met an acquaintance, a Tibetan policeman. He rebuked her, saying she should not risk her student status by taking part in a protest. She shouted back at him, and a Chinese policeman took her picture. Later, the Tibetan showed up at her home, and she was about to close the door in his face when he held out his palm, displaying her photograph, cut to shreds. They renewed their friendship, she said, but she couldn't help asking him, "Why didn't you tear up the rest of the pictures?"

In Lhasa, Tibetans and foreigners are constantly assessing who is to be trusted, who is undercover, who is only an apparent collaborator. Guests at Snowland would tell me to watch out for a certain woman employee or a man who came by on his bicycle or Tibetans who openly wear Dalai Lama photos and strike up conversations in fluent English. The air was so heavy with suspicion that I began to follow the example of friends and avoid giving out seemingly innocuous information, like the name of my hotel or how long I planned to stay.

Western tourists, especially the youthful backpackers who lodge in central Lhasa, find themselves drawn into this aura of intrigue and whispered warnings. Many Tibetans view the West as their last hope, and they wage a lobbying campaign to gain the sympathy of foreign visitors. Their cause, I agree, is just, but their propaganda can be as misleading as that emanating from Beijing. The young Westerners often swallow it whole, and some of them come to Tibet already afire with the Tibetan cause and steeped in misinformation. A young Englishwoman told me one evening that she had visited a private school where the children were learning Tibetan. "They don't allow them to learn the language in [public] school," she said. I tried to set her right, but I knew that many left Tibet believing such claims. (Those who had spent more time in Tibet, however, were less naïve. One who had passed months at a time in Lhasa, Shigatse, and western Tibet told me she no longer had the "illusions" she once had; now, she said, she refused to listen to every complaint.)

Westerners may also be ready to condemn China and side with the Tibetans because they have come up against a series of insolent, money-grubbing Chinese agents and bureaucrats—all too common in the People's Republic—and have had no dealings with unassuming peasants and other decent Chinese. A German medical student—driven to near frenzy by the delays, blunders, and loutish intransigence of the Chinese travel industry—told me, "I'm an easygoing guy, and when I came to China I was eager to learn about the country and people, but now I'm fed up. They just want to get as much money out of you as they can, and we are just students." He found the Tibetans more willing to help and less greedy for cash. "When I came to Tibet for the first time I found kindness," he said. The German student was one of many who were ripe to hear the worst about the Chinese. It was easy to understand. I often had to remind myself that not all of them were like the surly clerks who made life miserable for travelers as well as ordinary Chinese. When you experience the rudeness of petty agents, pay out government-mandated fees up to ten times the amount charged residents, and wake in the morning to martial music blaring from loudspeakers, you are primed to fall in with the most embittered Tibetan dissidents.

But in spite of the heavy cloud of hostility that lies over Lhasa and the tense encounters between Tibetans, Chinese, and Hui, many Tibetans frown on the spitting and name-calling and icy demeanors that some adopt. And many Tibetans form bonds of trust and friendship with the outsiders. In a Shigatse restaurant where Xiao Jin and I used to hang out, Chinese and Tibetans kidded each other with the light-hearted insults of good friends. "You're all descended from monkeys," a Chinese said, and a Tibetan woman laughed and took a swipe at him. The young Amdowa who posed as Chinese said that in Lhasa he met a Chinese factory worker in his thirties who preferred to date Tibetan women instead of Chinese. Tibetans were more trusting, the worker said. He also agreed that Tibet should have its independence and recognized that most Tibetans longed to be free from China. "Then why don't the Tibetans fight?" the Amdowa-passing-as-Chinese asked. "Because," the worker said, "they are kinder and more religious than we are."

A Lhasa woman also told me of a sympathetic Han teacher who told his students that he knew now, after coming to Tibet, that China did not belong there. "Your culture is so different," he said. He apologized for the way his government had taken over their land, and soon after that he disappeared from Lhasa. Some Tibetan students had informed on him, the woman said, shaking her head sadly.

When I traveled to Guchok Village with my friend Tashi Tshering, he talked at length with our Sichuanese driver. The man had spent twenty years in the TAR, and the two of them spoke frankly about Tibet and Tibetans. Tashi was pleased. "The Chinese who've been here a long time," he said, "have more sympathy and understanding of our problems." A Tibetan woman from Qinghai made the same observation. Some Chinese in her province look down on the nomads, she said, because they find them dirty and ignorant. "But," she added, "those Chinese who have been there a long time have grown to appreciate them and their culture."

These comments may help explain why relations between Tibetans and Chinese appear to be better in the east, in Amdo and Kham, than in the TAR. The eastern regions have seen protests, and most there hope for independence or at least some form of genuine autonomy, but residents of Kham and Amdo have told me that Tibetans, Chinese, and Hui treat each other with a courtesy and respect missing in Lhasa. In some areas mixed Chinese-Tibetan marriages are not unusual, and one Tibetan woman from the east told me her mother advised her to marry a Chinese because they were more faithful to their wives than Tibetan men.

Outside the TAR, great numbers of Chinese have moved into Tibetan farming villages. The two groups have lived side by side over time, and this may have allowed friendships and mutual respect to form. And the heavy military presence apparent in central Tibet is absent in the east, and few residents of Qinghai, Gansu, Sichuan and Yunnan have witnessed security forces assaulting monks with bullets and cudgels. But even the Tibetans from Kham and Amdo spoke to me of their fears for Tibetan culture and their despair over the future.

The tension is electric in Lhasa, where conflicts between Han and the natives are constant, but also in the adobe and stone houses of the peasants and the yak-hair tents of pastoralists, the fear remains that the government may step in once again to suppress religious practice and exert more control over their daily lives. One TAR peasant said, "We have more food now, after the reforms, but what good is that when the food has lost its taste? I cannot find the sweetness that I found in the old days." When I asked an elderly nomad about the Cultural Revolution, he reached behind him for his prayer wheel and turned it in his hand until we changed the subject; he acted on reflex, as if to reassure himself of his rediscovered rights and keep the enemies of faith at bay. Among the Pala nomads, several days travel away from major roads, researchers found feelings of "vulnerability, anxiety, and anger."[10] The nomads liked the latest reforms, but they knew they had no real power, that leaders in Beijing could trespass in their lives whenever they chose.

In the east as well, memories of the Cultural Revolution and the government's brutal response to the uprisings of the 1950s have left Tibetans anxious. Nomads in Qinghai told an Amdowa friend of mine, "The Chinese raped and killed people. The Chinese don't have a human heart." They told him they knew their culture was in danger, but they also knew they were helpless against the strength of the People's Republic, which claimed to own them and their land.

Government interference in monasteries has also angered Tibetans in rural areas in and out of the TAR, and monks, nuns, and students have held protests in Qinghai and the TAR countryside. In the spring of 1993, according to TIN, the military was sent to southern Tibet to seal off an entire group of villages called Kyimshi, including the local monastery. A nearby nunnery and monastery also joined the protests.[11]

A friend from Qinghai told me that in the 1980s he spent a year canvassing Tibetans in farming and nomad areas, and he found that two thirds of them wanted independence, though they disagreed on the best way to go about it. Others, he said, believed the government's claims that separation from the People's Republic would bring back the old serf system, and a small minority had no opinion at all. Harsh and even violent verbal attacks on the Dalai Lama, which have appeared in the media and in official pronouncements since the Third Forum of 1994, have certainly embittered rural Tibetans even more.

My Qinghai friend was the same one who used to listen to radio programs from Lhasa and dream of visiting that stronghold of Tibetan culture where the Potala and Jokhang stood as intact symbols of a thriving culture. His faith in the survival of the Holy City was an instinctive response, and he was not the first Amdowa to see the capital city as a refuge. During the early years of the People's Republic, when the Communists began to force eastern Tibetans into communes, the residents of entire villages abandoned their homes in Kham and Amdo and journeyed en masse to central Tibet.

Among them was a band of nomads from a remote county of Qinghai called Shi Qu Xian who left their ancestral land and began a desperate march toward Lhasa in the late 1950s. They were running from the Communists' demands that they turn their livestock over to the state—sheep, goats, horses, and yaks. Rather than join the revolution, they headed for Lhasa, driving their flocks before them into the forbidding mountain ranges beyond which the Dalai Lama still reigned supreme. They were Golok tribespeople, rugged nomads with a reputation for toughness and ferocity, but after two years of wandering through the wilds, only one hundred out of the thousand who had set out arrived in central Tibet. Many had died from disease, privation and the guns of PLA soldiers who took them for rebels; and many had set off on their own. The survivors reached Bange County in the Changtang, and there, destitute and starving, they were forced to stop. They never made it as a group to Lhasa, but by then it was 1959, the Dalai Lama had fled, and they had no choice but to labor for the regime they had hoped to escape.

My Qinghai friend and the Golok had acted on their faith that Lhasa would remain a safe haven beyond the mountains. They left all behind and set out toward a final sanctuary of last resort. But in both cases their efforts proved futile. The Chinese had arrived before they did.

When my friend from Qinghai arrived in Lhasa, he saw Chinese restaurants and shops, Chinese in the streets and apartment buildings, and he said to himself that Lhasa was dying. He was expressing the sorrow and rage many Tibetans felt, and this sense, that Tibet is endangered at its core, accounts for much of the rancor in Lhasa. If the Abode of the Gods can lose its soul, what is left? Those in Amdo and Kham and the remote areas of the TAR may look to the ancient capital as a secure retreat where they can immerse themselves in their culture and faith, but if the center of their longing and devotion is no longer truly Tibetan, they have nowhere left to go, no refuge at all. As Lhasa residents watch the buses roll into town from the north and east, packed with Han Chinese and Hui, they see the heart of Tibet under siege. They are embittered and despondent, and they are trying in many ways to say so.

11

"Outwardly Calm" (Human Rights)

It rains before dawn on September 27, the fifth anniversary of the first demonstration, held on this date in 1987. The peaks about Lhasa lie under a dusting of snow, and the air holds the chill of early autumn. I emerge from my hotel and find the streets silent—no tractors putt-putting over the cobblestones, no peddlers setting up their carts and stalls, only the Chinese scarf-sellers standing with hunched shoulders, waiting for morning worshippers to buy their wares. Few police are in sight, but a plainclothesman is standing on the balcony of the Barkor Cafe, speaking into a portable telephone.

An hour later a tourist bus arrives from the Holiday Inn and disgorges a cluster of foreign visitors armed with cameras. They are little aware of the tension in the air, the undercover police, the empty spaces where vendors normally station their carts, and the two jeeps which have just today parked near the Barkor. My friend and I pass a Tibetan woman who says quietly, "Most of the vendors won't show up today." It's a silent protest, my friend explains, a show of solidarity with the sixty monks who marched here five years ago to demand freedom from Chinese rule.

Last night the Barkor was thick with Tibetans circumambulating the Jokhang at sunset; the illegal peddlers were busy hawking shoes and clothing; and a dance group was performing in the square. An apparently normal day, but a sense of impending crisis had been growing for weeks. Tibetan friends had invited me to a picnic arranged for the following weekend, but in the atmosphere of alarm they dropped their plans. After dark on September 12 a half dozen Public Security police showed up at Snowland Hotel and checked the passports and visas of foreign visitors. They were smiling and meticulously polite, but I found their presence menacing. Since then Lhasa has been humming with rumors: The city will be sealed off on the 27th; the underground is planning a big demonstration for the 28th, when the security forces let down their guard; the police will step up their surveillance of foreigners; they were at the Kyirey Hotel last night; they will surely come to Snowland again this evening; they already came but just to check the registry.

I am cautioned to stay in my hotel on the 27th and above all, to stay away from monasteries. I avoid the Jokhang and Ani Tsamkung nunnery, but I disregard the other warning. If something happens, I want to be there. So I spend most of the morning away from the hotel. At noon, when I leave Snowland with a friend, a woman on the staff asks us where we are going. No one has questioned me like this before, but today, my friend says, the police came by and told the workers to keep tabs on foreigners.

At 6:30 in the evening I am draped over the third-floor balcony of my hotel, watching the intricate comings and goings about the courtyard pump, when I hear high-pitched shouts from the plaza. I look across the housetops to the gilded Jokhang roof and see monks come running to peer into the square below, and at this I hurry down the stairs and into the plaza, passing vendors who are folding up their tables and taking flight. Pushing against the current I find myself in front of an unmarked Public Security station. Police, some with two-way radios, are milling about, and a crowd has gathered before the storefront garrison. I ask a trio of Westerners what is going on, and they say, "We only came at the end of it. Someone was yelling something." A plainclothesman with a two-way radio shouts in Tibetan, gesturing at the crowd, and the onlookers melt away.

Later I hear from a man who was circling the Barkor that evening that the crowd suddenly began to run, then slowed down and came to a stop. The people looked at each other nervously and laughed. "I hear someone was arrested," the man says. Still later I learn what the lone demonstrator was shouting. It was, "Independent Tibet!"

No one needed to tell me what happened next. The semi truck parked in front of the security police stronghold hauled the protester off to prison—to Drapchi, Gutsa, or Sangyip, all near Lhasa—and there he was tortured and interrogated. This is routine treatment for demonstrators who dare to challenge China's hold on Tibet, and the man who raised his voice that evening knew what was in store. It is even possible he had been arrested for such a crime before.

But nothing about this demonstration will appear in the newspapers or on radio or television. News of this brief act of defiance will, at most, pass by word of mouth throughout the city and perhaps beyond, to human rights groups and Tibetans in exile. It is one of several I have heard of since I arrived in Lhasa, none of which received any notice in the government media: In mid-August, I was told, security forces arrested members of a small group which unfurled the Tibetan flag in front of the Jokhang; the following day they visited a monastery and nunnery and took more than a dozen into custody. A Chinese television crew from Yunnan, which happened to be on hand, was forced to turn over its film. "Hardly anybody knows about this," my source said. But many were talking about the follow-up arrests. In time I hear of another demonstration on the 27th: Before dawn a small group raised the Tibetan flag on a pole near the Jokhang Plaza. Police moved in immediately and hauled all of the demonstrators away to prison. I have no way to verify the separate accounts, but monitoring groups who keep track of political prisoners report that many arrests are due to quickly suppressed demonstrations like these.

Tension remains high after the 27th because hard on that date comes October 1, a double anniversary. It marks the both founding of the People's Republic and the first bloodshed of the resistance which emerged in the late 1980s. When demonstrators took to the streets on that date five years ago, demanding the release of monks imprisoned in the first protest, police opened fire on the crowd. Many died, many were wounded, and cars and shops burned.

The center of Lhasa is quietly transformed during this anniversary period. Public Security police take the place of traffic cops, and most of them are Chinese. The rickshaws hung with bright fabric disappear from their usual positions at the entrance to the plaza. When a driver tries to approach, police wave him away. The space is to be kept clear for surveillance and possible action. More jeeps appear, lined up outside the Public Security station. But no protests—at least none large enough to attract notice—take place on October 1. I hear only that a group of monks was arrested. No one can say why. As the days pass, the rickshaw drivers return and the rumors abate, but many of the Public Security police remain on hand.

Undeclared martial law prevails in Lhasa, even though the state officially suspended military rule in 1990. By then the city had spent a full year under PLA control, the result of a three-day rampage in March 1989. Soldiers manned roadblocks, foreigners were expelled, the military patrolled the streets, and Security Bureau spies openly tailed Tibetans and visitors as they passed through the byways of the capital. When the decree was lifted a new policy was in place. Tibetans call it "outwardly calm but inwardly strict." One friend puts it this way: "They want to give the impression to the outside world that all is well and they have no worries." Today the tourists are back and the roadblocks have come down, but Lhasa is infested with undercover agents. "If you talk to a foreigner now," a Tibetan said, "they still follow you, but they do it secretly."

During the first years of protest, demonstrators managed to circle the Barkor and march on the TAR government buildings a quarter of a mile away before police turned out in force. Today Lhasa is under round-the-clock surveillance by a swarm of plainclothes and uniformed agents lurking in ambush. Video cameras are trained on the Jokhang Plaza, the Barkor, and other sites around the city where trouble has erupted in the past. The cameras and the security forces are ready to record and squelch the first glimmer of dissent. Police are ever on hand to nab protesters at the first shout, the first raised fist, the first brave unfurling of the Tibetan flag. "Our protest," recalled a nun who later made her way to India, "lasted only ninety seconds." Today only a few protesters—a dozen at most—act together at one time.

The fear that weighs so heavily in Lhasa, the whispered rumors, the trucks ready to haul prisoners away—all are the bitter fruit of human rights abuses in Tibet. Tibetans have neither the right to free speech nor to its companion, the right to be informed. Prisoners are tortured and denied the right to a fair trial. Cadres and common folk alike know that their government lies and denies them access to the truth, but they are forced to repeat the official line. To keep its tight control over Tibet, China chooses to trample on many rights that international bodies have upheld as basic to a free life, and when the government-in-exile accuses China of brutality and political repression, they have the weight of evidence on their side, documented by human rights groups, Western governments, and the United Nations.

China's response is to redefine rights to its own advantage, to indulge in finger-pointing, to charge the West with interfering in internal affairs, and to ignore the charges altogether. It says that Tibetans now have the "right to subsistence," that free speech would lead to chaos, and that Tibetans are better off now than under the old serf system, which was a reign of terror.

These responses fail to silence the monitoring groups, who point to abuses throughout China but single out Tibet as a special case. There, nationalist protests have brought on the heavy weight of state repression with a special twist, the "outwardly calm" strategy, and there the ratio of political prisoners to the general population is reportedly more than seventy times that of China as a whole.[1]

China, however, denies that it holds any political prisoners in Tibetan jails. One official publication explains it this way: "There is no such term as 'ideological crime' in China's Criminal Law. So there is no so-called 'ideological criminal' in China." The demonstrators are therefore charged with "counterrevolutionary incitement," which is listed as a crime. They are derided as "splittists," a word which sputters with indignation and describes anyone suspected of trying to sabotage the unity of the motherland.[2]

In fact, the government claimed in a 1989 publication, the entire TAR maintains only one prison and two re-education-through-labor camps. (More recently China has acknowledged two TAR reform-through-labor camps.) Altogether, the document insisted, the work camps and prison held nine hundred prisoners in all, and not one of them was held for political reasons. All were common criminals.[3]

No one in Tibet—official, cadre, or commoner—really believes this. Lhasa actually has (besides the official prison, Drapchi) two detention centers, one reform-through-labor center, and four re-education-through-labor centers, all of which function as prisons. The TAR also has detention facilities in each of the six prefectures outside of Lhasa, more at the county level, and a second reform-through-labor center east of Lhasa in Powo County. At one time a Public Security official admitted that the TAR had twenty to thirty detention centers. Prisoners are also held in police stations and in the People's Armed Police headquarters in Lhasa.[4]

Detention centers are for prisoners undergoing investigation before being released or sentenced. Reform-through-labor centers hold male prisoners who have been tried and sentenced to terms of less than five years, according to Chinese officials, and re-education-through-labor centers are for prisoners sentenced without trial by government committees. Sentences in these facilities are three or four years. Drapchi, the one officially recognized prison, houses convicts who have been tried and sentenced to five years or more, but TIN reports that many prisoners there are serving lighter sentences.

China has also come out with an account of life inside the lone Tibetan prison. It's really quite comfortable, according to two visiting Chinese reporters whose story appeared in a government magazine. Families can visit once a month, and prisoners can write letters, under supervision. They drink butter tea, read periodicals in Tibetan and Chinese, subscribe to correspondence courses up to the university level, and take part in prison recreational activities such as movies, dances, and sports. Each convict receives a stipend to use at the prison store, medical care is available, and those with serious illnesses can visit hospitals in Lhasa. Prisoners work at gardening and car repair. And any prisoner who complains of mistreatment can file a grievance.[5]

But this is not the way former prisoners describe their experiences. One of these who has spoken of her days in Gutsa, the detention center for Lhasa, is Tsultrim Drolma, a young Khampa woman from the Chamdo area. After she escaped to India and came to the United States, she told me of her experiences in a series of interviews.

She is a slender woman, soft-spoken and polite, and she now wears a luxurious crop of black hair which falls in waves down her back. But when her ordeal began she was a nun with a shaven head, spending her days in prayer and meditation at Chupsang Nunnery outside Lhasa. Tsultrim had longed to join a convent ever since she was a child herding yaks and sheep in her seminomadic village of Pembar. In 1985, at the age of seventeen she made her way to Lhasa and soon entered Chupsang, a small convent behind Sera Monastery. During her initiation ceremony, surrounded by a crowd of other aspiring monks and nuns, she found herself overcome and wept with joy and gratitude. The monasteries of her native Chamdo had been razed during the Cultural Revolution, and when she was a child she rarely saw a monk or nun. But now she was in the Holy City, and she would spend the rest of her days praying, meditating, and studying in the mountain retreat of Chupsang.

But Tsultrim happened to be in Lhasa during the first demonstrations of 1987, and she was there again when rioting broke out during the New Year festivities of 1988. She saw a young monk shot down by a policeman's bullet, and she saw the security forces tossing prisoners like stacks of cordwood into a truck. And now she was enduring the intrusion of "work teams" which had moved into her convent and were subjecting the nuns to political indoctrination and surveillance. It was too much to bear, and by the spring of 1988 she and five other nuns had determined to hold a protest of their own. "We decided to sacrifice everything," Tsultrim Drolma said. "We knew what would happen to us because other nuns had been arrested before, but I wasn't afraid. I knew in my heart what I wanted to do for my nation, and I knew they had tortured so many people. I couldn't take it any more."

Before dawn one spring morning the six women left Chupsang for Lhasa and walked to the Jokhang. There they prayed before the shrines, committing themselves to their task and gathering courage before they stepped into the Barkor. It was nine o'clock in the morning when they emerged, a time when Lhasa residents are manning their market stalls, shopping, and circumambulating the pilgrim route around the temple. Tsultrim Drolma and her fellow nuns raised their fists and began to shout, "Independence for Tibet! Independence for Tibet!" They entered the Barkor, attracting passersby who stopped to watch the tight group of young women, easily identified as nuns because of their shaven heads and woolen robes. Many laypersons joined the nuns as they marched along the cobbled street, between the stalls and storefronts, and out into the square once more. They passed the doors of the temple and re-entered the Barkor, shouting all the time.

The growing group of protesters managed a second circuit before a phalanx of troops appeared suddenly, tossing tear gas canisters into the crowd and scattering protesters and onlookers alike. Two policemen grabbed Tsultrim, pinned her arms behind her back, and dragged her to a truck already filled with armed men in uniform. She and the other nuns were piled inside and driven to a building on the outskirts of Lhasa where their captors shoved them into a hallway lined on both sides with men. The men formed a gaunt-let, a corridor of bullies, who kicked, punched, and cudgeled the women as they stumbled down the hall. Those were the first blows Tsultrim was to endure over months of abuse. She had entered Gutsa.

The nuns were stripped and all their body orifices inspected; then they were handcuffed and led outside, still naked, and made to stand facing a wall. Tsultrim was not allowed to turn around and see her tormentors, but she felt their kicks and blows. They beat her with fists and truncheons, they broke a wooden chair over her back, and they applied an electric baton to her anus and vagina. The shocks from this instrument of torture were the worst of her ordeal, Tsultrim Drolma said later, and the round of torments continued, first one assault, then another, throughout the day. She was not allowed to sit or turn around, and when she fell, they stomped on her hands.

After dark they stopped at last, and Tsultrim Drolma was led to a solitary cell and dumped inside the door. She fell to the floor and saw a cot a few feet away, but she was too weak to climb onto it. The handcuffs bit cruelly into her wrists, and her body was swollen and bruised. This cannot be my own body, she thought. It was distended and bloated, something she had never seen before. She spent the night lying on the floor.

The following day her interrogations began. Again, she was not allowed to look about her. She had to answer with her head bowed and her eyes on her lap, but she was aware of perhaps three people in the room. One of them was an interpreter who translated her replies into Chinese. "Why did you demon-strate?" she was asked. "For what cause?" She answered, "For our rights. We want freedom." And at this, her tormentors would strike her with their fists, slap her, and pull her ears and hair. Sometimes they threw foul-smelling gar-bage in her face.

Every day she faced interrogations. Often the sessions went on for hours, but occasionally she was allowed to leave after a few minutes. At times she got a glimpse of her interrogator's uniform, and according to routine, the one in charge would identify himself by rank. As the days went on the questioners seemed to increase in status, as if they were trying to intimidate her, but they were never satisfied with her answers.

Tsultrim Drolma believed she might spend the rest of her days in Gutsa. No one told her otherwise. She was never tried or sentenced, and she could only appeal to her protective deity, Palden Lhamo, and other beings for help. Even when she was barely able to stand, she managed to make prostrations, but when the guards took notice they told her to stop. Then she concentrated her mind and visualized the Dalai Lama and the Green Tara, the motherly aspect of compassion who sits on a lotus flower. She recited mantras, and thus passed her days alone in the cell. Twice daily the guards brought her food—weak black tea without butter and half-cooked vegetables. She was constantly hungry.

One day in midsummer, without warning, Tsultrim Drolma was released along with some thirty other nuns and stepped, squinting, into the sunlight again. She had no money, but she walked into Lhasa and spent the night in a small monastery; then with four other nuns she returned to Chupsang. When the local people learned that the nuns had returned, they made their way to the convent with gifts of food—butter tea, yogurt, stuffed dumplings, and tsampa—but Tsultrim Drolma could only look at this bounty. She was unable to eat, too weak from her months of semistarvation in Gutsa. After a few days passed it was clear that the prison diet and constant beatings had damaged her health. She spent a month recuperating in Lhasa First People's Hospital before she could eat normally again.

Tsultrim spent a year at home in Kham, but the local Public Security office continued to call her in for questioning and visited her home to take photographs. Her family and neighbors in Pembar were tense and fearful, and Tsultrim left for Lhasa once again. She was afraid that her family would suffer if she stayed at home, and she wanted to rejoin Chupsang Nunnery. But she had been in the convent only a few days when officials told her she had been expelled and would have to leave. Confused, unsure of where she would go next, she set out for Lhasa late that night, and as she passed a Public Security post outside of town a group of uniformed Chinese accosted her, gagged her so she couldn't cry out, and took turns raping her. It seemed she could no longer claim to be a nun. Although she had resisted, that violent act had broken her vow of celibacy. Now, she decided, there was nothing to keep her in Tibet, and with a friend she left on a pilgrim truck for Mount Kailash, a sacred site near the Nepalese border. From there she made her way into exile.

The files of Amnesty International, Human Rights Watch, the London-based Tibet Information Network, the UN Committee on Torture, and the

Dalai Lama's government-in-exile contain many stories like Tsultrim Drolma's. Her account of non-violent protest followed by arrest, torture, near-starvation, and abusive interrogation conforms to those of hundreds more who have openly defied the Chinese claim on Tibet and to those of dissident and religious Chinese who have spent time in prisons, jails, and detention centers throughout the People's Republic. The monitoring groups have names and histories at hand: elderly Lobsang Tsondru, a monk from Drepung, beaten so badly he lost consciousness; Lobsang Chodrak, a trader whose jaw was broken in a prison beating; Phuntsok Yangkyi, a twenty-year-old nun, who died after guards beat her for singing a nationalist song.[6]

"Nearly all prisoners arrested for political protest are beaten extensively at the time of arrest and initial detention," TIN reports. And Amnesty International states, "In Tibet, people are frequently tortured and ill-treated when held on suspicion of supporting Tibetan independence or during police raids on monasteries."[7] Tsultrim Drolma's account is not an aberration; it fits the pattern of reports heard time and again by human rights monitors.

Her story is also a familiar one because she was never charged with a crime or brought before a court. She was, however, presumed guilty, interrogated, and punished before she was finally released. Monitoring groups know this is a common practice. "The vast majority of detainees are held incommunicado for anything between a few weeks and nine months and then released without charge," TIN stated in 1991. Since then, it says, the security forces have been trying a new technique: picking up suspected dissidents, torturing them, and releasing them after a few days, only to pick them up again later. TIN calls this "recurrent disappearance."[8]

But if Tsultrim Drolma had stayed in Tibet and continued to protest, she would be following a different route through the system. If she went into the Barkor once more to shout her slogans for independence, she would most likely find herself in front of a committee—not a court—made up of officials dominated by the Public Security Bureau. This is the usual pattern, monitoring groups report. The committee would sentence her to up to three years of re-education through labor and perhaps later extend her sentence to four years.[9]

If Tsultrim persisted in such criminal activities as joining protests, unfurling the Tibetan flag, or putting up independence posters, she would very likely appear before a court, charged with the crime of "counterrevolutionary incitement." Her trial would be held away from public view; if she saw a lawyer it would be on the day of the hearing itself or, at best, a week before; she would be found guilty and sentenced; and the verdict would be pretty much a verbatim copy of the prosecutor's indictment. From the court she would go to Drapchi Prison, perhaps for three to five years, and if she defied the prison authorities—by singing protest songs aloud, for instance—she would find her sentence extended.[10]

Three years is a light sentence for a political prisoner in Tibet. The average term in 1995 was 6.5 years, up from 5.7 in 1992, but some were serving sentences of twelve years or more. Four Drepung monks who founded a pro-democracy group got seventeen to nineteen years, for instance, and five villagers who organized a pro-independence demonstration got thirteen to fifteen years. Most long sentences, however, are the result of extensions, issued when inmates break prison rules. This was the case with fourteen nuns who received six additional years each for singing songs in praise of the Dalai Lama in 1993.[11]

These sentences are especially harsh compared to that handed to a Tibetan police chief who tortured a woman so badly she spent two months in the hospital. He received two years, but his sentence was suspended, which means that he will not have to spend any time in jail if he stays out of trouble for three years. The man was also convicted of illegally detaining four officials for three days.[12]

Many of Tibet's acknowledged prisoners—those officially tried and sentenced—are in jail for printing leaflets, forming pro-independence groups, passing information to exiles or foreigners, taking part in demonstrations, criticizing the government in public or private, and carrying the Tibetan flag. Out of one thousand unofficially reported political prisoners in Tibet, TIN states, only eighteen have been involved in violence. And yet, China says, none of the thousand are political prisoners.[13]

Police and soldiers have also killed unarmed Tibetan demonstrators without benefit of rubber-stamp trials. Although official news accounts tell of gun-wielding protesters and report that police acted with restraint, witnesses say otherwise. One Tibetan told me that during the riots of March 1989, he was visiting a hospital and within two hours saw the corpses of four young Tibetans dead from gunshot wounds. "It was horrifying," he said. "Only the police have guns. The people don't have any." Western and Asian witnesses have also said that the protesters were unarmed and that police shot into the crowds. And Chinese videotapes, smuggled out to exile groups, show police bludgeoning unarmed monks in the Jokhang while an off-camera voice shouts in Chinese, *"Da! Da!"* or "Hit! Hit!" Human rights groups say forty to 150 Tibetans were killed during the three days of protest in March 1989. The numbers are difficult to verify, but conservative estimates by groups like Amnesty International and Tibet Information Network suggest that during the protests of 1987 to 1989 up to 180 Tibetans were killed.

Tibetans have also died in prison or shortly after being released. TIN has counted thirteen who died in these circumstances, all of them apparently because they were beaten and denied medical care.[14]

China responds to publicity about its human rights record by denouncing past abuses in Tibet and present abuses in other countries, pointing to the region's economic gains, claiming that civil rights don't apply to developing countries, and charging that critics are interfering in China's internal affairs. *Beijing Review,* for instance, published an article titled "The Dalai Lama's Human Rights Records [*sic*]," a response to the Tibetan leader's attacks on China. It quoted old documents to prove that lords owned their serfs (serfs were actually tied to the land, not to the lord) and suggested that high lamas indulged in human sacrifice.[15] Dorje Tseten, former chairman of the TAR, also attacked the Dalai Lama during an interview in Beijing. "I can't agree with the Dalai Lama's comments on human rights," he said, "because he has no right to be talking about such things. It is a bit ridiculous. Before 1959, the Tibetan people suffered a lot."

The old Tibet did indeed break many standards of human rights (though it was not the chamber of horrors China likes to depict), and many countries, even those in the West that are most critical of China, are vulnerable to serious criticism themselves. But none of this excuses China's treatment of Tibetans.

At other times China puts its own spin on human rights, by saying that food and shelter are the primary rights and China has brought these benefits to the people of Tibet. After 1959, the 1992 white paper states, "The Tibetan people began to enjoy the right to subsistence, along with adequate food and clothing." Of course, these are basic rights, and they are recognized explicitly in the UN Covenant on Economic, Social, and Cultural Rights. But there is no evidence that Tibetans were left to starve in former times, and today beggars abound in Lhasa and other major sites in Tibet, many of them children and many of them homeless. Moreover, the government has begun to arrest demonstrators protesting solely for economic reasons.[16] Perhaps this is why no one raised the food and shelter defense during my stay in Tibet and Beijing.

I did, however, hear the argument that civil rights may be fine in some societies, but that China has different needs. "People have a different understanding of human rights in the West and East," Dorje Tseten told me. "You have to look back at history when you look at human rights. In a society like Tibet, rights are completely different from a developed country like the United States." Along with this contention goes the charge that the West is interfering in China's internal affairs and trying to impose its own cultural values when it brings up human rights.

But China itself has signed seven human rights agreements, such as the Convention Against Torture, which means it is accountable to the UN for upholding these contracts. It has also supported human rights scrutiny of other countries, such as Afghanistan and Chile, while it has complained about interference in its own affairs. And China was party to the Vienna Declaration and Programme of Action at the 1993 World Conference on Human Rights, which affirmed that "The universal nature of these rights and freedoms [referring to the UN Charter] is beyond question." Moreover, the Universal Declaration of Human Rights was not the product of one cultural tradition but of a worldwide consensus.

In a 1991 white paper, *Human Rights in China,* the People's Republic says that social unrest could threaten the people's right to subsistence and, therefore, China cannot conform to standards of civil and political rights. There may be historical reasons for China's fear of losing control, but this does not mean that breaches of basic rights are necessary or justified. China acknowledged this in approving the Vienna Declaration, which states that "the lack of development may not be invoked to justify the abridgement of internationally recognized human rights." And, as Amnesty International notes, "There is no evidence . . . anywhere in the world that denying people such a fundamental right as freedom of speech promotes or improves their right to subsistence."[17]

It is likewise true that torture does nothing to enhance anyone's right to subsistence, and China prefers to avoid the issue. Nevertheless, it is the most disturbing violation of human rights in Tibet and elsewhere in China. Its use is widespread and routine, according to many monitoring groups, even though the Chinese government has signed the 1987 Convention Against Torture. The government has also enacted a criminal code which forbids extracting confessions by means of torture and has adopted regulations on detention centers. The code outlaws beating, verbal abuse, corporal punishment, and mistreatment of prisoners. Amnesty International and the UN Committee on Torture, however, have both noted that Chinese law only forbids using torture in specific circumstances and allows for many loopholes. Both have called for China to adopt a total and explicit ban. Amnesty declared that in Tibet even children have been tortured. The UN committee also asked China to stop holding public executions, to set up a system to investigate complaints of abuse, and to notify families of those held in detention.[18]

In effect, prisoners have no protection against brutality once they are in custody. Amnesty International, Asia Watch, and other human rights organizations continue to gather accounts of inhuman treatment—beatings, burnings, scaldings, sexual molestation, dog bites, electric shocks, psychological torments—which are inflicted on the women and men who have dared to defy China's rule over Tibet. More recently, the reports say, the torture has often taken forms which are difficult to detect and which leave no scars, such as forcing prisoners to stand in cold water or in awkward positions for long periods of time.[19]

Although China has at times acknowledged the use of torture—condemning the practice in several 1993 newspaper stories and announcing the conviction of a police chief for torturing a woman—it usually overlooks the issue when it responds to human rights critics. It would rather talk about brutality in the old Tibet. The 1992 white paper, for instance, never mentions torture or any other violation of human rights, nor does the government booklet *One Hundred Questions About Tibet*. But another official publication, *Tibet: From 1951 to 1991*, makes this brief statement: "Tibetan law enforcement departments also ensure that prisoners are humanely treated."[20] Articles on the comfortable lives of prisoners in Tibet are also an oblique response to the charges of mistreatment.

China's usual response to criticism of its record in Tibet is to compare the past serf system to the present, but even in this regard China has made some contradictory claims. While spokesmen like Dorje Tseten have implied or said outright that Tibet is not ready for civil rights, official statements have at the same time claimed that Tibetans have indeed been granted these rights under Chinese rule. This indicates that China, while it denies these rights to its people, nevertheless recognizes them as valid.

Today, according to the 1992 white paper, Tibetans have full political and personal rights—true liberation. The paper cites China's constitution, which outlines a number of rights granted to its citizens—freedom of religion, speech, dissent, and assembly—and it claims that Tibetans now have the "right to vote and to stand for election." In fact, the paper says, in five prefectures of the TAR nearly 94 percent "of the people" turned out to vote for deputies to the Fifth People's Congress in 1988. "To enable illiterates to participate," it states, "beans were used in place of ballots in many places. Voters placed beans in the bowls behind the backs of the candidates of their choice." It is odd that China's leaders, who have vigorously opposed democracy movements, would boast of elections in Tibet. But the white paper's description of voting with beans (also replayed on propaganda films) seems to say that China has yet to grasp the concept of secret ballots.

Many of the Chinese and Tibetans who expressed outrage and sorrow at human rights violations in Tibet told me of officials who publicly defend China but condemn its actions in private. Still, some cadres seemed to believe the Party line. Twice in Tibet I heard loyalists assert, without my asking, that Tibet has no human rights problem. One was a Chinese soldier who boasted of China's power and complained of American hegemony. He knew all about rights, he said, because he used to work in a security office. "There is just a handful of Tibetans agitating for independence," he said. "Really, most of them don't want it. The few are instigated by the Dalai Lama." The second was an official at August First Farm outside Lhasa. His name was Dawa, and he diverged from our discussion of apples and cabbages to say that the party's reform policy is a boon to all of Tibet. "People here enjoy freedom and human rights, too," he said. Then he added, with evident pride, "None of our staff took part in the demonstrations."

But most Tibetans and Chinese know that the government ignores rights guaranteed on paper whenever it fears a loss of control. No one in Tibet has freedom of speech, dissent, or assembly when the issue is independence or support for the Dalai Lama or other "sensitive" topics. In 1993 Lhasa residents were able to protest inflation and rising taxes while troops looked on, but at the first shout of "Independence!" they were attacked with tear gas and cudgels. Since then, however, demonstrators protesting economic hardship have been beaten by security forces and hauled off to prison.[21]

Lhasa's Public Security Bureau, discreetly positioned video cameras, heavy military presence, jails crammed with political prisoners, and scores of undercover agents are evidence of the most obvious human rights abuses in Tibet, and the stories of torture, killings of innocent protesters, and summary trials cast a shadow of fear over the populace. Most residents are unwilling to take on this apparatus of control openly, and only a small percentage find themselves behind bars. But all Tibetans suffer from the state's repressive presence, and the most pervasive human rights abuses are silent and invisible. They are the many forms of censorship that deny everyone the right to speak openly and the right to be informed—two rights spelled out in the Universal Declaration of Human Rights and the Covenant on Civil and Political Rights.

Censorship helps maintain the "outwardly calm, inwardly tight" policy by blacking out news of public protests and other signs of discontent. And many social problems, like the swarms of beggars in Lhasa, are taboo subjects for newspapers and magazines. When a friend of mine suggested to a Tibetan reporter that he should interview beggars, as I had been doing, he shook his head. "Too sensitive," he said. It was not that he found the subject too delicate himself; it was only that he knew it would never be published. He gave the same response when my friend prodded him to write about the Chinese vegetable gardeners renting land near Lhasa.

Academics face the same controls. "I do my own research," said one Tibetan, "but I can't write what I really believe. It's very painful. I have to say what they want. They deny us our humanity." A Chinese student told me that historians working in China concentrate on the years before 1950, when the PLA invaded Tibet at Chamdo. "It's safer," my friend added. But even ancient history has its pitfalls. One researcher dared to write that the Tang dynasty Princess Wencheng, a Chinese wife of the seventh century Tibetan King Songtsen Gampo, was less influential than official histories maintain. Since the People's Republic upholds Wencheng as evidence that Tibet has long been part of China, the researcher came under heavy criticism, failed to receive a prize and a promotion he had earned, and saw his paper rejected for publication again and again.

Academics told me in many ways that they have no choice but to write what the Party dictates, and you need only glance at the titles of their works to see that this is true. During an interview with three Chinese specializing in Tibetan history at the Institute for National Minorities in Beijing, I asked them to mention some examples of the academy's work. A brief record of the Tibetan language, they answered, a book titled *Tibet Is an Inseparable Part of China,* some research on serfdom, a modern history of Tibet, and *The Biographies of the Dalai Lamas* by Ya Hanzhang. I had already read the last book and found it an irritating and detailed attempt to document China's claim on Tibet, full of political rhetoric and attacks on "imperialists." The other works, except for the apparently non-controversial treatise on language, were undoubtedly more examples of state-controlled propaganda on Tibet's past.

Most intellectuals I met were embarrassed and dismayed by the work they had been forced to perform. Tibetans told me repeatedly that I shouldn't hold researchers accountable for what they have written or what they told me during formal interviews. My friends had heard me complain when bureaucrats and academics spewed forth many words but little useful data, when they recited the shopworn Party line and false statistics. "Why do they expect me to believe that?" I asked. "It does me no good; you can read it everywhere." Tibetans and Chinese told me repeatedly, "They have to say that."

In order to preserve the "outwardly calm" facade, officials also drag Tibetan cadres into newspaper offices to write critiques of the Dalai Lama or his supporters. Again, the cadres have to produce what is expected of them, and the world then reads their bylines above articles that contradict their true feelings. One researcher told me he was sent to a news agency to write a "spontaneous" rebuttal to remarks made by the government-in-exile. "I was told what I was supposed to say," he said. "Did you do it?" I asked. "Of course," he answered. "I had no choice. They didn't give me the exact words, but they made me understand what they wanted." As an American I could ask him that naïve question, "Did you do it?" After months in China I was still finding it hard to believe that decent citizens were often forced to lie.

The officially sanctioned falsehoods not only humiliate researchers and others who are compelled to repeat them, but they also deny everyone access to the truth. Even educated cadres who know that the government systematically deceives its people cannot sort out all the lies. One intellectual, for instance, accepted the myth that Tibet has no problems with human rights—until he actually saw police beating unarmed monks. Others bought into government claims that Lhasa demonstrators had carried guns and shot at police—until they learned of the massacre of protesters near Tiananmen Square.

In spite of state efforts to censor the news, Tibetans manage to get their hands on forbidden literature and photos of the abducted child named as Panchen Lama, and many of them listen to Voice of America and the BBC in Chinese and Tibetan on the quiet. They do so furtively because they know that some Tibetans have endured torture and imprisonment for reading the Dalai Lama's autobiography or for possessing tapes of his speeches or videos that show him accepting the Nobel Peace Prize. Border guards have seized these items at frontier crossings.

China has also banned books by Western writers, if they criticize the Communists' role in Tibet or reveal facts which the Party prefers to hide. Only high-level cadres and officials are allowed access to these works. When they publish Chinese-language versions of such books, the authorities parcel out short passages to various translators so none of them will have the full text.

The security forces also use intimidation to keep Tibetans in line. After the 1989 riots, some said, agents made a show of tailing anyone who met with foreigners. They would also drop into offices and openly inquire about workers who had somehow drawn their attention. In 1992, Tibetan exiles visiting from abroad told me that they had to report to the Public Security Bureau when they arrived. There they were questioned about their lives outside Tibet and asked to list relatives still living in the TAR. Two days later police entered their hotel room at two o'clock in the morning to interrogate them. "I heard of one family that had this happen three times," one of the exiles told me. "And the police took video film from one of them."

The Chinese have slapped a gag order on Tibetan dissent, and censorship is worse today than it was before "liberation." In the bygone, backward times, wandering yogins and opera performers could openly ridicule those in charge, using mime and song to burlesque corrupt lamas and arrogant officials. Workers sang street songs criticizing officials, spreading the word about abuses and

255

crimes. Monks also delivered sermons calling for reform and decrying the greed and lack of charity too often found in religious orders. But public complaint about politics and the failings of leaders is taboo today. China imposes a crushing uniformity on all open comment. This is what the new rulers have brought the masses—fear of speaking openly, a tedious repetition of "correct" ideology and history, and, often, confusion and ignorance.[22]

Although the 1992 white paper claims that Tibetans "have obtained the right to be masters of their own affairs," this right is precisely what they lack. They cannot speak their minds about religion, their desire for independence, their veneration for the Dalai Lama, their anger at the influx of Han Chinese into their heartland. They cannot choose their leaders or system of government, nor can they decide for themselves how to manage their natural resources, rebuild their monasteries, or designate their reincarnate lamas.

When the insults to their culture and religion and the oppressive controls become too much for some to bear, the state uses torture, murder, intimidation, and blacklists to force them into silence. The central government must be spending enormous sums on its army of overt and covert agents and all their instruments of suppression while it continues to skimp on medical care and education. And Lhasa residents complain that so much money and manpower is spent on stifling public dissent that the capital's real criminals get away with more and more muggings and thefts, adding to the sense of unease and mistrust.

During a visit to Tibet in 1988, China's security chief, Qiao Shi, openly demanded that the state pull out all the stops and crush the "splittists." He called on the TAR government to treat dissidents with "merciless repression."[23] The security forces have been following these orders from above, torturing nuns and inundating Lhasa with agents. It takes a heavy hand to maintain outward calm in Tibet.

12

An Integral Part of the Motherland (Self-Determination)

Yin Fatang is an old soldier. He served in the People's Liberation Army during the early, heady years of the People's Republic and became a high official of the Communist Party. Now retired, he sits in his spacious Beijing apartment, a quiet spot far removed in time and space from the scene of his memories, but he is reliving a conflict more than forty years past, a confrontation which took place in October 1950. It is the battle of Chamdo, when the Chinese crossed the eastern frontier of Tibet and defeated the poorly armed Tibetan army. Yin, short and wiry with a wrinkled, elfin face, smiles and smiles, delighted to return once again to those moments of glory. He leans forward over the glass coffee table and arranges a plate here, an ashtray there, to illustrate the army positions.

Here are the Tibetan forces, Yin says, setting saucers to one side, and here are the Chinese. He points out the town of Chamdo, the river, and the troops of a Khampa defector who came over to the Chinese side; and he moves an ashtray to the rear of Chamdo to show me how the PLA encircled the town and cut off retreat.

Opposite the Chinese are the troops of the Fourteenth Dalai Lama, headed by a nobleman, Ngapo Ngawang Jigme. Some of his soldiers are local Khampa tribesmen, fierce fighters at home in the harsh climate and mountainous terrain. The Chinese, however, are bred in the lowlands and plains, and they are unaccustomed to the high, wild land of the Tibetans. So, says Yin, the Battle of Chamdo is harder, in a way, than the famous Long March of the 1930s, when Mao Zedong's troops traveled thousands of miles on foot. "We had to go into the hills to fight," Yin says.

In the view of Yin and his army, the Chinese at Chamdo are fighting more than Khampa guerrillas and Lhasa officers. They are fighting imperialists who are trying to wrest Tibet from its rightful place in the motherland of China, and they are fighting reactionary elements controlled by the British. Yin and his men believe they are on a mission to recapture soil which has slipped from China's grasp.

Yin recalls that the Tibetans were using British weapons, old World War I cannons and guns. As individuals they fought bravely, but they lacked strategy. "They coordinated poorly," he says. It took only two weeks to win the battle, with the help of Khampa defectors and superior arms and tactics. With the Chinese surrounding Chamdo, the Dalai Lama's troops had no means of escape. Their leader, Ngapo, surrendered.

To Yin those were splendid times. The People's Republic of China was a year old, and the Communists were already at work transforming their own society. Now they were coming to save the Tibetans. It was truly noble work. "Tibet was the last place to be liberated," Yin says. "We came as liberators."

"The peaceful liberation": That is the standard phrase for the events Yin was describing. Officials and commoners know there is no other acceptable way to refer to the battle of Chamdo and the events that followed—the march to Lhasa and the arrival of thousands of Chinese soldiers in central Tibet. "Before liberation" or "after liberation," they say. To call it the "invasion of Tibet" would be counterrevolutionary. They don't even use the phrase, "after the Chinese arrived."

But in private Tibetans often give a different twist to the events of 1950 and 1951. One said to me, "Oh, you're going to interview Yin Fatang. Very interesting. Hear what he says about the battle of Chamdo and then decide if it was really a peaceful liberation." He raised his hands in mock surrender. "Okay. Okay. You're right. This is a peaceful liberation. Don't shoot."

Although Yin Fatang and the other soldiers and cadres who marched into Tibet in the 1950s saw themselves as saviors, they were, in fact, invaders, and Tibet became part of China by force. But China prefers to phrase the takeover in other terms. It knows that establishing sovereignty is its major propaganda task concerning Tibet, and its tedious insistence—to the point of overkill—that Tibet has long been an integral part of the motherland reveals China's own insecurity regarding its rights of ownership.

Every Chinese exhibit on Tibet, every publication, every historical reference declares that Tibetan society was run by the Chinese central government from the thirteenth century to the twentieth. Museum displays and cultural tracts cite the age of Tibetan artifacts in terms of Chinese dynasties, not the reigns of Tibetan kings and Dalai Lamas. As China tells it, Tibetan officials never made a move without permission from the emperor or his representatives, and China molded the government, set the laws, and appointed officials in Tibet over the past seven hundred years. It's just that there was a small problem when imperialists gained control of Tibet after the fall of the Qing dynasty. At that time, the official version goes, the British managed to turn upper-class reactionaries against China, and in 1950 Yin and his peers had to liberate the region from their grasp.

In recounting this history China glosses over and ignores inconvenient facts and overstates those in its favor. Thus the 1992 white paper on Tibet upholds the marriage of Tibet's powerful King Songtsen Gampo to Chinese Princess Wencheng as the pivotal link forged between Tibet and China in 641, but it fails to mention the king's second wife, who came from Nepal. The same document likewise makes no mention of periodic uprisings against Chinese interference over the centuries or Tibet's ouster of Chinese troops in 1912.

Even the original records of past events are often no more reliable than official "statistics" published today. There is, for instance, the matter of China's National Constitutional Assembly of 1946. Tibet, at the time, hoped to deal with China's nationalist Kuomintang government over the return of land in Kham and Amdo (which had come under Chinese rule in centuries past), and the Lhasa government tried to open negotiations by sending a mission to congratulate the nationalists on their victory over Japan. The envoys managed to present their gifts and compliments, but they made no progress with the talks. Instead of listening to the Tibetans' demands, the Chinese delayed and put them off and finally persuaded them to bring their concerns before the coming assembly. The ingenuous Tibetans agreed to attend as observers only; and Lhasa instructed them to refrain from voting or even clapping their hands.

With this understanding, they appeared at the assembly and soon discovered that they were now to be enrolled as subjects of the Chinese government. They protested, they refused to sign the final document, and they asked for a public retraction, but it was too late: Their names had gone into the historical record as delegates from that Chinese region called Tibet.[1] Today, China's archives, textbooks, and propaganda pamphlets continue to repeat this fiction—conveniently provided by their enemies, the Kuomintang—as "proof" of Tibet's willing subordination to China.

But China's wearisome insistence on its centuries-old ownership of Tibet fools few, outside the boundaries of the People's Republic, with its rigid censorship and airbrushed histories, and even there a few canny dissidents have been able to see through the lies and distortions. Most Western academics and knowledgeable Chinese realize that Tibet, at most, functioned as a protectorate of China (although the Chinese had no concept of that relationship at the time) from the early eighteenth century until 1912.[2]

For two centuries China kept a small garrison in Lhasa with troops who accompanied a Chinese representative called an *amban*. Tibet called on China to help repel Gurkha invasions, the Lhasa government paid tribute to the emperor from time to time, and the imperial court occasionally called for reforms in Tibet. But by the mid-nineteenth century Qing rulers had almost no influence in Tibet, and even during the height of the dynasty's control, Tibetans were left to pass their own laws, maintain their own army, and issue their own currency. Chinese histories report that Dalai Lamas and other leaders were in power only at the pleasure of the emperor, but often the imperial court did no more than confer titles after the fact, after Tibetans had named their own leaders with their traditional methods.[3] Tibetans were willing to put up with these demands for ceremonial vassalage as long as the distant ruling court left them alone in their mountain retreat to run their own affairs. Korea, Mongolia, Burma, and Vietnam, all independent countries today, once had similar connections with the Chinese empire.

In 1912, when the Qing dynasty collapsed, Tibetans took advantage of the disarray and quickly ejected the Chinese from Lhasa. The Thirteenth Dalai Lama proclaimed his country to be independent, and until 1950 it functioned as a fully sovereign state. But Tibet was a somnolent and backward land, clinging to its conventions and preferring seclusion over the challenge of joining the modern world. It had de facto independence, but it failed to try for legal sovereignty in the eyes of the international community until too late. Only when the Communists were about to invade did it begin a frantic effort to muster support from the West. But this failed to halt the Chinese who soon took Chamdo.

Naïveté and isolationism did the Tibetans in. Because of Tibet's hide-bound conservatism and rejection of the outside world, China today can declare that no modern state has ever recognized Tibet as an independent country. But, as Chinese dissident Wei Jingsheng wrote in an open letter to Deng Xiaoping, "The reality [of Tibet's de facto independence] is there whether you admit it or not." Wei, one of China's most eloquent and courageous pro-democracy spokesmen, wrote the letter in the fall of 1992, just after he had been released from prison and before he was arrested again. Wei tears into the official history of Tibet and dissects it with scorn. "It would be ridiculous," he writes, referring to the imperial court's attempts to control the selection of Dalai Lamas, "if we defined [Canada and Australia] as Britain's colonies or even Britain's territory by arguing that the head of state of these two countries is the Queen of the United Kingdom and top government officials must be approved by the Queen." He also upbraids China for attacking colonialism elsewhere in the world but practicing it at home.

Wei draws on his own reasoned analysis of Tibetan history to attack China's claims, and he also uses the best weapon possible in the face of China's detailed but suspect records. That weapon is simple common sense. My friend Ngawangthondup, who escaped from Tibet during the 1959 rebellion, also manages to restore sanity to the debate by means of no-nonsense observations. "If Tibet is truly part of China," he says, "why is it necessary to prove it? No one tries to prove that Shanghai is part of China." And then he notes, "If China was in control of Tibet for all those years, why was Tibet so barbarous and backward as they say?"

When I was faced with the tangle of historical claims and all the archives of evidence that Tibet was an integral part of China, I also tried to rely on the most obvious testimony at hand, and that way I likewise came to reject China's obdurate stance on Tibetan history. I could see the Tibetan language in trouble, Tibetan culture threatened by an influx of Chinese, and the Tibetan religious establishment struggling to pass on its ancient learning. And I knew from

261

Chinese and Tibetans who had lived in the old society and from histories written by authors on both sides that neither language, culture, nor religion had come up against such hazards before the invasion of 1950. It was then, when Yin Fatang and his colleagues crossed the Yangtze and took Chamdo, that Tibet first faced the threat of assimilation. Only then did Tibet become a minority region in a larger whole. Now it displays the problems typical of a subordinate state, difficulties it never faced before the 1950s. And as the Chinese grip on Tibet has tightened, the threat has increased. I also knew that Tibet's colorful currency had been replaced by the Chinese yuan and the Tibetan army of men in sheepskin and woolen wraps by the olive-drab PLA: more evidence of radical change. The old Tibet was never a part of China the way it is today.

But China's censors and propagandists are so vigilant that many Tibetans have grown up ignorant of their own history, and almost all Chinese are convinced that Tibet has belonged to China for centuries. They routinely call it "our Tibet." The soldiers who crossed the Yangtze in the fall of 1950 believed that the mountain region they were invading was their own legitimate territory, and they were also on fire with other righteous causes—to oust the imperialists, free the serfs, and install a socialist state.

When Yin Fatang described the battle of Chamdo he portrayed the PLA as a union of heroes, bent on serving the Tibetan masses and bringing them justice, simple decency, and generosity to the point of sacrifice. His men, he said, were disciplined and trained to treat the Tibetans with respect and courtesy. When a hungry soldier stole some radishes, he was officially reprimanded and told to pay the peasants for their loss. Mao Zedong had instructed them, "Don't take even one needle from the people. Honor the monks. Show respect for the Tibetan religion and customs." So, Yin insisted, the commoners supported them. In the Gangze area of Kham they contributed yaks. Yin heard that they gave the PLA ten thousand yaks during those early months.

He was twenty-eight years old at the time and deputy commissar of the Fifty-Second Division of the Eighteenth Army, and once the battle of Chamdo ended, Yin and his men camped among the rugged, forested hills and sat back to wait. With the PLA deployed inside its eastern boundary, Tibet had no choice but to negotiate, and finally, in May 1951, the Chinese and Tibetans signed a contract, the Seventeen Point Agreement, allowing the troops to begin their trek to Lhasa and reclaim the territory which—they believed—had been stolen from the motherland.

Many of the Chinese walked all the way, some seven hundred miles through mountains, forests, and precipitous ravines. "We carried everything on our backs," said Yin, "according to what Mao said. We didn't depend on the local people." They took horses and yaks with them. He had been given five horses, so he could have ridden. But he felt it was unfair. He gave one of his horses to a wounded soldier and set out on foot.

The PLA had little food, and many horses perished along the way, but the troops, Yin said, still maintained discipline. When the local people ran away in fear, the PLA followed them into the forests and canyons and wooed them with song and dance to show that they came in peace. They never looted or commandeered supplies; they bargained with the nobles and monks for barley. The first Chinese troops thus made their way to Lhasa in the fall of 1951, and Yin's unit arrived the following spring. They delayed to avoid overtaxing the capital's food supply. All, as Yin told it, was done with the good of the Tibetan people in mind.

When Yin arrived, Lhasa was a cluster of flat-roofed houses in a wide river valley dominated by the towering Potala Palace and inhabited by some thirty thousand people. Yin saw the commoners of the capital as living in bondage to the silk-clad nobles and high lamas while outcasts, called "black bones," worked as butchers, blacksmiths, and collectors of the dead, and lice-infected beggars lined the Barkor.

But now, with the Communists there, he knew their lives would improve. "We taught the people," Yin said. "And we built the Sichuan-Tibet Highway." The Chinese also built schools, set up clinics, and paid wages to beggars and runaway serfs who joined them working on the roads.

In all, Yin spent twenty-seven years in Tibet, rising to become regional Party secretary in the 1980s. "I was there so long I felt I was Tibetan," he said. "I was very moved by the experience. I loved Tibet."

Yin is not the only Chinese to speak in heroic terms of the PLA's early years in Tibet, and even Tibetans, who resented the invaders from the start, admit that the troops were on their best behavior in those days. There is no doubting the sincerity of the first cadres and soldiers who made their way to that rugged and backward region. They worked devotedly to learn the language, and many of them planned to spend their lives in Tibet, helping the downtrodden build a true socialist state. These Chinese—and many of the Tibetans who joined them in the first flush of victory—reject the notion that Tibetans would now spontaneously raise their fists in the Barkor and cry "Chinese go home!" "Independent Tibet!" They are stung when Tibetans privately refer to them as *gyaro*—"Chinese cops" or "Chinese invaders," depending on whom you ask—and when they call the PLA soldiers, those one-time heroes, *khyi serpo*—"yellow dogs." They shake their heads and say, "It must be the Dalai Lama who is causing all this trouble. The people are happy with China there. Just see how much we've done." And then they point to the schools and hospitals and compare today to the old society. They seem to forget that all of China has lost the idealism of the early years; that they, too, suffered through times of famine, chaos, and persecution; and that many of them have also become opponents of the present government.

These Chinese, like Yin, say they love Tibet. Some of them grow misty-eyed expressing their love of the Tibetan people and culture. At yet, at the same time, they can dismiss Tibetan values, as Yin did when he said that "too much religion" held the people back, not just in the old society but in the 1980s when Tibetans could once again enter the monasteries to worship before the altars. These Chinese display an ingrained and unchallenged paternalism which allows sentimental indulgence and self-congratulation because China has given so much to these ignorant folk.

Yin Fatang, in fact, gave a lot to Tibet, in his way. He labored to relieve the victims of a disastrous flood in Gyantse; he lived with nomads and peasants; he tried to educate the masses in "correct" ideology; and he built roads and power lines. One dissident Tibetan told me he saw Yin as a man who genuinely cared for Tibet and tried to promote its best interests. And another dissident praised Yin, saying, "He worked very hard, and he even visited all the counties in Tibet; he can speak some Tibetan; he lives simply and can eat tsampa."

Nonetheless—even though he claims to know what they wanted then and what they believe today—Yin was out of touch with the people he governed during his long career in Tibet. During our second interview in Beijing, he said, "Most people don't want the Dalai Lama to come back because they are afraid they will suffer again." But even as he spoke, Tibetans were stopping foreigners to beg for photos of His Holiness. Any photos they can glean from tourists they touch to the crowns of their heads and place reverently on home altars. Small children on the street are able to speak these few words of English: "Dalai Lama piksha. Dalai Lama piksha." And when I heard Yin's avowal, I thought of an elderly pilgrim I met during one of my first circuits of the Barkor. The man tugged on my arm, and I automatically offered him money. But that was not what he was asking; he only wanted a photo of the Dalai Lama, so he shook his head at my mao notes and walked away. When Yin told me that Tibetans fear the Dalai Lama's return, I also thought of the Tibetan Party member who said, "If you want to make Tibetans happy just give them a Dalai Lama photo. They will love it; any Tibetan will."

Possibly, Yin didn't believe what he was saying; it may have been just one more formula he was expected to mouth. But he stated it with an air of confidence and conviction, just as he had recited to me the oft-told fable of the imperialists' hold on Tibet. In this accounting, the trade mission to Tibet—operating from the early twentieth century until the 1940s—becomes a front for British schemes to take over the entire region. These accusations are especially overblown because after India gained independence in 1947, Britain withdrew from the region even more, and Tibet had no more than four Westerners within its vast boundaries by 1950. But Yin apparently believed this rationale for the invasion of Chamdo.

Yin and others who took up the cause of Tibet in the 1950s have strong motives for continuing to believe the official line. They worked zealously to build socialism; they believed in the nobility of their cause; they made sacrifices. They can't accept the fact that Tibetans today resent China's presence and that much of what the Communists tried to do has ended in failure. Thus, aging Tashi Wangchuk, who joined the Chinese when the Long March passed near his Khampa village, told me complacently that in the old days there were many dogs in Lhasa and many, many beggars. I answered that the city is overrun with dogs and beggars once again. "What?" he asked, cupping his hand to his ear. I said it once more, louder. That time he heard me but did not respond.

Tibetans know better than to speak their minds before an official, and they are wary of any Chinese. They are wise in keeping their thoughts to themselves, but their silence adds one more barrier to getting at the truth. A

Chinese friend in Beijing, for instance, heard a Tibetan say, in response to a question, that life is better under the Communists than it was in the old society. This was enough to convince my friend that the Tibetan was being candid and also that he spoke for the majority.

So even many well-meaning and educated Chinese fail to recognize the fear that prevents Tibetans from speaking their minds. And when the systemic ignorance of most Chinese is added to the authoritarian mindset of Chinese officialdom, it means that common folk have little chance of getting through to the men at the top.

Tibetans not only face a wall of intransigent authority concealed behind layers of command and secrecy, they also face an alien people who claim to own them and their land. Although the government is a remote and arbitrary force in the life of ordinary Chinese, it is even more so for Tibetans. Those in charge, who claim to know what's best for Tibet, advocate an atheist creed and speak for a culture and viewpoint directly opposed to the most sacred values of the Tibetan people. A Drepung monk put it this way: "As the Chinese reject the existence of future lives, that is one difficult point. If freedom is only to eat and drink, it doesn't have much significance. That can by done by any animal, such as a dog or a cat which only worries about food and drink. So human beings are not the same. To be human has deeper meaning."[4] The monk had zeroed in on the gulf between Chinese and Tibetan worldviews. Tibetans are deeply religious; Chinese as a rule are determinedly materialist, even those who reject the atheist dogma of Marxism.

Tibetans want to live by their own values, make their own choices, and decide what they really need. But China insists on imposing its own values and deciding for them, and when Tibetans take to the streets in protest, the government leaders are baffled and insist that Tibetans should be grateful. Their paternalism is blind and deaf. It expects gratitude for taking away the people's freedoms and reserving the right to decide what is best. It refuses to hear what the Tibetans are saying, and it can't understand that dependency causes resentment and takes away the dignity of choice. As one Lhasa resident said, commenting on the renovation of rundown dwellings in the Barkor, "If the old houses are to be knocked down, it's up to us Tibetans to decide. The Chinese cannot decide for us, and we will only be able to decide when we are independent."[5]

In name Tibet is an autonomous region, but in fact it is run from Beijing. Although all the TAR chairmen have been Tibetan, the region has never had a Tibetan First Party Secretary. China explains away this obvious deficiency by saying that "there is no difference in nationality in the organizations of the Chinese Communist Party."[6] In other words, it claims that ethnicity is not an issue—although it boasts of giving the TAR chairmanship to Tibetans. Even the most thoroughly Tibetan of institutions, the Buddhist religious establishment, is controlled by the central government. As I made the rounds of government agencies I found Chinese appearing as spokespersons for Tibet. In the TAR Cultural Bureau, where you would expect at least a token Tibetan to take charge, Vice Bureau Chief Hu Jin An acted as spokesman even though a Tibetan vice bureau chief was present.

And then there is the military presence, which is overwhelmingly Chinese. This ostensibly autonomous region is occupied by outsiders who can't speak the local language. They are the descendants of the PLA which Yin Fatang joined so proudly in the early years, but they have none of the missionary zeal of former times. They are present now in good part to keep Tibetan dissidents in check and preserve the unity of the motherland. They are difficult to count. China keeps military statistics under tight cover, and estimates of the number of soldiers in the TAR vary from 60,000 to half a million. TIN has put the number at 150,000 to 250,000.[7] I know only that they are always around Lhasa, Damzhung (on the main highway north), and Shigatse, and huge convoys of PLA trucks, some loaded with troops, often pass along the major routes.

A small percentage of these soldiers are Tibetans, and those who join, I'm told, are usually poor peasants who are hoping to escape farm life and earn a good wage. But the PLA wants to be sure they are solid patriots before it allows them to sign up. In 1990 *Tibet Daily* announced an army recruitment drive that required "political investigation in order to ensure the quality of the new soldiers." "Never let those . . . who are resentful of the Chinese Party and the socialist system be recruited," it went on. "No youth who believes in religion will be recruited." In all, according to TIN, up to 10 percent of the army officers in the TAR may be ethnic Tibetans, and of that small portion, 95 percent are Party members.[8] I heard only one semiofficial confirmation of Chinese dominance in the military: An educator told me that August First

School, for the children of PLA members, is "mainly Chinese." But anyone who has seen a group of soldiers in Tibet knows at once that most of them are Han.

If, as the official reports claim, the "masses universally declared" that they would "completely smash the separatist conspiracy,"[9] then why aren't the masses patrolling the streets? Why is the great majority of soldiers imported from China proper? And why are there so many troops in the region?

It is true that Tibet is a border area and of strategic importance to China because it overlooks the Indian subcontinent. China and India have fought over the frontier, most notably in 1962. But there is another reason these troops are in Tibet, and that is to crush any signs of rebellion and to fight "splittism." This role becomes evident at times of unrest. During the 1989 demonstrations, Hong Kong's *South China Morning Post* reported, 170,000 soldiers were deployed to "within striking distance" of Lhasa, and the army was in charge during the martial law which followed. Again in the summer of 1995, just before the denunciation campaign against Tashilhunpo's abbot, some five thousand troops were moved to Shigatse. The town already had four military camps, and a fifth, behind the walls of the monastery, was hastily set up with tents to house the new soldiers. Further evidence that the troops are in Tibet to put down protests is in the words of Deputy Party Secretary Ragdi, who said in 1994 that stability in the TAR depends on "stepping up construction of contingents of troops stationed in Tibet" and strengthening other security branches.[10]

Whenever it clamps down on signs of rebellion, the Chinese government claims that it is protecting Tibet against a return of the old feudal society. But in spite of what Yin Fatang and other Chinese officials say, none of the advocates for independence or autonomy wants to reinstate the serf system of Tibet. In fact, a group of Drepung monks, formerly among the most conservative members of the old society, came out with the concept of a modern, free, and democratic Tibet in a 1988 pamphlet. They titled it "The Meaning of the Precious Democratic Constitution of Tibet" and distributed it to villages around Lhasa. The monks tried to define democracy and describe a future Tibet run by Tibetans. They listed individual rights as laid out in the Universal Declaration of Human Rights, and they denounced the excesses of the old society and promised to create a government accountable to the people which would guarantee them the right to speak freely. Democracy in Tibet, they said, would "embody both religious and secular principles," in the true Tibetan tradition. They also called on all Tibetans to work to restore freedom in their land.[11]

The Chinese responded by arresting every monk suspected of having a hand in this nonviolent call to action, and in November 1989 the government held a mass rally to convict ten of the Drepung monks of "the wicked goal of splitting the motherland" by printing "reactionary leaflets to propagandize the idea of independence for Tibet." The ten were sentenced to up to nineteen years of incarceration, at the time the harshest sentences handed down in Tibet for counterrevolutionary crimes.[12]

The monks wrote the pamphlet before the 1989 riots brought martial law to Lhasa, but they were sentenced during the period of overt military control. Since then the mood in the capital has become bitter and despairing. Several Tibetans told me they believe demonstrations do no good; the Chinese only come down harder after each one. But they could understand why others were driven to speak out. "I don't join," said one, "because that would just be for a moment. Then I would be in jail a long time. One moment of glory and then you disappear for maybe seven or fourteen years. I can do more by staying here. But the ones who do it, they are frustrated. They have been waiting and waiting for Tibet to have freedom again. Now, they think, at least they can do something. So they pray hard first. They go around to all the temples and pray, and then they just go out into the street."

In such circumstances many Tibetans look for hope in the West or in prayer. They are waiting for an outside force to rescue them because they feel they have no chance for justice under the Chinese, and they are encouraged because the Tibetan cause has received support from the U.S. Congress, the European Parliament, and other legislative bodies of the West (although they have found little support for self-determination from executive branches). One Tibetan showed me a photo of former President George Bush with the Dalai Lama and said, "This is the most important of all." Others begged me to "help the Dalai Lama."

Early in the history of the Chinese Communist Party, when the struggling Marxists announced the party constitution of 1931, Mao and his peers guaranteed minorities "the full right to self-determination." Tibetans, Mongols, and others, the constitution declared, could "either join the Union of Chinese Soviets or secede from it and form their own state, as they may prefer." But by the Sixth Plenary Session of the Central Committee in 1938 this provision had disappeared. Mao announced that minorities would enjoy specific rights; they could not be forced to study the Chinese language; they could administer their own affairs; but they would belong to a unified China together with the Han.

During those seven intervening years the Communists set out on the fabled Long March and made their way into minority terrain. In eastern Tibet the natives fled into the hills, rolled rocks down on the Chinese troops, and sniped at the soldiers from under the cover of boulders and trees. The Communists also met stubborn resistance from the fierce Yi of Yunnan and the Hui of Gansu. Although Party officials never explained why they rescinded the offer of self-determination, some have said it was the resistance they encountered from the non-Han along the way. Now they realized that the minorities would very likely choose to secede, and that gave their ill-considered promises a different aspect. Better not to risk defection; better to declare them all members of one family under the People's Republic of China and allow for no dissent.

The same attitude prevails today. The Chinese government has no faith in its own people. Its strict control of information, obdurate resistance to genuine democracy, lack of legal due process, abuses of political prisoners, and ever-present security forces reveal China's fear of letting the Tibetan masses have their way. In the government's view, this would bring disaster. The government only feels secure when the Tibetans are cowed and beaten into submission. As one young Tibetan said, "This is not the People's Republic. The truth is, we are the republic's people."

Unfortunately for Tibet, Chinese leaders changed their minds after the high-sounding constitution of 1931. While countries that once paid tribute to China have since become fully independent states and while former colonial powers have granted sovereignty to their one-time dependencies, China has stubbornly held on to Tibet. "I know that the Western countries took land and made colonies in the old days," a young Tibetan academic told me. "But now we are in different times. Now the world knows better. Only China

270

continues to act this way." He was overlooking the case of East Timor and other dark moments of late-twentieth-century colonialism, but his attitude was understandable in light of recent history. Informed Tibetans recognize that China's claim of past sovereignty is harder to combat than openly acknowledged colonialism, but they still take heart from the example of other lands—many of them also poor, landlocked states with few resources of their own—which were once dependents of Western powers.

This sentiment reappeared when I asked another young Tibetan what benefits China has brought to his land. He paused, stared at the floor, and said, "The Chinese built roads; they brought in Western medicine and education; they taught people about hygiene and agriculture; they built irrigation canals. The most important of all, I think, was Western medicine." This was a generous assessment because he was also aware of the losses; he had lamented them at length and told me of his fears for Tibet. I could see him struggle with this as he paused again; then he raised his eyes to my face and said with feeling, "But why couldn't they bring all of that and leave?" Such, he knew, was the experience of many other countries which had gained material benefits under their alien rulers and then won the freedom to manage on their own.

His question was a poignant one under the circumstances, and Westerners often pose it as well, shaking their heads in bewilderment. Why did China want arid, remote Tibet in the first place, they ask, and why, with all the expense and trouble Tibet causes them, don't they give it up? The answer, when anyone tries to come up with one, is always guesswork, but a common take on the issue is that China hopes to find resources in all the vast area of Tibet and it sees the land as more space for its teeming population. And then, many say, there is the question of defense, and Tibet overlooks the Indian subcontinent.

China expert Orville Schell has provided yet another theory. He states, "The reason they haven't [pulled out of Tibet], I think, is because of their titanic pride. It is very difficult for a country as insecure as China to consider giving up something to which they have committed so many resources and so much of their ego." It is, he says, the "fear of being made to look weak that makes them cling so tenaciously to Tibet."[13]

Tibetans inside China recognize the tenacious, determined stance the People's Republic assumes at any challenge to its claim on their land. They have learned just what happens when they call for independence or show support for the Dalai Lama. Even purely economic protests have brought out the SWAT teams and landed demonstrators in jail, and Tibetans have few choices when they look for a way out.

None of the Tibetans I met advocated violence, although members of the small underground may favor taking up arms (as the Tibetan Youth Congress in Dharamsala has at times). A Tibetan who had been present at one of the bloodiest riots said, "We think now that force does not prevail. It didn't prevail for Hitler. It's no use to depend on that kind of power. People mostly want happiness and peace, so we want peace with the Chinese. We don't want to fight with them. Moral power works best; this is my outlook. The Dalai Lama says we shouldn't hate the Chinese, so I put my hope in this."

But often my Tibetan friends failed to summon up even that much tenuous optimism. When I heard them express their fears and anguish over the future of Tibet, I would ask, "What can you do?" A few said "Only pray," but virtually everyone else said, "Nothing." This reply never failed to jolt me. I found it hard to believe that they had nothing in mind at all. It was only after months of hearing this bleak response that I finally understood why I found their answers so difficult to accept. Scores of times I have interviewed Americans with a grievance, and as many times I have heard them lay out their plans of action: lobbying, petitions, election campaigns, appeals through the media, foundations, neighborhood groups; they had dozens of options. But none of these were possible in Tibet. Tibetans had almost nowhere to appeal and no way to speak out. They knew that those in charge held all the political power and they themselves had none. When they held peaceful demonstrations, they were arrested and beaten and they lost their jobs. Even when they took up nonthreatening issues, they had no success: They had complained, for instance, about the razing of old homes in the Barkor, but their protests had no effect.

The only plan of action I heard came from a young Tibetan woman who had spent time in the West. She hoped that someday she could gather women together and give them vocational training. She would try to foster a sense of competition with the Chinese and work to spread this sense beyond her original group of women to men as well. Eventually, she said, Tibetan repairmen and shop owners would begin to beat out the Chinese in the marketplace, and as a result the Han and Hui would drift back to their villages in China proper. This would be better than organizing a boycott, she said, which would be politically risky and wouldn't succeed anyway, not without real economic incentives. A boycott would only take away the Tibetan customers, who are a decided minority now in Lhasa.

But even this humble plan, she said, was hatched during her time in the West when she was exposed to new possibilities for action and removed from the paralyzing tension and despair in her homeland. "If you had asked me before what we can do," she said, "I also would have said 'Nothing.'"

As for political action, informed Tibetans agree that the present climate leaves them almost no room to maneuver. The most they can do, they say, is to prepare for a time when the Chinese leadership is more receptive. Then they will be able to move quickly to take advantage of whatever opening they can find.

Almost all Tibetans want outright independence. They retain a deep-seated sense that they are a people separate from the Chinese, that in the past they ran their own affairs according to their own values without interference from China. But many know at the same time that complete independence is an unrealistic goal for now. They will take whatever autonomy they can get.[14] As one Lhasa resident said, "If you can get a big house, fine, you will take it. But if you can only get a few rooms of that house, then you will say 'all right' and go live in those few rooms." Moreover, many Tibetans support whatever the Dalai Lama proposes, and he is asking for a "middle way," without full independence but with Tibetans in charge of their internal affairs.

A young Tibetan academic told me, "Independence is impossible; the Communist Party won't allow it. So I just hope for this: that the Chinese will be fewer and fewer in Tibet, that Tibetans can wear their own shoes and their own clothes, speak their own language, take responsibility for themselves, and have real autonomy."

The majority of Tibetans place their hope for self-rule in their exiled leader and his efforts to secure their freedom. They also hope the forces of history will bring the dissolution of the Chinese republic, or new reform-minded leadership in Beijing, or united pressure from Western governments which could compel the Chinese to capitulate at last.

They are not alone in looking outside Tibet for solutions. Western experts also say it will take a change at the top of the People's Republic to bring any move toward real autonomy, let alone independence. "Until there is a change in this leadership, and China's perception of itself, it is doubtful there will be any real kind of solution to the problem of Tibet," writes Orville Schell, who has advocated Tibetan autonomy in local affairs, with China managing defense and foreign affairs.[15] Tibetologist Melvyn Goldstein has called for an "ethnic" rather than a political policy on Tibet, with Tibetan officials in charge, most of the Han returned to China proper, and the Tibetan language the major idiom of government but Tibet still run under the PRC system. He likewise states that it will take Chinese leaders of "vision and energy" to bring this about.[16]

Goldstein maintains that the West has a role in this scenario. He notes that China resents Western criticism of its record in Tibet and China's leaders feel that their efforts to improve the economy in that backward region have been ignored while many outspoken Westerners have taken up the most exaggerated claims of the exile groups. Thus, Goldstein says, influential groups in the West will have to stop repeating the exiles' charges of a Tibetan "holocaust" and throw their support behind something like his ethnic solution before China will risk any major changes. Dawa Norbu, the former Sakya resident who is now a professor at Nehru University in New Delhi, states that joint U.S.-Russian pressure on China to negotiate with the Dalai Lama, as well as progress toward genuine democracy in China, could bring greater autonomy to Tibetans in the PRC.[17]

The Dalai Lama is also looking to the West in his search for a winning strategy. Since 1987, when he addressed the Human Rights Caucus of the U.S. Congress, and 1988, when he proposed his "middle way" in a five-point plan to the European Parliament in Strasbourg, he has been sending signals to the Chinese through his public comments in the West. The Strasbourg proposition calls for all of the Tibetan ethnic areas—the TAR along with Kham and Amdo—to become democratic and self-governing. China would keep its control of major foreign policy and would be allowed to maintain some troops in Tibet until, after a regional peace conference was held, Tibet would become a demilitarized zone. Tibetans would vote on all of this in a national referendum.

The Dalai Lama's proposal has run into trouble with a vocal segment of the exile community which says it is a betrayal of the long-suffering Tibetans who deserve full independence, no matter what it takes. The Chinese, on the other hand, have refused to discuss the five-point plan, saying it is a stratagem for bringing up the forbidden topic of self-determination. The Chinese response to government-in-exile efforts to negotiate has toughened since the earliest contacts in 1978, and the 1987–1989 riots gave fuel to China's hardliners. Although both Hu Yaobang and Zhou Enlai once said they might consider the creation of a "greater Tibet" beyond the boundaries of the TAR, Chinese leaders now say this is impossible. They likewise reject demands for the establishment of a separate, democratic territory within the borders of the PRC and for the removal of PLA troops. The Chinese have insisted on setting the terms of the debate and therefore, according to Dawa Norbu, the government-in-exile can do little more than create media events.[18]

But the Dalai Lama is still bringing up the terms of the Strasbourg proposal, saying that time is running out, that Han Chinese continue to flood into Tibet, and something must be done to reverse the tide. In 1996 he was asking Western governments to urge the Chinese to negotiate with his government-in-exile. "I wish to reiterate our willingness to start negotiations anytime, anywhere, without precondition," he told the British parliament in July 1996.[19] "Our basic request," he said to Foreign Secretary Malcolm Rifkind and other British officials, "is to please help us get China to the negotiating table." He took a conciliatory stance toward the Chinese, saying that the country's leadership is growing more benign, and that this gave him hope for peaceful change. He even hinted at a willingness to coexist with the Han who have come to Tibet to seek their fortunes. "When more liberty comes, many of these Chinese will appreciate the Tibetan culture," he said. "So if the number of those Chinese who respect Tibetan culture is okay, then I think we can find some way to manage."[20]

These comments were mild and appeasing compared to his earlier speeches which charged the Chinese with razing the environment and killing off more than a million Tibetans. His remarks contrast utterly with the Chinese attacks on the Dalai Lama himself, whom the official press characterized in 1995 and

1996 as a demogague and a deceiver and the cause of discontent, "splittism," and economic stagnation in Tibet.

The shrill tone of these invectives has gone up several registers since the Panchen Lama affair. Chinese officials were outraged when the exiled leader announced his choice for the Panchen Lama, and even some of his staunchest supporters have said off the record that the government in Dharamsala handled the affair badly. TIN also states, "The Dalai Lama's announcement may have been preemptive and undiplomatic, but nevertheless [Beijing's response] has been extreme."[21]

Some Tibetans concede in private that the affair set back chances for negotiations; others maintain an optimistic stance, as the Dalai Lama himself has done during his visits to Western countries. Their optimism appears to be part of the conciliatory approach, a way of saying, "We expect the best from the Chinese." To underscore his peace offering the Dalai Lama held a teach-in in Los Angeles in the summer of 1996 expressly to bring Chinese and Tibetans together. Tibetans who attended the affair said that their leader spoke of his hope to someday perform a *Kalachakra* initiation (a three-day tantric ceremony held before a large public audience) in Tiananmen Square, where Chinese also suffered the repressive measures of the state.

Since the mid-1980s the Chinese government has declined, at least in public, to negotiate with the government-in-exile. After the Dalai Lama's visit to Britain, a Chinese foreign ministry spokesman rejected the call for negotiations. And the PRC continues to open the doors wider to the floating population of Han in Tibet while it censures the Dalai Lama at every opportunity, thus infuriating Tibetans in the TAR by ignoring their concerns over assimilation and by trampling on their religious and nationalist feelings. Any hopes for a solution seem, in late 1996, to be a long way off.

And yet there is the example of the now-sundered Soviet Union, which at one time appeared to be an unassailable fusion of states, welded together for all time. And there was the black period of the Cultural Revolution when it appeared that Tibet had, in the words of the old abbess, "come to the end of prayer." In both instances new leadership brought dramatic change and new freedoms. It can happen again, and it is still possible that it can happen in time for Tibet's resilient culture to survive and develop on its own, liberated from the threat of assimilation.

Notes

Chapter One: Abode of the Gods

1. *Tibet: Its Ownership and Human Rights Situation* (People's Republic of China white paper), (n.p., 1992), 29; Cultural Palace of Nationalities, *Social History of Tibet, China: Documented and Illustrated* (Beijing: Photograph Publishing House, 1991), 62–66; Thubten Jigme Norbu and Colin Turnbull, *Tibet: Its History, Religion and People* (Harmondsworth, U.K.: Penguin, 1972), 358; Tashi Ragbey, "The Case for Rangzen," in *Tibet: The Issue Is Independence,* ed. Edward Lazar (Berkeley: Parallax Press, 1994), 13, 15.

2. The overview of Tibetan society before 1959 that follows in the text is based on interviews with Tashi Tshering, Ngawangthondup Narkyid, Zhang Jichuan (all identified in the introduction or chapter one), and Liu Shengqi, research fellow, Institute of Nationality Studies, Beijing, all of whom lived in Tibet during this period.

   It also makes use of these firsthand accounts: Heinrich Harrar, *Seven Years in Tibet* (Los Angeles: J.P. Tarcher, 1981); Dawa Norbu, *Red Star Over Tibet* (New Delhi: Sterling, 1987); Dorje Yudon Yuthok, *House of the Turquoise Roof* (Ithaca: Snow Lion Publications, 1990); H. E. Richardson, *Tibet and its History* (London: Oxford University Press, 1962); Shen Tsung-lien and Liu Shen-Chi, *Tibet and the Tibetans* (Stanford: Stanford University Press, 1953).

   And it also draws on the following scholarly works: George Ginsburgs and Michael Mathos, *Communist China and Tibet: The First Dozen Years* (The Hague: Martinus Nijhoff, 1964); Melvyn C. Goldstein, "Serfdom and Mobility: An Examination of the System of 'Human Lease' in Traditional Tibetan Society,"

The Journal of Asian Studies 30, no. 3 (1971), 521–34; "Taxation and the Structure of a Tibetan Village," *Central Asiatic Journal* 25, no. 1 (1971) 1–27; _____,"Reexamining Choice, Dependency and Command in the Tibetan Social System: 'Tax Appendages' and Other Landless Serfs," *The Tibet Journal* 21, no. 4 (1986), 70–112, Goldstein and Cynthia Beall, *Nomads of Western Tibet: The Survival of a Way of Life* (Berkeley: University of California Press, 1990); and A. Tom Grunfeld, *The Making of Modern Tibet* (Armonk, N.Y.: M.E. Sharpe, 1987).

3. *Concerning the Question of Tibet* (Peking: Foreign Languages Press, 1959), 213, 215; cited in Grunfeld, 13.

4. Dorje Yudon Yuthok, 165–6.

5. Harrer, *Seven Years,* 184.

6. The historical summary that follows in the text is based on information in Melvyn C. Goldstein, *A History of Modern Tibet, 1913–1951: The Demise of the Lamaist State* (Berkeley: University of California Press, 1989); Grunfeld; and Richardson.

7. The accounts of the protests, including the estimates of casualties, are based on several eyewitness reports, which must remain anonymous, and the following publications: Amnesty International, *People's Republic of China: Repression in Tibet, 1987–1992* (New York: Amnesty International, 1992), 46; Asia Watch, *"Merciless Repression": Human Rights Abuses in Tibet* (New York: Human Rights Watch, 1990), 9, 15; The Law Association for Asia and the Pacific Human Rights Standing Committee and Tibet Information Network, *Defying the Dragon: China and Human Rights in Tibet* (London: Tibet Information Network, 1991), 22–3, 26, 28–9.

Chapter Two: The Land and Its Survivors

1. Elmar R. Reiter, "The Tibet Connection," *Natural History* (September 1981), 70; S. Dillon Ripley, "Tibet: The High and Fragile Land Behind the Ranges," *Smithsonian* (January 1981), 101.

2. Galen Rowell, "The Agony of Tibet," in *The Anguish of Tibet,* eds. Petra Kelly, Gert Bastain, and Pat Aiello (Berkeley: Parallax Press, 1991), 213.

3. Tibet Information Network, "Hydroelectric Project: Tunnel Collapses," London, August 10, 1996 in World Tibet News (online news service), August 11, 1996, available from listserv@vm1.mcgill.ca. August 11, 1996.

4. Tibet Information Network, "Hydro-Electric Project."

5. Xinhua, "Lhasa power to stop burning of dung, sod," *China Daily,* April 26, 1990.

6. Daniel J. Miller, "Wild Yaks of Kunlun," *Himal* (Lalitpur, Nepal) 5, no. 3 (1992), 35–6.

Chapter Three: Village, City, and Pastureland

1. *Wen Wei Po*, May 12, 1996 (in Chinese), "Pro-Beijing Hong Kong newspaper defends Chinese role in Tibet" in World Tibet News, May 15, 1996.
2. Ibid.
3. Tenzin Gyatso, 14th Dalai Lama, "An address to members of the European Parliament," Strasbourg, June 15, 1988.
4. John Grey [pseud.], "Modernise, Or Else!: Building the New Lhasa," *Himal* 8, no. 1 (1995), 18.
5. Ibid., 13.
6. Ibid.
7. Tibet Information Network and Human Rights Watch/Asia, *Cutting Off the Serpent's Head: Tightening Control in Tibet, 1994–1995* (New York: Human Rights Watch, 1996), 21.
8. Wang Jiwen, Jiang Weiyang, Basang Zhuoga, "Establishing and Improving the New Tax System for the Tibetan Socialist Market Economy," *Tibet Studies*, no. 1, 1995.
9. Goldstein, *Nomads,* 166–71.
10. Ibid., 162.
11. Ibid., 48.
12. "Dharamsala Responds to China's White Paper," *Tibetan Environment and Development News* (June 1993), 2.
13. Tibet Information Network, *Serpent's Head,* 107–114.
14. "Dharamsala Responds," *Environment News.*
15. Orville Schell, "Chinese Attitudes to Conservation and to Tibet," in Kelly, *The Anguish of Tibet,* 204.

Chapter Four: Keeping Well in the Land of Snows

1. Israel Epstein, *Tibet Transformed* (Beijing: New World Press, 1983), 391.
2. White Paper, 53–4.
3. "Infant Mortality Hits All-Time Low in U.S.," Associated Press, in *San Francisco Examiner,* September 5, 1993.
4. The data on infant mortality and life expectancy (except for that cited for the U.S.) comes from Central Intelligence Agency, *The World Factbook, 1992* (Washington: Central Intelligence Agency, 1992).
5. White Paper, 53.
6. "Tibet: The Facts," *The New Internationalist* (London), December 1995, 19.
7. UNICEF, "League Table of Maternal Death," *The Progress of Nations 1996* (Wallingford, U.K.: UNICEF, 1996) 8–9.
8. Stuart and Roma Gelder, *The Timely Rain: Travels in the New Tibet* (New York: Monthly Review Press, 1964), 94.

9. Patrick E. Tyler, "In Heavy Smoking, Grim Portent for China," *New York Times,* March 16, 1996.

Chapter Five: Schools for Tibetans

1. White Paper, 48.
2. Ibid.
3. Ibid.
4. Susan L. Shirk, *Competitive Comrades: Career Incentives and Student Strategies in China* (Berkeley: University of California Press, 1989), 60.
5. Xinhua, "Shanghai Donations for Project Hope," April 19, 1996, in World Tibet News, April 21, 1996.
6. *Tibet: From 1951 to 1991* edited by Chen Ray (Beijing: New Star Publishers, 1991), 85; "Special Census of the Population of Tibet," *Tibet Daily,* February 16, 1996.
7. *Tibet: 1951–1991,* 81.
8. Richardson, 14; Goldstein, "Re-examining Choice," 101–2.
9. The Amdowa was apparently referring to Tucci's book, *To Lhasa and Beyond: Diary of the Expedition to Tibet in the Year 1948,* written originally in Italian. It was published by Snow Lion Publications, Ithaca, N.Y., in 1987.

Chapter Six: Dorje Talks, I Talk

1. Tenzin N. Tethong, "Report on the Second Delegation to Tibet," in *From Liberation to Liberalisation: Views on "Liberated" Tibet* (Dharamsala: Information Office of His Holiness the Dalai Lama, 1982), 105–6.
2. Melvyn C. Goldstein, "The Dragon and the Snow Lion," in *China Briefing, 1990* (Boulder: Westview Press, 1990), 144; Tibet Information Network, *Defying the Dragon,* 83–4.
3. The International Campaign for Tibet, *The Long March: Chinese Settlers and Chinese Policies in Eastern Tibet* (Washington: The International Campaign for Tibet), 1991, 17–18.
4. Kathryn Woolard, *Double Talk: Bilingualism and the Politics of Ethnicity in Catalonia* (Stanford: Stanford University Press, 1989), 124–5; Wolfgang U. Dressler, "Acceleration, Retardation, and Reversal in Language Decay?" in *Language Spread: Studies in Diffusion and Social Change,* edited by Robert U. Cooper (Bloomington: Indiana University Press and The Center for Applied Linguistics, 1982), 324.

Chapter Seven: A Pearl of the Motherland

1. Nicholas D. Kristof, "Cultural Conquest: Tibetans Yield," *New York Times,* September 23, 1991.

2. Tenzin Tethong, 105; Heinrich Harrer, *Return to Tibet* (New York: Schocken Books, 1985), 67; Christina Jansen and Suzette T. Cooke, "Tibet: A Chinese Province?", *Liberation to Liberalisation*, 193.

3. Harrer, *Return*, 15, 72.

4. Ibid., 172.

5. Goldstein and Beall, *Nomads*, 151.

6. White Paper, 50.

7. Harrer, *Seven Years*, 164, 237; Richardson, 25; R. A. Stein, *Tibetan Civilization* (Stanford: Stanford University Press, 1972), 153.

8. *Tibet Daily* (in Chinese), August 14, 1994, quoted in Grey, 14.

9. Pamela Logan, "Renaissance Man: Artist adds contemporary strokes to traditional Tibetan painting," *Far Eastern Economic Review,* April 11, 1996, 86.

10. Milarepa, quoted in Stein, 266.

11. Kristof, "Cultural Conquest."

Chapter Eight: The Children of Chenrezi

1. Tibet Information Network, *Serpent's Head;* Amnesty International, *China Report—No One is Safe: Political Repression and Abuse of Power in the 1990s* (March 1996) in World Wide Web, http://www.io.org.amnesty; International Campaign for Tibet, *A Season to Purge: Religious Repression in Tibet* (Washington: ICT, 1996). The Shen quote is from Elaine Kurtenbach (Associated Press), "Tibetan Buddhists Enduring Worst Wave of Repression," April 16, 1996, in World Tibet News, April 17, 1996.

2. Propaganda Committee of the TAR Communist Party, *A Golden Bridge Leading into a New Era* (n.p.: Tibetan People's Publishing House, 1994), in Teresa Poole (*London Independent*), "China tries to stop spread of Tibet Buddhism," *San Francisco Examiner,* January 6, 1995; and in a slightly different translation in Tibet Information Network, *Serpent's Head*, 25–9; Tibet Information Network, "China Admits Holding Panchen Lama Child 'For Protection,' " June 1, 1996, in World Tibet News, June 1, 1996.

3. T. C. Palakshappa, *Tibetans in India: A Case Study of the Mundgod Tibetans* (New Delhi: Sterling Publishers, 1978), 16, cited in Grunfeld, 185.

4. Goldstein, *Reexamining Choice,* 111 n. 37; Dawa Norbu, *Red Star,* 162, 201, 220.

5. Dawa Norbu, *Red Star,* 221, 217.

6. Xinhua, "Tourism Turns Booming Sector in Tibet," April 12, 1996, in World Tibet News, April 12, 1996.

7. See Stein, 240–1, for a discussion of the persistence of Bon, and Stein, 147, on a fifteenth-century Buddhist leader putting an end to feuds between Buddhist and Bonpo monks.

8. "Lamaism," *Pictorial China* 128 (Beijing: New Star Press, 1991).

9. Cultural Palace, *Social History of Tibet,* 67.

10. Epstein, 404–5, 411, 230–1.

11. The account of the Panchen Lama controversy is taken from ICT, *Season to Purge,* 48–57; Tibet Information Network, *Serpent's Tail,* 52–70; Isabel Hilton, "The Boys Who Would Be Lama," *Independent* (London), April 21, 1996, in World Tibet News, April 25, 1996; Seth Faison, "China Battling Dalai Lama, Picks Rival, Also 6 Years Old," *New York Times,* November 30, 1995; "One Boy's Arrest Shows a Broad Repression in Tibet," *New York Times,* March 26, 1996; Patrick E. Tyler, "China Rejects Boy Chosen by Dalai Lama as 'Living Buddha,' " *New York Times,* November 13, 1995; "China Installs Its Choice As Reincarnated Lama," *New York Times World News Briefs,* December 9, 1995.

12. Uli Schmetzer (*Chicago Tribune*), "Human rights groups say China holding six-year-old," April 3, 1996, in World Tibet News, April 3, 1996; Xinhua, November 29, 1995, in Tibet Information Network, *Serpent's Tail,* 63, and in Faison, "China, Battling Dalai Lama"; Tyler, "China Rejects Boy"; Tibet Information Network, "China Admits Holding Panchen Lama Child 'for Protection,' " in World Tibet News, June 1, 1996.

13. Xinhua, "Xinhua cites Buddhist scholar on support for 11th Panchen Lama," March 29, 1996, in World Tibet News, March 30, 1996; Reuters, "China says Tibetans accept its choice of lama," March 29, 1996, in World Tibet News, March 30, 1996.

14. Tibet Information Network, *Serpent's Tail,* 47, 95.

15. The higher number for the monk population in 1959 is reported in International Campaign for Tibet, *Forbidden Freedoms: Beijing's Control of Religion in Tibet* (Washington: International Campaign for Tibet, 1990), 86. The lower figure was cited by Tibetan official Ngapo Ngawang Jigme in a speech made in April 1960, cited in Grunfeld, 167, in which Ngapo also gave the count for 1960. The data for the end of the Cultural Revolution comes from the Nationalities and Religious Affairs Commission, Lhasa.

16. The Lhasa government at that time listed 7,700, but during major festivals the Dalai Lama would distribute alms to 10,000. The actual populations of the monasteries were generally known in spite of the official counts.

17. "The Basic Viewpoint and Policy on the Religious Question During Our Country's Socialist Period" (Document 19), Art. VI, March 1982. The full document is reprinted in Donald E. MacInnis (Ed.), *Religion in China Today* (New York: Orbis Books, 1989), 8–26; "Large Offerings to Monasteries Must be Curbed," Public Security Bureau Document, Markham County, Meba Shang, Chamdo Prefecture, TAR, February 12, 1993, in ICT, *Season to Purge,* 33–4; Xinhua, in English, May 31, 1994, in Summary of World Broadcasts (BBC) June 4, 1994, cited in ICT, *Season to Purge,* 34–5.

18. Goldstein, *Demise*, 24.
19. Wang Rong, "Monk tires of secular duties," *China Daily*, August 13, 1992.
20. Tibet Information Network, *Serpent's Tail*, 29.
21. Tibet Information Network, "Lhasa Monasteries Closed after Monk Shot, 40 Detained," May 17, 1996, in World Tibet News, May 19, 1996; "Second Serious Incident in Lhasa Area: 30 Nuns and up to 50 Others 'Severely Beaten,' " May 18, 1996, in World Tibet News, May 19 1996; "Tourist Account of Monks' Protest, Police Search for Photographs," May 24, 1996, in World Tibet News, May 24, 1996.

Chapter Nine: "The Final Solution"

1. Grunfeld, 218–9; Zhong Quan, "Figures and Facts on the Population of Tibet," *About Tibet*, no. 6 (Beijing: New Star Publishers, 1991); "Special Census," *Tibet Daily.*
2. International Commission of Jurists, *Report on Tibet and the Chinese People's Republic,* Geneva, 1966.
3. Melvyn C. Goldstein and Cynthia M. Beall, "China's Birth Control Policy in the Tibet Autonomous Region," *Asian Survey* 31, no. 3, (1991), 285–303.
4. Ibid., 295.
5. International Campaign for Tibet, *Long March,* 13.
6. Tibet Information Network, *Defying the Dragon,* 199.
7. See Roderick MacFarquhar, *The Origins of the Cultural Revolution,* vol. 2, *The Great Leap Forward, 1958–60* (New York: Columbia University Press, 1983), 330; Penny Kane, *Famine in China, 1959–61: Demographic and Social Implications* (New York: St. Martin's Press, 1988), 84–5. Kane cites several estimates of excess deaths. For discussions of the effects of policy on the famine see MacFarquhar, 330–36, and Jean-Luc Domenach, *The Origins of the Great Leap Forward: The Case of One Chinese Province* (Boulder: Westview Press, 1995), 166–8.
8. Dawa Norbu, *Red Star,* 167–171.
9. Asia Watch, *Merciless Repression,* 73–4.
10. Grey, 11.
11. The population data for Han in the TAR in the 1970s and in 1980 are all cited in Grunfeld, 222.
12. Tibet Information Network, *Defying the Dragon,* 79.
13. International Campaign for Tibet, *Long March,* 7–10.
14. Nicholas D. Kristof, "In Corner of Tibet Chinese now Predominate," *New York Times,* November 3, 1991.
15. Tibet Information Network, *Defying the Dragon,* 78.
16. Grey, 11.

17. For the Third National Forum statements, Tibet Information Network, *Serpent's Head*, 23. For *China's Tibet* quotations, Grey, 17.

Chapter Ten: Han Go Home!

1. White Paper, 17; "Military Implements Martial Law" (in Mandarin), *Lhasa, Tibet Regional Service*, FBIS-CHI-89-044, March 8, 1989.
2. White Paper, 23.
3. Tibet Information Network, *Serpent's Head*, 94, 91.
4. Amnesty, *No One Is Safe*, 30; Tibet Information Network, *Serpent's Head*, 27, 46–7, 76, 83.
5. Tibet Information Network, *Serpent's Head*, 85, 92–4.
6. Ibid., *Serpent's Head*, 35–6, 42, 48.
7. June Teufel Dreyer, *China's Forty Millions: Minority Nationalities and National Integration in the People's Republic of China* (Cambridge: Harvard University Press, 1976), 168; Dawa Norbu, *Red Star*, 155. Also see Grunfeld, 145.
8. Dawa Norbu, *Red Star*, 203–13; Ginsburgs and Mathos, 147–53; Goldstein and Beall, *Nomads*, 151. Goldstein in "Dragon and Snow Lion" maintains that Tibetan peasants controlled their own incomes before 1966, but this contrasts sharply with Dawa Norbu and Ginsburgs and Mathos. The discrepancy may exist because Goldstein is describing the entire period 1959–1966 while the other writers are covering the period before 1962, when Party policy took a more moderate turn.
9. Ginsburgs and Mathos, 152.
10. Goldstein and Beall, *Nomads*, 155.
11. Tibet Information Network, *Serpent's Head*, 27.

Chapter Eleven: "Outwardly Calm"

1. "Tibet: The Facts," *New Internationalist*, 18.
2. Tibet Information Network, *Serpent's Head*, 79; Jing Wei, *100 Questions About Tibet*, (Beijing: Beijing Review Press, 1989), 40.
3. Jing, *100 Questions*, 39.
4. Tibet Information Network, *Serpent's Head*, 86–7; *Defying the Dragon*, 37.
5. Liu Zhiquan and Yang Xinhe, "Xizang jianyu jianwen," *Liaowang* (Overseas Edition), November 28, 1988, in Asia Watch, *Merciless Repression*, 38.
6. Amnesty, *No One Is Safe*, 1, 29, 52; Tibet Information Network, *Serpent's Head*, 142.
7. Tibet Information Network, *Serpent's Head*, 89; Amnesty, *No One Is Safe*, 46.
8. Tibet Information Network, *Defying the Dragon*, 34; ___, *Serpent's Head*, 72–3.
9. Amnesty International, *No One Is Safe*, 17; Tibet Information Network, *Defying the Dragon*, 34–6.

10. Tibet Information Network, *Serpent's Head,* 90–91.
11. Tibet Information Network, *Serpent's Head,* 90.
12. Reuters, "County police chief in Tibet sentenced for torture," April 29, 1996, in World Tibet News, April 29, 1996. The case was reported in China's *Procuratorial Daily.*
13. Tibet Information Network, *Serpent's Head,* 80.
14. Tibet Information Network, *Serpent's Head,* 90.
15. Bu Wen, "The Dalai Lama's Human Rights Records," *Beijing Review,* May 20–26, 1991, 5–6.
16. Tibet Information Network, *Serpent's Head,* 10, 11, 80.
17. See Amnesty, *No One Is Safe,* 68, for excerpts from the Vienna Declaration and quotation on "no evidence."
18. Amnesty, *No One Is Safe,* 54, 47; Reuters, "China should have an anti-torture law, U.N. body says," May 6, 1996, in World Tibet News, May 10, 1996.
19. Tibet Information Network, *Serpent's Head,* 73.
20. *Tibet: From 1951–1991,* 99.
21. Tibet Information Network, *Serpent's Head,* 6, 10, 80.
22. Richardson, 25; Stein, 153–4, 275–6; Harrer, 164, 237.
23. Asia Watch, *Merciless Repression,* 1.

Chapter Twelve: An Integral Part of the Motherland

1. Richardson, 166–8; Goldstein, *Demise,* 550–558.
2. Ginsburgs and Mathos, 1; Goldstein, *Demise,* 44; _____, "The Dragon and the Snow Lion," 130–131; Richardson, 50–72; Stein, 85–90. Also see Grunfeld, 231, for a different interpretation.
3. Dreyer, 39; Richardson, 71; Stein, 88.
4. Tibet Information Network, *Defying the Dragon,* 4.
5. Ibid., 3.
6. Jing, *100 Questions,* 73–4.
7. Tibet Information Network *Defying the Dragon,* 77; Tibet Information Network cited in "Tibet: The Facts," *New Internationalist,* 17.
8. Tibet Information Network, *Defying the Dragon,* 77, and 77 n. 11 and 12, quoting *Tibet Daily,* October 28, 1990 and citing data from *Wen Wei Po,* March 30, 1990 and *People's Daily,* November 9, 1989.
9. See note 1, chapter 10.
10. *South China Morning Post,* March 18, 1989, in Tibet Information Network, *Defying the Dragon,* 77 n. 8; Tibet Information Network, *Serpent's Head,* 69; *Tibet Daily,* August 2, 1994, in Grey, 10.
11. Tibet Information Network, *Defying the Dragon,* 115–6.
12. Ibid., 39–40.

13. Schell, 204.
14. See Goldstein, "Dragon and Snow Lion," 149. In 1985–6, he estimated, 10 percent of Tibetans in Lhasa favored Chinese rule, another 10 percent were die-hard advocates of independence, and the rest were bitter about China's treatment of Tibet but believed full independence was impossible. Since then, with the riots and the attacks on the Dalai Lama, nationalist sentiment is even stronger.
15. Schell, 204.
16. Goldstein, "Dragon and Snow Lion,"167.
17. Ibid; Dawa Norbu, "China's Dialogue with the Dalai Lama 1978–1990: Prenegotiation Stage or Dead End?" *Pacific Affairs* 64, no. 3 (1991), 371.
18. Dawa Norbu, "China's Dialogue," 371.
19. "Beijing Rejects Dalai Lama Talks," *Hong Kong Standard,* July 18, 1996, in World Tibet News, July 20, 1996.
20. "Dalai Lama Optimistic on Tibet but Says Time Runs Out," Reuters, London, July 21, 1996, in World Tibet News, July 24, 1996.
21. Tibet Information Network, *Serpent's Head,* 52–3.

Bibliography

Amnesty International. *People's Republic of China: Repression in Tibet, 1987–1992.* New York: Amnesty International, 1992.

Asia Watch. *"Merciless Repression": Human Rights Abuses in Tibet.* New York: Human Rights Watch, 1990.

Central Intelligence Agency. *The World Factbook, 1992.* Washington, D.C.: Central Intelligence Agency, 1992.

Cultural Palace of Nationalities. *Social History of Tibet, China: Documented and Illustrated.* Beijing: Photograph Publishing House, 1991.

Dawa Norbu. *Red Star Over Tibet.* New Delhi: Sterling, 1987.

Dressler, Wolfgang U. "Acceleration, Retardation, and Reversal in Language Decay?" In *Language Spread: Studies in Diffusion and Social Change,* edited by Robert L. Cooper. Bloomington: Indiana University Press and The Center for Applied Linguistics, 1982.

Dreyer, June Teufel. *China's Forty Millions: Minority Nationalities and National Integration in the People's Republic of China.* Cambridge: Harvard University Press, 1976.

Epstein, Israel. *Tibet Transformed.* Beijing: New World Press, 1983.

Gelder, Stuart and Roma Gelder. *The Timely Rain: Travels in the New Tibet.* New York: Monthly Review Press, 1964.

Ginsburgs, George and Michael Mathos. *Communist China and Tibet: The First Dozen Years.* The Hague: Martinus Nijhoff, 1964.

Goldstein, Melvyn C. *A History of Modern Tibet, 1913–1951: The Demise of the Lamaist State.* Berkeley: University of California Press, 1989.

———. "Reexamining Choice, Dependency and Command in the Tibetan Social System: 'Tax Appendages' and Other Landless Serfs." *The Tibet Journal* 21, no.

4 (1986): 79–112.

————. "Serfdom and Mobility: An Examination of the System of 'Human Lease' in Traditional Tibetan Society." *The Journal of Asian Studies* 30, no. 3 (1971): 521–34.

————. "Taxation and the Structure of a Tibetan Village." *Central Asiatic Journal* 15, no. 1 (1971): 1–27.

————. "The Dragon and the Snow Lion: The Tibet Question." In *China Briefing, 1990,* edited by Anthony James Kane. Boulder: Westview Press, 1990.

Goldstein, Melvyn C. and Cynthia M. Beall. "China's Birth Control Policy in the Tibet Autonomous Region." *Asian Survey* 31, no. 3 (1991): 285–303.

————. *Nomads of Western Tibet: The Survival of a Way of Life.* Berkeley: University of California Press, 1990.

Grey, John. "Modernise, Or Else!: Building the New Lhasa." *Himal* [Nepal] 8, no. 1 (1995): 10–18.

Grunfeld, A. Tom. *The Making of Modern Tibet.* Armonk, N.Y.: M.E. Sharpe, 1987.

Harrer, Heinrich. *Seven Years in Tibet.* Los Angeles: J.P. Tarcher, 1981.

————. *Return to Tibet.* New York: Schocken Books, 1985.

International Campaign for Tibet. *A Season to Purge: Religious Repression in Tibet.* Washington: International Campaign for Tibet, 1996.

————. *Forbidden Freedoms: Beijing's Control of Religion in Tibet.* Washington: International Campaign for Tibet, 1990.

————. *The Long March: Chinese Settlers and Chinese Policies in Eastern Tibet.* Washington: The International Campaign for Tibet, 1991.

International Commission of Jurists. *Report on Tibet and the Chinese People's Republic.* Geneva: 1966.

Jansen, Christina and Suzette T. Cooke. "Tibet: A Chinese Province?" In *From Liberation to Liberalisation: Views on 'Liberated' Tibet.* Dharamsala: Information Office of His Holiness the Dalai Lama, 1982.

Jing Wei, ed. *100 Questions About Tibet.* Beijing: Beijing Review Press, 1989.

Logan, Pamela. "Renaissance Man: Artist adds contemporary strokes to traditional Tibetan painting." *Far Eastern Economic Review* 11 (April 1996): 86.

Miller, Daniel J. "Wild Yaks of Kunlun." *Himal* [Nepal] 5, no. 3 (1992): 35–36.

————. "China's Dialogue with the Dalai Lama, 1978–1990: Prenegotiation Stage or Dead End?" *Pacific Affairs* 64, no. 3 (1991): 351–72.

Ragbey, Tashi. "The Case for Rangzen." In *Tibet: The Issue is Independence.* Berkeley: Parallax Press, 1994.

Reiter, Elmar R. "The Tibet Connection." *Natural History,* September 1981, 65–70.

Richardson, Hugh E. *Tibet and Its History.* London: Oxford University Press, 1962.

Ripley, S. Dillon. "Tibet: The High and Fragile Land Behind the Ranges." *Smithsonian,* January 1981, 97–104.

Ross, Lester. *Environmental Policy in China.* (Bloomington: Indiana University Press) 1988.

Rowell, Galen. "The Agony of Tibet." In *The Anguish of Tibet,* edited by Petra K. Kelley, Gert Bastian, and Pat Aiello. Berkeley: Parallax Press, 1991.

Schell, Orville. "Chinese Attitudes to Conservation and to Tibet." In *The Anguish of Tibet,* edited by Petra K. Kelley, Gert Bastian, and Pat Aiello. Berkeley: Parallax Press, 1991.

Shen Tsung-Lien and Liu Shen-Chi. Tibet and the Tibetans. Stanford: Stanford University Press, 1953.

Shirk, Susan L. *Competitive Comrades: Career Incentives and Student Strategies in China.* Berkeley: University of California Press, 1989.

Stein, R. A. *Tibetan Civilization.* Stanford: Stanford University Press, 1972.

Tenzin N. Tethong. "Report on the Second Delegation to Tibet." In *From Liberation to Liberalisation: Views on 'Liberated' Tibet.* Dharamsala: Information Office of His Holiness the Dalai Lama, 1982.

Thubten Jigme Norbu and Colin Turnbull. *Tibet: Its History, Religion and People.* Harmondsworth, U.K.: Penguin, 1972.

Tibet Information Network and Human Rights Watch/Asia. *Cutting off the Serpent's Head: Tightening Control in Tibet, 1994–1995.* New York: Human Rights Watch, 1996.

Tibet Information Network and the Law Association for Asia and the Pacific Human Rights Standing Committee. *Defying the Dragon: China and Human Rights in Tibet.* London: Tibet Information Network, 1991.

Tibet: From 1951 to 1991. Beijing: New Star Publisher, 1991.

"Tibet—The Facts." *The New Internationalist,* [London] December 1995, 18–19.

Tucci, Giuseppe. *To Lhasa and Beyond.* Ithaca: Snow Lion Publications, 1983.

Woolard, Kathryn. *Double Talk: Bilingualism and the Politics of Ethnicity in Catalonia.* Stanford: Stanford University Press, 1989.

Yudon Dorje Yuthok. *House of the Turquoise Roof.* Ithaca: Snow Lion Publications, 1990.

Index

INDEX

INDEX

Y

Yadong, 38
yaks, 59, 60–63; wild, 62
Yamdrok Tso hydroelectric project, 40–44;
  environmental impact report on, 42; fail-
  ure of, 42–43
Yarlung-Tsangpo, 58
Yin Binggao, 38
Yin Fatang, 257–258, 262, 264–265
Yogurt Festival, 147, 149
Yunnan Province. *See* Kham
Yuthok Yonten Gongpo, 92

Z

Zhalu Monastery, 178, 183, 184
Zhang Chunyong, 88
Zhang Jichuan, x–xiii, xv
Zhou Enlai, 275

Barbara Erickson is a journalist whose experience includes teaching in Uganda, writing about Chile, El Salvador, and Honduras for regional and national publications, and teaching journalism at the University of California, Berkeley. She lives in Northern California with her husband.

VIETNAM
BUSINESS OPPORTUNITIES AND RISKS
by Joseph P. Quinlan

A concise guide to one of the world's hottest new markets, offering a quick, comprehensive snapshot of the country.

Paper, $19.95, 1-881896-10-2

Books for Children

LONG IS A DRAGON
CHINESE WRITING FOR CHILDREN
by Peggy Goldstein

A Parents' Choice Award–winning introduction to the Chinese written language.

Hardcover, $17.95, 1-881896-01-3

RED EGGS AND DRAGON BOATS
CELEBRATING CHINESE FESTIVALS
by Carol Stepanchuk

An enchanting look at China's festivals that includes stories, folklore, recipes, and much more. Illustrated with beautiful folk paintings from China.

Hardcover, $16.95, 1-881896-08-0

MADE IN CHINA
IDEAS AND INVENTIONS FROM ANCIENT CHINA
by Suzanne Williams

Young readers explore ancient China's scientific discoveries and technology in this lively account of people, ideas, and social change.

Hardcover, $18.95, 1-881896-14-5

KNEELING CARABAO AND DANCING GIANTS
CELEBRATING FILIPINO FESTIVALS
by Rena Krasno/Illustrated by Ileana Lee

A charming introduction to the complex history and culture of this beautiful country through its festivals. Stories, activities, and beautiful illustrations.

Hardcover, $19.95, 1-881896-15-3

For a complete catalog, write:
Pacific View Press
P. O. Box 2657
Berkeley, CA 94702